Also by Mark Roseman

The Wannsee Conference and the Final Solution:
A Reconsideration

A Past in Hiding:
Memory and Survival in Nazi Germany

LIVES
RECLAIMED

LIVES
RECLAIMED

A STORY OF
RESCUE AND RESISTANCE
IN NAZI GERMANY

MARK ROSEMAN

METROPOLITAN BOOKS

Henry Holt and Company   New York

m

Metropolitan Books
Henry Holt and Company
Publishers since 1866
120 Broadway
New York, New York 10271
www.henryholt.com

Metropolitan Books® and m® are registered trademarks of
Macmillan Publishing Group, LLC.

Library of Congress Cataloging-in-Publication data

Names: Roseman, Mark, author.
Title: Lives reclaimed : a story of rescue and resistance in Nazi Germany /
    Mark Roseman.
Description: First edition. I New York : Metropolitan Books ; Henry Holt and
    Company, 2019. I Includes bibliographical references and index.
Identifiers: LCCN 2018059534 I ISBN 9781627797870 (hardcover)
Subjects: LCSH: Bund—Gemeinschaft für Sozialistisches Leben—History. I
    Anti-Nazi movement—History. I World War,
    1939–1945—Jews—Rescue—Germany. I Government, Resistance
    to—Germany—History—20th century. I Socialists—Germany—History—
    20th century. I Germany—History—1933–1945.
Classification: LCC DD256.3 .R575 2019 I DDC 943.086—dc23
LC record available at https://lccn.loc.gov/2018059534

Our books may be purchased in bulk for promotional, educational, or business use. Please
contact your local bookseller or the Macmillan Corporate and Premium Sales Department at
(800) 221-7945, extension 5442, or by e-mail at MacmillanSpecialMarkets@macmillan.com.

First Edition 2019

Map by Jordan Blekking

Printed in the United States of America
1 3 5 7 9 10 8 6 4 2

To Roberta

People think of history in the long term, but history, in fact, is a very sudden thing.

—Philip Roth, *American Pastoral*

That was a small lesson I learned on the journey. What is interesting and important happens mostly in secret, in places where there is no power.

—Michael Ondaatje, *The Cat's Table*

CONTENTS

LIVES
RECLAIMED

Introduction

Flowers for the Heinemanns

November 10, 1938: Tove Gerson brought flowers. In Essen as elsewhere in Germany during the previous night—Kristallnacht, as it came to be known—Jewish homes, businesses, and places of worship had been ransacked and destroyed, and their occupants terrorized. Violence continued to swirl and eddy in neighborhoods across the city. Tove, herself not Jewish, had come to check up on the Heinemanns, a wealthy and cultured Jewish couple, now retired. Tove had met them through her parents-in-law and had attended many a chamber concert in their imposing villa. On the square outside the Heinemanns' home, Tove was confronted by a baying mob. A slight and, by her own admission, somewhat fearful woman in her mid-thirties, Tove found herself barked at for bringing "flowers to the Jews." She stammered some excuse, fought her way through the crowd, and made it inside, where she found the aging couple cowed and crushed amid the torched paintings and shattered glass of their home.

December 4, 1939: Sonja Schreiber spoke up. Ever since the Wehrmacht had invaded Poland in September, stories about atrocities had been circulating in Germany. News bulletins reported the massacres Poles had ostensibly perpetrated against the Germans and the actions the Germans had carried out as "reprisals." Sonja, an elementary school teacher in Essen in her mid-forties, was also working as a volunteer at the local ration office and found herself engaged in conversation by a Frau Gross, a fellow volunteer. When it came to atrocities, Frau Gross said, she knew who was really responsible: the Jews. Sonja, gentle and idealistic, someone almost too naïvely good to impose order on the classroom, could not stand this twaddle, and spoke up strongly in defense of the Jews as a persecuted people. A shocked Frau Gross told her husband—and her husband told the Gestapo.

November 8, 1941: Artur Jacobs brought a woman to tears. Artur, a spritely sixty-year-old former teacher in Essen with time on his hands, had made it his business to follow the worsening fate of Germany's Jews. Over the last few weeks he had registered with dismay the first major deportations from his region. Ignoring the increasingly severe sanctions against those who helped Jews, Artur ventured what moral and physical support he could. When a "Frau K," about to be deported to Minsk, thanked him for his solidarity, Artur said it was he who should be thanking her. She had given him a chance to discharge some of the guilt he felt at what was happening to his fellow countrymen. At this point Frau K broke into tears. "You have no idea what consolation you have given me."

December 1942: Else Bramesfeld took a risk. Back in April, her Jewish friend Lisa Jacob had been assigned to a deportation and since then had been "hiding in plain sight." From time to time Else sheltered Lisa. Now, however, Else offered something more, a lifeline in the form of an official piece of ID that Lisa could present when asked for her papers on a train or tram. Else had obtained it by writing to her professional teachers' association, saying she was on holiday and had lost her ID card. In requesting a replacement, she included a photo—of Lisa. The association never caught on to the ruse and duly mailed back a new ID card bearing Else's name and Lisa's likeness. It was, as Lisa would later write, a priceless "Christmas present," one that lightened the psychological load every time Lisa had to move between addresses.

February 1944: Grete Dreibholz disclosed a forbidden friendship. Forty-seven years old, the daughter of a prosperous businessman in the manufacturing town of Remscheid, until 1933 Grete had been passionately involved in Remscheid's left-wing scene. Her beloved sister, Else, another free spirit, married the well-known playwright Friedrich Wolf, a Communist Jew, and followed him to the Soviet Union after the Nazis came to power. Under the Nazis, Grete's radical connections became a liability. She was dismissed from her well-paying administrative position and took up factory work to make ends meet. By 1943 she was working alongside Polish and Russian forced laborers housed in appalling conditions. Ignoring the risks, she befriended their interpreter, a formerly well-to-do woman from Warsaw. In a letter in February, Grete wrote about this friendship, describing with a fearless lack of self-censorship what the forced laborers endured. If it had not been for the clothes she had found for the interpreter and her daughter, she wrote, they would have had literally nothing to wear.

July 29, 1944: Hermann Schmalstieg opened his home. Hermann was a handsome, romantic thirty-something, a working-class boy who had managed to qualify as a master craftsman in precision engineering. The Great Depression had made it hard to find a job, and he eventually landed a position as a technician at the Braunschweig Technical University's Acoustics Institute. During the war, the institute was employed on military contracts and moved to an isolated site on the Auerhahn Mountain, in the Harz Mountains near Goslar. Here Hermann had use of a lonely forester's cottage. Friends asked him if he would allow a young woman on the run to take refuge there for a while. And so, toward the end of July, a twenty-one-year-old Jewish woman, Marianne Strauss, came to stay with him in the cottage for a few days.

Lives Reclaimed is about a small group of idealists living in Nazi Germany, many of them women, who recognized the plight of others and acted on that knowledge, despite the risks of retribution. Tove, Sonja, Artur, Else, Lisa, Grete, and Hermann were all connected to the Bund: Gemeinschaft für sozialistisches Leben. The name translates to League: Community for Socialist Life, but its members referred to it, simply, as "the Bund." Although they have been largely unheard and unseen till now, the record of their voices and actions has nevertheless been preserved. This book looks at not only what they did but also what motivated them to reach out to others, including complete strangers, and how they found the freedom

and courage to act. It explores the consequences of their actions for those
who received their help and for the helpers themselves, both during and
after the war.[1]

Even in the rarefied company of the few groups that helped Jews in Nazi
Germany, the Bund stands out—not least because it was not in any sense
created to oppose the Nazis. It both predated and outlasted the regime.
When originally formed in 1924, amid the cooling hopes of the Weimar
Republic's revolutionary years, the Bund had no conception of the brutal
dictatorship that was to come or any sense that within a decade its members would be living a life of danger and clandestine action. For many on
the left, the climate in 1924 was still one of optimism—albeit tempered by
the recognition that achieving social transformation would take longer than
expected. Based in the Ruhr, and founded by some of the teachers and
pupils at Essen's adult education institute, the Bund grew to perhaps as many
as two hundred members—workers, teachers, middle-class women with a
social conscience, and others, among them quite a few Jews. Through meetings, joint study, physical exercise, and excursions, this new group sought
to develop a holistic and uplifting communal life. It also reached out to
others through adult education, experiments in alternative schooling, gymnastics training, and political meetings. Its members were hoping to be
the crucible for a future, better Germany. They were certainly not preparing for life under a future fascist dictatorship.

Looking back after 1945, however, the Bund's members believed that it
was the principles and structures they had established in Weimar's climate
of radical experimentation that had equipped them to resist the Nazi tide.
But how could this circle of vegetarian, teetotaling utopians be prepared
for a dictatorship? Were the gentle teacher Sonja Schreiber and the sheltered middle-class housewife Tove Gerson in any way steeled to withstand
the terror and intimidation of the Third Reich? Though the Bund was perhaps stricter and more all-encompassing than many movements in terms
of the demands it placed on its members, it resembled thousands of other
organizations in Weimar's lively alternative scene—youth groups, "life-
reform" associations, dance and exercise schools, and left-wing splinter
groups of every shade of red. Within a very short time after the Nazis came

to power, this whole scene was brutally dismantled—some of its activists imprisoned or killed, others intimidated into silence, still others lured into joining the new powerful national movement that had swept Germany with such force and élan. The Bund itself looked supremely ill-equipped to resist. Its collection of idealistic souls were neither hard-boiled street fighters nor practiced in clandestine conspiracy.

Yet the group survived, for the most part evading the Gestapo spotlight and maintaining a striking degree of associational life. Sometimes its actions do not seem very remarkable—a handful of rather quirky souls meeting in a rainy Sauerland forest to celebrate the summer solstice. No doubt such meetings took courage, but carefully choreographed get-togethers in the drizzle hardly hastened the Nazis' demise. Yet somehow a collective was preserved that evaded detection and saved lives. Had the Bund found a formula for survival and action that eluded the other oppositional groups crushed under the Nazi boot? Or was it just exceptionally lucky?

Whatever the case, transforming from an open community to an illegal group and then maintaining its integrity under threat cannot have been easy. Survival in opposition meant hard choices and unpalatable compromises. As it adjusted to the new rules of the Third Reich, the Bund's program of assistance evolved, moving from sheltering political dissidents on the run in 1933, through arranging visits to local Jews after Kristallnacht, to riskier actions. Alongside material aid, it tendered moral support in letters, offering kind words to victims who did not realize there were still people in Germany willing to record the injustice of their persecution. Bund members dispatched hundreds of parcels to deportees in Polish ghettos and the Theresienstadt ghetto, and even tried to assist deportees in Auschwitz. They provided a lifeline and hiding places for Jews, several of whom survived inside Nazi Germany thanks to their help. *Lives Reclaimed* traces the group's shared path into and out of the Third Reich.

What makes the Bund stand out for the historian are not just its achievements but also its archive, not just its wartime record but also the trove of wartime records. For example, Tove described her gesture after Kristallnacht with which this book opened in a 1942 speech in Bartlesville,

Oklahoma, after she immigrated to the United States. Her original notes are stored in a U.S. archive. The transcript of Sonja's interrogation, after she so boldly defended the Jews, can be found in some of the rare Gestapo records that survive. Artur's conversation with Frau K, as she readied herself for deportation, was noted down by him that evening in a diary, much of which has been preserved. Marianne's encounter with Hermann is captured in a chronicle she wrote while on the run and then kept, untouched, throughout her life. No fewer than four diaries or diary fragments offer testimony about the group. In the historical scholarship about rescue, nothing like this exists. That rich source base enables the Bund to offer more than just an exceptional story. It allows us to see, up close, what it was like to defy the Nazi regime.

"Resistance" is in some ways not a fashionable word in the historiography of Nazi Germany, the appeal of *Inglourious Basterds* or *Valkyrie* notwithstanding. Twenty to thirty years ago, true enough, scholars were finding opposition in every corner of the Third Reich. Study after study uncovered a spectrum of resistance, ranging from unresponsiveness to Nazi initiatives to active attempts at bringing down the regime. All kinds of actions were included, from angry parishioners protesting the removal of crucifixes from local schools to groups of young people who wanted to dance to banned swing music. Working-class regions like the Ruhr and the Saar were portrayed as being largely immune to Nazi propaganda.[2] Viewed against such a landscape, the Bund would appear to be merely a tiny part of a groundswell of opposition.

But given the undeniable signs of popular enthusiasm for the Führer, this interpretation of German society proved impossible to sustain. It is not surprising that scholarship has swung in the opposite direction, emphasizing the degree to which the population embraced the regime. Hitler's rule has come to be dubbed a "dictatorship by acclamation."[3] We now know the degree to which even police actions were triggered by popular denunciation. Nazi persecution of Jews enjoyed considerable popular support, and some scholars even claim that the population learned to embrace genocide.[4]

This recent emphasis on societal mobilization provides the backdrop for the present book. It helps us understand the Bund's story—above all, the group's experience of encirclement and isolation. Denunciations by neighbors were just as much a threat as direct surveillance by the Gestapo.

The Bund offers vivid testimony of the challenge of opposing a dictator-ship so well anchored in society, of the painful but necessary daily choices about when and how far to compromise, and of the courage required to make even small gestures of opposition. The Bund also reminds us that not everyone supported the Nazis. Apart from their own example, we learn through the Bund members' eyes that the society around them was not monolithic. On both the home front and battlefronts, they observed fluc-tuations in the popular mood, finding relief and hope when opinions seemed to be turning against the regime. Above all, they were aware that even the seeming enthusiasts were subject to the same pressures to conform as they themselves.

Surrounded by an atmosphere of acclamation, the Bund found it in itself to challenge the regime—most notably by providing practical help to vic-tims of persecution and by saving lives the regime was committed to destroy. Here "resistance" shades into "rescue."[5] Looking at Tove, Sonja, Artur, Else, Grete, Hermann, and others, we see how a network was able to operate under Nazi rule, providing help and sustaining lifelines for Jews in a way that individuals would have been hard put to do on their own. We can trace the fragile but resilient threads, woven in the 1920s under very different expectations and conditions, that made it possible for a group to be informal enough to elude persecution and, at the same time, tight-knit enough to survive and stand up to the Reich.

It may seem a perverse claim, given the library shelves of books on the sub-ject, but in fact the history of rescue is only now being written. As a sub-ject of scholarship, rescue has until recently been the preserve of psychologists, ethicists, and, to a smaller extent, social scientists.[6] The first group, in particular, has understandably treated rescue less as a historical than as a psychological phenomenon. Even now, popular awareness and public commemoration continue to be dominated by the rescuer as an indi-vidual impelled by ethical predisposition and empathetic personality. His-torians have, however, begun to expose the limits to this kind of analysis. Recent work has suggested that different social, cultural, and geographi-cal environments so dramatically determined the opportunities for and risks of rescue that rescuer personality types can offer at best a very partial

explanation for what happened. Studies have begun to explore group
action—not only the small number of organizations that made help for Jews
their priority but also the many more informal networks. They have shown
the complex mixture of motives involved in transactions that were dependent on the resourcefulness of both helpers and helped.[7] Yet few group
studies have been able to offer such a sustained and intimate analysis before,
during, and after the Nazi years as the Bund allows us to do.

Until very recently, the overwhelming majority of rescue accounts has
relied on the memories of the protagonists, recorded in later life. Such testimonies have the virtue of offering a mature perspective delivered in
freedom. My own interviews with twenty-five individuals in Germany,
Holland, the United Kingdom, Israel, the United States, and Australia left
an indelible impression on me.[8] Surviving Bund members—in their late
eighties or nineties by the time I spent time with them—were in a way living documents themselves. Their physical bearing and moral stance still
conveyed a hint of the mission that had once imbued them.

Yet, vital though such encounters were, the Bund's rich trove of contemporary documents, recorded during the years of the Holocaust and
total war, reveals worlds that interviews cannot access. Denunciations from
neighbors in Gestapo files, diary entries and letters in the Bund's own
archive, Prussian education ministry files on the removal of Artur Jacobs's
teacher's pension, and many other records together show the unfolding
apparatus of persecution. Records from the time reveal that the Nazi
period was far from uniform, sometimes changing markedly from one year
to the next. As the Bund noted immediately after the war, when memories
were still fresh, the way you had to respond to an arrest in 1933 was no
longer valid in 1939 and different again in 1942. The diaries, secret
speeches, and family correspondence—supplemented by the Bund's very
early postwar publications—give us a sense of how Bund members adapted
their way of life, practicing subterfuge, learning reluctantly to lie, and, in
short, changing their mission and modus operandi.

As well as presenting the history of a remarkable group, *Lives Reclaimed*
offers a disquisition on the relationship between experience and memory. Its central concern is the question of vantage point—the difference
between choices and perceptions in the moment and events and experiences as remembered and represented later.[9] Bund members not only

recorded their thoughts at the time but produced several postwar accounts of life in the Third Reich. Some were informal, some more formal, ranging from speeches delivered just after liberation to a full-length book published in 1990. Unusually, we can observe close-up not only lives lived opposing the regime and helping Jews but also the twists and turns that splintered and recolored this experience after the war. In tracing the transformation of experience into memory, we learn how challenging it proved to make sense of and articulate life under Nazi rule. This was partly because the experience itself had been so unprecedented and so hard to grasp, even for the protagonists. But it was also because the postwar world would accept only certain kinds of stories, making it doubly hard to render a truly authentic account.

After 1945, the Bund's inspirational leader, Artur Jacobs, hoped that the courage, generosity of spirit, and resilience the group's members had demonstrated would earn them an influential place in the reshaping of postwar Germany. Yet within a couple of years, the Bund was feeling almost as out of place as it had during the Nazi period. In 1950, Ellen Jungbluth, the last Bund entrant to swear an oath of commitment to the group, was writing impassioned notes to her fellow members, asking, "Why are there no young people in the Bund?" Soon she and the others had to resign themselves to simply aging gracefully together. Just as painfully, their status as political opponents of the Nazi regime was questioned, and their role as rescuers went unacknowledged. The group produced lengthy accounts of its wartime actions but to little avail. In the 1960s, the Bund even found itself accused of having exaggerated its record. Artur died unrecognized in 1968, his wife, Dore, eleven years later. In the 1980s, an attempt to obtain recognition for them at Yad Vashem, in Jerusalem, yielded little fruit. A second attempt by one of their beneficiaries, including a visit to Jerusalem to talk to the director of Yad Vashem personally, had no more success. The disappointment of postwar hopes provides the sad coda to our story—but it also helps us see something central: namely, how changing postwar climates and assumptions have limited and colored our understanding of resistance and rescue in the Third Reich.[10]

This book, then, seeks to reclaim the lives of an idealistic group of

Germans who, in a small way, did something remarkable. They sustained their community and upheld their values. At risk to themselves, they reached out to help others—and they saved lives. They left behind the resources for us to rediscover their achievement and to learn how and why they acted as they did.

1

Years of Innocence

Origins of the Bund

An explosion of revolutionary hopes followed the fall of the Wilhelmine monarchy in November 1918. No one embodied the radical aspirations of the moment better than Artur Jacobs, a charismatic thirty-eight-year-old with boundless optimism and self-confidence. Born in 1880 into modest circumstances in Elberfeld, a small town in the Wupper Valley, Artur went on to attend higher secondary school (in German, "Gymnasium") and university, and eventually found his vocation as a high school teacher. Artur was inspired by socialism's promise of social justice and by the verve and independence of the burgeoning German youth movement. In the spirit of the latter, he aimed to do away with the obligation of formal respect traditionally accorded the teacher, hoping instead to inspire his students with his magnetism and mentorship. Personality, not credentials, would affirm his claim to lead. Impatient, impassioned, careless about propriety (he once, for example, took a group of girls on a hiking trip during which teacher and pupils all slept in the same barn), compelling to those who accepted his leadership and dismissive of those who did not, Artur was a controversial figure among staff, pupils, and parents alike.[1]

In the turmoil after World War I, Artur's hope for an educational revolution that would lead to societal transformation was widely shared in

Germany. The radical mood briefly permeated even the Prussian educational administration (in Germany, education remained the responsibility of the individual states). In November 1918, Gustav Wyneken, an influential educator and the spiritual father of the Entschiedene Jugend ("Youth of Conviction"), Germany's "first revolutionary pupil and student movement,"[2] was given an official appointment by the new socialist education minister and charged with transforming the school curriculum for the new republic.

In Essen, Artur was a tireless advocate of educational change, mobilizing pupils in his school to force through the revolutionary idea of a "school council," which gave pupils a say in running the school. However, despite Artur's protestations, just a few months later the teaching staff voted by a large majority to end the experiment. Undaunted, Artur briefly pursued the grander project of a citywide pupil-teacher council. In August 1919, Essen became the center of the Entschiedene Jugend movement and Artur one of its most influential activists. After he helped organize a major conference of students from across the city, the local Catholic press incited a backlash among conservative pupils, teachers, and parents. In the ensuing battle over school politics, Artur, though still relatively young, was placed on extended sick leave and eventually forced to take early retirement, albeit with a generous pension. It was at this low point, with his hopes for revolutionary pedagogy crushed and his career brought to an untimely end, that Artur discovered the possibilities of adult education and called the Bund into being.[3]

In a wave of enthusiasm for widening mass access to higher education, 1919 saw the founding of *Volkshochschulen* (adult education institutes) across Germany. In Essen, Artur played a significant role in creating the new institute, which, unusually, offered courses in four separate religious and political divisions: Protestant, Catholic, "free" (i.e., nondenominational and, in fact, socialist), and "scientific-neutral" (i.e., liberal). Artur became the coordinator of the "free" division. Just as earlier in the Gymnasium, Artur sought to create a close bond between inspirational teacher and motivated students that would extend beyond the classroom. Here, in this new world of adult education full of idealistic teachers and students, his ideas fell on fertile ground.[4]

In March 1924, Artur and eight other teachers and pupils from the school, aged between twenty-five and forty-five and most of them women, formed a new group, to which they swore a solemn oath of commitment. Though they would eventually settle on "Bund: Community for Socialist Life," the name remained in flux for a while, changing from "Free Proletarian Bund" through various permutations, including "International Socialist Order: Bund." The designation "international" may seem grandiose for a community whose membership never exceeded two hundred, but in the parlance of the time it meant simply that they were hostile to nationalism and felt part of an international community of socialists. Whatever the official name, to the members it remained, simply, "the Bund." Among the original nine were several whom we have already met. Else Bramesfeld and Sonja Schreiber were teachers or teachers in training, inspired by the idea of a new kind of inclusive pedagogy. Lisa Jacob was one of three Jewish women in the original circle, the others being Artur's wife, Dore, and Else Goldreich.[5]

Politics of the Personal

The vast majority of the Bund's members lived in the Ruhr region—and the city of Essen, the sixth largest in Germany at the time, was the center of the group's activities. In the 1920s, the Ruhr was one of the most important industrial regions in the world. Its major industries were coal, iron, and steel, and its economy was dominated by giant companies like Krupp and Thyssen. Over the previous half century, towns and suburbs in the northern part of the region, where deeper, richer seams of coal were to be found, had grown at a speed that rivaled the explosion of gold-rush towns in the American West. After the First World War, Ruhr towns like Hamborn, Gelsenkirchen, and Oberhausen continued to support a radical population of coal miners and steelworkers. Living and working conditions here resembled the dark industrial scenes of a Dickens novel—or the grim world uncovered by the reportage of Alexander Stenbock-Fermor, the "Red Count"—a world that to many Germans seemed profoundly alien.[6]

Farther south, however, the region was more urbane and settled, with Essen well on its way to becoming an administrative and commercial hub. Towns and subdivisions along the Ruhr River, including those in the Essen-Stadtwald area, where Artur and Dore lived, and where the Bund would build its central meetinghouse, were leafy, attractive, and middle-class. South of the Ruhr, along the Wupper Valley, several small towns with textile or metallurgical specializations had been the cradle of Germany's industrial revolution. After Essen, the city of Wuppertal was home to the second-largest concentration of Bund members. During the early 1920s, the Ruhr region was rife with unrest: frequent strikes, a bitter standoff with the French forces that occupied the western part of the region after World War I, and a major left-wing uprising in the wake of the failed Kapp Putsch of 1920.[7]

The Bund shows the influence of so many contemporary trends that it is hard to imagine it emerging anywhere but in Weimar Germany.[8] For one thing, it drew heavily on the ethos of the German youth movements. Most of the members had belonged to one or another of the youth groups that were popular at the time, whether the prewar Wandervogel, the left-wing Naturfreunde ("Friends of Nature"), or Zionist groups. The term *Bund* can mean many things, including "league," "federation," or "covenant," but in the youth scene of the 1920s, it acquired a very specific meaning. The so-called *bündisch* youth movement that took shape after the First World War anticipated many of the features of Artur's group. Almost all *Bünde* were united in their mission of bringing together a group of men (and sometimes women) closely bonded by loyalty and common values. They also shared the sense that their groups represented natural fellowships, which stood in opposition to what they considered the artificial forms and conventions of modern society. Each *Bund* was supposed to form organically around a natural leader, whose inspiring personality would serve as the group's center. This meant that in the case of "our" Bund, regardless of Artur's natural gifts, the youth movement values with which many Bund members had grown up had prepared them to seek and accept a charismatic leader.[9]

To understand the Bund as experienced by its members, we have to imagine an entity that was part political group, part 1960s commune, and part Quaker society. Like a political party (though it did not stand for elections), the Bund had clear goals for societal change, advocating above all for socialist principles, including public ownership of the means of production. Artur's Bund felt close to the main parties in the working-class movement, the Social Democrats (SPD) and the Communists (KPD), and, like other left-wing splinter groups, aspired to be an elite vanguard, helping to influence the larger workers' movement. To do this, it sent members into both the SPD and the KPD in order to maintain connection with those parties.

However, the term "Socialist Life" in the Bund's name also referred to the organization's desire to experiment with new ways of living, to pursue what was known in Weimar as "life reform." Bund members sought to create their own community, living by their own rules. Many resided together in houses owned or rented by the group. Unlike the communes of the 1960s, the Bund did not intend to withdraw from the world. In a 1920s pamphlet, the group presented itself as "a socialist life-and-struggle community in the industrial heartland"[10] whose members' mission was "to take socialism seriously" in their own lives "and to put truth into practice— without fear of the consequences or of clashes with the world around us."[11] It demanded from its members a degree of self-denial that no 1960s collective ever would. There were to be no drugs; Bundists were expected to do without alcohol and even nicotine, though caffeine seems to have been an addiction they could not renounce.

As with many other so-called life-reform groups in the Weimar period, the Bund made no distinction between the personal and the political. Thus, its members applied their shared principles not only to questions of national importance but to all aspects of daily life. When Artur, Dore, Lisa, Sonja, Else, and others came together, they were as likely to discuss marital relationships, work problems, difficulties in raising children, or failure to fulfill obligations to the group as the development of the world economy.

"For the Bund member," declared a Bund publication in 1929, "there is no private life separate from the Bund."[12] At the group's annual *Verpflichtung* ("commitment") ceremony, which took place around Easter, members deemed ready would solemnly swear to uphold the Bund law. The law began with a preamble stating that all who committed themselves to the Bund placed their lives and all their capacities unconditionally at its service. "Those making the commitment," it went on, "must be ready to place the calling above all else and to serve it to the best of their ability. Everything else in life (job, family, personal relationships, worries about one's livelihood) should be secondary to this central purpose."[13] Members' relatives often found it difficult to accept second place behind the organization. Else Goldreich and Tove Gerson, for example, became estranged from some of their family members, and Meta Kamp-Steinmann grew increasingly alienated from her spouse, who did not belong to the Bund.[14]

Surviving records from the 1920s and early 1930s reveal how aggressively the group's leadership intervened in the personal lives of its members. Young couples were required to practice a "test marriage" under the eyes of the Bund before they could wed. (Though the exact implications of this remain shrouded in secrecy!) In some cases, the group took children away from parents when they felt that doing so would better enable the children to mature as independent beings. Indeed, for a few years in the late 1920s, the Bund experimented with removing all members' children to have them board and learn under supervision of Bund members in a secluded schoolhouse in the woods.

As the Bund expanded the range of its activities, members' lives increasingly belonged to the group. On Sundays in Essen, they would spend the whole day together, discussing, eating, walking, playing music, and exercising. In the later 1920s, branches were set up in Mülheim, Wuppertal, Remscheid, and elsewhere in the Ruhr. Each branch held meetings at least once a week. Once a month, Essen would host a tightly choreographed weekend of studies, discussion, and physical exercise for members from all the branches. At Easter there would be a five- or six-day retreat somewhere in the Ruhr, which everyone would attend—it was here that the commitment ceremony took place. In early summer, the Bund held a two-day festival, and in August all Bund members were expected to join a two-week retreat in the Sauerland or the North Sea region, wandering, debating, and exercising in heathland or hilly landscapes. At Christmas, the group would hold its own "festival of light," which incorporated some of the rituals of a German Christmas celebration, though divorced of any explicitly Christian element, and with the addition of their own literary and philosophical touches.[15]

During the 1920s, Bund members presided over at least three communal "Bund houses." The group's central meeting place and residence in Essen, which its members called the "Blockhaus" (or "Log Cabin") was built in 1927. The house still stands—it is virtually the only all-timber building in Essen to have survived the war. Upstairs there was a small apartment, in which Sonja Schreiber lived for many years. In Essen's Eyhofstrasse (later renamed Dönhof Street), Artur and Dore owned the house they lived in—

and it also became a place for many Bund members to practice communal living on a rotating basis. Another house in Wuppertal-Barmen, on the Schützenstrasse, served a similar function. Here, core residents included Ernst and Pia Jungbluth, Liesel Speer, and Walter and Gertrud Jacobs. Here, too, beyond the more or less permanent occupants, residents would come and go, giving many the opportunity to experience daily life in the group.

Beyond such experiments in communal living, the Bund also threw itself into educational work at all levels. Recent educational reforms allowed the development of non-confessional elementary schools for the first time and imposed relatively few regulations. The Bund took advantage of these new opportunities by working with parents in a number of schools to replace conventional curricula with holistic learning and to extend school instruction into the family. The Bund also expanded adult education courses into several surrounding cities and spent a great deal of energy organizing lectures, cultural meetings, festivals, and other public events with the goal of winning new recruits. In addition, the Bund also produced a significant number of pamphlets, brochures, and small booklets designed to inform the wider public about its philosophy.[16]

As with its view of politics, the Bund's concept of freedom also takes some understanding. Like later alternative movements, Bund members rejected what they saw as bourgeois convention. Unlike their post-1968 counterparts, however, the Bund espoused neither sexual freedom nor untrammeled self-expression. It has often been said of Weimar *bündisch* organizations that they sought freedom for the collective rather than for the individual, but this was not true of Artur and friends, who were deeply concerned with individual freedom. Indeed, they called on one another to renounce claims of ownership over spouses—not for free love but to avoid limiting each other's spiritual capacity. At the same time, they believed that true freedom required the individual to rise above the tyranny of her drives and whims, and to align her own wishes with the needs of the whole. True freedom thus required practice, self-discipline, and self-denial—and it was the group's task to help the individual on this path. From 1929 on, the Bund styled itself an *Orden*, or "order," and in 1931 it renamed itself the Internationaler Sozialistischer Orden: Bund. The monkish overtones of "Order" and the emphasis on daily acts of self-control reflected the Bund's explicit aspiration to replicate the strength of commitment and the asceticism of religious orders, reminding us of a religious sect or of German Quaker movements at the time.[17]

For all the emphasis on individual liberty, the Bund was profoundly hierarchical. In a 1928 publication, Dore wrote that the true leader should stand above the group, which could never achieve its goals if it were a democratic organization.[18] This is striking language for a community sincerely committed to creating a "socialist" lifestyle and shows how strongly the notion of an organic hierarchy was embedded in the Bund and, indeed, in the wider youth movement—influenced milieu. In some other similar organizations, the internal hierarchy was so pronounced that tensions between the democratic impulse and the acceptance of leadership developed into open conflict.[19] In the Bund, although Artur was without doubt primus inter pares, the leadership was more shared and seems to have been less contentious, at least until 1945. A nine- or ten-person "Inner Circle," drawn largely from the original members, met, often weekly, to plan activities, deal with problems, and supervise all aspects of group life.[20]

From the outset, the Bund's underlying philosophy sought to reconcile the ideas of Kant and Marx. At first glance this seems a strange ambition, since Marx's writings were an explicit repudiation of the German "idealist" tradition that Kant had founded. For Kant, freedom was possible only when humans recognized the true requirement for a life lived in society— namely, that individuals learn to act in such a way so as not to impinge on others. This was what Kant described as the categorical imperative: that one should act "only according to that maxim whereby you can, at the same time, will that it should become a universal law." For Marx, however, Kant's philosophy was blind to the real forces that drove human history. Ethical imperatives divorced from the hard facts of social and economic development were just empty philosophizing. Marx's "dialectical materialism" predicted that a just society would result not from individuals voluntarily subscribing to moral maxims but from the liberating power of class conflict, as capitalism foundered on the inequalities, exploitation, and alienation that were its inevitable consequence.

If the Bund was to combine Kant and Marx, it would have to reconcile Kant's emphasis on the individual's ethical stance as the basis of liberty with Marx's emphasis on the determining historical role of material forces and the collective struggle of the social classes to which those forces gave rise.

In aspiring to just such a reconciliation, Artur's ideas bore the imprint of Hermann Cohen, with whom he had studied philosophy at the University of Marburg. Cohen was among the most profound and influential of the Neo-Kantians who sought to reinterpret Kant in the light of Marx's insights. What Cohen could not accept in Marx was that the just society of the future would inevitably arrive as the result of historical forces, with no universal ethical justification. For the Neo-Kantians, socialism was a question of morality and ultimately had to make sense for all, not just for the proletariat. The Bund, however, did not abandon Marx's belief in the historical role of the proletariat and called for institutional changes, such as public ownership of industry. It probably never succeeded in fully reconciling its different philosophical elements, but whatever the ultimate theoretical incoherence, the group felt empowered by its philosophy to press for socialist transformation at the societal level and for individual ethical improvement at the personal level.[21]

A distinctive element of the Bund's philosophy and daily practice was the work of Artur's wife, Dore. The daughter of two highly acculturated, educated German Jews, Berta and Ernst Marcus, Dore had been one of the seven schoolgirls who, back in 1909, had gone hiking with their teacher, Artur Jacobs, and scandalously overnighted in a barn. Artur came to know Dore, fourteen years his junior, while giving lessons in math and physics to her and a group of other girls. Dore's father, a judge, was also a noted Kant scholar, and he formed an instant bond with Artur. Dore herself was idealistic and intelligent, and as a young teenager was already a youth movement enthusiast. When Artur appeared on the scene, she became a lifelong admirer; after some years the couple became secretly engaged, and they married in 1914. She was one of the Bund's founder-members.[22]

Dore's gift to the Bund was *Körperbildung*—literally, "body education"; the modish word had been coined for new forms of physical exercise regimes. Here again, the Bund was part of a larger trend. The period spanning the late nineteenth and early twentieth centuries was a great age for seeking a new, ostensibly more natural relationship to the body. Sun worship, nudism, excursions into nature, new forms of physical exercise and gymnastics, and revolutionary, self-consciously primal forms of dance flourished. Their practitioners saw them as reclaiming the body from the depredations of industrial society and as symbols and harbingers of societal renaissance. Dore's induction into this world had come when she was a child, in the form of the eurhythmics of Émile Jaques-Dalcroze. Dalcroze sought to deepen access to music through exercises in physical rhythm, and like many of his contemporaries, he hoped thereby to achieve a new liberation of the human spirit. In 1911 Dore began studying at the Bildungsanstalt, Dalcroze's newly established center for eurhythmic gymnastics in Hellerau, which very soon attracted innovative figures in dance and music from all over Europe. During the early 1920s, Dore evolved her own highly distinctive approach to physical movement in tandem with the development of the Bund—and in 1925, she founded the Essen-based Bundesschule für Körperbildung und Rhythmische Erziehung (Bund School for Body Training and Eurhythmic Education), which would hold classes in the Blockhaus.[23]

Dore aimed to forge a new relationship to the body in a technological age. For those taking her adult education courses and Bund school classes in the 1920s, the experience resembled a kind of physical psychotherapy. The individual was gently but firmly compelled to rethink the most fundamental aspects of her relationship to her physical self. Posture, movement, engaging with an object, negotiating a physical space—all were subject to scrutiny. Dore also introduced another recent dance innovation, the so-called *Bewegungschöre*, or movement choirs, to create a kind of modern dance in which the individual would find his natural place in the larger group. Unlike the pioneer of the Bewegungschor, Rudolf von Laban, Dore was less interested in aesthetic performance than in achieving a natural relationship between the individual and the collective. Many found this to be a transformative experience. Many, in fact, became aware of the Bund after seeing group performances led by Dore or her pupils.[24]

The Bund and Its Members

Given the Bund's emphasis on education, it is not surprising that many schoolteachers joined. Ernst Jungbluth was one of them. Like Artur he came from a modest, pietistic background in the Wupper Valley, in Ernst's case in Barmen. (When Artur and Ernst were young, Elberfeld and Barmen were two separate industrial towns adjacent to each other along the Wupper River. In 1929, along with a number of other smaller communi-

ties, they were merged into a new city given the name of Wuppertal.) Ernst
grew dissatisfied with the church's stance on social issues and became a
Communist after the First World War. Encountering Artur soon after the
war, Ernst quickly became a devoted admirer, as well as a founding member of the Bund. He remained an irrepressible optimist all his life and would
take over as the group's leading figure when Artur grew frail in the 1950s.
Sonja, also a teacher, was the daughter of a city councillor and, like several
other women in the group, came from a more solidly middle-class background. Born in 1894, she was one of the group's older members. Sonja
was a gentle idealist, remembered with affection by her pupils half a lifetime later, and devoted to the Bund; for decades she lived in the Blockhaus.
A significant share of the members were workers, some seeking to improve
themselves through education, others inspired by performances of the
Bund's movement choirs. Indeed, for the middle-class Tove Gerson, the first
classes with Dore felt revolutionary precisely because workingmen and
middle-class women were occupying the same intimate space, without airs
or embarrassment.[25]

Partly because of the central role played by Dore's school in generat-
ing recruits, partly because of the group's emphasis on education, and perhaps also because of Artur's presence and leadership, from the beginning
the Bund attracted many women. Of the founding group of nine, we know
there were at least five and probably six women. (The identities of seven
Inner Circle members are securely established: Else Bramesfeld, Ernst Jungbluth, Artur and Dore Jacobs, Lisa Jacob, Sonja Schreiber, and Else Goldreich, who died young in 1928. We are not sure if the other two were Käthe
Franke and Berthold Levy.) Dore's work offered women the chance to train
as *Körperbildung* and gymnastics teachers, a career increasingly recognized
as a profession during the 1920s and 1930s. The presence of so many
women went hand in hand with a keen awareness of gender inequality.
Among the Bund's many publications was the 1932 tract *Man and Woman
as Comrades in the Struggle*, which, in keeping with contemporary socialist
feminism, insisted on female employment as the means to equality and
independence. Unlike many contemporary publications, it acknowledged
that female employment would call for a new male role in the home, though
women who joined the Bund without their partners found this hard to
put into practice. In fact, gender issues were often the most direct and

challenging area of daily life in which to apply and test the movement's
principles.[26]

Like Artur and Ernst, several Bundists came from strongly Protestant
or pietistic backgrounds—particularly the sizable contingent from the
Wupper Valley. Many of them felt that organized religion had failed to
address social injustice and left the church in protest, though for others,
such a significant break proved extremely difficult and involved painful
battles of conscience. In any case, despite the Bund's hostility to Chris-
tianity for what its members saw as its obscurantism, as well as its inculca-
tion of political passivity and deference to the powerful, much of the group's
style and values were informed by Low Church Protestantism. Writing in
1922, the sociologist Hermann Schmalenbach noted that, in fact, *bündisch*
organizations generally were characterized not just by close emotional ties
between members but also by a religious spirit. The German word *Bund* is
also the term for the biblical covenant, and this was no doubt part of its
appeal for many. In Artur's Bund, the spiritual element was particularly
marked, given the group's festival of light, its search for inner truth, its use
of the word *Sendung*, or "calling," in describing its mission, its asceticism,
and its sense of community—all strongly reminiscent of German pietism.

The membership also included a significant minority of Jews or people
with Jewish connections. Dore, having grown up in a very acculturated
German Jewish family, had felt no strong bonds to Judaism as a child. Nevertheless, she became an enthusiastic Zionist as a student, and at one point
considered moving to Palestine. When she returned to Essen after her studies in Hellerau, she founded a branch of the Zionist youth group Blau-
Weiss (Blue-White), one of the first youth groups in the city in which boys
and girls could go on trips together and as equals. Dore's basement was
full of the paraphernalia of her Blue-White Zionist youth group, which
expressed a Jewish-socialist identity more than a true desire to go to Palestine. Through Dore, other left-wing or Zionist Jewish youngsters found
their way to the Bund.

Dore's star pupil in the school, for example, was Lisa Jacob, five years
her junior. The daughter of an Upper Silesian Jewish businessman, Lisa had
been a Blue-White member in her hometown and joined Dore's group
before becoming one of the Bund's founders. Other Jews included Else
Goldreich, a middle-class mother of three, who was also there from the

beginning; Berthold Levy, the son of a distinguished Jewish couple, who met Artur through adult education classes; Erna Michels, the daughter of a well-known Wuppertal judge; Mikscha Brandsdorfer, who trained under Dore and taught at the school until 1933; and Wasja Enoch, the daughter of Eastern European immigrants, who trained with Dore in the early 1930s. Many of the Jewish members came from solid bourgeois backgrounds, but there were also working-class and Eastern European Jews in the group. Some non-Jewish Bund members had strong Jewish connections. One example was Grete Dreibholz in Remscheid, who, as we know, was the sister-in-law of the Jewish writer Friedrich Wolf (Wolf's son Markus would become the East German spymaster after the war). Another was Tove Gerson, who came to the Bund in 1933 via Dore's school and was married to a man with part-Jewish ancestry.[27]

Seeing the Dangers?

When I interviewed an already very frail and ill Änne Schmitz, she said reverentially, in a quivery voice, "Artur saw the dangers, saw the dangers early on."[28] Maria Briel made a similar claim about Ernst Jungbluth. "He really fought against the widely held idea that the Nazis' hold on power would be brief," she said. "The Bund was always very clear on this point."[29] Dore's recollections affirmed this view. "The Nazi seizure of power did not find us unprepared," she wrote in her history of the Bund. "We had no illusions about the supposed 'weakness' of this demonic movement."[30]

This claim that the Bund had been able to weather the storm because it had so clearly anticipated the Nazi threat was one the group was already making soon after the war. But how prepared had it really been? It had not in any sense formed to fight the Nazis. Certainly, Artur was an outspoken opponent of any kind of ethnic nationalism, but when he and his friends swore the oath of commitment to one another in 1924, the Nazis were an insignificant force.[31] After an abortive putsch attempt in November 1923, Hitler was languishing in jail. From the end of 1930 up to the Nazi seizure of power in January 1933, however, it took no great insight to see that the country was in the grip of a major crisis. The Nazis' September 1930 electoral breakthrough and their stunning results in the regional elections of

April 1932 and the national election in July of that year made it all too obvious that democracy was threatened by a radical right. By the summer of
1932, the Nazis were by far the largest party in the national parliament
and a major force in many Ruhr cities. Long before obtaining power, they
represented a physical threat to anyone on the left. The Essen police, among
others, showed extraordinary tolerance of the right, allowing the Nazis'
paramilitary arm, the Sturmabteilung (SA), to act on the streets with impunity from early on. Violence against property and persons, even murder,
went unpunished.[32] To that extent, the threat was obvious.

Like other small left-wing groups, the Bund tried to broker a rapproche-
ment between the increasingly estranged Social Democratic and Communist Parties in order to strengthen opposition to the Nazis. In the fall
of 1931, the International Socialist Order (ISO), as the Bund then called
itself, organized a series of public meetings to present its platform and plead
with the working-class parties to join together. Not surprisingly, local party
leaderships were skeptical. Discussions at Bund meetings resulted in Communists and Social Democrats hurling insults at one another. In Mülheim,
the local KPD branch forced Bund members to choose where their loyalties lay. While some stayed with the Bund, others agreed to follow the party
line. Half of the twenty members of the Mülheim group bowed to the party
and left, and in Wuppertal, Social Democratic and Communist papers publicly denounced the Bund.[33]

The Bund was undoubtedly correct about close cooperation between
the left-wing parties being Germany's best hope for stopping Hitler. Yet it
is hard to see its program as contributing to that end. Despite militant rhetoric about being an "absolutely reliable storm troop," the Bund program
remained what it had always been: dedicated to working toward a better
society through "conferences, lectures, weekend meetings, scientific, ped-
agogic, political, and artistic classes and study groups, choirs and movement choirs, a network of adult education circles," and other programs. The
discrepancy between its meetings calling for urgent action and its actual
program of piecemeal self-improvement is almost touching. This was not
a group preparing for battle with the Nazis. Bund members were idealists,
not street brawlers. Their kind of action was education, day-to-day ethical choices, and subordination to the cause. How on earth would they cope
with Nazi terror?[34]

2

The Assault

Hitler's first war was fought against the German Left. As with his later war against Britain, this one, too, began with a "phony war." For a few weeks after Hitler was appointed chancellor, on January 30, 1933, there were skirmishes here, a police directive there, but political life continued with some semblance of normality. An ominous sign came on February 22, when the Prussian minister-president, Hermann Göring, enlisted SA thugs as auxiliary police. They could now pummel their political opponents with impunity. But it was not until after the Reichstag fire on February 27 that hostilities began in earnest. The following day, the Decree for the Protection of People and State was issued, allowing the indefinite "protective custody" of political opponents. Within a week, one thousand Communists had been imprisoned in the Düsseldorf administrative region alone (where Essen and other western Ruhr cities were located) and more than ten thousand across the nation. Violent repression of Social Democrats soon followed. By the end of April, forty to fifty thousand opponents of the regime had been incarcerated. In towns throughout the Ruhr, police and SA combed neighborhood after neighborhood and house after house for wanted men. The lucky ones were interned in prisons and workhouses, the unlucky ones in makeshift concentration camps, run-down hotels, youth hostels, sports grounds, even a converted restaurant.[1]

The Bund, too, soon found itself in the spotlight, though initially the new rulers' resentful brutality was tempered by their clumsy amateurishness. Shortly after the seizure of power, Essen's *National-Zeitung* newspaper denounced the Bund's adult education work as Communist propaganda. A few days later, armed SA men surrounded the Blockhaus. Bund member Karl Heilwagen was stopped as he came out of the building, hustled back inside, and interrogated. We even have a report from one of the SA stalwarts who took part in the raid, the appropriately named Herr Bruchhaus, who happened to live close by. According to his report, he and others ransacked the Bund's quarters that evening and were about to raise the Nazi flag over the building when five policemen, summoned by Dore, appeared and put a stop to the raid. Bruchhaus also claimed that the SA had found photographs on the premises showing three couples in compromising positions: "apparently three Jewish men and three Christian girls—all three were completely naked and the men and girls were embracing." Unfortunately for Herr Bruchhaus, the photos had been "mislaid" and could not be produced in evidence.[2]

Dore's call to the police is an indication that in these very early weeks the Nazis had yet to gain complete control of the forces of law and order. Bruchhaus noted that the SA members were "extraordinarily angry" that the police had stopped them and "exposed" them in front of the civilian population.[3] Artur, too, found that not everything had been Nazified when he wrote to the director of the Essen Volkshochschule to alert him to the *National-Zeitung*'s critique. The director responded that he had received assurances from the paper's editor that in the future, any articles about adult education would be submitted to the director for comment. But the truce proved short-lived. The elections of March 5, 1933, confirmed the National Socialist German Workers' Party (the NSDAP or Nazi Party) as the strongest party in the Reichstag, albeit still lacking the hoped-for absolute majority. Hitler accelerated the offensive against the left. The Bund now endured what Dore described to her son as a lengthy period "with the heat turned up."[4]

In early April, police raided the house on Eyhof Street in Essen where Dore and Artur were living with other Bund members, noting the names of those present and confiscating books and letters. Dore was interrogated at police headquarters the next day. Fearing that the police were planning to arrest him, Artur went on the run, spending several uncomfortable weeks tramping through the Sauerland. From time to time he showed up at Bund friends' houses. Then, in June, the police raided the house of a Bund supporter in Essen, the Krupp manager Martin Schubert. Confident that he would be above suspicion, the group had entrusted him with three suitcases stuffed full of documents, including minutes from meetings of the Bund's Inner Circle. All of this was discovered and confiscated during the raid. Schubert himself was placed in "protective custody" and released only toward the end of August. Authorities used the documents to begin legal action against Artur. On September 14, 1933, the police issued a decree dissolving both the Bund and Dore's school and confiscated their books and equipment on the grounds that they "worked for the Marxist cause."[5] For the rest of the Nazi period, the Bund would operate illegally.

Many of the Bund members, particularly the Communists among them, now found themselves in the regime's sights. Ernst Jungbluth, a schoolteacher and Communist, was arrested when he went to obtain a passport to visit Switzerland for medical treatment. His house was searched, his books taken, and he was sent to one of the many brutal improvised concentration camps, in his case in Brauweiler, where he suffered two tough months, including some weeks in solitary confinement, before being released. Berthold Levy, who was not a Communist but was Jewish, was taken into protective custody, as was Georg Reuter, one of the most talented graduates of Dore Jacobs's school. In Remscheid, Grete Dreibholz, with close family links to the Jewish playwright and left-winger Friedrich Wolf, was interrogated by the Nazis. She was dismissed from her well-paid job as personal secretary to a steel industrialist. Tilde Stürmer was similarly forced out of her promising administrative post with the Krefeld Chamber of Commerce.[6]

Fearing political action against them, other Bund figures left the region altogether. Some headed to Göttingen, others to Hamburg. Erna Michels crossed the border into nearby Holland; as a leftist Jew, she was particularly under threat. Another member, Doris Braune, who had encountered the Bund through Artur's adult education classes, went down to Meersburg, on Lake Constance, to stay in the small guesthouse run by Käthe Franke

and Julie Schreiber, Sonja's sister, a little establishment that would later play
a key role in many comrades' survival. At some point, Artur himself considered immigrating to Switzerland, but it seems that his old colleague Anna
Siemsen, in precarious Swiss exile, told him that immigrants were having
a very hard time and that he should stay where he was. To lessen the pressure on the Jacobses' thirteen-year old son, Gottfried ("Friedl"), Artur and
Dore sent him up to Dore's sister in Hamburg. Before long, Dore's sciatica
flared up. Throughout the Nazi years it would be an indicator of acute
stress, becoming so paralyzing that for long periods she was barely able to
move.[7]

Grudges and Politics

The group suffered considerable violence in the opening weeks of the
regime, but not all of it meant that the regime saw the Bund itself as a particular threat. Dore's school for physical education was targeted as much
because she was Jewish as because it was seen as subversive. Artur had made
political enemies well before starting the Bund because of his public visibility as part of a radical youth movement. As a former high school teacher,
he also had to contend with resentful former pupils who had not liked his
revolutionary teaching style and were now in positions of influence—most
notably Essen's newly appointed "Commissar for School Matters,"
Dr. Bubenzer. Ernst Jungbluth and others were targeted as Communists,
and Berthold Levy was imprisoned in place of his father, the well-known
left-wing lawyer Friedrich Levy, who was allowed out of protective custody on grounds of ill health while his sons were taken instead. However
varied the reasons, the fact was that the group was full of people who one
way or another were under suspicion.[8]

   The notion of totalitarian rule conjures up faceless violence, and of
course in many ways the relentless procedures of the police and the Gestapo
were just that. Yet in the small- and medium-sized towns of the Ruhr area,
where people knew one another, there were plenty of old scores to be settled, too. The aggression of the party and the police against the Bund was
often grounded in personal grudges. In a note sent to the police in September, pleading for her school to be allowed to remain open, Dore said

the continuous persecution they had faced since March was the result of rumors and slander circulated by individuals in the neighborhood. This was not just a story for officials—she later wrote to her son, Friedl, about the "rather wild rumors" that had been spread by a hostile neighbor. Dore's fears are confirmed by records of the Prussian education authorities. As part of the city of Essen's efforts to strip Jacobs of his pension, it forwarded to the education authorities a series of denunciations that had been made by ordinary citizens against Jacobs and the Bund. Conservative neighbors, some of whom had tried to prevent the Blockhaus from ever being built, back in the 1920s, now found a willing ear for their complaints. And the authorities were quick to put them to good use. It was Artur's former pupil Dr. Bubenzer, for example, who conceived of the operation to deprive Artur of the teacher's pension he had been receiving since being forced into early retirement in the 1920s.[9]

Thanks to letters the Bund sent to the police, preserved in the archives, we can see the group's defensive strategies forming very early on. As the city authorities grew more aggressive, the group tried to present Dore's school and even the Bund as apolitical and to emphasize their distance from the Communists. Members—even when newly released from protective custody and thus with every reason to keep their heads down—were courageous enough to submit affidavits confirming the Bund's lack of political involvement and Communist hostility toward them.[10] Taking for granted even at this stage that the mail was intercepted, they wrote seemingly naïve letters to each other, assuring each other that they had confirmed to the police that the group was not in any way Communist and hoping that this would soon end the matter. This effort was clearly coordinated, as evidenced by the fact that all followed the same script. Thus Martin Schubert sent Dore a letter about his interrogation, noting that since "the police have been able to establish that I am not in any way involved in politics, your pure record must now finally be free of the shadow of rumors and denunciations."[11] This letter nicely matched the one Dore herself would send to the police a couple of weeks later, emphasizing the school's lack of political character. The group was not afraid to lie and, within certain limits, was also not afraid to appear loyal to the new regime.

The letters remind us, too, that while there were SA thugs ready to storm the building and raise a flag on the roof, much of the persecution now took more bureaucratic, routinized forms. Sometimes this offered limited opportunities to avert the worst. One could still write letters to the police president, and occasionally achieve something by doing so. Dore was able to have some of her confiscated books and equipment returned, and even though her school had been shut down, she was free to rent out the Blockhaus to other gymnastics teachers, ostensibly operating under their own steam. The work of her school could thus continue in the guise of these self-employed teachers offering hourly instruction in the Blockhaus.

But these concessions were minor. Despite Artur's efforts to defend himself, the three suitcases of papers confiscated from Martin Schubert were used to show that he was a Communist (though in fact he had probably never been a member of the Communist Party). Under the Law for the Restoration of the Civil Service, his pension was withdrawn, effective as of 1934. Dore similarly found herself in a losing battle with Essen and Reich authorities over the right to maintain her school. In a 1934 decision, the school's closure was reaffirmed and Dore banned from training non-Jewish pupils. Other Bund members in state service found themselves under duress. Sonja Schreiber, for example, was repeatedly interrogated by Bubenzer and was threatened with dismissal because of her links with the Bund. She also faced a crisis of conscience when all nondenominational schools were closed and primary school teachers were required to belong to a church. A celebration of Sonja's life produced by the Bund decades later suggests that supportive superiors kept extending her "grace" period. It no doubt helped that one of her sisters was an active Nazi and that her father had been a well-known deputy in the city assembly. No such protection existed for Berthold Levy, who, as a left-wing Jew, was sacked from the Humboldt-Realgymnasium, where he was a trainee teacher (the school now carries the name of his mother, Frida Levy).[12]

The Nazi assault ushered in difficult financial times for many. With Artur having lost his pension and Dore her school income, the Jacobses' earnings were reduced to the rent from the Blockhaus and Dore's private physical education lessons for Jewish pupils. It's hard to determine whether Artur had any other income—under Gestapo interrogation, he mentioned the rent from his wife's property (presumably the Blockhaus and the house on Eyhof Street) and gifts from relatives. It is more likely, however, that these payments and gifts came from other Bund members—some, like

Sonja Schreiber, living in a Bund property, others simply helping to keep Artur and Dore afloat. Georg Reuter and Karlos Morgenstern gave physical education lessons in Göttingen. Doris, living in the guesthouse in Meersburg, learned to manage orchards and earned money working as a gardener for various families in the neighborhood. In the mid-1930s she moved to Berlin and trained as a secretary in estate management at the Lette-Schule, a vocational school for women.[13] While many members faced financial difficulties, however, skilled workers in the group profited from rising employment and the modest wage growth of the 1930s.

A Chill Wind in the Schoolyard

The Bund learned, as did many other oppositional figures in Nazi Germany, that the chill new wind was often felt hardest by the children. In the rough-and-tumble of the playground, where Hitler Youth members saw their social muscle enhanced by their uniforms, and in the classroom, where Nazi enthusiasts among the teaching staff relished their new mission and fellow travelers felt the need to prove their credentials, children were soon exposed to the realities of the Nazi state. For Artur and Dore's son, Friedl, the dispatch to Hamburg to stay with his aunt and cousin was initially a welcome departure from his parents' stern eye, and his letters indicate that for a few weeks he enjoyed himself greatly, not least because he had not yet been placed in a new school. Though worried about the whereabouts of his father, who was at the time living rough for fear of persecution, Friedl hoped the stay in Hamburg might be extended. Despite their other troubles, however, his parents were unlikely to indulge such idleness for long, and in May they sent Friedl to a boarding school in the Harz Mountains. His mother had long expressed concern about his physical fragility and wanted him toughened up; Friedl was soon complaining about the amount of exercise he was having to do at the new school. He also faced a new concern: Were the boys he wished to befriend politically reliable? A sad note in June informed his parents that he intended to avoid getting into false relationships: "One never knows who one is dealing with." Meanwhile, worried about any kind of material getting into the wrong hands, his parents urged him to pass all their letters on to a relative for safekeeping.[14]

For another Bund child, Friedl Speer, the son of Bund member and teacher Liesel Speer, there was pressure at school to participate in religious instruction, even though a law requiring it had not yet been passed. Artur wrote to his son about the matter:

> Friedl [Speer] now has an important task, which requires cour-
> age. In general, school is increasingly becoming a trial of char-
> acter and courage for you. And that is for the best. Nothing is
> more terrifying today than people's cowardice and hypocrisy.
> They give in before they are even attacked. In a time of such
> groveling, every courageous person is doubly important.[15]

Artur's letter makes clear that the Bund was already considering where it could and should take a stand. His son responded, alarmed at the degree of courage on which his parents seemed to be insisting:

> You write that every courageous person is doubly important.
> Why? Resistance is surely pointless! Why make life difficult for
> oneself? I feel that it is perfectly all right to bend outwardly. You
> know that in my innermost self I will never bend. Explain to me
> why one has to make a stand externally too.[16]

Maria Briel recalled in later years that Friedl Jacobs suffered very badly at school. Fellow pupils played all sorts of nasty tricks on him.[17] How far this was directly attributable to the Nazi climate is, of course, hard to say. Bund children already felt like outsiders at schools even before 1933. Friedl was not an easy individual—part small child, part old man. But, certainly, the stakes had been raised. Even where there was no direct assault, there was the insidious fear of letting slip something incriminating. One of the Bund children, Margarete (not her real name), eight years old when the Nazis came to power, was acutely conscious of the discrepancy between what counted as true at home and what was said outside.[18] It was much harder for a child to know what constituted a dangerous or incriminating statement than the adults might have realized. Margarete remembered an incident from 1937 in which she was sitting in the classroom, reading Arabian fairy tales. The teacher asked her why she was not reading German ones. She panicked, fearing that her "un-German" behavior might have betrayed the family. In retrospect, she was struck that her twelve-year-old self had been unable to see that the question was not meant as a threat.

Denunciations and the Diffusion of Terror

For many Germans, the unsettled weeks after the seizure of power rapidly gave way to a sense of normalcy. As the insightful observer Sebastian Haffner noted, they had been expecting so much more violence than actually transpired that the predominant emotion was relief: "First came creation of fear by wild threats, then severe terror measures but nevertheless falling somewhat short of the threats, and finally gradual transition to a near-normalcy, but without complete renunciation of a little background terror."[19] For the Bund, too, the convulsions of the spring and summer of 1933 soon died away, although what emerged in their place was neither safe nor normal. For one thing, the police and, particularly, the Gestapo remained active. Investigations, interrogations, and arrests plagued the Bund throughout the Nazi years. In the second half of the 1930s, perhaps as a result of cross-border mail interception, Reinhard Heydrich's Sicherheitsdienst (SD) was periodically involved in monitoring the group, including checks of various Bund members' mail. In Wuppertal alone, Bund members were incarcerated in 1933, 1936, 1937, and 1938. In the last of these cases, August Schmitz was imprisoned when an incriminating pamphlet was found during a search of his house. Maria Briel, in Remscheid, escaped the same fate only because of her mother's quick thinking. While the Gestapo was in the house and Maria under orders not to move, her mother fiddled around with the fire and threw an underground newspaper on it.[20]

Many of these actions were not part of the concerted assault against the left but, rather, individual investigations triggered by denunciations from the public. "The people around us," the Bund wrote in an early postwar pamphlet,

> were strangers, enemies. In Germany, every "people's comrade" was a potential spy. In every tram, at concerts, at school, at the

factory, even in private homes, we felt surrounded by enemies. The informer was everywhere, right next to us. As a result, even in the thick of these turbulent times, one lived cut off, like an outcast, buried alive, as it were.[21]

In Wuppertal, soon after the seizure of power, Bund members occupying the shared house on the Schützenstrasse found hostile slogans painted on an exterior wall. Frightened, they decided to move to a different part of town where no one knew them, with neighbors who were very conservative but not out-and-out Nazis.[22] In Essen, the group had reason to fear its neighbors, both at the Jacobs house on Eyhof Street, now renamed Dönhof Street, and at the Blockhaus. In 1937, for example, one of Artur's resentful former pupils, Max Fross, who lived on the same street as the Blockhaus, helpfully kept the Gestapo informed about Bund activities.[23] Fross's statement captures his resentment, and it is full of inaccuracies (among many other errors, he mistakenly claimed that Artur was Jewish):

> I know some of the Communist Clique from the System time [a Nazi term for the Weimar years], and as his former pupil I know the notorious Jewish retired teacher Jacobs. I realized that some of his supporters, whom I know by sight, were going in and out of the basement of the temporary church (formerly Communist building) . . . I therefore would like to suggest that these people be closely monitored to see if the meetings are a danger to the state.[24]

Overall, the Bund's experience is a reminder that even in working-class heartlands like the Ruhr or Saar regions, the Nazis rapidly destroyed the cohesion and solidarity of the milieu. While particular streets or blocks of houses remained safe spaces in which to grumble about the regime (Änne Schmitz, for example, lived among trusted neighbors), most neighborhoods were not.[25] The Blockhaus and the Jacobses' home were located, in any case, in solid middle-class neighborhoods that were more likely to be pro-Nazi and anti-Communist. Even if there was only one pro-Nazi family on a street—or, worse, if one suspected that there might be such a family but was unsure which one it was—that was enough to undermine easy sociability. The Nazis proved adept at encouraging denunciations from neighbors, workmates, and even fellow drinkers at the pub. Many were motivated by resentments and conflicts that predated the Third Reich or had little to do with Nazism, as the examples of Artur's former pupils show. Letters of denunciation reveal a confused mix of motives, sometimes citing clothing, lifestyle, and beliefs to convey a sense of a threatening other. Rumors and murmurs about supposed misfits and regime opponents circulated and grew, and eventually were relayed to the Gestapo.[26]

The men and women of the Bund feared hostile reactions not only from strangers but also from friends and family. Some had openly pro-Nazi relatives. One person I interviewed remembered that her mother, a Bund member, was estranged from her own parents. When her mother reluctantly attended a family celebration at the parental home, she found it gay with Nazi flags. Margarete, the interviewee who preferred to use a pseudonym, had a good relationship with her mother's parents but felt that Oma and Opa disapproved of everything her mother did. In another case, Ellen Hube-Brandt (later Ellen Jungbluth), who came to the group in the late 1930s, was alienated from her pro-Nazi family before she ever encountered the Bund. She remembered her father "standing up from the sofa and making a gesture of obeisance whenever the *Horst-Wessel Lied* was played. It was so awful."[27]

Even when relatives and friends were not Nazis, they often looked askance at the Bund members' unwillingness to fit in. Many in the Bund had already brooked family opposition in the 1920s because of their unconventional lifestyle choices.[28] Making difficult decisions in the face of family disapproval had undoubtedly steeled Bund members psychologically for the new challenges of the Nazi era. But one should not, for that reason, fail to appreciate the tensions, particularly when the group embarked on actions carrying serious risks of official reprisal. In an interview in 1990, for example, Maria Briel spoke of the pressures relatives brought to bear. She still remembered a little ditty her family would often recite about how only the stupid go against the flow. In her case, the conflict did not lead to a permanent rift, although she endured a great deal of psychological stress, and at the time she felt able to speak openly only with her sister.[29]

An Existential Crisis

Though they might claim to have been prepared for the challenges of Nazi rule, Bund members never sought to underplay the shock of 1933 and the blows and threats that rained down on them. Suddenly, they found themselves at war. As Tove told me, and as Artur and friends wrote after the war ended, they were not by nature the sort of physically courageous individuals who relished the heat of battle. They were gentle souls, fearful of suffering, torture, prison, and death.[30] The more the group got to know of the regime, the more intimidating it seemed. Most of us, thankfully, have never had to experience the naked fear occasioned by a nighttime knock at the door, still less exposure to interrogation and threat of torture. We can barely imagine the anxiety of those early weeks and months, when the forces of law and order could no longer be relied upon—indeed, were increasingly feared—nor the grinding anxiety occasioned by the constant threat of denunciation.

But the most dramatic impact of the Nazi assault is one that is never mentioned in the Bund's postwar writings. In these sources, we see the Bund attempting to present its development from the 1920s through the Nazi years as a seamless whole, and to argue that the group's distinctive project and character in the 1920s laid the foundation for its strength in the 1930s and 1940s.[31] There was, as we will see, much about its utopian experiment that proved its worth under Nazi rule. Yet it is obvious there could be no easy continuity after the seizure of power. After all, the Bund's raison d'être before 1933 was *Bildung*, education. Within the group itself, *Bildung* meant educating the members to live ethical lives on a higher plane of spiritual freedom. As it turned out, this dimension could, with daring and difficulty, be sustained even in the Third Reich. But given its larger ambitions, the little community made sense only if it was an agent of transformation beyond the group's confines—reforming elementary schools, teaching and inspiring others in adult education institutes, holding public meetings, or promoting its own example of a lived utopia via pamphlets, talks, dance, and the steady recruitment of new members. Curiously, nowhere in its postwar accounts did any Bund member acknowledge the impact of the fact that in 1933 this mission as "multiplier" and as vanguard abruptly came to an end.

The group must have faced the stark question: What was its purpose now? If it could not influence and guide others, did it even deserve to exist? After the war, in hindsight, the Nazi years could be presented as the ulti- mate trial, one in which the group's resolve and commitment were hard- ened and sharpened. That was a plausible story for the Bundists to tell in retrospect, when they knew that the Nazi period had been finite and tem- porary. Yet for a while at least, and particularly when hope faded that the regime would quickly collapse, there must have been profound uncertainty about the group's purpose and function. Only in a handful of speeches toward the end of the war, as the prospect of Nazi defeat at last seemed near, did Artur speak openly about the challenges they had faced.[32] "All activity for the outside world stopped," he acknowledged, "and with it all success, all resonance, all affirmation."[33] Under the Third Reich, the Bund was on its own. Could it survive? And even if it could, what was the point of doing so?

3

From Vanguard to Refuge

It did not take long before the Nazis were making inroads even into social groups that had not supported them before 1933—above all, the working class. As early as December 1933, Neu Beginnen (like the Bund, a small, well-informed, and clear-eyed left-wing group) noted that the Nazis were enjoying a much more positive reception across the social spectrum than had been expected. The party's very favorable results in the November Reichstag elections and in the plebiscite on leaving the League of Nations in November 1933 were not, the group argued, the result of electoral fraud and terror.[1]

By 1935 there were strong signs of economic recovery, and by the end of 1936 Germany was approaching full employment. Years of crisis and chaos were giving way to a sense of energy and purpose, and Germany now projected an image of confidence and power on the international stage. Few Germans, even anti-Nazis, and even German Jews subject to brutal exclusionary pressures, were immune to a sense of triumph at the reassertion of national sovereignty against Versailles's rules—a resurgence manifest in the reintroduction of conscription in 1935, the remilitarization of Germany's Rhineland territory in 1936, and the incorporation of Austria into a greater Germany in 1938. Alongside these achievements, the reestablishment of strong authority and leadership and the apparent creation of a more classless society also appealed to elements in both the socialist and the Catholic milieus that had previously been staunchly anti-Nazi.[2]

Finding that even formerly friendly territory was now in the enemy camp took a heavy toll on the Bund's morale. "It was hard not to lose one's faith," an early postwar Bund publication explained, when the socialist movement had collapsed "like a house of cards" and everything and everyone seemed to be conspiring against them and their beliefs.[3] The grinding weight of isolation and threats bore down on the group. For Artur, the psychological low point came not in 1933 but a year or two later. In a speech given on the eve of the Third Reich's collapse, he recalled that for a while the group had been able to sustain its earlier momentum, despite the danger and the isolation. Only then did their mental reserves run out. In the pre-Nazi era they had sometimes talked themselves into believing that their life was hard because it was strict. But after a couple of years of Nazi rule, Artur said, they had learned what a hard life truly meant.[4]

Burning Issues

To survive, the group had to rethink everything. The Bund was lucky to have a leader like Artur—an idealist yet at the same time very much a realist—who made a sober appraisal of the threats they faced. The group formed a commission to identify new procedures for ensuring their safety. It seems that some members were deemed to be too careless to be kept in the loop. Joseph Blümer (known as "Pilz-Jupp" because he knew everything there was to know about mushrooms), for example, was deemed a firebrand and ejected. Other pre-1933 enthusiasts simply wanted to keep their heads down and dropped out of their own accord.[5] Where there had been a couple of hundred people in the Bund's orbit before 1933, the active membership during the Nazi years dropped well below one hundred.[6]

Then there were all the incriminating papers that needed to be destroyed. Because the Bund was worried that its members might try to keep sentimental memorabilia (no doubt photos from group outings were treasured possessions), all were assigned a monitor to oversee what would be kept and what discarded. Fritz Denks remembered that you were not allowed to use your spouse as your monitor, since he or she would be tempted to preserve the same dangerous treasures. In kitchen ovens and living room stoves, address lists, photos, and group papers were destroyed.[7] Ernst's daughter Ursula Jungbluth, then seven years old and a resident in the Bund's house in Wuppertal, recalled the exhilaration of being allowed to stay up late for a "bonfire night" in the utility room.[8] What this means for us today, of course, is that fewer traces remain of group life before 1933 than might otherwise be expected. The group may have destroyed more even than it needed to.

The Bund was already practiced in self-policing. Now this willingness to override personal privacy (and to accept the invasion of one's personal space) took on a new meaning.[9] No one, not even the most reliable, was to be spared checks on their room, their letters, their papers, and "the most private corners of their lives."[10] The Bund called these periodic checks "housecleaning." "We found so many things," the Bund reported after the war, "which no one had noticed, and which might have put us in grave danger during the next house search."[11] The group became its own "Gestapo," searching, censoring, and applying peer pressure to minimize its vulnerabilities.

But housecleaning was not enough. Artur felt it imperative to anticipate all potential threats. How should they react if a meeting was suddenly interrupted? What were the correct responses during a house search? Critical situations were reviewed over and over. Using role-playing, the group enacted mock interrogations, practicing how to respond, while Bund friends observed and criticized their acting. Lisa remembered rehearsing what to say, again and again, until she could give the correct answers in her sleep.[12] What impressed Maria Briel was that despite being such a high-minded theorist, Artur always had an eye for details.[13] He never treated any incident or mistake as an accident, and always sought to understand its cause.[14] Moreover, because the regime's rules were changing, the group found that responses that had worked in 1933 needed updating in 1939 and again in 1942.[15] In 1933, for example, Dore had dared to call the police to stop an SA unit from terrorizing the Blockhaus. But given the Gestapo's increasing power and the intensification of the regime's anti-Jewish policy, such a call would have been useless—and unwise for a Jewish woman—just a couple of years later.

"We learned to be silent, to lie, conceal, and deliberately mislead," Lisa wrote after the war, recalling the difficulty of convincing this high-minded bunch that they could not afford to maintain the honesty they otherwise regarded as essential for an ethical life.[16] "Artur Jacobs taught us (and there were more than a few tears shed in this class) to fight the enemy with his own weapons."[17] They learned not to assume that the Gestapo knew anything more about the group than was obvious. In 1940, Lisa was subjected to an interrogation that lasted for hours, during which she was repeatedly threatened with incarceration.[18] She later claimed that by the end of it, she "was almost merry" at having managed to convincingly recite "this impressive construction of lies."[19]

Seventeen Points

Not long after the Nazis came to power, the Bund felt it necessary to articulate its critique of the party's ideology, even if it could not do so publicly. The result was a list called "The Seventeen Points," in which the group picked apart what it saw as the tenets of National Socialism. We no longer have a copy of the list, but we know that the seventeen points tackled the party's thinking about race, biological materialism, "fatalism," and what the Bund dubbed its relativism, although the Nazis presented themselves as an answer to the relativism and uncertainty of the Weimar years. The Bund's theses challenged the party's emphasis on the "Führer principle." They portrayed the regime as a modern incarnation of the Inquisition and exposed the way it was undermining the rule of law. They also took aim at the idea of a "Nordic race" and its "cultural mission," as well as the "blasphemy"—a term they used—of Nazi religion. Like the philologist Victor Klemperer, the Bund was alive to the way the Nazis were redefining and corrupting morally positive terms such as "honor," "effort," "courage," "socialism," "people's community," and so on.[20] The Bund would later expand these critiques in pamphlets, drafted in secret for future publication, with titles such as *The Authoritarian System*, *Race Madness*, and *The Performance Cult*.[21]

The list clearly had enduring importance for the group. Years later, in 1945, just a day or two after he, Dore, Lisa, Käthe, and others were liberated, Artur gave a moving address in which he reminded those around him how significant this analysis had been.[22] Even decades after that, in the early 1960s, Ernst, still very active in teaching young adults about the Nazi years, wrote to Artur to express once again his appreciation of the "17 points."[23] And in 1969, a memorial service for Artur's brother, Walter, recalled Walter's weekly visits to Essen in the early 1930s to work on the seventeen points.[24]

Given that the absurdity and iniquity of Nazi ideology seems so obvious to us today, we may wonder why even decades after the end of the war it seemed so significant to the Bund that it had been able to formulate the seventeen points. Ernst's letter gives us one clue. After praising Artur for getting to the heart of the Nazi beast, he wrote that the analysis had been so important because "from then on what stood before us was not just an object of terror, but a historical phenomenon, an object of study. We saw the inner contradictions and sensed the unnatural basis of this movement."[25] In other words, the group gained some mastery over the menace. Where once the Bund had offered to strengthen its members against the "relativism" of the Weimar years, now it inoculated them against the strident claims of the Nazi regime. All the surviving Bund members I interviewed later on stressed the confidence they gained from these insights and the comfort they derived from the belief that the regime would inevitably founder on its own contradictions.

On one level, this makes sense. On another, it raises new questions. Did the group really need persuading that the regime was "unnatural and all wrong"? It seems so. In the talk he gave just days after liberation, Artur reminded his fellow Bund members that intensive study had proved to all of them that there was no space in the Nazi regime for any decent human being.[26] The biggest threat to the group had come, he said, not from the Gestapo but from the regime's ability to co-opt support. Ernst similarly emphasized that "continuous educational and information training in all questions of political and spiritual life" was essential to "protect ourselves against the nationalsocialist poison."[27] We need to remember that during the 1930s, even longtime socialists grew giddy over Hitler's diplomatic feats.[28] In wartime, the moral pressure to defend the fatherland was even more intense.[29] Artur and Ernst were acknowledging a powerful undertow against which almost all German oppositional groups had to struggle. The challenge was to maintain absolute conviction that the Nazi movement had nothing good in it, despite the enthusiasm and energy it mobilized on all sides, despite the experts and scientists it had found to endorse it, and despite the opportunities it offered.

Consider Fritz Denks, one of the Bund's youngest members, born in Mülheim in 1911. The son of recent immigrants from the Baltic, both of whom had died by the time Fritz was twelve, he battled through a childhood of poverty with the help of his two older brothers. He became a plasterer, and in his late teens or early twenties, along with other Mülheim friends, he began traveling to Essen to hear Artur's lectures. A trade unionist and member of a Socialist Workers Youth movement, Fritz narrowly escaped a drubbing from the SA in 1933, thanks to friendly neighbors who alerted him that a troop was on the way. That same year, he lost his job and was faced with the choice of signing up for the new Reich Labor Service, a Nazi public works program, in East Prussia or losing his unemployment benefits. So, Fritz moved to East Prussia. The local administrators, recognizing his talents, invited him to teach the political reeducation class the men were required to attend as members of the Labor Service. Responding to the "Socialist" label in the National Socialist Party and believing that he could perform this task without being an active Nazi, Fritz was tempted. It was only the opposition of his wife, Guste, and perhaps other Bund members, that persuaded him not to pursue this course. He found another job back in the Ruhr, one that allowed him to leave the Labor Service. Fritz, it should be added, would have an impeccable record as a Social Democrat after the Second World War. He would later become an SPD deputy in the North Rhine-Westphalian parliament and mayor of Mülheim. Yet even he was close to signing on to the Nazi cause.[30]

Moreover, anti-Semitic prejudices and racism were by no means absent on the left. In an early postwar Bund report describing what it had done to help Jews, the Bund noted that it had organized a series of study groups for members intended to combat these impulses. Participants would analyze every aspect of the Nazis' racial ideology and learn about the history of the Jews through the millennia. "By this means some were prompted to reflect for the first time on such matters, while others were able to clarify confused ideas," noted the report.[31] We can see from these statements that not all Bund members started out with a full sense of the dangers of anti-Semitism or of the wrongness of Nazi racial thinking. Decades later, even

Maria Briel, an implacable radical completely committed to the group and its ideals, felt the need to point out how important these sessions had been.[32]

We now approach this history with the knowledge of what the Nazis were capable of, but it is important to remember that this was not the case for most people at the time. Bund members were confronted with the heavy personal costs of not going along with the regime; they saw the great number of their fellow citizens expressing enthusiasm about this new movement; and they themselves sometimes held latent prejudices, which the Nazis were in an ideal position to exploit. Maintaining an attitude of consistent opposition required study and, above all, will. During the Nazi years, the Bund added a series of six new paragraphs, or "laws," to the commitment oath. Nearly all of them were about not taking the easy way out, not going with the flow, and sticking with one's conscience. Thus, the second law read, "I am ready to subject my daily actions to more serious and careful scrutiny in order not to succumb to the particular danger of our time— the danger of denying my true beliefs and living as a private individual rather than serving as a steward of the mission." The third law followed with "It is my firm will not to allow unacknowledged worries about my livelihood to lead me to acts of omission and commission that I cannot condone. I am ready to keep testing my courage with small challenges, so as not to succumb to the general cowardice and lack of character." The next two laws continued in the same vein.[33]

It is also important to remember that the Nazis represented the legal authority, controlling the reins of government, and that Bund members, even though they espoused radical ideas, were upright, law-abiding individuals. This mind-set was something else they had to overcome. Lisa wrote shortly after liberation that "a really important step for us was to gain the inner conviction—on no account must we have a bad conscience; rather we should live confident that we have done nothing bad. We, not our enemies, are right. We are legal, they are illegal."[34]

Hidden Choices

A fact often forgotten is that even staunch opponents of the regime had to make compromises. To be sure, there were issues for which one had to be willing to go to the barricades.[35] But the Bund seems to have reasoned that there was no purpose in needlessly sacrificing life when careful choices might bring one through. The Bund seems to have made a choice early on, for example, not to engage in leafleting, distributing underground news-papers, scrawling slogans on walls, or other risky strategies that aimed to influence the wider public. (Some Bund members, however, by dint of their intergroup links, did at times engage in such leafleting. And during the war, the group did circulate some highly incriminating information about the regime's Jewish policy.)[36]

One reason the Nazis were so effective is that they were able to infil-trate left-wing groups with spies, who then denounced their members. But what often initially aroused the Gestapo's attention was the discovery of illegal newspapers and posters. During the first three years of the dicta-torship, exiled socialists, for example, smuggled some two million printed items into the Reich.[37] It was on the basis of such activities that the Gestapo was able to track down and round up left-wing groups. The first attempt to create an underground Communist Party organization for the city of Essen had already been smashed in May 1933. The regional Communist leadership, based in Dortmund, was crushed around the same time. A new organization was put together in August 1933, but arrests led to its disso-lution just three months later. The Communists created yet another under-ground organization for the Ruhr in January 1934, this time based in Essen; it, too, lasted only two months before meeting the same fate. The same pattern could be seen all over Germany.[38] By 1934, exiled Social Democrats had nearly given up on the idea of reaching out to the unper-suaded with written propaganda material. They continued to distribute leaflets underground to fellow socialists, but even this carried immense risk, and by 1936 the Social Democrats had stopped the practice altogether.[39] The Communists continued to bring illegal materials into the country, although the party itself acknowledged that they had very little impact and that very few were read.[40] As late as January 1943, by which time the Communists had learned to be extraordinarily cautious, the Gestapo nev-ertheless decimated the party's most recent effort to influence workers in the Ruhr.[41]

The Bund's choices about leafleting were thus entirely realistic.[42] Another choice we know they must have made related to service in the army. Apart from Artur and Ernst, most of the Bund men were of an age that made them eligible for conscription. Unlike the Christian nonconformist group called the Bruderhof or, indeed, the Jehovah's Witnesses, none resisted the draft. Even before compulsory military service was introduced in 1935, the members of the Bruderhof recognized that their determination not to serve would force them into exile. Contacts made with coreligionists abroad eventually allowed group members to leave the country.[43] By contrast, Jehovah's Witnesses did not leave the country and continued to refuse military service, with the result that many were prosecuted and interned in concentration camps. Non-Jewish Bund members seem by and large not to have considered leaving the country, lacking the necessary language skills, resources, and contacts. Refusing military service, then, was a life-threatening choice, and the Bund did not ask its members to sacrifice themselves. At the same time, not a single person in the Bund joined the Nazi Party, even though some resistance circles made a case for having members on the "inside" to find out what was going on and to understand the enemy's thinking. We do not know whether Bund members simply found the prospect too abhorrent or whether they recognized that none of them, given their background, were likely to be allowed admittance. (The child of one Bund member did join the SS, but this was not at the group's behest.)[44]

At the time, the group was understandably reticent to record on paper its discussions about what to go along with and where to draw the line. Even from the safe vantage point of the postwar years, Bund members remained tight-lipped on such matters. In an interview toward the end of her life, Tove Gerson recalled the timbre of Bund conversations on sensitive topics like these:

> What about a young worker who is offered a job opportunity if he joins a Nazi organization, should he join or not? And what about teachers, what should they do? Those were difficult decisions. And the group was there to help, to counteract what one's own wishes or needs might otherwise lead a person to do. To put it in old-fashioned terms, the group would reveal what one's conscience said was right.[45]

But such an open acknowledgment was the exception.[46]

Since neither Bund publications nor the people I interviewed touch on the subject, it is only through Gestapo and postwar denazification records that we can learn about some of the other compromises Bund members made to fit into the new order. Ernst, for example, joined the National Socialist Teachers' League (NSLB) and National Socialist People's Welfare (NSV), in which, as he informed the Gestapo in an interrogation, he actively worked as a volunteer. He also joined the Reichsluftschutzbund, or RLB, an air defense association, and organized the distribution of the Nazi youth newspaper in a local school. In his Gestapo file we find a statement from him dated January 1938, probably the result of an interrogation, in which he said that he would volunteer for service if ever war were declared, but given that he was forty-nine, it was probably an offer the regime would be unlikely to take up (though men of his age would in fact be mobilized toward the war's end). Even so, the *Gau* leadership continued to declare him politically unreliable (the Nazis revived the medieval term "*Gau*" for each party district). In 1937 his effort to receive a passport to travel to Holland had been rejected and a blanket ban issued to prevent him ever receiving a passport.[47] Sonja joined all the same groups—the NSLB in 1934, the NSV, and the RLB—suggesting that these were what the Bund took to be the most harmless pre-Nazi organizations, ones its members could join easily and without unnecessary compromise for the purpose of not sticking out. Sonja contributed one Reichsmark a month to Nazi charities and, like another teacher in the Bund, Liesel Speer, also joined a non-Nazi patriotic interest group, the Reichskolonialbund (RKB).[48] Liesel, in turn, was also a member of the People's Association for Germandom Abroad (VDA), yet another pre-Nazi patriotic body that had survived into the Third Reich. After the war, British authorities found a Nazi letter saying that Speer was "not suitable for education of the youth of the NS-State," suggesting that she, like Ernst, had not managed to persuade the Nazi authorities that she was on their side. As a result, even though she was allowed to remain a teacher, she was transferred to a distant school.[49] Ellen Hube-Brandt joined the NSV and the German Women's League. These memberships are not evidence of hypocrisy or a betrayal of values. But as dues-paying members of the VDA and the RKB, the Bund's teachers could not help but contribute to the image of a totally mobilized society, even while resisting it.

From these files, then, we gain a glimpse of the moral complexities and emotional tangles of life as a left-wing activist in Nazi society. But only a glimpse. When it comes to conversations and gestures in the street—the raised arm, the "*Ja, ja*" to some obnoxious bit of Nazi rhetoric—we have very little insight as to how Bund members behaved. As some would find, failure to take the necessary precautions could land one in serious trouble with the Gestapo.[50] But, for the most part, we are aware only of the infractions the Gestapo uncovered. We know of a couple of cases—and there must be more—in which Bund members adapted their behavior to blend in. In one official document, for example, Liesel Speer signed her name "with German greeting," the new Nazi valediction that was an alternative to "Heil Hitler."[51] She was seeking to establish the "Aryan" ancestry of her son. One Bund member, a bookbinder, said that at one point she fulfilled a contract for the SS.[52] But these are just tiny scraps of knowledge and only hint at the larger collage. One particularly fraught question was how the group should approach the conformity of its children in school and elsewhere. Should they join the Hitler Youth, for example? Membership was theoretically made compulsory in 1936 and, in practice, legally enforced after 1939.[53]

The Bund as Refuge

When Ellen Hube-Brandt encountered the Bund through her lessons with Dore in the late 1930s, she felt at ease for the first time in years. Finally, she could put into words why she found herself so alienated from the world around her.[54] The more she and her Bund friends were estranged from German society, the more the group became their lifeline. After the war, Germans who had not left the country but claimed to have always opposed Nazism liked to talk of "inner emigration," of maintaining a private psychological territory. But with rare exceptions, it was not possible to maintain such a stance without being part of a collective.[55]

Even more important than providing an account of Nazism's failings and weaknesses or helping individuals chart a moral course in an immoral soci-

ety was the simple fact that the Bund created a collective space, a counter-
weight, to the world outside. In this way, the Bund's meetings both
endangered the participants and offered them security. Members knew that
coming together was essential for their well-being, but they also knew they
were most conspicuous and endangered when they did so. As a result, all
aspects were carefully choreographed. If Bund members met accidentally,
they were trained to pretend not to know each other, in case one or the
other was being followed.[56] The arrival of each participant at group meetings was timed to the minute to avoid drawing the sort of attention that
two or more people turning up at the same time might. Reinhold Ströter
remembered that because the train often brought him into town early, he
would have to walk around the neighborhood for a quarter of an hour to
arrive at the appointed time.[57] A 1940 letter from Tilde Stürmer asking
Grete Ströter to pass on details of a meeting to Mathilde Zenker survives
because it was captured by the Gestapo. The letter conveys the sense of a
casual family get-together involving a few people but does propose a very
definite time of arrival. After the letter was intercepted and evidently led
to some Gestapo inquiry, a follow-up letter from Tilde's husband, Alfred,
apologized to Grete for causing any inconvenience. It was, of course,
designed to be read and misinterpreted by the Gestapo, and indeed we find
it preserved in the Gestapo files.[58]

We may wonder whether such tactics could have been effective.
Neighbors were aware of Bund members' comings and goings, as denunciations show. More important than such stratagems, probably, was con-
juring the illusion that this was a loose and harmless group of friends.
Importantly, the Bund had a large number of women, a group the Nazis
did not take seriously as political actors. Furthermore, it was sufficiently
informal and family-like to allay suspicion—and the interest in gymnastics and dance helped reaffirm this impression. Other small left-wing
groups tried similar techniques. Hilde Paul, a former member of the
Socialist Arbeiter Jugend, remembered that she and her friends had discussed the possibility of arrest and decided to "make [ourselves] as politically unimportant as possible and explain our meetings as get-togethers
of old friends."[59]

The group benefited from access to spaces where it could meet largely
removed from scrutiny, above all at the Blockhaus in Essen. Because a local

Catholic church was renting the hall for services, the building was somewhat protected from Nazi seizure. The character of the downstairs hall as
a gymnastics training space also provided a modicum of cover. The building was several yards away from neighboring houses, so sound was unlikely
to travel. Other houses also hosted group meetings on a smaller scale—
the Jacobs house on Dönhof Street, the Bund house on the Ottostrasse in
Wuppertal-Barmen, and the guesthouse on Lake Constance in Meersburg.

Even after they had made it safely inside, participants in meetings had
to have a cover story about their relationship to one another in case a
stranger came to the door.[60] Bund members liked to relay what happened
during a Gestapo house search in Wuppertal when a meeting was in progress. As Tove Gerson recalled, at the first aggressive thump on the door,
Jacobs took action:

> He was an absolutely fearless man. As they came in and began
> [the search], he sat down at the piano and played songs. Then
> he stood up, picked up the briefcase with everything in it, walked
> through all the people, and left the house. And no one laid a
> finger on him![61]

The degree to which the Bund was able to maintain its associational
life through the Nazi years was nonetheless remarkable.[62] In addition to
the annual get-togethers and the regional meetings in Essen, local Bund
groups continued to meet in Mülheim, Wuppertal, and elsewhere. There
were also various kinds of study groups within the organization. Lisa, for
example, led a small circle of younger members.[63] The Inner Circle also
continued to convene.

One striking example of the group's continued commitment to its project of ethical improvement was that it still insisted on holding "probationary marriages" for younger members. This was taken so seriously that
Reinhold Ströter, who had gone to Hamburg in pursuit of work, returned
for a while with his sweetheart, Grete, so that they could absorb the atmosphere and be observed in one of the Bund houses.[64] Three Bund marriages
were celebrated simultaneously in 1938, those of the Morgensterns, the
Briels, and another couple. Reinhold and Grete's marriage followed; a sign
of the Bund's control of its members' lives was that theirs was the first of

these supervised marriages where the group allowed the bride and groom's parents to attend!

The Solace of Nature

Whenever they could, but particularly around Pentecost and in the summer, Bund members would "take to the hills" to hike, to discuss philosophy, ethics, and politics, and to commune with nature.[65] Ever since the 1920s, the Bund had made the Sauerland, the rolling wooded country to the east of the Ruhr region, its own. Little villages such as Kirchhundem and Albaum were the group's second home, and the Bundists formed a deep connection with the landscape. Many knew the flora and fauna intimately, the red foxglove and the yellow arnica, the delicate bellflower and the red-tinted canary grass, the golden gorse blooms, and the delicious wild things to eat—cèpe mushrooms, blueberries, and blackberries.[66] Building a fire was a solemn business. Reinhard referred to it in an interview, without irony though with a smile, as a "sacred act."[67] Sometimes stones would be warmed in the fire and then extracted to provide a warm bed to lie on. The group liked to return to the same isolated spots, finding their improvised fireplaces still intact after weeks or even months.[68]

Reading the Bund's accounts, we begin to find it perfectly normal that one could have serious debates amid the pine trees. But even in the forests, group events were not without risk. Trips were carefully planned, with small groups traveling to the region separately and then meeting up, as if accidentally.[69] At the climax of each outing, all the Bund members would gather on some lonely hillside and, for a precious few hours, enjoy the experience of solidarity.[70] In the evening, the smaller groups would separate again, returning to different accommodations. If they were in the same town, Bundists would walk past each other without acknowledging that they knew each other, except, as recorded in a poem by Walter Jacobs, with "a quiet smile."[71] In an anonymous Bund member's diary (which, as we'll see below, was probably written by Lisa Jacob), the writer expresses gratitude at the end of a day that had been full of overwhelming impressions— for the opportunity to walk home alone on a peaceful path and reflect quietly on the day's experiences.[72] The concern that they might be found and the tense choreography of seemingly accidental encounters added emotional significance to every meeting.[73]

Anti-Nazi Movement

Körperbildung played a surprisingly important role for the Bund under Nazism, lending it a convincing cover, enhancing its cohesion, and, even more significantly, improving its ability to reach and influence the outside world. Until 1938, both Dore and Lisa could legally give private gymnastics lessons—though only to Jewish pupils. Still, in this way, they were able to earn some modest income while also providing Jews an opportunity to engage in physical training and exercise, which they otherwise would have been denied. Dore and Lisa also continued to give illegal classes to non-Jews. In fact, a number of non-Jews who later became key Bund members were drawn to the group during the Nazi years because of their studies with Dore or her former pupils. Ellen Hube-Brandt was one of them:

> The sessions with Dore began with what I'd call the purely technical elements of body training. . . . They were very important for me because they always started with us as human beings: our ability to see, to hear, to visualize, as well as our anatomy. But then the lessons moved on to issues that concerned the whole person and the idea that once you recognize the way things really are, you are bound to act accordingly. I found this idea more and more compelling, and I realized I couldn't avoid making the connection between this body training and the way I lived my life and my strong opposition to Hitler. There was no other choice.[74]

When Ellen first said this in an interview, it was difficult for me to understand how physical exercise could have acquired such deep philosophical and political meaning—how it could have compelled her to take the dangerous step of joining the Bund during the Nazi years. But this is exactly what happened. In 1936, newly divorced and seeking perhaps to start a new career, Ellen had moved to Essen and sought out lessons in *Körperbildung* with Dore. Dore was wary of this stranger and did not agree to teach her at first. Seemingly by coincidence, Ellen became acquainted with some other women in Dore's orbit and ended up practicing with them for two years. Evidently Dore had orchestrated all of this as a silent test of reliability. In 1938 Ellen received a coded letter indicating that Dore was willing to teach her.[75] From here she was gradually admitted into the Bund proper, and her *Verpflichtung* was solemnly celebrated in 1943.

Ellen was not the only person to enter the Bund's orbit in this way. In Göttingen, Hermann Schmalstieg was initially drawn by the gymnastics lessons offered by Georg Reuter. Wasja Enoch, who had begun taking classes with Dore just before the Nazi seizure of power, joined the Bund in the 1930s, and she even became part of its Inner Circle before leaving Germany for the United States with her husband in 1938.[76] In the 1930s, Meta Kamp-Steinmann—who, like Hermann, was living in Göttingen— was introduced to the Bund through gymnastics lessons from Karlos Morgenstern.[77]

Perhaps most importantly, *Körperbildung* gave the Bund the appearance of being apolitical. When Gestapo raids uncovered materials relating to gymnastics and dance, for example, the brochures suggested to the officers that they were dealing with some harmless earth-movement kind of sect. Maria witnessed a couple of puzzled Gestapo agents shaking their heads, unable to make sense of the materials.[78] *Körperbildung* was even, in some cases, able to give the Bund the appearance of being somehow in the Nazi camp, since it had some similarities with movements and aesthetic tendencies that the Nazis found convivial or that had aligned themselves with the new regime.[79] Yet, as Ellen's testimony indicated, beyond the protection *Körperbildung* afforded the group, the participants found some kind of political and spiritual meaning encoded in the physical movement itself. Some years after the war, Tove looked back on the special significance of the movement choirs.[80] First, there was the experience of complete but natural incorporation within a group. But then there was the added dimension of what this meant during the Nazi period. In her imperfect English, she wrote:

A second effect upon me I would like to mention that this group experience came at a time when the outer reality was more and more threatening and uprooting. . . . In contrast to the Nazi groups I got the concept that the individual in this new group is not dissolved and does not become part of a mass but functions as a highly alert personality that at the same time serves and adjusts to the needs of the group without loss of identity.[81]

Was there something about Dore's approach that by its very nature was inimical to Nazism? After all, the Nazis did not ban expressive dance as they did many other forms of avant-garde art. Several leading dance practitioners became enthusiastic Nazis.[82] But there were important differences between the kind of spectacle and movement the Nazis endorsed and what Dore had to offer. The spontaneity and gender mixing in Dore's approach clearly differed from the tenets of the pro-Nazi society Kampfbund für deutsche Kultur, which called for clear spatial alignment of the dancers and a distinct separation of men and women.[83]

Dore's work undoubtedly gained additional political significance from the simple fact that both she and Lisa were Jewish and their instruction of non-Jews illegal. For Dore's pupils who participated in the public performances, one in particular took on a very explicit meaning. In 1934, Erna Michels, now with a growing gymnastics practice of her own in Roermond, Holland, invited Bund members to cross the border and perform for a Dutch audience. Her guests, all carrying their dark red dance suits, crossed the frontier at different places and times, on bicycles and motorbikes, by train and bus. The group performed a covertly anti-Nazi piece, *The Grand Inquisitor* (doubtless an allusion to Dostoyevsky's *Brothers Karamazov*, though adapted to the current moment), and Tove recalled the enormous impact on performers and audience alike of the dramatization of a symbolic stand-off between the group and an authoritarian leader. The following day, while still in Holland, the Bund members used their brief moment of freedom to read one of the first books about the Nazi concentration camps, *Die Moorsoldaten* by Wolfgang Langhoff. Decades later, Tove still remembered the dread they all felt as they crossed the border back into Germany.[84]

4

Calls to Arms

Standing By

Between 1933 and 1938, the Bund's energies were focused largely on keeping its little vessel afloat. Its top priorities were to offer an alternative to the Nazi vision and to provide its members with a safe space. In small ways, it is true, Bund members did confront the regime, sometimes separately, sometimes together. Several in the group felt called upon to take more substantial risks—most notably in offering temporary hiding places to left-wingers on the run. But on the whole, the Bund was engaged in only cautious outreach. From an outsider's perspective, its subversive activity was mostly invisible.

As Germany grew more prosperous and powerful during these years, the Nazis intensified their assault on the Jews. The escalation of anti-Jewish policy was not, however, continuous. In the early weeks of the regime, the war against the Jews took second place to the war on the left, though Jewish left-wingers were singled out for particularly brutal treatment. In 1933 and 1934, Jews were ejected from the civil service, law, medicine, and journalism. The protection for former veterans, on which President Paul von Hindenburg had insisted, allowed a significant number of Jewish civil servants and professionals to remain in their posts, but younger Jews were soon barred from any kind of higher education or professional advancement. In

1935, the Nuremberg Laws reduced Jews from citizens to subjects and made intermarriage—and sexual relations—between Jews and gentiles illegal. Subsequent regulations also introduced the concept of the mixed-race Jew, a category that would now face a confusing mix of prohibitions and exemptions. In economic terms, anti-Jewish measures were introduced very unevenly, varying from one trade to another and from place to place. Some regions quickly became off-limits, with shops even unwilling to sell to Jewish customers, let alone buy from Jewish merchants or employ Jewish labor. In some towns and trades, however, Jewish entrepreneurs were able to operate relatively unhindered. After 1936, the pressure on Jews to close or sell out intensified. Non-Jewish firms also found themselves nudged more and more aggressively to remove their Jewish employees. By 1938, even highly valued senior executives like Wasja Enoch's husband, Otto, or Tove's Christian but "racially" half-Jewish husband, Gerhard, were being edged out. Everywhere Jews were shunned, their interactions with non-Jews reduced to commercial or official transactions. Despite the fits and starts, the extent to which Jews were excluded from German society in a mere five years was astonishing.

Throughout these years, the Bund remained largely on the sidelines, though it provided moral support and sometimes a place of refuge for Jewish members seeking to leave the country. The Dutch town of Roermond, where Erna Michels now lived, was within easy reach of the Ruhr, and one Bund friend after another traveled there to enjoy a few days of freedom. Liesel Speer, for example, visited Erna repeatedly between 1934 and 1938; Ernst apparently spent five days there in 1937, and Sonja followed him in 1938, as did Gertrud Jacobs, Artur's sister-in-law, and other Bund members in 1939. In 1938, Sonja also took the train to Zurich to ask a contact there, Reja Farbstein, about the possibility of arranging for Dore to live and work abroad.[1]

Even when it wanted to, the group found it had little ability to affect the situation of those who remained behind in Germany. The Jacobses could do little to protect their son, Friedl, for example, now officially a first-degree mixed-race Jew (i.e., a child possessing two Jewish grandparents and, thus, subject to increasingly restricted opportunities in education, training, and employment), who lurched from one miserable school experience to another. For a while he attended a school in Kettwig, but he was forced to leave by Easter 1934. His attempt to study at the Essen Engineering College in 1936 was thwarted by several members of the Nazi German Students' League, who bullied and harassed him. Former classmates later recalled shouts of "Windows open, Jews out" and "It stinks of garlic." (The notion that German Jews used lots of garlic in their cooking was absurd by any measure.) According to the classmates, Nazi students damaged Friedl's drawing instruments and, as one witness remembered it, threw a full wastepaper basket at him across several rows of benches. After a few weeks of this, Friedl moved to an engineering school in Duisburg, but with the same miserable outcome.[2] In the spring of 1938, the Jacobses sent Friedl to stay with relatives in Holland.

As for Jews who were not members, the Bund also made some efforts in their behalf. Else visited the nurse in the Jewish community offices in Düsseldorf to ask what help the group might offer. The Bund was systematic in its operations and tended not to engage in one-off efforts, so similar visits may have taken place in other cities. One well-documented individual recipient of help was twenty-four-year-old Eva Seligmann, a half-Jewish woman who in 1936 came to Essen to live in the Blockhaus for a year. The Seligmann case is interesting because it shows that even in the mid-1930s the links with leftist or left-liberal Jewish milieus that had been a feature of the Bund's pre-Nazi world were not completely broken. The connection came through Gerda Simons, who, as a socialist, had been ousted from her position as a professor of education in 1933 but continued trying to assist former Jewish students. In introducing her former student Eva Seligmann to the Bund, Gerda doubtless recognized that the young woman's background in the youth movement, her commitment to pacifism, and her interest in educational reform were all reminiscent of the Bund's intellectual spirit.

Unable to find a job as a teacher after 1933 because of her "racial status," Eva took a series of short-term positions before moving to Essen. At the Blockhaus, she earned board and pocket money in return for cooking and providing housekeeping and child care. Unsurprisingly, Eva found the Bund an inspiring community and formed friendships that would last a lifetime. But she could not advance in Germany in her chosen field, and the Bund was not in a position to provide financial support indefinitely. Luckily, she managed to immigrate to England before the outbreak of war.[3] Some

Jews, particularly Jewish women, took advantage of the professional training Dore and Lisa were able to offer in gymnastics, and as late as March 1940,
when interrogated by the Gestapo, Lisa was still listing half a dozen Jewish women as pupils.[4] In addition to the professional qualification, the training no doubt provided moments of respite at a time of ever greater anxiety.

The Bund may have done more to help outsiders, although we lack the
evidence. It is also possible that in these early years of Nazi rule, the Bund
simply did not feel compelled to act. What Jews in distress needed was
material help or connections abroad, and the Bund could provide neither.
After the war, its members also admitted frankly that they had not been
on the same wavelength as much of the Jewish community in the region.
The Ruhr's Jews, like the majority of those in Germany, were solidly middle-
class and engaged in trade. They were patriotic, respectable, and for the
most part socially conservative; their lifestyle bore no resemblance to the
Bundists'.[5] In an interview, Gustav and Mathilde Zenker both remembered
having to overcome their reluctance to help people with such different
political views and from a radically different social milieu.[6] It thus seems
likely that the Bund's efforts to help Jews remained limited during this time.
It is surely no accident that Eva Seligmann had so similar an intellectual
orientation to their own.

Overcoming Their Reserve

The events that came to be known as Kristallnacht were shocking and
unforgettable, yet they also had a clear prehistory. The first half of 1938
had seen ominous changes. In March of that year, German Jews looked on
fearfully as their counterparts in Austria were subjected to a brutal assault
following the Anschluss. In April, German Jews were ordered to supply the
authorities with a comprehensive list of all their assets. Jews' ability to obtain
and use passports was restricted, and in the summer a new Jewish ID card
was announced. All this and more created a profound sense of foreboding.
With increasing frequency and vehemence, Hitler had also been publicly
accusing "international Jewry" of blocking Germany's foreign policy ambitions. As tension mounted over the Czech crisis in the autumn of 1938,
Jews again found themselves on the receiving end of Nazi violence. The

crisis was resolved by the end of September with the Munich Agreement, but many Nazi radicals had been hoping for war, and now, having been denied it, they were spoiling for a fight. In October 1938, responding to pending administrative changes in Poland that would deny Jews with Polish citizenship living in Germany the right of return, the Nazis brutally rounded up Polish Jews in Germany and drove them across the border. Yet even these attacks paled in comparison to the violence on November 9 and 10.[7]

The immediate catalyst for Kristallnacht was the death on November 9 of an official in the German embassy in Paris, Ernst vom Rath. The Nazis never needed evidence to blame events on the Jews, but in this case, there was a direct Jewish connection. Vom Rath died from gunshot wounds inflicted days earlier by Herschel Grynszpan, a young German Jew of Polish descent who was furious at the deportation of his parents from Hanover in the nationwide roundup. When the news of vom Rath's death reached Germany, the Nazi leadership happened to be assembled in Munich, celebrating the twenty-fifth anniversary of Hitler's Beer Hall Putsch—so it was easy for Propaganda Minister Joseph Goebbels to urge the regional party bosses to exact revenge. They, in turn, telephoned their subordinates back home to take action.

Mobs set synagogues on fire, forced rabbis and other Jewish leaders to parade through the streets, and desecrated and burned Torah rolls. Jewish shops were smashed, looted, doused with gasoline, and set ablaze. Jewish welfare homes, orphanages, and other public institutions were invaded, and their inmates terrorized and brutally assaulted. The doors of Jewish homes across the country were broken down, as rampaging hordes smashed, burned, stole, and battered. Police and fire services were ordered not to intervene unless non-Jewish property or lives were at stake. Hundreds died in the violence.[8] Many older Jews never recovered either psychologically or physically from the events of that night.

In the fevered atmosphere of the days between the news of the attack on vom Rath and the announcement of his death, Artur foresaw that there might be trouble and traveled with Dore to Wuppertal, where they were less well known.[9] Tove Gerson and Hedwig Gehrke stayed behind at the Jacobses' house on Dönhof Street, where someone had scrawled on the steps that it was a "Jew house." Tove later recalled her hesitancy to do anything

about the graffiti, in contrast to what she saw as Hedwig Gehrke's no-
nonsense working-class readiness to take a bucket and mop and wash it
away.[10] In Wuppertal, Artur and Dore were unmolested. "You will have
been very worried about us," Artur wrote to Friedl on November 12, 1938,

> and therefore you should know that we are healthy and fine and
> apart from small disturbances at the house have not experienced
> anything bad. . . . You will have learned about the events from
> the newspaper. I don't want to say anything about them at the
> moment. These were days that we will never forget. Not only
> the wonderful synagogue, but the beautiful youth center too
> was a victim of the flames.[11]

The Jacobses learned later that the Blockhaus had only narrowly escaped
destruction.[12]

In 1942, hoping to alert the sleepy little oil town of Bartlesville, Oklahoma, to the reality of Nazi Germany, Tove dwelled at length on the events
of those days. She had immigrated to the States in 1939, a few months after
Kristallnacht, to join her half-Jewish husband, who had been there alone
for a year while she'd continued her *Körperbildung* training with Dore and
her political education with the Bund. Speaking to an American audience
in her imperfect English, Tove described an incident that had occurred during the violence on November 10 and 11, 1938. Even as the assaults and
vandalism continued, Tove had taken it upon herself to visit some family
acquaintances who had been affected, a wealthy Essen Jewish couple, the
Heinemanns, to express her solidarity in the face of the violence. She
arrived at their home with flowers and much anxiety, was snarled at by
someone in the crowd, but managed to get safely inside to find the old
couple and their house in a state of utter devastation. Tove's English notes
for her 1942 speech survive in Harvard's Schlesinger Library:

> Fine old couple. Cultivated home. Serkin, Busch, Furtwängler
> have played in this home. How the home looked after the
> "action," How people acted during and after the action: crowd
> curious and sensational—satisfied over misery of "the wealthy";
> the neighborhood-friends watching from the window without

helping (high city-official), the craftsmen refused to take over repairs; man of the crowd menacing me because "flowers to Jews"; woman for cleaning refuses to come any longer. . . . Why could fright so completely defeat their humanity? Because they did not believe really in anything except their own security and happiness. The only exception was a Protestant minister who picked the couple up in their garden and took them mid through the crowd, home in his house. When the old couple asked him "how can you do this, this is dangerous for you." He answered I have no time to think about what is dangerous for me or not.[13]

In later interviews, Tove filled in some of the details that are missing from this abbreviated version of her account. When she reached the Heinemanns, a mob of jeering onlookers was still milling around outside. She could not yet see the full extent of the damage, but the front door had been beaten on so badly that it would not open.

> Awful the way people look when they act as a mob. The front entrance was completely destroyed so I went through the tradesman's entrance. I was naïve, I had no experience of such a situation, I brought flowers, and a man ran out of the mob towards me and said "and you want to bring them flowers!"—I was frightened! When someone comes out of a mob directly at you. I mumbled something about "if you are yourself married to a Jew you are surely allowed to . . ."[14]

The Heinemanns' maid opened the door, and Tove walked in. The damage was indescribable. Windows had been smashed, and the mirrors downstairs were now simply shards on the floor. The carpets had been cut up and ruined. Sofas had been torn apart, their stuffing spilling out through jagged tears. The curtains were blackened where the mob had tried to set them on fire. The evidence of malicious, manic energy was almost unreal. Upstairs, Tove found the Heinemanns devastated and emotionally paralyzed, though still able to describe lucidly what had happened to them.

When the mob had arrived, the couple had been ordered into the garden. Frau Heinemann had asked if she could at least grab a coat for her ailing husband, and this had been granted with abusive laughter. The police came and escorted her husband away, not unkindly, leaving Frau Heinemann alone in the garden while the mob rampaged within. After her husband returned, the couple were still not allowed into the house. Their neighbors, with whom they were on good terms (he was a city official), looked on timorously from behind their curtains but did not feel able to intervene. Finally, a courageous pastor arrived with a young friend of the Heinemanns' and took them to safety. Now they were back in their ruined home. In one respect, Herr Heinemann was better off than many of his younger male contemporaries, thirty thousand of whom were being interned in concentration camps in the wake of the Kristallnacht pogrom, in order to increase the pressure on their families to emigrate.[15]

Tove's gesture of bringing flowers was not isolated; nor was it one she undertook completely of her own accord. The Kristallnacht violence had prompted the Bund to reconsider its own role and, ultimately, to decide that it was time for its members to raise their heads above the parapet. On November 10, Artur called on Bund members to act, with words that, Tove recalled, "became a mantra for us, namely, 'overcome your reserve and end the isolation of the Jews.'"[16] To avoid exposing the Bund, Artur cautioned everyone to offer help as individuals rather than as representatives of a group.[17]

After visiting the Heinemanns, Tove went with Lisa Jacob and others to the Jewish orphanage in Dinslaken, where both the staff members and the children had been subjected to the most brutal and humiliating treatment.[18] The orphanage's director, Yitzhak Sophoni Herz, and his charges had been driven into the street and made to watch the assault on their home. A jeering mob of over a hundred, among them individuals who just a week before had cheerfully done business with the orphanage, looked on. In a scene that resembled a public ritual of humiliation from the Middle Ages, the traumatized children were forced to process through the streets; they were then herded into a schoolyard and into the school hall, along with some older men and several Jewish women, some of them barely dressed.[19]

Elsewhere in the town, Tove met a distraught, impoverished older Jew who said that no store would sell him food. Tove bought what she could at a local shop and returned to find him hunched over on a trunk in his darkened apartment. Jews' houses in Dinslaken had been vandalized, and in many the electrical lines had been damaged, leaving them without power. The man told her how he had been dragged out of his house by SA men and forced to watch the synagogue burn.[20] Tove learned that many women and their children in the city had not dared to go home and had spent the night wandering around in the cold. She saw children returning to their wrecked homes, so traumatized that they were hiccupping and literally gasping for air.[21]

Because the orphanage itself was in such a terrible state, Tove went back to the Heinemanns a few days later to see if they could contribute financially toward at least making it livable. The door was opened by a distraught housekeeper; she told Tove that the old couple had committed suicide. Even if they had remained alive it is doubtful that they could have helped. The orphanage had been so thoroughly pillaged, and local policy toward the orphans was so heartless, that the institution could not be saved, and the children were transferred to Cologne.[22]

In Remscheid, Maria Briel and Grete Dreibholz also sought out Jews in need. Maria remembered having great difficulty in reassuring the people they visited that they meant no harm. One family was especially wary; the Sternbergs were so alarmed by the women's visit and so suspicious of their motives that Maria and Grete had to leave before they could even offer any practical assistance.[23] In Mülheim, the Zenkers similarly sought out local Jewish families with offers of help.[24] Others crossed the border into Holland to mail letters abroad on behalf of Jews, presumably so that they could tell relatives what was really happening and plead for assistance without fear of the censor.[25] In Düsseldorf, Else Bramesfeld made the rounds visiting assorted acquaintances and again called on the Jewish Community Center nurse. She also visited close friends of Dore's, including a distinguished former social worker, who gave her yet another dreadful account of the previous days. Else recalled:

> When I arrived, she was sitting upstairs in a room that had been half cleared up and told me with astonishing composure what had happened. In the evening an SA troop had arrived, pushed her and the housemaid into the bathroom, and started its work of destruction. On the ground floor I saw a demolished room,

and upstairs too, furniture smashed to bits, pictures out of their frames, the portrait of her husband hung out the window, a cupboard with valuable glassware tipped down the stairs to the floor below, beds and upholstered furniture cut to pieces. Once the troop had gone, there were shards of glass underfoot everywhere.[26]

Across the Ruhr, Bund members sought to reassure, offer solidarity, and provide moral and practical support to Jews. In January 1939, Artur wrote to his son, Friedl, now safely out of Germany and living with relatives in Holland:

> You can well imagine that under such conditions we have our hands full trying to help, advise, console, keep people from despair and keep the little spark alive. All our energies and those of our friends are focused on this. Often, we can manage only little things, the big things are beyond us. But at the right time in the right way little things can sometimes work wonders.[27]

After the war, Artur would write that Kristallnacht acted as a wake-up call to the world, alerting other nations not only to what the Nazis were doing to the Jews but to what might at any time be done to any state, any people, any church. The barbaric acts had awakened not only compassion and moral outrage, he argued, but also an instinct of self-preservation, paving the way for the common front against Hitler.[28] It is true that the violence unleashed on November 9 and 10 did attract a great deal of international attention; still, Artur probably overstated the lessons the international community had drawn. For the Bund, however, Kristallnacht was transformative.[29]

Motives and Barriers to Action

We shall probably never know how many members of the Jewish community the group helped in those days, weeks, and months. Many of those assisted did not survive to tell the tale, and others dispersed across the world. Had the recipients been able to record their memoirs in later life, would they have considered such actions worthy of remembrance? The gestures were often small, even if they conveyed to the recipients the invaluable knowledge that someone still cared about them. But would the elderly Dinslaken Jew whom Tove assisted remember that she had gone shopping for him because the local stores were refusing to sell him food? Would an elderly Essen lawyer who made it to the United States at the last minute have remembered that Bund members had crossed the border into Holland to mail letters for him?[30] On an even smaller scale, would a Jewish family have recorded the visits of solidarity Artur Jacobs made before they immigrated? Probably not. The Bund was careful to conceal its identity, and consequently, the recipients rarely discerned the group impulse behind such seemingly personal gestures. At most they may have heard something vague from the visitor about well-wishing "friends" with whom he was connected. Mindful of the censor, in his letters to Friedl Artur referred to the Bund in the same way.

What kind of risks was the group running? Helping Jews was not yet criminalized, and there was thus no predictable penalty. There is little evidence that those who helped Jews on Kristallnacht were pursued by the authorities. Yet the Gestapo had long made it clear that loyal people's comrades were expected not to mix with Jews. Even those who simply shopped in Jewish stores might find their photograph published under denunciatory headlines in the local press. During Kristallnacht itself, the atmosphere of violence made everyone fearful of stepping forward. Peeking out from behind the curtains, onlookers like the Heinemanns' neighbors were undoubtedly worried that they would become targets themselves. Those like Maria Briel and Grete Dreibholz who reached out to strangers, only to be regarded with suspicion, must have felt triply isolated—at risk from the regime and the mob, unsupported by friends and neighbors, and feared as potential malefactors even by those whom they were seeking to reassure and support.

Why did they do what they did? A great deal has been written about the motives and factors that drove helpers or rescuers. After the war, the Bund itself would devote much thought to the question. But their answers were different from their observations at the time. The most revealing contemporaneous sources are the letters exchanged between the Jacobses and their son, Friedl, in Holland, many of which have been preserved. Parents and son were cautious, mindful of the censor, yet still had much to say.[31] One of Artur's most striking ideas was that beyond just bringing comfort, the Bund might also help the victims gain new insights from adversity and rid themselves of a bourgeois fixation on material well-being. In a January 1939 letter to Friedl, after describing how much the Bund had on its plate, Artur wrote:

> If anything in these dark times can set our spirits in motion once more and remind us of that spark of spiritual strength within, it is these small moments when we see our words landing upon fertile soil. People learn to see their lives from a completely different perspective. Hammered by fate, the old quest for a pleasurable life, a good position, security and affluence, suddenly falls apart. In its place, real life emerges, with other goals and possibilities.[32]

In another 1942 talk in Bartlesville, this one to the American Association of University Women, Tove sounded a similar note:

> I saw rich Jewish women sitting in the rubble of their homes. . . . What I was most conscious of was that these women, who like all of us had once clung to their possessions and their homes, seemed no longer to even see their destroyed home, and seemed to be completely uninterested in "stuff," seemed to have completely moved beyond "stuff," and had space within them for only one thing and that was the question: how is this possible? How is it possible that human beings can do this to people who have never done anything to them, whom they don't even know. How is this possible?[33]

Bund members continued to express the idea that adversity was liberating the victims from materialism until 1942. Artur, for example, made similar comments about Jewish community leaders eking out a life in Essen. But as the Bund came to fully apprehend the murderousness of the Nazi project, the notion that hardship might be beneficial in any way became unpalatable. There is no record of any Bund member expressing it after the war. Tove's comments in 1942 probably reflect a moment of transition. She begins with the theme of leaving materialism behind, but she moves on, not to the "spiritual liberation" of former materialists but to search for the reasons for the violence.

Something that emerges clearly from Artur and Dore's letters to Friedl is the extent to which their own experiences and Dore's family and personal connections alerted them to the suffering of others. This might seem both obvious and banal, but the Bund's postwar account of its actions denied that such personal ties played any role at all. The reality was, however, that as parents of a first-degree *Mischling*, Artur and Dore had from 1933 onward seen Friedl subjected to what Artur described in his diary as the most destructive kind of pressure, public ostracism. For a confident, secure individual, this would be hard enough, Artur felt, but for an insecure young man, it was a poison for which there was virtually no antidote. Unable to finish high school and forced to leave technical college under miserable circumstances, Friedl remained without a secure foundation, despite his multiple talents—without professional prospects of any kind and, in fact, without any kind of life goal.[34]

Moreover, Artur and Dore themselves were having to deal with the increasing barrage of measures aimed at Germany's Jews. In a letter to Friedl on July 20, 1938, Artur, never one to dramatize, acknowledged, "We are so looking forward to getting away for a bit. Times have been hard lately and one needs some respite from the challenges and the unsettling events."[35] After the summer break, Dore wrote to a friend about how difficult it was to keep calm. One knew in the end who would win, at least in one's head, she wrote, but the events of the day had become so threatening and so hideous as to overshadow everything. The feeling of powerlessness was overwhelming. You could see disaster approaching, and there was nothing you could do.[36]

Dore's relatives and the couple's Jewish acquaintances were leaving the country one after the other. By 1938, most of the Jews in the Bund had immigrated—among them Erna Michels to Holland, Berthold Levy to Sweden, Mikscha Brandsdorfer to Palestine, Wasja Enoch to the United States. In August 1938, Dore wrote to Friedl that her sister, his aunt Eva, had sold her business and would be leaving Germany soon for England. In the same

letter she mentioned other friends, "Ernst und Hedwig," who were leaving
to join their children abroad. "The decision came very quickly once Ernst
lost his profession," she explained.[37] Friends and relatives continued to
be uprooted. From one week to the next, the Herzfelds, parents-in-law of
Dore's brother Robert, departed for Palestine without managing to sell their
house. One son was in Brazil, the second in Paris, a daughter in Palestine,
another in transit, and now the old couple had left, just like that.[38] On September 6, 1938, responding to the continuing convulsions around them,
Artur told Friedl, in language that was undoubtedly guarded, given that
the letter would be intercepted by the authorities,

> I have to say that I think you've actually been incredibly lucky,
> when I see how difficult it is for people trying to get out now.
> Even in the time since you left, our lives and choices have dimin-
> ished significantly. Every day there are new obstacles. In this
> tense atmosphere, which places a large question mark over every
> kind of work and every life plan, you are able to work and study
> freely. You have people who are willing to help and offer advice
> at any time. All this gives you a big advantage over others.
> Whenever you find things difficult and have to do something
> unpleasant or overcome small difficulties, think about that.[39]

Germany's Jews were subject to a huge levy, amounting in the end to
more than 25 percent of their assets, to pay for the damage inflicted on
Kristallnacht. The Blockhaus was listed as Dore's property, and Artur
thought they might have to sell it, but as an "Aryan," he was able to transfer Dore's property from her name to his own and, thus, protect it from
confiscation.[40]

"Life here is hard," sighed Artur on December 2, 1938, in a rare moment
of vulnerability. "Every day brings new surprises. One's heart is so heavy.
Even if you remain reasonably composed through the day, you are vulnerable to all the demons at night." By reaching out to others, helping them,
and seeing how steadfastly they coped with the blows fate rained on them,
Dore wrote, it was possible to gain courage, strength, and new faith.[41] Of
course, many Bund members were not Jewish and so did not have the same
kind of encounters and challenges. But for them, Dore and Artur's experi-

ence made palpable what Jews were going through. Observing Dore and Artur worrying about how their son was doing in Holland, Karlos Morgenstern wrote that they were combatants in a kind of war:

> What you and Gottfried [Friedl] are going through—and we experience through you—is truly a battlefront. On one side is the individual with his spiritual mission, and on the other all the entanglements which society and nature impose on him.[42]

Despite Karlos's vagueness (he was surely trying to elude the censor), his meaning is clear. As leaders of the Bund and a mixed-marriage couple, the Jacobses kept all Bund members attuned to the Jewish fate under Nazi rule in a visceral, personal way. There were good reasons for many members to feel disconnected from Jewish suffering, particularly since the Bund had consciously rejected organized religion. But Karlos's note shows that through Artur and Dore, other Bund members had a deep connection to the Jewish lot. Such personal links were vital, and yet they remain invisible in the group's postwar pamphlets about its wartime achievement.

On November 18, 1938, Dore wrote to a relative in Holland that she wanted to leave Germany. Given her loyalty to the Bund, this was striking evidence of the toll persecution had taken on her health and psyche. In February 1939, Artur told Friedl that they were trying to get Dore to Denmark or England. In April, they obtained a quota number for immigration to the United States, though it seems likely that they took this step not out of a serious desire to cross the Atlantic but, rather, because it would encourage the Dutch authorities to give Dore temporary residential rights by demonstrating that she would not be a permanent burden on the public purse. As far as America was concerned, in retrospect, we know there was no chance that this quota number would have been processed before emigration out of Germany was halted in October 1941. Evidently, Dore and Artur had also been arranging to have friends or relatives provide financial guarantees to facilitate immigration to England—again, not with the aim of actually going there but instead to make Dore acceptable to the Dutch authorities.[43]

In the end, Dore's health stalled their efforts to leave.[44] In the wake of Kristallnacht, Dore's sciatica worsened to the point of paralysis.[45] In

March 1939, her condition deteriorated so dramatically that Artur was obliged to take her to a hospital, an event that involved considerable expense.[46] Dore did not leave the hospital until late July, and she then stayed with Artur's brother and sister-in-law in the Bund apartment in Wuppertal, where several members cared for her. Not until October 1940, more than eighteen months after falling ill, did Dore return to her own home on Dönhof Street, though she still needed two canes and a helping hand as she once more had the pleasure of visiting each room in the house.[47] This was doubly difficult for a woman whose whole life and philosophy had centered on physical movement.

The Outbreak of War

The war would be the Bund's finest hour. But the months between Kristallnacht and the outbreak of war were anything but auspicious. In addition to dealing with his wife's continued ill health and seeking guarantors abroad, Artur was still involved in negotiating the transfer of Dore's property, which "took a great deal of effort and worry—and expense," as he communicated laconically in July 1939.[48] Artur, never particularly fit in these years, succumbed to the pressures in the spring of 1939 and became so ill that for weeks he kept having to defer a trip to Holland to visit his son. Dore would not venture onto a train again until April 1941, and she remained unable to take part in Bund excursions until the summer of 1942.[49]

The outbreak of war brought rationing, which gave the regime a new tool with which to discriminate against Jews. Jews were denied clothing coupons from the outset, and after December 18, 1939, they were allowed only basic food rations, whereas others received a supplementary card. The precise rules changed with each ration period. In December, Jews received less meat and butter than others, no cocoa, and no rice; in January 1940, they were permitted no meat or vegetables. In addition, they were forbidden from buying non-rationed foodstuffs, including chicken, fish, and smoked foods.[50] On top of all this, Dore and Artur had an additional worry that the war might limit their ability to communicate with their son.[51]

The war also soon reduced the group's cohesion and ranks. Male members were subject to call-up, and in December 1939, the Bund's celebration of Gustav and Hedwig Gehrke's marriage took on a special poignancy since Gustav, who had already been drafted, had to rejoin his unit in Poland immediately after. Gustav, Karlos Morgenstern, August Schwab, Reinhold Ströter, and Alfred Stürmer, among others, were drafted in 1939 or 1940, as were the sons of older members, including Käthe Franke's son, Hans Hermann; Walter and Gertrud Jacobs's son, Dieter; Ernst Jungbluth's son, Eberhard; and Liesel Speer's son, Friedl. As the war went on, even men who were exempted from call-up as skilled craftsmen were affected, as the authorities moved them and their factories from the Ruhr region to more remote areas in central Germany less exposed to the intensifying air raids. As a result, the Bund became a group even more reliant on women—as well as older men like Artur, Walter, and Ernst. Just a few younger men in protected occupations, such as Hermann Krahlisch, Erich Nöcker, and Gustav Zenker, managed to stay in the Ruhr for the duration of the war.[52]

In one respect, the outbreak of war provided the Bund with a brief sense of consolation: it threw much of the population into the same state of profound anxiety they had inhabited for some time. But this was short-lived. In April 1940, Denmark and Norway fell to the Germans, and on May 10, Germany invaded France and the Low Countries, placing Friedl once more under Nazi rule. To the horrified Bund, it looked as if the whole of Europe would be at Hitler's feet and nothing could stop the Nazis from ruling indefinitely. Compounding this disaster were cheering neighbors, celebrating an unbroken string of victories bought with relatively few casualties, seemingly oblivious to the true nature of the regime they were endorsing. Whereas resistance groups abroad could often profit from a shared sentiment of patriotic resistance against an invader, in Germany opponents to the regime seemed disloyal traitors, impervious to the appeal of a resurgent fatherland.[53]

The Bund and Its Children

When, in later years, the Bund described the challenge of feeling so isolated in wartime, it referred to the incessant drone of regime propaganda and the roar of public acclamation. But at no point did these postwar accounts suggest that the group's own children were susceptible to this barrage. The reality was, however, that non-Jewish Bund members could not prevent their children from being exposed to Nazi influences. In January 1940, Artur wrote to his son, Friedl, in Holland; avoiding commentary in a letter that might be read by the censor, he noted that Ursula ("Ursel") Jungbluth, Ernst's fifteen-year-old daughter, "is a BDM [the Nazi girls' organization] leader and completely absorbed by her role. She has grown very tall and pretty."[54] Talking to a youthful audience in Bartlesville in 1942, Tove offered an account of the activities of an enthusiastic member of the Hitler Youth, without quite specifying whether she was referring to a real individual. But the name she used was surely no accident: "Ursula J is doing her homework after school. A telephone call informs her that she must report immediately to such and such a place. Without hesitation, she drops everything and leaves."[55]

Tove explained how the Hitler Youth groups appealed to children and described the dilemma of parents who opposed the regime, whose children would ask, "Mummy, why don't you like our Führer?" Revealing one's true opinions, even to one's children, could be dangerous. Did one, in any case, have the right to involve a child in one's own crisis of conscience? Tove concluded the talk with a question to her young audience: "Do you have some issue that is so important to you, to which you are so devoted, that you are willing to devote your free time, your strength, your whole being to it, just as the 'Ursulas' do for their bad thing?"

Meanwhile from Holland, no doubt with a caustic undertone, Friedl wrote to Ernst Jungbluth: "From your daughter Ursel I learned some time ago that she has become a BDM leader. Please tell her that I congratulate her. She will surely be very proud of her achievement."[56] With the outbreak of war, the regime's grasp on Germany's youth intensified. Membership in the Hitler Youth became compulsory, as did labor service for young women. At least one of the Bund sons, Friedl Speer, accepted conscription even though he could have been deferred as a student.[57]

Powerful as the regime was, its influence within the Bund might not have been so divisive had there not already been tensions between the generations. For the children, the fact of growing up in families more devoted to the larger cause than to their needs had been challenging, as had growing up with values that were at odds with those of their peers. In Friedl Jacobs's case, his childhood had been dominated by his parents' moral mission and their leadership role in the Bund. In my interviews, only a few former Bund children explicitly expressed negative feelings about their parents' devotion to the group, but it seemed revealing that many did not want to talk about it at all, and Margarete, the one who was most critical, chose to speak only under a pseudonym. Other than Friedl Jacobs, none of the children joined the Bund after the war.

Looking at Artur and Dore's correspondence with Friedl, one cannot help sympathizing with both sides of their unhappy exchanges. Friedl appears immature at times, petulant, needy, alternately critical and self-abasing. But to his parents, the most troubling aspect of his behavior was that he was slow to respond, often failing to acknowledge receipt of letters or information at moments when communication was critical.[58] In 1939 Friedl was a crucial intermediary with the Dutch relatives who might have been able to help his mother leave Germany, but his poor communication with the relatives in Holland evidently made a bad impression, and hampered the Jacobses' ability to elicit aid.[59] The most bitter recriminations came from Artur on December 15, 1938, when the couple was still recovering from the aftermath of Kristallnacht: "We are very unhappy with you and feel completely disconnected from you."[60] Friedl was dilatory, too, in dealing with his own affairs, including his draft status. Although of "mixed race," he was still legally obliged to register for military service.[61] His parents were thus by turns deeply worried, irritated, and disappointed, and they became even more hectoring and interventionist, to a degree unexpected between parents and a son in his twenties.

Yet away from the relationship with his parents, we know that Friedl was in fact an impressive young man. Milo Anstadt, later a celebrated Dutch journalist and writer, was a Polish Jewish immigrant to Holland and part of a circle of young Jews in Amsterdam. He became friendly with Friedl in early 1939, and it is clear that Friedl impressed Anstadt—the latter's 1996 autobiographical novel *De verdachte oorboog* (the title translates roughly as "The Suspiciously Shaped Ear," referring to an allegedly Jewish physical characteristic), devotes an entire chapter to him.[62] If the author's account is correct, in March 1939 Friedl was an astute enough observer of the international scene to have predicted that the Nazi invasion of the remaining Czech lands of Bohemia and Moravia would be the last acquisition Hitler could attain without war.[63] Another member of the young Amsterdam circle, Susi Cohen, who already knew Friedl from Essen, similarly remembered his clear-sightedness.[64] To his peers, Friedl seemed intelligent, serious, thoughtful, and kind, even if socially awkward and at times obsessed with his difficulties in making contact with the opposite sex.[65] He was certainly in a difficult position—in addition to dealing with the German authorities, he did not have a proper job in 1940.[66] His parents, particularly Artur, seemed always to know better. In February 1943, for example, responding to Friedl's dire prognostications about the Holocaust, Artur allowed himself to make fun of his son's remarks, writing, "No, my wise son." Friedl's predictions, as it turned out, would prove all too accurate.[67]

One challenge, not just for Friedl but for other Bund youngsters, was that they rarely dealt with their parents alone but, instead, faced an adult collective. There was no privacy. In January 1940, Karlos Morgenstern wrote to the Jacobses that "E" (probably Else Bramesfeld) had visited him in Braunschweig. "Since E's visit," wrote Karlos, "I have thought of you a lot. E read letters from Gottfried [i.e., Friedl] to you and from Erna to him."[68] Evidently, Else was traveling around with Friedl's letters in her luggage. This kind of sharing allowed the parents to gain group backing for their approach to their children, who were, of course, put in a very unequal position.[69]

The clearest sign of the parental generation's unease is the self-congratulatory way Artur and others seized on any sign that despite everything, something of the way they had raised their children was shining through. After receiving a letter from Käthe Franke's daughter Ilse, for example, Artur commented that the "pure air" of her childhood still made itself felt.[70] Similarly, in January 1941, Artur's brother, Walter, wrote to his nephew expressing his pleasure that Friedl had acknowledged the value of his parental home.[71] He only wished that his own son, Dieter, felt the same. In June 1941, Walter exclaimed, "Ach, Gottfried, if you could all get together sometime and tell each other about your lives. I think then you would really know how to value some of your childhood memories. Because through the experiences that you have been forced to suffer, all of you now have enough perspective and distance to recognize the value of your family and childhood."[72]

But these moments of affirmation often gave way to open concern at their children's trajectory.[73] When Friedl Speer was home on leave in March 1942, Artur lamented in his diary that the times were taking the children away from their parents and that the youngsters were failing to see through the regime's rhetoric.

> Listening to Friedl Speer
> Still completely absorbed by his personal experience.
>
> For him, war is still an exciting experience that gives impetus to life, satisfies one's yearning for adventure, one's desire to see the world and experience new things. One can tell, despite the frenzied retreat at the end and a couple of difficult days: he still has not experienced the real nature of war.
>
> It is hard to listen to him.
>
> No horror at everything that is terrible in this war, no question about the general fate, about meaning, causes or broader connections. . . .
>
> How rare it is that all the good that children stand to inherit from their parents—the convictions and wisdom their parents have acquired by dint of hard struggle—actually comes to life and blossoms anew.
>
> How many countervailing forces there are in our age! How many countervailing forces in man![74]

A visit from Käthe Franke's son, Hans Hermann, en route to deployment in France, occasioned a similar bout of reflection. Artur admired the energy and down-to-earth character of the younger generation but, at the same time, despaired over its lack of idealism.[75] A few days later, he was still worrying that all the care and thought the Bund had invested would go to waste. Would the children return to their spiritual roots? he wondered.[76] At other times, he was more vehement. "And one day the cause is supposed to rest on *them*?!" he exclaimed bitterly.[77]

How adrift Artur and other Bundists must have felt on their fragile raft—not only at war with the regime and alienated from their neighbors but also unsure whether their own children would support them or carry on what they had started. Still, never once in the group's postwar memoirs did the starkness of their wartime anxieties emerge.

Rock Bottom

In addition to their isolation, members of the Bund were always at risk. Working as a volunteer at the local ration-card distribution center in December 1939, Sonja Schreiber made an unguarded comment to a colleague about the fate of the Jews, as mentioned at the beginning of this book. A few days later, Friedrich Gross appeared at the Essen Gestapo headquarters to announce that his wife had been "deeply surprised and offended" by Sonja's defense of the Jews. On March 8, 1940, the Gestapo brought Sonja in for interrogation. There was no doubt, the Gestapo officials reported, "that the accused has adopted the Jewish-Communist ideas of the married couple Jacobs. There is therefore no reason to doubt that she actually made the remarks reported by the witness Gross."[78]

Aiding Sonja's cause, however, was a supportive letter from fellow educators who were members of the National Socialist Teachers' League. Following interrogations, the Bund had the practice of going over what had been said and noting what should be amended or clarified. As a result, Sonja submitted to the Gestapo an additional statement to add to her sworn testimony. In it, she listed the names of two colleagues who had supposedly witnessed the conversation with Frau Gross, and she asked the Gestapo to interview them to determine whether Sonja had said anything political or critical of the state. The colleagues mentioned were indeed subsequently interviewed, and nothing negative emerged. Nevertheless, education officials admonished Sonja, placed an official warning in her personnel file, and withdrew the additional rations that she received because of her work. But, perhaps in view of the fact that Sonja had a sister who was well connected in local Nazi circles, the Gestapo did not take the punishment any further.[79]

Around the same time, Lisa and Artur fell foul of the authorities after a neighbor of the Jacobses', a sixty-two-year-old widow named Anna Gellingshausen, denounced them. Probably prompted by an Essen Gestapo officer seeking more material against the Bund in the wake of the Schreiber affair, Gellingshausen reported a series of suspicious goings-on, including suitcases being brought in and taken out at all hours, both at the house on Dönhof Street and at the Blockhaus. Even though she lived adjacent only to the Dönhof house, Frau Gellingshausen seemed to have knowledge of activities at both locations, which suggests that this was a put-up job, as does the fact that a series of other denunciations were recorded at the same time. What added to her suspicions, she said, was the clothing worn by those doing the carrying—namely, the kind of clothing that before the Nazi seizure of power had been worn by those in the Wandervogel (the free-spirited youth groups that had emerged in the nineteenth century). "My impression was that these were former Communists," she continued.[80] That impression led to a combined Gestapo-SD search of the house on Dönhof Street and the seizure of forty books and thirty-two brochures. "Jacobs gave his agreement to the confiscation," the Gestapo memo records dryly.[81] Both Artur and Lisa underwent several hours of intensive questioning. In a restitution court hearing after the war, Lisa described the good cop, bad cop routine: "They tried to frighten me, threaten me, and also in a jovial way to get something out of me."[82]

For the Bund, this early phase of the war was the spiritual low point. In an uncharacteristically gloomy mood, Artur wrote to Friedl in April 1940, "No one has any control anymore over what happens to them, at least externally. All the more important that we prepare our inner selves for whatever comes. Life is hard."[83] A couple of months later, in an old ruined hut on an isolated hillside in the Sauerland, the group, normally so confident about the direction of history, was worrying about the future. Artur described the scene to a friend. Trying to ignore the rain coming in through the roof, they asked themselves, "Is the human race moving forward at all? Do we have any reason to believe that it will one day be different, better, more just?"[84] Or was the idea of progress just an illusion, a self-deception to make life more bearable? Were the horrors of the old barbaric times destined always to return? Were violence, evil, lies, and brutality the inescapable lot of humanity?

Sometimes, the only way to cope with the misery was to reach out and help others.

5

Lifelines

In October 1942, Artur and Dore were staying in Julie and Käthe's little guesthouse in Meersburg, near the Swiss border, enjoying a brief respite from the increasingly war-torn Ruhr. On October 14, Artur wrote in his diary about a visit to an acquaintance's home. The conversation had turned to the "tragic fates of people today." "They listen attentively," Artur noted, "and perhaps they're even upset—but no more than after watching an upsetting film." He continued:

> The idea that this concerns us—that we share responsibility for everything that's happening, and that we might be able to do something about it—this doesn't even occur to them. And yet they see themselves as "open-minded" people, more knowledgeable and more profound than the rest. They simply have no sense of the morass into which they've allowed themselves to fall.[1]

The subtext of this conversation was undoubtedly the persecution of the Jews. After various mutterings about his hosts' philistinism and bourgeois desire for comfort, Artur concluded his diary entry with the words "upsetting and disappointing." Artur's stance is understandable and, indeed, admirable. In the wake of Kristallnacht, his group had faced the challenge the Nazis posed head-on. But as the regime's policies grew more brutal and lethal, we might ask whether the Bund's unwillingness to look away had any practical consequences. Was Artur's belief that one could make a difference, in the end, as deluded as the couple he was complaining about?

Gifts of the Spirit

Back in 1940, Lisa had approached the Duisburg rabbi, Mannes Neumark, to ask what she could do to help those in distress. Though a longtime resident of the Ruhr region, Neumark had been born in Posen and alerted Lisa to the plight of Jews in that area. A German province until the end of the Great War, when it became part of the newly created Polish state, Posen was reclaimed by Germany after Poland's defeat and absorbed into the new administrative area of the Warthegau. In December 1939, most of Posen's Jews had been brutally expelled, along with hundreds of thousands of non-Jewish Poles, into an area known as the General Government, the part of Poland that had been neither absorbed into Germany nor occupied by the Soviet Union; instead, it was administered by the Nazis with the utmost brutality. Many of the Jews ended up in the little community of Ostrow-Lubelski, part of a region near Lublin that the Nazis briefly conceived of as a Jewish reservation. Neumark's brother David was one of the deportees, and he, in turn, put Lisa in touch with another deportee, Gertrud ("Trude") Brandt, with whom Lisa remained in correspondence until Trude was murdered in 1943.

Significantly, at the time deportees were still able to use regular mail. And though many of Trude's letters were destroyed in a bombing raid in 1943, a substantial number survived.[2] It's not entirely clear if they were all intended for Lisa. In the letters, Trude writes sometimes to a person she calls "Mitzi" (probably a cover name for Lisa) and sometimes to a "Heidi Bruchsal," using a cover name for Hanna Jordan, a young woman who moved in the Bund's orbit during these years.[3] It's not clear how closely Hanna was involved or whether this was just misdirection. What we do know is that Lisa initiated the correspondence.[4]

David Neumark probably chose Trude Brandt for the exchange because of her dedication to the community in Ostrow-Lubelski. Among other things, Trude had been in charge of providing nourishment for the displaced children, distributing food acquired with help from the American Jewish Joint Distribution Committee. The deportees had very little with which to barter for food on their own, since before they had even arrived in Posen they had been robbed of almost everything they'd brought with them. With inadequate clothes and bedding, many had died during the first winter. Trude's own husband, Georg, had died in January 1940, just weeks after their deportation, and she had been left as the sole caretaker for their handicapped child, the youngest of their five children and the only one who had been deported with her.[5]

Lisa sent more than just letters. With the aid of some thirty to forty people, she orchestrated an effort to supply the Jews in Ostrow-Lubelski with food and other essentials.[6] Trude then distributed these goods to those most in need. Her letters return again and again to the extraordinary value of the Bund's parcels. The Bund's help, Trude wrote, constituted "the last remaining possibility" for her "to offer some small measure of private assistance" to others. The parcels brought joy in so many different ways, she found it hard to put her thanks into words. Many of the clothes and other goods the Bund sent were not used directly but were bartered with local farmers for food. In a whimsical moment, Trude chuckled over the fact that the bread she was eating had been "baked from your cardigan," and the potatoes had been "underwear in a previous life."[7]

Trude continually wrestled with the task of adequately expressing her gratitude:

> If I could do as I wished, then I would hug you and give you a kiss—and that would express what I'm feeling much more accurately than the longest letter. "But since that cannot be, I remain here"[8] and must use this dry and boring medium to tell you how much pleasure you have given me. . . .
>
> I feel a strong conviction that I must pass on to others all the love I have received, and that this goodness will be a powerful, living force. That thought calms me and keeps me from feeling shame. This is why I can thank you with an open, unencumbered heart, you dear!
>
> Two packages have arrived. I cannot tell you how much they

warmed my heart. The first to arrive was the parcel with the cardigan, sofa cushions, etc., and yesterday the coat. What a beautiful coat you gave up for me! How kind of you, and it's just right for me. It's such a rarity here to find something in such good condition—that alone is a source of pleasure. And, it's of such high quality. But everything else gave me great pleasure, too. For example, I have been suffering from a pulled muscle. Probably I pulled it carrying the boy, and this "medicine," which I had not known of previously, was just the thing. I used it straightaway and it brought me a great deal of relief. Not being able to bend properly is a real problem for me, so I am enormously grateful to you.[9]

Almost as enriching for Trude was the intellectual and spiritual exchange. "How much your letter pleased me and forced me to think," Trude wrote, before remarking on the way her correspondent's understanding of history aligned with her own.[10] For a certain kind of high-minded, politically left-leaning German Jew, the Bund's language and ideas were instantly recognizable and appealing, conveying the sense that the ethical and intellectual world they had felt themselves to be a part of still existed and still accepted them within its fold. This must have been of incomparable psychological value. As Trude observed in 1942, after talking about the effort and pain it cost to continue living:

And so it is important that new strength flows in from somewhere; in fact, it is essential for survival. To feel the warmth and proximity of people so similar to myself is like having a transfusion after losing a lot of blood—it is lifesaving. This is not just a metaphor, or a turn of phrase; it is the purest truth. Do you sense what you are giving me, how much you are helping me with the only kind of help I can use?[11]

Perhaps because it was safer to keep Jewish matters out of letters that would be inspected by the authorities, and perhaps because these matters did not seem particularly relevant to the women's life philosophies, neither correspondent referred to her Jewish background. No doubt, the connection via the Neumarks had already made clear to Trude that she was dealing with someone who had Jewish ties, and of course Lisa knew full well why Trude had been slated for deportation. But what we know from the reminiscences of Trude's son Heinz (who spent the Nazi years in prison and a concentration camp) and other sources is that the atmosphere and values of the Brandts' home in Posen had been very similar to those of Lisa and the Bund's other Jewish members. Trude's father, Ludwig Krause, had been a rabbi in the German Jewish reform tradition, observant in practice but concerned to understand Judaism's revolutionary, socially progressive potential. Heinz remembered Passover Seder evenings in which Judaism's radical and humanist dimensions emerged from the story of the exodus from Egypt. Trude and her husband, Georg, ran a cosmopolitan, unconventional household. They were not practicing Jews, but they were nonetheless inspired by the ethical teachings of the Jewish philosopher Martin Buber. The Bund's mixture of romanticism, social democracy, high ethical standards, and universalism was not uncommon in progressive Jewish households, and had much in common with the intellectual world in which Dore had been raised. Like many Bund members, the Brandts had been firm opponents of the First World War.[12] When Trude described her son Heinz as "an honorable character with an idealistic, perhaps too idealistic bent," she could not have known the degree to which her praise would overlap with the values of her correspondents.[13]

Evidently, Lisa made an effort to give Trude the sense of having something to offer in this exchange, asking her for parenting advice. "Your letter moved me deeply," Trude wrote back. "I did not expect you to respond to me like this—it touched me to my core. This sudden reversal of things—that you should seek to anoint me, someone who stands before you in such great need, as giver rather than taker, is almost overwhelming."[14] Trude's advice—that one should learn to have no expectations, even of loved ones, and that however they behave, one should not impose one's own demands upon them—was similar to the Bund's own philosophy of giving others freedom within a relationship (though whether it quite matched the Jacobses' actual approach to their son is another matter).

We do not know how many others like Trude were the beneficiaries of the Bund's letters and parcels. Trude and her letters to Lisa figure in Artur's diary, and in documents the Bund later published in the book *Gelebte Utopie*, in a way that few other individuals do. It is possible Lisa decided to focus her help on this one individual and those around her, rather than spreading the group's limited resources among many. It is also quite possible that she contacted other deportees but, for any number of reasons, did not establish such a close connection with them. Trude probably also stood out because she was like-minded, literate, and morally upright. Though Bund members knew Trude only through correspondence, Lisa later wrote, she became something of a friend (and the Bundists did not use that word lightly). A note in the Bund files observes, "We were able to bring a spark of light into her darkness and were richly rewarded with the gifts of personal strength and inner freedom that flowed back to us."[15]

Deportation and Dissemination

Decades after the war, the Bund handed over its surviving copies of Trude's letters to her son. But at least one copy survived separately. During the years Trude was confined in Ostrow-Lubelski, a German soldier, Franz Chales de Beaulieu, was working for the Wehrmacht in Berlin. (The missing *r* in "Charles" was the spelling mistake of a Prussian bureaucrat; nevertheless, it remained de Beaulieu's official name until after the war, when he moved to France and adopted the name François Charles.) A theology student, future cleric, and covert anti-Nazi, de Beaulieu was part of an army section monitoring enemy activities, Fremde Heere West (Foreign Armies West). Because of this he was granted access to all sorts of material, including papal speeches and anti-regime sermons from the bishop of Münster, documents he collected and secretly circulated to opposition circles. In February 1943 he was caught carrying some of these papers as he left the barracks. Additional incriminating documents turned up during searches of his home. A court-martial followed, and de Beaulieu was lucky to be only demoted and sent to a penal battalion. He had no connection to the Bund as far as we know; nor is there any evidence that they knew of him. But, intriguingly, among the documents found in his possession was a lightly edited, typed copy of one of Trude's letters to "Heidi Bruchsal."[16]

Another intriguing fact is that the copies of Trude's letters the Bund handed over to the Brandt family after the war consisted of both handwritten versions and typed copies. The typed copies are undated, but they seem to have been produced during the war, because in every case the name of the addressee has been removed, a step that seems to suggest that the letters were meant to be circulated without compromising the recipients' identities. It is likely, therefore, that the Bund was reproducing and circulating letters from Trude Brandt, presumably to inform others, whether Bund members or outsiders, about the conditions deportees were facing.[17] We do not know how the typed copy made its way to de Beaulieu, but it seems probable that he received it from outside sources rather than having intercepted it as part of his military activities. We do know that he was connected with Quaker circles in Berlin that were helping Jews, and also that he fell in love with an eighteen-year-old Jewish girl, Eva John. Several Bund members had direct or indirect ties to such networks, including Hanna Jordan and Doris Braune.[18]

This is not the only hint of the Bund's hidden but concerted effort to disseminate information about Nazi persecution. A chance reference in a Bund newsletter from 1953 reveals that in 1941 the Bund was in contact with Gertrud Luckner, another Quaker involved in rescue work.[19] But perhaps the most significant testimony is provided by a single sheet of paper in the Bund's archive, a typed wartime letter (or a typed copy of a handwritten letter) preserved by Lisa.[20] The letter is undated, but a reference in it to the fact that the first major transport from the Ruhr had "just taken place on Sunday" helps us identify when it was written.

At the end of 1939, when Trude Brandt and other Jews were being expelled from Posen, the deportation of German Jews remained the exception rather than the rule. Despite increasing pressure from regional leaders and other lieutenants, Hitler was slow to authorize the removal of the Jews. From the fall of 1940 on, SS circles (knowing that war was secretly being planned against the Soviet Union) were canvassing support for a future plan to send all of Europe's Jews to Soviet territory. Once Operation Barbarossa began, in June 1941, clamor for Jewish removal grew. Hitler, however, wanted to defeat Stalin before he acceded to such demands. For complex reasons, in September 1941 Hitler did finally agree that the German Jews could now be expelled, even though the USSR was far from being defeated. The first major deportations left the Ruhr in the last week of October—and this is when the letter must have been written. It is unsigned, and the addressee is not named. Postwar notes written in pen on the typed copy make clear that the "Berta" and "Ruth" in the text were in fact pseudonyms for Dore and Lisa.

The letter begins, somewhat mysteriously, "I wrote you how concerned we are about our friend. You know nothing about it and ask what has been happening." What follows is a strikingly clear and comprehensive account of the deportations. In Cologne, 1,600 Jews had been ordered to prepare themselves for transport, the letter states, along with 1,300 in Düsseldorf and 275 in Essen ("that is a quarter of all the Jews here")—altogether more than 20,000 in the whole of the Reich. No one knew where they were headed, the letter continued:

> People are saying that it is Litzmannstadt [Lodz] (provisionally) but probably they will be sent on from there. They can take with them (out of their entire possessions) 50 kilos (as long as they are able to carry it themselves) and 100 Mk (which will be needed largely for the long journey). All other property, including money, bank savings and so on, falls to the state. Those affected must sign that they are voluntarily handing over their property to the state.

The letter makes it clear that the Bund had close connections to local Jewish community leaders, since only they could have provided such detailed information about the transport's destination and the fact that the destination itself was probably a way station.

In some sense, the letter is cautious. It offers no judgment about the brutal policies it describes. While forthright about the tragedy of those affected, it devotes not a single word to the authorities responsible. Nevertheless, it does not content itself with cold statistics but asks the reader to imagine what it was like:

> To venture into an uncertain future, branded and ostracized, with no means of support, in winter in the East, along with the elderly, the sick, and children in conditions of hygiene so bad that even our young and healthy soldiers succumb—to be without ration cards, without the assurance of even the most basic

nourishment, confined in camps or in ghettos, cut off from all contact with the outside world and with society, and from any source of spiritual nourishment . . .

No one knew how long the detention would last. The unfortunates were thus denied the one thing that could make internment bearable even under the worst conditions: certainty that one day they'd be able to resume their normal lives. Meanwhile, all those left behind were in despair. "Because," the letter noted, "what's not in doubt is that no one will be exempted, and the rules are becoming ever more severe. The next group is supposed to go much further to the East and is allowed to take only 20 Kg of baggage with them!"

In vague terms, the letter then turns to the Bund's own particular concerns, naming "Berta" and "Ruth" as potential deportees and expressing deep anxiety about the situation of "Ruth," as a Jewish woman not protected by marriage to a non-Jew. Without so much as hinting at the group's existence, it alludes to all the Bund was doing. In one respect, the letter reveals the limits of the group's knowledge at the time. The official rationale for the deportations, we read, was "labor deployment in the East." On this, the letter commented, "This will be true but is only a camouflage for the fact that one wants to be rid of them." In other words, while it was clear to Bund members that the regime's priority was getting rid of its Jews, they, like many German Jews at the time, could not yet conceive that a policy of mass murder was crystallizing in regime circles.[21] Rather, their concern was that even someone as resourceful as "Ruth" (Lisa) might not survive the cold and hunger. If she were ten years younger, the letter observes, perhaps things would be different.

With its openness, clarity, and depth of knowledge, this was by any standards a remarkable letter to be sent in October 1941. The coded references to Dore and Lisa make clear that it came from the Bund, but to whom was it addressed and what was its purpose? Because the Bund filed it along with Lisa's notes about Trude Brandt, one might conclude that she was the recipient, only that is scarcely possible. It contains much information she would already have known. Moreover, it is unlikely that the group would have risked sending such a letter via the regular German post. If intercepted, it would have revealed to the authorities that Essen Jewish community officials were leaking information, and the consequences would have been dire.

The letter contains few clues about how it was sent, but one denunciation offers a hint: in 1944 two women, who revealed themselves to be very well informed about the Bund, reported to the Gestapo that some of its members were exploiting their freedom of movement to cross the border into Switzerland and to send mail abroad from that neutral country.[22] This is plausible. From the guesthouse in Meersburg, on the German side of Lake Constance, trips into Switzerland were relatively uncomplicated. It is possible, therefore, that this letter was indeed intended to be mailed in Switzerland to Bund members abroad, both to inform them and to disseminate the information as far and as wide as possible. The opening of the letter, addressed to an uninformed and somewhat distant well-wisher, would thus be designed to conceal the group's identity and its relationship to the letter's recipient.

The most likely destination of such a letter would have been the Bund members in the United States, Tove and Wasja. Yet Tove's well-preserved papers offer no evidence that they received it. Tove was avidly following events, trying to keep abreast of the news from Europe. The files she left behind include clippings she kept from the *New York Times* about reports on the slaughter of Jews.[23] Years after the war, Tove commented to a friend how conscientiously she had followed the news at the time.[24] But there is no hint in her wartime papers or later correspondence that she had learned the truth about the deportations from Bund communications. In a short account of her life as a Bund member, Wasja indicated that she had received news from the Bund via friends in Switzerland and Sweden only a handful of times.[25] The other possibility is that the Bund was indeed engaged in a more systematic dissemination campaign within Germany. Either way, it was clearly learning a great deal more detail than we find in Artur's diary and was seeking to spread that knowledge where it mattered.

The Bund and the Onset of Mass Deportations

What would happen to the deportees? It was not immediately apparent to even insightful observers like Artur Jacobs that with the assault on the

Soviet Union in the summer of 1941, the Nazis were rapidly moving toward outright genocide. For key Nazi figures, mass murder was becoming a thinkable and acceptable solution to the Jewish problem. However, even now it remains unclear to historians when the wholesale murder of European Jewry was established as definite policy. In September, when Hitler agreed that German Jews could be expelled, he might not yet have intended the deportations to be the prelude to mass slaughter.

We know that when Hitler gave the nod, no destination for the transports had been established, and a hasty series of efforts followed to find places where the deportees could be dumped. The first trainloads of German Jews were consigned to the Jewish ghetto in Lodz, a city the Germans had detached from Poland and incorporated into the newly created German region of the Warthegau. Later transports that autumn went to the Baltic and Byelorussian destinations of Kovno, Minsk, and Riga. There seems to have been no consensus among Nazi policy makers about what was supposed to happen to the deportees, although they clearly were not expected to thrive. Over the next few months, officials involved with the deportations seem to have moved from assuming that the endpoint was some punitive territorial solution to understanding that the object of the exercise was to bring about the death of the deportees through dire treatment. As early as November 1941, some deportees were shot on arrival.

If the regime itself did not yet quite know what its next actions would be, the situation was, of course, all the more uncertain for the deportees. What no one doubted was that conditions would be miserable. Clear, too, was that by dint of extended immiseration and repeated forced moves while still in Germany, the deportees did not possess even those bare essentials they had been allowed to take with them on their journey. The Bund, with some sense of the conditions Trude Brandt had confronted, assisted in furnishing some deportees with what they needed. By collecting from friends and drawing from their own reserves, they rustled up lightweight aluminum plates and bowls, rucksacks, bread tins, cutlery, warm clothing, and food.[26] As Artur noted appreciatively in his diary in November 1941, Dore also drew up a small booklet with medical advice.[27]

Bund members even accompanied deportees to the holding centers and carried their bags. Such gestures, though seemingly small, took enormous courage. The introduction of the yellow star for all German Jews in

September 1941 made the Bund's interaction with them much more visible. While the Gestapo had always pursued those who were friendly to Jews, a new regulation enacted on October 24, 1941, raised the stakes: "Persons of German blood, who demonstrate friendly relationships with Jews in public, are to be taken temporarily into protective custody, as an educational measure, and in serious cases are to be sent for a period of three months to a concentration camp, grade 1."[28] This was not a law but a regulation, which meant that instead of being given their day in court, the offenders were dealt with summarily by the Gestapo. Initially secret, the ordinance was widely publicized beginning in November. Goebbels fulminated in the press that since "the Jew" was a sworn enemy of the German people, "everyone who deals privately with him is one of them and must be treated and dealt with as a Jew."[29] In practice, however, the Gestapo's handling of such offenses was unpredictable. For the most part, helpers were not risking their lives; even so, the fear they must have felt cannot be overstated. Historians know of at least twenty cases from across Germany in which helpers were killed for their actions.[30] And for the Bund, there would soon be disturbing warnings close at hand. Hanna Jordan's friends Eva and Carl Hermann were arrested for hiding a Jewish couple and sentenced to three and eight years of prison, respectively.[31]

Someone, possibly one of the Bund's overseas members, cautiously asked Artur in a 1943 letter, "Can one visit a patient with an infectious disease without being infected oneself?" Artur answered, "Yes, one can, if one does it with sufficient caution and care."[32] It is clear that the group was not deterred by the threat of persecution. In November 1941, Artur recorded in his diary his conversation with Frau K, as she was about to be deported to Minsk, that appeared at the beginning of this book. His comment—that it should be him thanking her for allowing him to discharge a tiny portion of his guilt and that one "suffocated" if one did nothing—brought her to tears.[33]

The Bund's postwar comments that its actions were merely "a drop in the ocean" and could have "no impact on the tragic overall fate of the Jews" sound like a preemptive concession to address anticipated criticism of the group's small-scale efforts.[34] But Artur's comments during the war make clear something we can easily lose sight of: namely, the enormous psychological barrier to any kind of action posed by the systematic and comprehensive

character of Nazi policy. It is easy to see how one's sense of the utter arbitrariness of helping just one person in thousands, or of being able to ease
burdens only a little, could prevent one from doing anything at all.

The painful sense of powerlessness is a theme that appears again and
again in the Bund's writings. On November 9, 1941, as a wagonload of
deportees huddled overnight in the Essen synagogue, awaiting transport
the following day, Artur set out to visit them, to offer consolation and support. But then, suddenly, somewhere on a dark street along the way he
stopped:

> I was en route to the prayer hall where they were told to assem-
> ble today. I don't know what drove me—perhaps some mute
> conviction that no one has the right to stay peacefully at home.
> But I turned back around when I realized that there was no one
> I could help.

When Artur spoke to Frau K, he not only acknowledged how little he
could do but also suggested that his help was of greater benefit to himself
than to her. To be sure, this in itself was a kind of psychological gesture—
meant to remove any sense of dependence that his charity might cause.
We see the same kinds of gestures in Lisa's letters to Trude Brandt. Even
so, the idea that the helpers are the ones actually being helped recurs sufficiently often that it must have been central to the Bund's self-understanding.
Lisa Jacob spoke movingly of how, when confronted with particularly worrisome or threatening situations in her own life, she would regain her
composure by putting together parcels to be sent to Trude. She kept a suitcase under her bed, and over time, she would fill it with things for the next
set of parcels.[35] Artur, too, wrote that in those moments when one felt so
horribly lost and powerless, the only thing that helped was to "Work, create, do something meaningful!"[36] Artur's commitment to action also had
another dimension: it offered some relief from that sense of complicity, the
sense that all those citizens of Nazi Germany who were not being persecuted were guilty for allowing such a system to continue and for being its
beneficiaries. Only through action could they alleviate some of their guilt.
This was a remarkable notion for a man who had lost so much at the hands

of the Nazis, whose wife was under threat, and who was not in any way an executor of Nazi policy or a servant of the state.

When the mass deportations started, the Jews remaining in the region were forced out of their miserable accommodations and into even more primitive communal barracks before being dispatched east. In April 1942, for example, Essen's Jews were sent to the barracks on the site of the former Deimelshof coal mine in Essen-Steele. Again, ignoring the regime's threats to helpers, Bund members visited the occupants to offer what assistance they could. Artur's diary records the scene:

In the barracks:

How many challenges they have to face! Overnight 300 people from every class, every age group, every occupation have been thrown together, in a mad rush, without even the most basic things. (They can bring with them only what they'll later be allowed on the journey East—that is essentially nothing, compared to what they had in their normal existence.) No furniture, no cupboard, no table, no mattresses (instead, straw sacks, sometimes filled with paper), one big stove (on which almost 100 women are supposed to do their cooking!) In such conditions— how could anyone expect things to go smoothly? Among people who are not used to each other and who have to learn almost everything about living together—how can anyone be surprised that there's constant collision, friction, discontent, and demands both reasonable and unreasonable?

They <u>have</u> to fix up their living area (in order to live at all), but who has any desire to make everything nice and comfortable when tomorrow it could all be over?

A devastating scene—the old headmaster, who is supposed to look after the children (there are still some here), sits in despair among his piled-up books, unable to come to terms with his fate.

"We live like dead men," he said, "spiritually adrift, in dirt and misery. When I think how we used to live . . ."

Tears welled up in his eyes.

What consolation can one offer? Every word of false comfort only aggravates the injury.[37]

In Düsseldorf, Else Bramesfeld was a regular visitor to a house where
Jews were quartered. She would go in the evening, when it was dark, mindful that the local SA headquarters was next door. She vividly remembered
her first visit there. She wanted to call on a couple she had last seen when
they were still living in their comfortable and well-appointed home.
Directed to a room in semidarkness, she "saw a large wide frame on which
the occupants had laid down to sleep, one next to the other, wrapped in
their blankets." She located her acquaintances among this miserable, form-
less huddle. The woman was seriously ill and would die soon afterward.
Even so, Else kept visiting others there and was sometimes able to bring
rations she had "diverted" from the meal plan of the trade school where
she worked.[38]

In Duisburg, Jews were forced to live in very rough conditions in the
building of the former Jewish-owned Winter department store on the Bau-
strasse. Mathilde Zenker visited this group and managed to smuggle in
clothes and food. By her account, one evening she found herself trapped
inside and was able to get out only because of a bomb attack that caused
the guards to run away. The episode was sufficiently unnerving that her
husband, Gustav, burned all the Bund papers they had kept until then.[39]

In these months of mass deportations between October 1941 and the
summer of 1942, the Bund's activities seem to have been at their most
intense. Artur consistently followed what was happening to the region's
Jews, courageously staying in touch with Jewish community leaders. He
cultivated a close connection, for example, with David Krombach, a distinguished lawyer and the leading figure in Essen's shrinking Jewish community. The Krombachs were the kind of bourgeois family for whom he
would have had little time in the past. Now not only did the urgency of
the moment override such considerations, but in the Krombachs' response
to adversity Artur discovered qualities he much admired. David Krombach's willingness to work for the common good revealed to Artur an
estimable and kindred spirit. When the Krombachs, too, were included in
a deportation in April 1942, Artur noted down what he said were David
Krombach's last words before they parted:

A final word from Dr. Krombach (as, drained and overtired, he bade me farewell. Tomorrow they start on their journey):

"We have had to shoulder many burdens. We often thought we would go under. But we have also experienced much that gave us hope. Selfish feelings fade away—one is simply ashamed of them. Instead, we've pulled together and discovered something of the power of the whole."

"It may be," he added after a pause, "that later, when all this is behind us, we'll look back on it as the most important time of our lives and won't regret having gone through it, brutal as it was."

If Artur recorded his words accurately, it seems that David Krombach, like him, also saw some virtue in the tests posed by adversity.

On April 21, 1942, the Krombachs and the other Esseners were sent to Düsseldorf in preparation for a major eastward transport of Jews from the Rhine-Ruhr region. They did not know where they were headed; it would turn out to be the little town of Izbica, southeast of Lublin. "Today is the deportation," Artur observed sadly. "There have been some difficult hours. Inspection of suitcases. Farewells. For many, farewell forever. What goes through people's minds in such moments? It's haunted me the whole day." In the following months, the Bund would sustain its connection with Essen's Jewish community through Marianne Strauss, a striking nineteen-year-old who worked for the community and was engaged to the Krombachs' son Ernst, who had been deported along with his parents.

Visits to the deportation centers, keeping up connections with local Jewish community leaders, and drumming up foodstuffs and equipment for the deportees—all this was intended to help a larger group, not only those personally known to the Bund. At the same time, of course, the fate of individuals close to Bund members was of particular concern. One such person was Dore's aunt, Sara Auerbach. On one occasion, the Jacobses rushed down to Cologne, to the old convent where she was housed, after some obscure and worrying comments in a letter she'd sent had led them to fear the worst. But in this case, it seems the reality was not quite so grim.[40]

Then, in June 1942, Sara Auerbach's turn came. On Saturday, June 13, Dore received an "alarming telegram" from her aunt announcing that she had been ordered to leave on Monday and asking to see Artur and Dore once more.[41] The Jacobses hurriedly traveled to Cologne in a rattling train. Bombing had disrupted the Cologne transport system, so it was only late Saturday afternoon that they were able to reach the convent. Outside, everything was peaceful. Inside, uproar and confusion. The Gestapo was there, and Artur, as an "Aryan," was not allowed in. After quickly shaking hands with Sara Auerbach, he had to leave her in the care of Dore, who had only recently become well enough to travel herself. To Artur in that brief moment, Aunt Sara seemed reasonably composed, despite the impending deportation.

Dore wrote a few days later that this was one of the most demanding days of her life.[42] The sight of the enormous dormitory, beds stacked against beds, the room full of elderly people in despair—it was all heartbreaking. In just a matter of hours, they were supposed to make important last decisions, pack, and get ready to leave—but how could these people even keep their wits about them in all the noise, confusion, and overcrowding? Two beds over from Dore's aunt lay an eighty-two-year-old woman, expelled from her old-age home just four days earlier, deaf, and stunned by the storm raging around her. They had all recently endured a massive bombing attack. Mountains of personal possessions were piled on the beds. From these last remnants of their former lives, the occupants had to choose what could fit into a single kit bag and a suitcase, and which valuable goods—umbrellas, hot water bottles, duvets, coffeemakers—they would leave behind.

Like her husband, Dore observed the way the stress of the moment brought out the best in people. (No doubt, it was only possible to have this thought because what actually awaited the deportees was still unknown.) Even though most came from "philistine" backgrounds, Dore wrote ("loads of butchers' and bakers' wives according to the aunt," Artur noted), she admired their ability to tolerate distress, their willingness to help others, and their sloughing off of material concerns.[43] She was impressed by the general mood—without hope but composed, and sometimes with a touch of gallows humor. Everyone was generous with one another and shared what they had. Dore was touched that despite the strict limits on baggage, her aunt still insisted on packing a volume of Schopenhauer's aphorisms and one of Marcus Aurelius.

Was there ever any discussion about saving Dore's aunt, the last blood relative on German soil of the Bund's cofounder? By the time Aunt Sara was in the convent, and certainly once the deportation process was under-way, with Gestapo officials supervising every move, it would have been impossible. But in the run-up to the deportation, had there been any thought about perhaps spiriting her away, shedding the yellow star, and finding an address where she could live unobtrusively in safety? There is no evidence that there was.

We know of the Bund's efforts on behalf of the other case of particular personal concern in these times—namely, Lisa, the only Bund member under imminent threat of deportation. True, beyond the reference to "Ruth" in the typed letter about deportations we discussed earlier, we have few contemporary sources detailing efforts to help Lisa; much of what we know derives from her own postwar account. So it is perhaps not surprising that any discussions about Dore's aunt are also not documented. But there are some early hints about the Bund's concerns for Lisa's safety. In the fall of 1941, Friedl Jacobs elliptically expressed anxiety that Lisa might be endan-gered, and his mother confirmed that she, too, was worried.[44] According to the Bund's code, members' bonds of loyalty to the group were supposed to override even the call of family. It would certainly have been easier to ask the group to pool rations to assist a member of the Inner Circle, Lisa, than one of its members' aunts. Perhaps at a time when no one could pre-dict how long Nazi rule would last, it simply did not seem realistic to arrange for this elderly woman, a stranger to most of the group, to spend an indefinite period in hiding. Whatever the prime consideration, the fact is that alongside the significant risks the Bund took, it also had to make agonizing choices of exclusion and inaction. For Dore, nothing was more painful than seeing her beloved aunt being readied for dispatch to the bru-tal unknown.

The Parcel Service

Even after the deportation trains rolled out of the stations, crammed with their cargo of "unsettled, helpless people—conscious and yet blithely unaware at the same time,"[45] as Lisa described them, the Bund did not give up its commitment. One set of beneficiaries was the Krombach family.

Ernst Krombach's fiancée, Marianne Strauss, working in the Jewish Community offices in Essen, was able to obtain the Krombachs' address in Izbica and soon began dispatching letters and parcels to the family. The surviving copies of the young lovers' correspondence show that she was putting parcels into the mail at a rate of more than twenty a month. As she acknowledged in postwar interviews, the goods she was able to send were provided with help from the Bund and sympathetic members of the clergy. In addition to donating some of their own rations, the Bund also obtained rations from Else Bramesfeld, who had access to the reserves at her trade school. After that closed, she began working at the Düsseldorf food supply office—where she was again able to hive off small amounts of food, including semolina, rice, and fat. Ernst Krombach wrote repeatedly that the Bund members who helped arrange the parcels simply could not imagine the lifesaving value of the goods they contained.[46]

In July 1942, while on one of the Bund's excursions, Artur copied into his diary a letter, most likely one he had sent to David Krombach in Izbica. The letter contained many themes that are by now familiar to us. After noting that he could not stop thinking about what his correspondents were enduring, Artur indicated, at least implicitly, that he had been forced to reappraise the Krombachs' personal qualities. They were, after all, people whose lifestyle and background he had once seen as bourgeois and hidebound. He thanked them for so generously and openly engaging with him, despite the gulf between them.[47]

We know, from a message the Krombachs were able to send back, that letters had the best chance of getting through when they were secreted in parcels. If the Krombachs received Artur's missive, his contemplative sentiments, so wildly out of kilter with the extremity of their lives in Izbica, must have seemed to come from another planet. At the same time, the evidence that there were German gentiles whose ethics remained intact may have offered some reassurance. But it could do nothing to avert catastrophe. By the end of the year, the Krombach parents were dead, and Ernst had been blinded in an accident. Though we do not know with certainty, it is quite possible that he, too, was dead by that point.[48]

In July, Artur and Dore received a distraught notification from Friedl that his girlfriend, Regina "Gina" Gaenzel, had been deported, along with her mother, Anna Gaenzel.[49] As soon as Friedl received a card from her bearing the address "Lager Birkenau, bei Neu-Berun in O.-Schlesien," he passed this on to his parents. Rumors about Auschwitz were beginning to circulate, and the Nazis used this address to disguise the origin of the postcards inmates were forced to send to allay suspicion. Further letters Friedl sent to his parents at the end of September and the beginning of October imply that before her deportation, he and Gina had agreed on a code. By this means she had been able to convey in her postcard that she and her mother were going to be killed. (We don't know exactly what the code was.) In his letter to Dore and Artur, Friedl wrote that Gina was in the hospital—an obvious euphemism—and continued, "but for me, who knows her, it is unambiguously clear that she is convinced that she will now become healthy."[50] The response from his parents and his succeeding letter make clear that this meant that she was certain she would be murdered. "The thing that is happening now," Friedl wrote, "can never ever be made good."[51]

Undeterred by Friedl's fears, however, and with an address now in hand, the Bund sent package after package to Gina and her mother for at least six months.[52] "How good that we now have the address for the friend," wrote Ernst Jungbluth, on October 8, 1942. "The first parcel has just gone, the second will go off this afternoon."[53] On October 12, Dore, on a brief visit to the Meersburg guesthouse, confirmed to Friedl that the Bund had now written and sent several small parcels, and that she was about to mail a package containing some cake and fruit. In all, Bund members sent several parcels and letters in a single week—to Auschwitz! As late as February 1943, Artur was still assuring his son that the group continued to mail goods without pause to Gina, and because nothing was being returned, they were hopeful that at least some had reached their destination. Sadly, the record suggests that she had been murdered in September 1942. (Her mother, however, was still alive. But while non-Jewish Poles in the Auschwitz main camp were able to receive parcels, this was not true for Jews, or for anyone in Auschwitz-Birkenau. Even so, Gina's mother survived the war and immigrated to the United States in 1951. There is no evidence that this was ever known to Friedl.)[54]

Money and food were so scarce that sending even unrationed dry goods was a sacrifice. But more impressive still was the courage it must have taken to bring the letters and parcels to the post office. Ever since Jews had been forced to adopt the additional middle name of Sara or Israel, it was immediately clear when a letter was being sent to a Jewish recipient. In any case, the destinations—the ghettos and camps in the East—made this doubly obvious. It was no small thing to stand in line at the post office, to have the parcel franked by an official and the paperwork checked, perhaps to return a few days or weeks later to the same office to do the same thing—even if the senders often used fake return addresses. Such civil courage could pay surprising dividends. Even though changing regulations progressively limited what could be sent and where, Bund members were continually surprised by what the German postal service would accept, and what actually arrived at its destination. Outside the extermination centers, packages did, in fact, reach deportees in Poland, at least until regulations changed, sometime in 1942, and continued to be delivered to Theresienstadt even after that.[55]

In addition to sending parcels, Artur sought to reassure his son in a different way. Responding to Friedl's agonized breast-beating over not having acted before Gina was deported, Artur tried to offer consolation by listing some of the negative consequences that would have resulted from such an intervention:

> To be permanently dependent on the help of others would probably be intolerable in the longer term, particularly now, where everyone has enough to do simply taking care of themselves and where everything is so difficult. The only exception would be if one could live with close friends who are very reliable, and who simply take it for granted that they would share everything they owned. But where can one find that, unless one has already created it through a long life of selflessness and mutual help?[56]

It is doubtful whether such obvious self-satisfaction in the Bund's superior qualities could really offer Friedl consolation. But it does reveal how strong, even now, were the group's scruples about creating a situation of dependency, with its moral and psychological costs. Perhaps these scruples had played a role in deterring the group from protecting Dore's aunt. It was a kind of thinking still possible when one did not yet know (or not yet for sure) that the government was in the business of mass murder. The absence of that knowledge had the positive effect of encouraging the group to perform all kinds of small acts of solidarity, even though in hindsight they might seem futile. But it also allowed scruples to play a role whose time had definitively passed.

Forced Labor

Jews were not the only beneficiaries of the Bund's assistance. By the fall of 1941, there were some two million foreign laborers at work in Germany, and three years later, there were almost eight million, a quarter of the workforce. The conditions in which they worked varied enormously, depending on the basis on which they had been brought to Germany and the racial category ascribed to them by the Nazis. While some workers from the Low Countries enjoyed contractual terms that approached those of their German counterparts, the concentration camp inmates, numbering well over half a million, and the even larger number of Soviet POWs worked as slave labor under brutal conditions that in many cases proved fatal. In between were groups like the mostly female Eastern European civilian workers, drafted under duress, who worked under poor conditions but were not for the most part starved or worked to death.

In February 1944, Artur received a letter from Bund member Grete Dreibholz, who was working in a factory after having been dismissed from her clerical position because of her left-wing background. Despite her primitive living conditions, Grete wrote, she felt immensely privileged compared with the Polish forced laborers who were housed on-site in barracks. She had made a close connection with the Polish woman who was the interpreter and leader for her fellow conscripts. "If she had not received things from me and E.," Grete related, perhaps referring to Else Bramesfeld, "she and her daughter would have <u>one</u> shirt between them! I organized shoes for her, but they are already worn out."[57]

Most of what we know about the Bund's help for foreigners is from postwar testimony. Shortly after the war, Marianne Strauss wrote to municipal welfare authorities about the substantial aid the Bund had given prisoners of war and forced laborers.[58] In her autobiography, the Göttingen Bund member Meta Kamp-Steinmann records at some length her own efforts to assist local forced laborers. After learning that Eastern European workers could be employed at least part-time in the household, Meta claimed to the authorities that she was unable to work her market garden alone and was thus allowed to employ "Anna," a young Ukrainian woman. Another Bund member and friend of Meta's, Ellie Schlieper, acted as interpreter, and Anna became the linchpin of a distribution network that provided clothes and other essentials to her fellow conscripts, housed in the local labor camp. Before long, however, the local authorities moved all the foreign workers into factories. After that, Meta and Anna had only very limited contact. Shortly before the end of the war, according to Meta, after forced laborers had looted freight trains following an air attack, Anna turned up at the house with gifts of bacon and some other foodstuffs.[59] Decades later, Meta's son, Ernst Steinmann, still recalled the close contact his mother had maintained with local Eastern European workers.[60]

Bund members Gustav and Mathilde Zenker helped a Belgian prisoner of war, and their support was evidently so memorable and meaningful to him that he invited them, years later, to visit him in Belgium, which they did at least once, in September 1954.[61] Similarly, Wolfgang Briel told me in an interview that his parents, Fritz and Maria, had become so close to some Yugoslav workers in Remscheid that, years after the war, they were invited to visit them in Yugoslavia. He remembered stories of his parents being driven around in a horse and cart and feted by the local community.[62] Doris Braune, too, had a recollection to offer. As a regular visitor at the Youth Residential Home in Finkenkrug, founded by the educator Anna von Gierke, Doris was involved in helping Polish forced laborers at a nearby factory. Like Meta Kamp-Steinmann, she established contact via workers who came to their home to do small repairs; through them she was able to reach others in the labor camp. At the end of the war, according to Doris, the only building in the area not plundered by the forced laborers was the Anna von Gierke house.[63] It seems almost certain that the Bund did much more for local foreign workers than has been documented.

You Must Hear It from Me Again and Again

A moving coda to the Bund's efforts arrived on Else Bramesfeld's doorstep in October 1945. It was a letter sent from a DP camp in Bavaria by Isa

Hermanns. Elisabeth Marianne ("Isa") Hermanns was a Jewish doctor from Bonn, born in 1910, who had ministered to the Jews of Düsseldorf before she and her parents were deported to Theresienstadt in July 1942. Isa and her mother both survived. Now Isa had the chance to put pen to paper. Else, she wrote, was someone to whom she had felt "closer through all the terrible years than almost any other living person." First, because of the uncomplicated sympathy and support Else had offered while Isa was still in Düsseldorf, but also because of the many parcels Else had sent. It was not even so much their contents as the statement they made: "We are here, we are thinking of you, you are not forgotten." From Isa's letter we learn that Bund members sent parcels from Hamburg, from someone called Lotte Wolff in Düsseldorf (Wolff was in fact a cover name for Else, as Isa well knew), as well as from Stuttgart (we know this was Reinhold Ströter), Überlingen (Karin Morgenstern), Meersburg, and Constance. They contained straw shoes, soup cubes, dried fruit, soap powder, soap, cornmeal, and even cheese ("wonderful"). On one particularly memorable occasion, Isa had received seven parcels at one go. Another day, she received a marvelous long letter from Else that had been held up in the mail for two years. "You courageous woman," Isa said. She continued:

> You must hear it from me again and again and allow me to tell you again and again that these parcels from outside gave me the will to survive, gave something so horribly meaningless some meaning, somehow held me steady, in short, they helped immeasurably. And on top of that they brought us all those little things to eat, which we needed because we were really starving—particularly in 1942–43 and in fact until my father's death in March 1944.[64]

Else had done wonders. Yet it is a sobering reminder of the limits to what even the Bund could achieve that, soon after this letter was sent, Isa's mother died from the aftereffects of deprivation. And despite the moral reassurance Else's contact had offered, Isa could not shrug off her wartime experience and committed suicide a year or two later.[65]

6

In Plain Sight

From Offering Aid to Providing Refuge

By the war's outbreak, only two of the Bund's Jewish members remained in Germany. One was Dore, who as the wife of a non-Jewish spouse was protected from many of the Nazi measures. Her marriage fell into a category the Nazis called a "privileged mixed marriage," which had nothing to do with the regime's racial theory and everything to do with public morale. Mindful of the repercussions on the non-Jewish relatives of Jews, Hitler was wary of subjecting families who retained strong connections to the gentile world to the punishing restrictions of the anti-Jewish laws. Since couples' social relationships were assumed to be determined by the husband, mixed marriages with an "Aryan" husband were seen as more connected to gentile society.

Starting in December 1938, though, without a law to the effect ever being passed, officials began making a clear distinction between these privileged couples and other Jews, and even between them and other mixed marriages. Even couples where the husband had a Jewish background might be deemed "privileged" if their children had been brought up as non-Jews (and, conversely, an "Aryan" husband was no protection if the children had been given a Jewish upbringing). "Privilege" was, of course, a relative term. It meant that for the time being Dore was spared some of the increasingly punitive measures affecting other Jews. She did not have to wear the yellow star, for example, and was not subject to deportation. In many regions (it's not clear if this was true for Dore), the Jewish partners were not subject to the same reduced rations as other Jews. Only later in the war, and with significant regional variations, would Jews in mixed marriages begin to be targeted more severely.

The other Jewish Bund member left in Germany was Lisa Jacob. As a single woman, she was subject to the full rigor of Nazi measures. Beginning in September 1941, Lisa was required to wear the yellow star, and by October it was clear that this public marking of German Jews was a prelude to deportation. In November, Friedl asked in coded form, though clearly in a state of high anxiety, how things stood. His mother responded:

> We understand your worries. You are right to be concerned. True, I am not doing so badly, thanks to Father's care. What I would do without him, I have no idea. But we have many concerns about Lisa. Her condition changes from day to day. Heart issues are so unpredictable. One day things look more hopeful, she feels very strong and cooks, but then days come where everything looks really bad. How lucky that Aunt Gertrud thinks so much of her. She can always rest there when the noise of the children here gets too much.[1]

(The "children" were of course irrelevant, though not entirely fictitious. Grete Ströter was staying in the Dönhof house with her two small children. If anyone was sensitive to their noise it was Artur, not Lisa.) For Lisa, this was the grimmest period of her life. In Essen, she barely ventured out near her own home during daylight hours. When she wanted to go somewhere, she would leave the house before dawn, walk long distances to catch trains from distant stations, or take long tram journeys, since tram passengers were less rigorously checked. She traveled without the star, since Jews were by now severely restricted in their use of public transport. When she could, she spent time in Wuppertal, where she was not registered and not known to the local Gestapo, though of course an ID check could be fatal.[2] The Bund house in Wuppertal offered Lisa a place of refuge (hence Dore's reference to Friedl's "Aunt Gertrud," who was, in fact, Artur's sister-in-law,

Gertrud Jacobs, one of the members of the Wuppertal group). Even there, though, it took an enormous act of will to master one's anxiety. Decades later, Ellen Jungbluth looked back almost with disbelief at the way Lisa managed to sustain a normal, productive existence even while living in the shadow of deportations.[3]

At home in Essen on Dönhof Street, time ticked by, heavy with dreadful anticipation. Two suitcases packed with clothes, food, and medication stood ready in the basement, in case Lisa was caught by surprise and taken away. Sometimes she would wake in the middle of the night with a cry of terror, roused by the sound of boots on the street outside. At the same time, she was making preparations to avoid deportation. Artur had ready a series of letters, ostensibly from her, posted from Berlin and Ratibor, her hometown in Upper Silesia; he planned to show these to the Gestapo if they came looking for Lisa. Another Bund member had managed to get the letters franked and sent, to strengthen the impression that she had left Essen long ago.[4]

On April 12, 1942, the summons came. Lisa was ordered to report for a transport on April 22, destination unspecified. (In fact it was Izbica, on the same train the Krombachs had been assigned to.) When the police came to the house to deliver the message, Lisa was in Wuppertal. Two hours later, a Bund member reached her there with the news. It might seem incredible, Lisa later wrote, but it came as something of a relief. The suspense was over. After the grinding interregnum, the time for action had come.[5]

It seems the letters sent from different destinations were not shown to the police. Possibly, when the summons came, whichever Bund member received it at the door did not say the right things, in that instant, to confirm the idea that Lisa was long gone. The records indicate that the Bund now adopted a different ruse. Lisa wrote a letter, dated April 12, which Bund friends "discovered" the following day:

> I am utterly in despair because you are not yet here for me to talk to. But I cannot wait any longer. There is no rest to be had for me. Terrible news from Mother—horrible—that someone so old and so sick should be having to carry a rucksack on her back.
>
> I cannot bear these images anymore. I am completely undone, my swollen legs, my heart. . . .

> Farewell, you good people. Everything that I am I owe to you. Will we ever see each other again? No, no, I must not think of that.[6]

The masquerade hinted at suicide. We assume that a version of this letter was given to the police—though a copy survives in the Bund's papers.[7]

"On this April 12, 1942, I became lost to myself, as it were," Lisa later wrote.

> Just as my friends changed my name (for various practical reasons I called myself Gert), so in effect was I struck from the list of the living. I no longer belonged to the citizens who had rights and duties, who had a name, an address, ration cards and passes, who had entitlements of all kinds. I became a non-person, a "nothing"—and a strangely unreal existence began.[8]

Although Lisa was the last single Jewish Bund member on German soil, she was not the only one subject to German persecution. Erna Michels had fled to Holland in the 1930s and now found herself under an increasingly menacing German occupation. Around the same time Lisa was evading deportation, Erna, too, went into hiding. She spent the next two and a half years holed up in a tiny room with two other people. She had to leave all her possessions behind, and virtually everything was lost. She would suffer particularly badly from hunger during the last winter of the war. But she would survive.[9]

The Bund Intervenes

For more than three years, from April 1942 to May 1945, Lisa's fellow Bund members would protect her. As far as we know, she was the first person the Bund sought to hide (if that is the right term for someone who traveled more after going "underground" than ever before). Before Lisa, the group had undertaken remarkable gestures of solidarity, generosity, and support, but no deportee had been offered a place of refuge. Why?

Reflecting on this question leads us to a simple insight, though one

seldom remarked upon: Everyone who saved a Jewish life failed to save
other Jewish lives. Everyone who acted passed up other opportunities to
act. To understand the helpers' experience, to write *their* history, we need
to note the decisive fact that every helper had the repeated experience of
standing by. Every conscientious observer, even those whose interventions
saved lives, endured the demoralizing experience of powerlessness in the
face of persecution, not once but again and again.

After the war, the Bund never dwelled on such dilemmas, just as it only
hinted at the other compromises its members had to make to get by in Nazi
Germany. We cannot be sure why the group chose to offer refuge to some,
while to others they extended only assistance in preparing for deportation.
Why did the Bund, in some cases, send parcels but not prepare hideaways?
We do not even know if this was a considered choice. (Of course, it is possible that the group offered help that was not accepted—an idea that is
not as absurd as it sounds, as we will see.) Even if I had thought of the question when those I interviewed were still alive, I am not sure I would have
dared ask it. It sounds disparaging—or, worse, oblivious to the massive dangers of helping Jews inside Nazi Germany.

One explanation might be the feeling that it would be painfully arbitrary to pick one stranger to be saved while allowing others to be taken.
More likely is that the group's sense of mission may have militated against
too much risk-taking. In postwar accounts, the Bund members spoke of the
group's strengths, of its flexible character, the solidarity and camouflage
it provided, the way it pooled resources—in short, the way, once the
group committed itself to act, it put steel in the spine of its helpers and
rations in the pockets of those they helped. But the blade cut both ways.
For its members, the group was a precious resource with a sacred mission
for the future. Did they have the right to endanger that mission for individual acts?

Writing from Holland, Friedl seems to have been unsure that the group
would protect even Lisa:

> That aunt Lisa is so ill troubles me a great deal. Is there no pos-
> sibility of making her life a little easier? Perhaps one of the rela-
> tives could have her stay with them and look after her, because
> it surely can't be so long until she is fully recovered. But if one

simply leaves her to her fate, she will certainly have a very difficult time of it, and we would be right to feel most seriously
worried about her.[10]

He need not have worried about their commitment. For the Bund, Lisa
presented a clear choice, a very different matter from the questions raised
by the strangers and relatives, such as Dore's aunt, they had allowed to pass
through their hands. There was no arbitrariness in helping *her*. She was a
founding member, one of its Inner Circle. She *was* the Bund. If the group
allowed her to be taken, its own integrity would be shattered. On a personal level, she was very close to Artur and Dore. She had built up the
Bundesschule with Dore, working intensely to develop new forms of physical education. More recently, with Dore still recovering from her sciatica,
Lisa had been one of her most loyal caregivers. Lisa and Artur shared close
ties of sentiment and possibly, according to the hints of some of my inter-
viewees, something even more intimate than that. There was no question,
once Lisa had decided to stay in Germany, that the group would take on
every risk and hardship necessary to protect her.

Lisa on the Run

On the first day of Lisa's life as a non-person, Artur gave her some crucial
advice. She recalled it years later:

> Artur invited me in his usual manner to accompany him to the
> station. I refused, horrified, but he insisted. That was how he
> taught me a powerful, unforgettable lesson. "Don't keep turn-
> ing around! You must get used to seeming untroubled and cheer-
> ful, even if you're feeling anything but," he said. "We will do all
> that is humanly possible to look after you, but it is you who has
> to engage in the battle with fear—that is the biggest danger."
> Then, after months in which everything had gone well, he evi-
> dently sensed some ill-founded optimism on my part, and dur-
> ing a walk suddenly said: "So, what will you do if they catch
> you? Are you really prepared for such a situation?"[11]

Thus, Lisa became an "illegal." It was possible for her to accompany Artur on his walks because, by the norms of the time, she did not look particularly Jewish. There were still women on the street who were not at work, and many of her age—she was forty-three—who were not in uniform. For men of a similar age, walking on the street, except at certain specific times, was not an option. Men were supposed to be either at work or dressed in a military or party uniform. But even though Lisa did not have to worry about her mere presence instantly raising suspicions, there were still spot checks to contend with, particularly while traveling. To avoid the attention of neighbors, she could never stay too long with any one host, and as more and more women, particularly single women, were enjoined to take on some kind of vital employment, the need for cover stories to explain her lack of occupation became more urgent. Thus she was obliged to simulate illness, disappear for days, and, above all, to keep moving from place to place.

Lisa spent much of the war on the move, traveling by train between western, central, and southern Germany. In Göttingen she stayed with the Gehrkes, in Wuppertal with Liesel Speer, Ernst Jungbluth, and Walter and Gertrud Jacobs; in Remscheid it was probably the Briels who put her up, and in Mülheim it may have been the Zenkers. She spent time at Bund addresses in Hamburg and Düsseldorf as well, and on several occasions also stayed with farmers in a rural area south of Essen, a hilly region dubbed Elfringhauser Schweiz. (She discovered only after the war that the farmers had suspected all along that she was Jewish but had not turned her in.)[12] In the final months of the war, she was ensconced in the Meersburg guesthouse.[13] According to Lisa, on all her longer journeys she did not travel alone but was accompanied by other Bund members. Sometimes she enjoyed the protection of a uniformed companion, as when Karlos Morgenstern or one of the other enlisted Bund men traveled with her.[14]

Other than these companions, one thing that made the risk of train travel easier to handle was the ID card Else Bramesfeld had miraculously managed to procure for her, which relieved the stress of spot checks. As we know, Else had written to her professional association claiming to have lost her papers while on holiday, and had asked for a replacement ID. Along with her request, she had submitted a photo—of Lisa.[15] There must have been some very anxious days waiting to see if the ruse worked, but the pass reached Lisa as a Christmas gift in 1942:

The pass was my most precious possession. Life and death depended on its existence. I carried it in my shoulder bag, which I never let out of my sight. At night the bag always lay next to me. To grab it during an air-raid warning or when a visitor arrived became a reflex. Thus, I managed not to lose the ID despite the years of disruptive bombing nights. When conditions became more threatening in the air-raid cellar, and my eardrums almost burst from the pressure of the falling bombs, I slipped the pass into my breast pocket. In this way I managed to rescue it even in the most terrible night, when the Bund house went up in flames, and I escaped with just pajamas, robe and shoulder bag.[16]

Ellen Jungbluth remembered getting a sudden insight into the enormous stress those like Lisa were under. She and Lisa were sitting together one evening when there was a ring at the door, and she noticed immediately how Lisa pulled out her identity card and checked the details. They could hear the sound of heavy boots coming up the stairs. A police officer did indeed appear, but he was there only to scold them for neglecting to black out the windows properly. Ellen was so relieved, she told me, she "wanted to give him a hug."[17]

According to Friedl Speer, Lisa benefited on more than one occasion from an unusual source of information. Ewald Kassel was the child of a Communist couple who had been Bund activists before 1933. Along with Friedl Speer and Friedl Jacobs, he had been among the oldest of the group of children the Bund had raised collectively, away from their parents, for a couple of years. Evidently, Ewald had a very fraught relationship with his stepfather, and in 1933, as a gesture of rebellion, he joined Hitler's elite SS bodyguard, the Leibstandarte, in which Ewald remained until he committed suicide at the end of the war. According to Friedl, Ewald's personal loyalties held firm, and during the war when on leave he would meet with Lisa and give her his sense of how the political situation was unfolding.[18]

For Lisa, escaping detection was one problem; another was getting enough food. Without gainful employment, she earned no money. In any case, acquiring food in wartime also involved ration cards, which as a non-person she was not entitled to receive. The Bund arranged for different families to anonymously donate ration cards each week.[19] Some of Lisa's hosts, including the Gehrkes in Göttingen, grew their own food, so feeding the visitor was less of a problem there. But most of the others did not, and as travel and post conditions deteriorated later in the war, it became harder to arrange for Lisa to receive food donations. The burden increasingly fell on those with whom she was directly quartered at the time. Particularly during the last months of the war, food was very tight, though Lisa did not starve.[20]

The Gift of Community

During this time when Lisa lived as a non-person, the Bund's most important gift to her, she felt, was an identity, a reason for living—more important even than the shelter or the food she received:

> What continually renewed my ability to resist was my life in the Bund and the awareness that although I was nonexistent in society, I was still an important link in a chain. Because in the Bund everything continued on its way, even in those off-kilter years.[21]

Looking back, Lisa felt that many potential regime opponents were unable to take action because they were paralyzed by their sense of isolation and the lack of "oxygen." Many Jews too, she felt, lost their will to resist because they lacked a supportive environment.[22] But Lisa remained in the thick of things, taking part in every Bund outing and continuing to work with others in honing the group's philosophy. This emerges not only from her early postwar memoirs but from another one of those eloquent but cryptic documents stuffed in boxes and folders in the Bund's archives—in this case, a small anonymous notebook, amateurishly bound with a striped paper cover.

The text is a kind of letter-diary. Only Tove is identified by name, but it seems to be addressed to all the young people in the Bund whom Lisa was mentoring, and there are a number of clues that Lisa is the author.[23] The writer is a woman and a poet, and Lisa was known for her love of verse. In the notebook, the author refers to having been working on her

"*Chorschrieb*," by which she means the choreography for one of the *Bewe-gungschöre*, or movement choruses. This is an activity in which Lisa surely would have participated.[24] The writer begins by noting that at the start of the summer she went on her "holidays," after having initially planned to stay home and care for the sick. "But," she adds, "things turned out differently, and now that the summer is over I must say I am more grateful than ever for the gift of being able to be with the others out in the open."[25] That would fit perfectly with Lisa's trajectory—as we know from Artur's letters to Friedl, in 1942 she had been caring for Dore until forced to go underground.[26] A photo pasted into the diary, taken from behind of a woman walking with a rucksack in the middle of a field, may depict Lisa. The timing also fits with a cautious reference in a letter from Else Bramesfeld to Karin Morgenstern, sent at the beginning of June. "My friend is doing well despite bile etc.," she begins, with the usual Bund formula of using health problems as code for Nazi threats. "You know that she was hiking for a couple of days. Now she looks brown and outdoorsy and strong and everything is better. I'm so happy!"[27] It seems, in other words, that within a couple of months of going underground, Lisa participated in her first Bund retreat as an illegal, and at the end of the summer she recorded her reflections on the experience in the notebook.

The notebook begins with a poem:

> Let this be a guide for those who wander
> past hills and fields and forests yonder,
> past blossoming earth to a smoking fire
> on the edge of the wood under summer sky.

> We glowed from within warmed by the sun
> and from wise words more happiness won
> what will come, how things will turn,
> from the master's vision we learned to discern.

> When no path was in view, and no hint of light
> The master kept the high peaks in sight.
> The truth we uncovered together us binds
> In darkest winter its light us finds.

With its mysterious, quasi-mystical language, the poem might be read as a paean to nature and God. For those in the know, however, it captured the psychological value of a Bund gathering in the Sauerland, and the insights and reassurance Lisa gained from Artur's wisdom. It is followed by pages effusing about the joys of nature, complete with rich descriptions of meadows full of flowers and of foraging for blueberries and mushrooms. The writer concludes, "I believe I have never felt quite so profoundly how everything is in flux, dying and being reborn, never finished, always emerging and every day somehow different; and how <u>that</u> is precisely what <u>life</u> is."[28]

For Lisa, the spiritual nourishment provided by these gatherings stood in great contrast to her life outside. In her notebook, she describes the spiritual barrenness of the everyday Germans she encountered, preoccupied by their own problems in a country at war. During her journeys on trains and trams, she was surrounded by people so self-absorbed they had become, in her words, "mere ruins" of their former selves, no longer fully human. The word *Trümmer*—"ruins" or "debris"—was particularly evocative, given the piles of rubble already common in Ruhr cities at the time.[29] On some days, she writes, she too got caught up in the self-absorption of the day, spinning in tight circles around her own concerns. But then came the "holidays," the fog lifted, and a beautiful landscape was revealed. That is how man should live, she felt: striving for clarity, consciousness, knowledge, beauty, and closeness to the divine.

The diary then goes on to ruminate on what was evidently the retreat's theme—namely, a religion for the new age, a system of belief connected closely to the Bund's philosophy of history. At the core of this philosophy was a faith that the underlying logic of history would compel humanity to move in the right direction. It was this faith in progress that lifted Lisa above the brutal threats of her immediate circumstances and, indeed, gave those threats meaning and purpose as dialectical harbingers of a better tomorrow.

Lisa, it seems, was determined to press on with her life despite the difficulties and isolation. During this time, she continued to act as mentor and leader for a group of ten or more younger Bund members. The risks of meeting, Lisa later observed, added to the intensity of the bond.[30] At a memorial service for Lisa in 1989, Ellen recalled almost with disbelief how Lisa, despite her precarious life, had resumed her physical training. Ellen

Artur as a young man

Artur and Dore as a young couple

Meeting of young Bundists, c. 1928

Winter meeting of the Bund at Hubbelrath, 1928

Lisa Jacob performing an expressive dance

Movement choir

Bund excursion, late 1920s or early 1930s. From left to right: Erna Michel, Artur, Georg Reuter (standing), unknown, Lisa Jacob, Tove Gerson, unknown, Gertrud Jacobs, Wasja Enoch, Dore, Karl Heilwagen

Bund excursion with children, 1932. Those pictured include: Friedl Jacobs, seated in the center under the tent; Sonja Schreiber, lying down to the right of the tent; behind Sonja, Pia Jungbluth; behind Pia, Julie Schreiber; Liesel Speer at the rear; and Gertrud Jacobs standing

Bund children, 1930. On the left, Eberhard Jungbluth with Dieter Jacobs on his back. In the center, Friedl Speer on the shoulders of another Bund child. To the right of them, also riding high, Friedl Jacobs held up by Gert Goldschmidt. On the right, the young Ursel Jungbluth on the shoulders of Hanna Reuter

A Bund excursion

Renaming the Rüttenscheidstrasse in Essen, April 19, 1933. This was one of many renamings in the period following the seizure of power

Political prisoners forced to remove a Soviet star—with their fingers—from a wall on Essen's Schwanenkampstrasse, August 1933

Crowds look on as the main Essen synagogue burns, November 10, 1938

ALTE SYNAGOGE, ESSEN

Artur writing in his house on
Dönhofstrasse, 1939

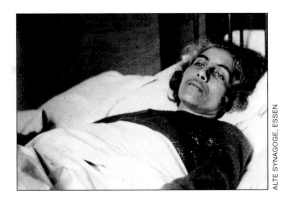

ALTE SYNAGOGE, ESSEN

Dore incapacitated with sciatica, 1939

by now had her own gymnastics practice, and she invited Lisa to conduct some master classes with her pupils—who no doubt had no idea of their guest teacher's illegal status.[31] Being on the run also did not prevent Lisa from continuing to provide support to Trude Brandt in Poland (though at some point parcels stopped being accepted).[32] And Trude was not Lisa's only beneficiary. She also sent postcards and small parcels to addresses in Theresienstadt.[33] Far from simply being the passive object of "rescue," Lisa was actively contributing to her own survival, and helping others at the same time.

Another Past in Hiding

For the first sixteen months of her illegal life, Lisa was the only person we know of whom the Bund sheltered for any length of time. But in August 1943 she was joined by a second fugitive, in February 1944 by a third, and in the fall of that year by several more. Of all the stories of those rescued by the Bund, the most striking is that of Marianne Strauss, Ernst Krombach's fiancée, who in 1942 worked for the Jewish Community offices and acted as an intermediary for Bund efforts to help the Krombachs. When she went underground in 1943, she was just twenty years old. Marianne was the daughter of a formerly well-to-do Jewish grain merchant, Siegfried Strauss, and his wife, Regina. Deprived by Nazi restrictions of other educational opportunities, she had trained as a kindergarten teacher in Berlin, returning to Essen in October 1941, when her family was assigned to the transport to Lodz. Thanks to special connections via their banker and through their backgrounds as patriotic and decorated World War I veterans, her father and uncle managed to save the family from deportation for the time being and continued to seek a way to leave the country.[34] While they waited, hoping for a miracle, Marianne, back at home with her anxious and conservative parents, was impatient to act and threw all her energy into working for the dwindling Jewish community. She worked as a kindergarten teacher with the community's children, then as a nurse with the elderly, and then after the elderly, too, were deported, as a clerk in the community office.

Marianne Strauss's wartime survival story represents the pinnacle of the

Bund's achievement. While other non-Bund members owed their lives to the group, she was the only outsider they protected over a long period, in her case for almost two years. She is also the only one whose years on the run are so well documented. Thanks to her wartime diary and her surviving letters, her case provides unique insights about the demands placed on both helpers and helped. The story begins in March 1942, in the weeks before the Krombachs' deportation. Through her relationship with Ernst Krombach, Marianne gained a sense of Artur's courageous initiatives. It may be that she first met him personally only on the evening before the Krombachs were sent east. Once Ernst was gone, Marianne divided her time between work for the community, sending parcels and letters to Izbica, and struggling to learn what she could about Ernst's fate. She kept a letter-diary of her actions and thoughts, nominally directed to her beloved. She may even have sent copies of parts of it to him. At some point when Marianne was working as a nurse in the Jewish old-age home, Artur came in with food and offered help. From time to time, other Bund members would bring food, too. Artur asked Marianne to keep him informed about what was happening to the community because, he said, he was compiling a dossier on Nazi policies. In the spiritual and emotional vacuum after her fiancé was deported, Marianne sought out the Jacobses, first hesitantly and then, as the news coming back from Izbica grew ever more dire, quite frequently. "They always made me very welcome," she said in an interview, "and for me it was an enormous moral help to be able to talk about this dreadful business and unburden myself."[35]

Artur gradually introduced Marianne to the Bund. For Artur, Marianne was admirable, a young woman doing exactly what the Bund advocated— that is, surmounting pain and fear by focusing all one's energies on helping others. No doubt he was gratified, too, by her obvious admiration for the Bund's teachings. In trying to help Friedl deal with the pain of seeing his girlfriend taken from him, Artur cited, without directly naming her, Marianne's example and her tireless work for the community:

> Yesterday evening a young girl was with me, whose best friend had to go to the East. She has always had a rich and varied life with many friends, books, music, etc. Now everything has been

taken from her. And how does she live? I asked her. She told me: From early to late I sit in the office, then at home, to help my mother, then I make up parcels[36] and then I think how else I can help. By then, it's usually after midnight. This is not the life I was used to, but it satisfies me. The only unsatisfying thing about it is that it is much too little.

Hers is certainly not a happy life in the usual sense of the term. But isn't it nevertheless worth living? And don't you think that it can yield moments of deep satisfaction that a carefree "happy" life can never offer? How different life seems when we triumph over such difficult conditions![37]

As Marianne's emotional bond with the Bund deepened, the rest of her world was collapsing. She had a brief moment of hope when she forged a connection with Christian Arras, a young man whose father's company provided trucks for the Wehrmacht. Arras was willing and able to visit the Izbica ghetto on her behalf. Because he delivered some parcels to the ghetto for her, she not only was in a position to send more than she could by mail—and be assured of the receipt—but received a remarkable report from her fiancé by return.[38] The hope this brought, however, quickly gave way to despair as she realized from the report how horrendous conditions in the ghetto really were. At the end of the year, when Arras made another trip to Izbica, he brought back the even more desperate news that Ernst's parents had perished and her fiancé had been blinded in an accident. It was clear that Ernst could not survive much longer. In the meantime, the group of elderly people she had been tending to in Essen had been deported to Theresienstadt. By the fall of 1942, the large majority of Essen's Jews had been sent east. Now, working in the community office, Marianne sometimes found herself tasked with informing people that they had been assigned to the next deportation. Her only source of solace came from the hours she spent with the Bund.

Back in September, when Arras brought back Ernst Krombach's first report, Artur's diary was full of news from the ghetto. Then on September 22, he noted that he was singing songs with Marianne Strauss. At least one Bund soldier on leave was in attendance:

Folk songs and more somber ones from Brahms.
That's what she wished for. But one sings along with ambivalent feelings.

How can someone so mired in this turmoil,* for whom life
consists of nothing but waiting for something terrible to happen or hearing about something terrible that's already happened,
how can she open herself up to this world of beauty and meaning, a world that seems so far away, so unreal, like a cruel joke?!

A front-line soldier, hearing these old songs for the first time,
suddenly began to cry—the contradiction was so terrible, so
unnerving, so unsettling . . .[39]

*She was awaiting her deportation. [Pencil addition at the bot-
tom of the page.]

In the next months, Artur's admiration for Marianne continued to mingle
with concern over the possible psychological effects of her iron self-control.
In November, she received a summons to report to Gestapo headquarters
that turned out to be harmless. In December she had to process the disastrous news about Ernst's accident.[40] Artur worried about her state of mind:

Strange the way the girl is, with her apparent calm.
Terrible things must be going on inside—how could it be
otherwise?

But on the outside she keeps up the conventions, like a suit
of armour that prevents the ailing body from collapsing.

A wild cry would be so much more natural. But perhaps this
is the salutary part of conventional behaviour. Without it, someone so young would surely fall apart.

Yet I sense that she is frozen, unable to find release in sorrow
and thus to experience new life and depth.

On the one hand total pessimism, which brusquely rejects
any offer of consolation, any tiny trace of hope, even the smallest sign of a possible way forward. On the other, a web of illusions in which the soul careens about like a drunkard, with no
sense of reality.[41]

If Artur was impressed with Marianne, she was doubly so by him. The Bund was, she said in later life, "the most formative influence on my life."[42] Of course, in her diary and in letters she was extremely cautious about mentioning her contacts with the group. But we have brief hints here and there. A friendly nurse indiscreetly wrote of her pleasure in hearing Marianne talk about her new connection.[43] From November 1942 on, Marianne's diary entries reveal a new interest in the changing political and military situation, which suggests Artur's intellectual encouragement. It is true that world news was now becoming the only source of hope and relief for all surviving Jews. Nevertheless, the Bund's influence is clear, and elements of their philosophy begin to appear in her writing.

At some point, it seems, Artur told Marianne that if her situation became desperate, she should turn to them. Tove said she learned after the war from Else Bramesfeld that Artur had said to Marianne, "You can't save your parents, but you can save yourself."[44] Perhaps the experience with Lisa had convinced him that they could accomplish something like this again. Marianne herself surely seemed a good candidate for assistance. She was resourceful and independent, and it was clear that she would not fold under pressure. Moreover, as a dynamic, serious, and very attractive young woman who was willing to be guided, she must have been irresistible to Artur, whose yearning for young followership was so badly frustrated during the Nazi years. There is some anecdotal evidence that Marianne was not the only person whom the Bund discussed being able to help. Hanna Jordan, herself not a Bund member, told me that the Bund declared itself willing to assist some distant Jewish relatives of hers, a young couple and their eleven-year-old son, who were on a deportation list. According to Hanna, when she gave them the good news, they were too frightened to respond and left with their transport. But there is no direct evidence of another instance in which the Bund helped someone for such an extended period of time.

The Bund's offer to Marianne would be put to the test at the end of August 1943. That summer, the powerful allies who had previously helped Marianne's father protect his family from deportation were themselves coming under suspicion. As a result, they were rapidly losing the ability to help anyone, even as the Strauss family was hoping against hope that they might soon be allowed to immigrate to Sweden.[45] On August 31, 1943, two of the most hated members of the local Gestapo turned up at the family house, giving them a couple of hours to prepare for deportation and remaining to supervise while casting a covetous eye over the family's possessions. At some point Marianne slipped out of the house unnoticed. She spent the day on the run, tried to phone the family's high-level connections to prod them into action, and by nightfall had made her way to a Bund address.

If Marianne Strauss's story shows anything, it is that being "rescued" depended not only on willing helpers but on initiative and courage from the person rescued, as well as a readiness to place one's life in others' hands. It also involved difficult choices for everyone. According to Marianne, her father had discreetly handed her a substantial wad of cash before she left. There is thus some evidence that her parents understood and sympathized with her wish to escape. They may also have hoped that Marianne would be able to call upon their connections for help, as she indeed tried to do.

It is less clear, however, whether there was any discussion about her brother, two years her junior, a less outgoing youngster and, by the standards of the time, a little more obviously Jewish in appearance. Was there a possibility that he might accompany her? Marianne told me that she had asked him to come but he had refused. A relative of hers heard from Marianne after the war that her mother would not allow it, fearing that Richard was too young. (It is worth remembering that the family would not have known with certainty that deportation meant death. The Strausses may have been aware that their transport was headed to Theresienstadt, but not that transports had been regularly leaving that ghetto for Auschwitz, or that there even was such a thing as Auschwitz.) There is some circumstantial evidence, however, that Marianne may not have given Richard a choice.[46] One thing we know for sure is that shepherding a young man through the war who was clearly not engaged in essential war work or in military service and was not wearing a Nazi Party or Hitler Youth uniform would have presented the Bund with a far, far greater challenge even than sheltering Marianne. We know of no men saved by the Bund (though as we will see, it is possible that some male partners in mixed marriages were protected by them toward the end of the war).

Lisa could never have doubted the Bund's commitment to her, but for Marianne as she slipped out of the family home, it was a gamble that Artur and the Bund really were willing and able to deliver. As she said in an interview decades later:

> Maybe somebody else would have felt squeamish about it and thought, Well, people say these things and they don't mean them. But I took that risk, you see. And I thought, If they don't want me, they can say so.[47]

Marianne could not even check, at that moment, if the Bund was willing. Most of the Bund members did not have a private phone, and they probably would not have trusted important conversations to it even if they had. There was nothing to be done but to turn up unannounced at one of the Bund addresses. Probably it had been prearranged that she should seek out Sonja. Sonja was living at the Blockhaus, in her small apartment upstairs. The ground floor was still rented out to a local Catholic church, but the Bund continued to use the basement for meetings. It was here that Marianne turned up after nightfall.

On the Run

Only Marianne's first few days resemble the life in hiding of Anne Frank—or of Erna Michels, holed up in her tiny room in Holland. During this time, Marianne was confined to Sonja's little upstairs rooms. During the day, the church kindergarten brought in many outsiders, and Marianne had to remain very quiet—should the rooms have been searched, there was nowhere to hide. She could venture out only after nightfall, and on several occasions she used these outings to again try enlisting the help of her father's connections—although eventually they warned her that any further contact would be extremely dangerous.

The Bund must have discussed what to do with their fugitive right away. As Artur wrote in his diary a day or two after her escape:

> Marianne is in the Blockhaus. She eluded disaster at the last minute.
>
> What an upright, mature, intelligent, active, courageous

young person! And one discerns hardly a glimmer of what she's going through!

What people like her have learned to deal with! And with undiminished spirit!

That young people of this caliber can still evolve in such an environment should make us think. It is proof, surely, that good seeds will germinate in even the most unpropitious soil.

Again and again, Marianne simply amazes me. The thought of all she carries on her shoulders! She stands there unbowed, with her heavy burden and an uncertain and difficult life before her . . .

What resources does she have to draw on? First, there is the boundless energy of the young; second, a certain caution in expressing her views, which she has learned to practice since childhood; and, not least, the strength she developed during a long period of suffering and growth.[48]

Almost immediately, the Bundists began to share their food with Marianne. For the first time in her life, Marianne became the cook, preparing vegetables and salads for Sonja and herself from Sonja's rations and the gifts from their Bund friends. Sonja also provided her with a sympathetic ear, and during those few weeks in the Blockhaus, the two of them formed what would be a lifelong friendship, despite the gap in their ages (Sonja was now almost fifty). But the most remarkable step the Bund made at this stage was to direct one of its members, Grete Ströter, to visit the Strauss family in prison. Marianne's parents, brother, uncle, aunt, and her aunt's mother were all being held there temporarily—the Gestapo hoped they would be able to find the wayward girl quickly and deport the whole family together. Grete passed the Strausses some token that indicated that Marianne was alive and safe—an extraordinary gesture that must have taken a huge amount of nerve. A few days later, the Gestapo gave up waiting and dispatched the Strauss family to Theresienstadt. All would perish before the end of the war, most of them in the gas chambers of Auschwitz.

Within a very short time, the Bund decided that the same risks that had induced Lisa Jacob to move from place to place also made it untenable for Marianne to remain in situ. If the house were hit in an air raid and had to be evacuated, Marianne's presence would be revealed. Since the Gestapo was on the lookout for her, the consequences for the entire group could be disastrous. Marianne began to travel, lodging with some of the same helpers who had assisted Lisa, and by the end of the war she had stayed with at least ten different Bund families. She made between thirty and fifty journeys in this time. Like Lisa, she had no official passport or state ID, but before going underground she had been able to renew a postal ID card that did not contain the obligatory middle name Sara and, thus, did not expose her as a Jew. This pass would not withstand every kind of check, and had the authorities scrutinized it to any degree, it would have been completely inadequate. In many contexts, however, it was enough. In theory, one needed a birth certificate to get a postal ID, which would list one's religious identity, but there were ways to get around this. The trick was to get your mailman to certify that you were who you said you were. Many Jews seem to have taken advantage of such subterfuges.[49]

Unlike Lisa, Marianne traveled on her own, and she was therefore even more dependent on her wits and her ability to appear calm and confident. When uniformed men boarded the train, Marianne sometimes went to the toilet and remained there until the next stop, where she exited. Once or twice she moved slowly through an overcrowded train ahead of the guards and managed to get off at a station before they reached her. In her deposition to the restitution authorities in the 1950s, Marianne mentioned two occasions on a train when she was caught by the police. Both times she managed to slip away, once because of police inattention and the second time by melting into a large crowd.[50] On trams, too, several times she edged slowly to the back as the police came in the front.[51] After the war, she told two fellow survivors that she had on at least one occasion declared that she was traveling on a secret mission for the Führer and could not talk about it.[52] It was just as Artur had said to Lisa: everything depended on the demeanor and savvy of the person being "rescued" (and, of course, the requisite amount of luck).

In the early months, when the Gestapo was still actively looking for Marianne, the Bund decided that she should get out of the Ruhr altogether. Most of her hosts were women on their own or with children whose husbands were away at the front or working in remote locations. Her initial hosts were both outside the Ruhr: the Morgensterns in Braunschweig and

Hedwig Gehrke in Göttingen. In the case of Änne Schmitz, in nearby Bur-scheid, where Marianne stayed in 1944, we know that Ernst Jungbluth traveled with her and made the introductions; but we do not know how the Bund alerted Marianne's first two hosts, or how much warning they had before Marianne turned up.

Both seem to have offered a warm welcome. The Morgensterns and the Gehrkes grew some of their own produce, reducing the challenge of feeding an extra mouth. In addition, Marianne had the advantage of possessing some money, and in Braunschweig there was a restaurant where it was possible to order a meal without having to hand in ration cards, so she ate there from time to time to avoid burdening her host. The Strauss family had also left a considerable quantity of goods in the care of a non-Jewish family with whom they were acquainted, and at various points Marianne was able to collect things for barter. In this way, she may have been in a stronger position to contribute to her upkeep than Lisa was (though presumably Ellen was paying Lisa for lessons). But Marianne, too, showed great enterprise. In addition to collecting family property and bartering it, she also made artificial flowers out of felt and leather and sold them to a shop in Braunschweig, which paid her mainly in ration coupons.

A stay with Bund friends required a cover story to explain the visitor's presence to the outside world—and sometimes even to the family. So, for example, Hedwig's mother-in-law, who was living with them and was not reliable, was told some kind of tale. In Remscheid, three-year-old Wolfgang Briel knew Marianne simply as "Tante," or Aunt, a courtesy term for close female friends of the parents'. The term may have been adopted so that little Wolfgang would talk of her to others as though she were a relative. The following year, Marianne stayed with a Göttingen Bund member, Meta Kamp-Steinmann. Meta's teenage children had a vague sense that she was some kind of political refugee but did not know that she was a Jew. One day, her older son, Ernst, a confident young man who, like many youngsters at this time, was engaged in antiaircraft defense work, was out walking with Marianne when they were stopped and asked for their papers. Ernst had no idea what was at stake. Marianne, for her part, was so relaxed and so quick to joke with the patrolmen that she never actually had to produce her ID. Later, however, Ernst's mother grasped how close to disaster they had come.[53]

The Ruhr bombing often made for useful cover, as Marianne could be presented as a bombed-out victim seeking respite. Meta invented the story that Marianne had lost her family in an air raid and had become psychologically unstable; her doctor had advised her to move to a new location to recover. The neighbors were fed this tale, and it rapidly made the local rounds. When Marianne appeared at times too cheerful for the cover story, Meta would "wink at the neighbor with a sad face and point to [her] head. Which was supposed to imply, 'The poor girl is completely confused!'"[54] Bund member Änne Schmitz, living in Burscheid, told the local mayor that Marianne was an Essen resident who'd lost her papers in the bombing and was coming to stay for a while. Since Marianne eventually planned on returning to Essen, Änne informed him, she didn't want to register properly in Burscheid. A cover story that Artur invented served Marianne well at the Briels', in Remscheid. One of the Bund members loaned their small child for the purpose, and Marianne was presented as a young mother taking refuge with friends. "When we had the child here," recalled Maria Briel, "the neighbors said, 'She's the spitting image of her mother'!"[55]

A major problem for the illegals—and, indeed, for their hosts—was the question of what to do if they fell ill. There are stories of Jews being hidden in Germany (not by the Bund) on the explicit condition that no doctor would be called if they became sick. This was in fact the message to Hanna Jordan's mother when she turned up at an address her contacts had found.[56] One of Marianne's biggest fears was that she might need medical treatment. In Göttingen she was stung on the eyelid while tending Hedwig's bees. Luckily, the swelling went down by itself. During air raids, Marianne was almost more afraid of being injured than of dying. As Maria Briel remembered:

> Marianne was frightened. . . . She must have been thinking, For God's sake, please don't let me end up in a hospital! And that was a time when there was an air raid every day, when the bombs fell every day.[57]

During the winter of 1943 in Wuppertal, a minor disaster struck. Wuppertal is a hilly town with many sets of steps carved into the steep streets, and in the icy weather that year, these steps became treacherous. Marianne was coming down some steps when she slipped, grabbed the iron banister, and wrenched her thumb. She was in agony, but she couldn't tell whether she had dislocated or broken it. Yet the risk of going to a hospital was too great. The injured thumb continued to swell and throb and began to look as if it would be permanently out of joint. After a couple of days, Marianne decided she had to do something.

When she arrived at a nearby hospital, the staff members were surprised when she said she was not covered by insurance and was there as a private patient. Surprise turned to horror when she asked the doctors to set the thumb without anesthetic: "Without an anesthetic—they couldn't *possibly* dream of doing that." Marianne explained that after an earlier experience she was terrified of anesthetics; what she didn't say, of course, was that she was fearful of betraying herself when semiconscious. Did they suspect anything? Marianne didn't think so. With her hair up in a bun, she looked every inch the German girl. Eventually the staff agreed. "It was like a medieval procedure," she recalled. "I don't think I made a peep, and they were absolutely staggered at this. . . . They set my thumb, but it never healed properly." In the longer term, stress and poor nutrition did no favors to her health. Her diet consisted chiefly of bread and potatoes, with a distinct shortage of fats and proteins.[58] But in this particular deprivation, Marianne was not so different from many other Germans at the time.

Between Spiritual Refuge and Emotional Turmoil

Among the many private papers that emerged after Marianne's death, probably the most remarkable was a diary she'd kept while on the run. It contains a number of entries from the late spring of 1944 through the early spring of 1945. Folded into the little volume are also some letters she received during that period. The diary offers striking parallels with Lisa's "anonymous" chronicle, revealing the freedom enjoyed by both of these women while living illegally, as well as the vital importance of the intellectual and spiritual nourishment offered by the Bund.

In May 1944, for example, Marianne described a trip to the countryside during Pentecost, presumably to attend some kind of Bund meeting:

The rain is streaming down, but still how beautiful it is to camp by the lake. How intensely one lives when close to nature, to weather and time, to the animals and the sounds of solitude. I can't tell you how beautiful it is! At first I was worrying about the weather and thinking I could enjoy it and feel happy only if everything were bathed in sunlight. But now I realize that's not true. Everything, oneself included, is more alive when the clouds and the rain and the wind are all about. I feel like the grass and the leaves, exposed, utterly open to the elements. It's beautiful! Beautiful, beautiful, beautiful.

To be totally oneself, without distortion, without a mask, without qualification. To open oneself fully, to forget oneself and only then to find oneself.

Like Lisa, Marianne reveled in the experience of nature and the sense of being free from everyday concerns. And because in the wilds of the Bergisches Land or the Sauerland one could engage in the normal peacetime activity of camping, it was paradoxically possible here, for a few days at least, to live a life of wandering and impermanence and yet feel rooted rather than uprooted, and not harried from pillar to post.

Also like Lisa, Marianne took up in her diary many themes arising from her conversations in the Bund. She wrote to an imaginary correspondent— probably her fiancé, Ernst, though she knew by this point that he was almost certainly dead. After her description of being in nature, Marianne mused:

You know, I'd like to say something about the Whitsun days. Those few days were beautiful. I keep thinking of the discussions about WA, a topic I'm sure you've often pondered and talked about. An endless topic. Much became clear to me, much more was touched on just enough to send one's thoughts rolling forward like a great boulder.[59]

"WA" was shorthand for *Weltanschauung*, or a way of viewing the world. Numerous pages of the diary are devoted to the necessary conditions to form a coherent *Weltanschauung*, and to the question of how to find the right

Maßstab, or yardstick, by which one might judge the world. For all the touchingly wooden quality of some of the discussion, it is clear that it meant a great deal to the writer. Like Lisa, Marianne sought a way to subsume her struggle to survive within the broader challenge everyone faced—specifically, the challenge of reaching a sound and authentic way of understanding the world:

> We live in a time that lacks a Weltanschauung. Lessons and slogans are taken from all corners, thrown together, jumbled up, and no one looks to see whether they really fit together. This is no basis on which to build a coherent worldview. The last two centuries, with all their technological developments, have confronted mankind with radically new challenges—challenges which have yet to be mastered. Technology has changed the whole structure of the world and dislocated basic concepts and values.
>
> That's why we can't talk of a WA in our time. Above all, a WA has to evolve organically.

There's no doubt that Marianne would have been careful not to make any anti-Nazi statements in the diary, in case it were ever to be found. But at the same time, her writing was very much in line with the Bund's search for some type of logic underlying history—a logic that could provide hope and reassurance in a time of great confusion.

Diaries are never easy documents for the historian to interpret. They seldom offer a direct window onto the writer's soul. What appear at first sight to be purely private reflections, unaffected by any ulterior communicative intent, are always shaped by genre, by a sense of who the (sometimes imaginary) audience might be, and by the emotional function the diary performs for the writer. Marianne, for example, seems to have been influenced by the model of a rather high-minded philosophical journal. There are no crossings-out or scribbles in her diary, and there are relatively few descents to the mundane. At least part of the diary was written as though addressing Ernst, who was now, sadly, beyond reach. So, what we find here is only one version of herself, and a great deal of her life—her experiences and her reactions to the changing times—has been left out.

And yet the ruminations do capture an essential element of those experiences—namely, the spiritual succor and grounding offered by the Bund. For Lisa, as we have seen, participating in such a philosophical quest for meaning was not just vital but natural, the logical consequence of twenty years in the Bund. For Marianne, it was an extraordinary invitation to take on a new identity, as a young recruit to the cause. After the war, this aspect of the Bund's assistance disappeared, and Marianne moved on, becoming a wife and mother in England. In conversations in later life, she remembered the Bund's wonderful assistance, but not quite that while on the run she had seen herself as a Bund disciple. For their part, the Bundists, once the enormity of the Holocaust was clear, could hardly foreground their achievement in having provided philosophical inspiration for those they helped. In retrospect, saving lives was all that mattered. But this focus on survival does not do justice to the wartime experience of the Bund's beneficiaries or, indeed, to the group's own sense of its mission at the time.

This is not to imply that life with the Bund was always easy. Marianne's diary tells of something else that disappeared from view after the war: it hints that living in close quarters with her helpers produced tensions that occasionally erupted into conflict and prompted soul-searching on her part. As a mature woman who had lived with Bund friends for twenty years, Lisa was in a different position than the beautiful and impulsive twenty-year-old who suddenly found herself cohabiting with strangers from drastically different backgrounds. Marianne's reflections in June 1944 on the marvelous days in the country and her thoughts about "WA" were accompanied by a cryptic comment: "One hopes that all the Easter wounds have been healed. But have they? The effort is too great! Only we three are aware of it."

A later letter with earnest advice from Sonja, which Marianne cites in her diary, makes clear that the "wounds" referred to tensions with her Remscheid hosts Fritz and Maria Briel. Fritz Briel would have been around thirty-seven at the time, considerably older than Marianne, though not so much older that there was no chance for some kind of emotional involvement. Sonja's letter does not imply any impropriety, but it does suggest that a kind of emotional intensity had evolved that had left Maria feeling angry and excluded: "I know this is not your intention, that you act from impulse. But we cannot simply follow our impulse and have to be able to

justify it to ourselves as responsible people."[60] Sonja's letter also expressed
concern that in relation to another young couple, the Krahlisches, Marianne
may have been too intrusive with her advice, in a way that left all parties
unsettled:

> And something else, while I'm dispensing maternal advice: I
> was somewhat perturbed by the fact that you ventured to
> advise Hermann on his personal relationships. Really, the only
> person who can and should give such advice is someone with
> maturity and experience, someone who has gained firsthand
> insights into such difficult problems. I hope you have not entan-
> gled yourself in difficulties. I also think you should be a little
> more circumspect toward a man who has an intimate relation-
> ship with another woman. You have known both sides for far
> too short a time.

"How right she is!" Marianne added with a note. "And that's why it's
doubly painful!" In the diary, Marianne berated herself and accepted the
criticism. Ironically, it seemed that in a number of cases, the cause of friction was Marianne's desire to involve herself in the lives of her hosts. Taking refuge in small apartments belonging to married strangers, it seems,
had the effect of roughly pushing aside the screens that would normally
shield family life from view. In addition, part of the Bund's philosophy was
that its moral and political values should be applied just as much to marriage and private life as to the public arena; its members were thus encouraged to engage in open discussion about relationships.[61] For Marianne, who
felt her inactivity and her dependence so keenly, here was a forum in which
she believed she could actively help. But the impact of the beautiful, head-
strong girl had evidently been explosive.

In fact, the diary reveals that in August 1944, after four weeks with Meta
Kamp-Steinmann, Marianne was not sure where to go next. She had been
anxiously awaiting a letter from Bund member Karin Morgenstern, with
whom she had been having some kind of disagreement. Marianne traveled
to the Harz Mountains, where Karin was camping with Hermann and Lene
Krahlisch, but the conversation did not produce the needed clarification.
Nevertheless, Marianne traveled back to Braunschweig with Karin. In her

later accounts, Marianne never hinted that the chain of helpers had been close to breaking, and, indeed, it might well have seemed petty to dwell on any discord, which certainly did not fit with her almost hagiographical memory of the Bund.

Around this time, she received another rather striking letter with advice. Although addressed to *"Liebe Anya"*—Dear Anya—it was clearly directed to Marianne (and occasionally even forgets the cover name, referring to the recipient as "M"). It was full of earnest, well-meaning advice about the delicate balance of living with others:

> Our whole lives consist of experimenting and testing.
> But laying down the law unilaterally, as you tend to do when living with others, is not ideal. This expresses itself in many small things.
> To be sure, M is young and the world is open to her. And she wants to conquer it all by "force." But that's not the right way.
> One must be able to adapt to other people—that has to be learned. One must listen to others, learn how to fit into their lives, and not always react critically to everything that doesn't suit you.[62]

There were pages and pages of advice, clearly written with love, but pointed and precise all the same. It is likely that Meta was the author. For a moment one wonders if the writer fully understood the predicament of a young woman who had been robbed of her family and was under permanent threat from the regime. Yet, obviously, living at such close quarters required tact from both sides. No matter how at risk the refugee was, her hosts had good reason to expect that she would fit in. One could also see the critique as a tacit invitation to be part of their community. This letter was full of affection, with its promise of a food parcel; and an invitation to "live and experiment" together undoubtedly reminded Marianne that there was a group of people who, far from seeing her as a "non-person," expected the same of her as of themselves. For all the distress the criticism caused, this must have been an immensely reassuring message to a Jew in Nazi Germany.

This episode reminds us again of the difference between lived experience and what could later be remembered. However beneficial to Marianne, such criticism was hardly something either side wanted to remember after the war. Amid the slaughter of the Holocaust, to have rebuked a young woman whose parents had been sent to Auschwitz for her impetuosity in giving personal advice! As important as they were in the moment, such things became unsayable after the event.

Another subject that became off-limits after the war, at least in these terms, is that Marianne did not always adhere to the implicit contract with her helpers. The same fearlessness that served her so well occasionally put Bund members needlessly in danger. The normally unflappable Maria Briel mentioned in an interview that the only time she had been really nervous was when Marianne developed a relationship with a French forced laborer in Remscheid. Since the authorities were on the lookout for every improper liaison between German women and foreign laborers (though French workers raised the least "racial" concerns about contact), this posed an unnecessary risk of attracting official attention.

Hermann Schmalstieg recalled another example. Like many in the Bund, Hermann came from a modest working-class background and was a graduate of the left-wing youth movement the Naturfreunde.[63] Having first encountered the Bund in the Nazi era through gymnastics, he soon recognized that there was more than simply physical exercise on offer: here was a movement seeking answers to fundamental questions about life.[64] He began to participate in Bund excursions, and the movement made such an impression on him that after the war he pursued an entirely new career path, giving up his job as a laboratory technician and becoming a youth worker in order to help shape a different generation of Germans.

During the war, Hermann's job as a lab technician for the Technische Hochschule in Braunschweig was declared essential war work. His section, which tested audio and radio equipment for the military, was moved to Auerhahn Mountain, near Goslar in the Harz Mountains. He was quartered in a lonely forester's cottage, in an isolated area, ideal for hiding the young Marianne. It was there that she was sent by the Bund in July 1944. One episode in particular engraved itself on his memory, as he recounted more than fifty years later. In the mornings, he would leave Marianne in the cottage while he went off to work. Her presence was a closely guarded secret in what was, after all, a highly sensitive military area. As Hermann was returning home one day, his blood ran cold. Marianne had opened the windows wide and was sitting with her legs dangling outside, singing happily.[65] Incidents like this one probably explain why the Bund never managed to find a permanent abode for Marianne until the very end of the war.

Marianne's diary does not record this episode. Yet her visit to the Harz Mountains is vividly captured all the same. On Monday, July 31, 1944, she looked back at the weekend and described a conversation that prompted her to consider whether "the only things of value in life are those one produces oneself, the insights that come from within." A little later, she recorded her emotional turmoil about being drawn to the person she'd been speaking with and the guilt she felt toward her fiancé, Ernst. That person is not named, so we cannot be sure that she was talking about Hermann, but it seems almost certain, since the conversation happened the previous day, when we know they were together. "Yesterday during our walk," she wrote, "we discussed Weltanschauung and the Jewish question: How is such an attitude possible given such intellectual ability and judgment! If only he knew! Oh, my stupid heart."

Hermann, looking back a half century later, was adamant that there had been no affair, and adamant, too, that he had known that she was Jewish. But Marianne wrote that her "stupid heart" had left her with strong feelings for someone with intolerable views, prompting the only entry in the diary making even an oblique reference to her Jewish identity. Her remark "If only he knew!" meant either that he did not know she was Jewish or that he did not realize she was so drawn to him. Either way, within a few days it was time to move on.

We will return later to Marianne and Lisa's experience of the closing months of the war. It is worth noting that, just like Lisa, Marianne did not stop providing help to others while she was on the run. As we will see, through the Bund's good offices, she helped a friend find a place to hide. Like Lisa, she also continued to collect foodstuffs and other goods to send to family members in Theresienstadt, as friends of her relatives acknowledged after the war (alas, no family members survived to give thanks). The "rescued" remained "helpers" throughout.

7

The Test of Total War

The Battle of the Ruhr

As long as the German army proved invincible, the Bund struggled to remain confident that Hitler would eventually fall. In 1940, all of western Europe lay at Hitler's feet. The spring of 1941 brought yet more painful news: the rapid rout of enemy forces in both Yugoslavia and Greece, Rommel's triumphs in North Africa, and a widespread feeling that Britain would be forced to capitulate. In June 1941, a German army three million strong swept into the Soviet Union. It was only in the fall of 1941, as Hitler's troops became bogged down in Russian mud, that the Bund at last found cause for optimism. We can see this new confidence in a November 1941 entry in Artur's diary, though it was couched ambiguously in case the diary fell into the wrong hands: "Worry about the final outcome, which earlier kept all one's emotions in thrall, has disappeared."[1]

It was just at this point, however, that Bund members began to be exposed more personally to the threats of war. The first to feel the heat were the Bund's men in uniform. Until the Russian campaign, German losses had been relatively light, and many German soldiers had had a comparatively easy time. But the eastern front proved more intractable than expected, particularly after the Russians mounted a counteroffensive in December. Through letters from the front and conversations with the soldiers while they were on leave, the rest of the group tried to gain a feeling for the actual conditions of combat. The gentle Reinhold Ströter was the correspondent most cited in Artur's diary, but we also have letters from August Schwab, Karlos Morgenstern, and Ernst Jungbluth's son, Eberhard. Bund members would copy out extracts from their loved one's letters and circulate them. These exchanges gave Artur and others some understanding of what was happening at the front, offered reassurance that the writers were still hale and hearty, but also provoked new concerns about risks and hardships in the field.[2]

Those concerns were something Bund members at home had in common with their neighbors. Unlike most of their neighbors, however, they found themselves in an ambivalent, indeed, paradoxical relationship to the war. While desperately hoping that the Bundists in uniform would come home unscathed, they wanted Germany to lose—indeed knew Germany *had* to lose. After November 1941, Artur might have felt more confident that the right side would triumph, but this also provoked new fears about the Bund friends placed involuntarily on the wrong side of history. In early 1942, Reinhold Ströter and Liesel Speer's son, Friedl, were both in the thick of the fighting. Those waiting at home simultaneously feared for their safety and experienced intense guilt at the unwarranted privilege of being spared the wrath of war.[3] As Germany's position grew more desperate, the situation on the home front became increasingly life-threatening. Here, too, Bund members found themselves caught in the same paradoxical mixture of hope and fear.

From February 1942 onward, the Ruhr became a central target for British Bomber Command. The region's western cities were easier for the RAF to reach, and Essen saw significant attacks in March, April, June, and September 1942, while Duisburg was particularly hard hit in July, August, September, and December. Initially, Artur tried to maintain a philosophical detachment. He explained to another Bund member suffering badly from anxiety that he and Dore had learned to sleep through the raids and not to race down to the cellar every time the alarm sounded. To rest, it was necessary to look death in the eye and make peace with it. If sleep proved really impossible, Artur recommended reading a history book and making detailed notes with a pencil.[4] By 1943, Artur's "white magic," as he put it, had lost its potency.

"We have decided to go down to the shelter when the siren sounds,"
Artur announced on June 4, 1943.[5]

On another occasion he noted:

> One gets used to a lot, even to bad things. But this insecurity
> and systematic threat of death and destruction hanging over
> us every night, as city after city is targeted with unearthly
> consistency—no one can get used to that.[6]

On March 5, 1943, British aircraft attacked Essen using new technol-
ogy that allowed them to hit a city center with unprecedented accuracy.
Nearly half the attacking force delivered high explosives and incendiaries
within three miles of the target zone. The total bomb tonnage was well
over twice what had been dropped on Coventry in the famously destructive German raid of November 1940. The result was a night of devastation of a kind Germany had not seen before. This was the beginning of
British Bomber Command's almost five-month-long Battle of the Ruhr.[7]

The Jacobses were not in Essen on March 5, but other Bund members
were. They wrote and circulated eyewitness reports so that those who had
not been in the blast zone could gain a sense of what had happened. "A
weight fell from my shoulders when I received word from home that my
loved ones were once again spared," August Schwab wrote from the front,
though he also noted that the future was now full of uncertainty.[8] Friedel
Kette, one of the many gymnastics teachers trained by Dore, produced
one such account, addressed, at least ostensibly, to her sister in Vienna. Friedel had been staying with a friend on the outskirts of town that night
(probably Sonja, who penned her own account), but even there the floor
had heaved and buckled beneath them as if in an earthquake. Crawling over
to the door and peering out, Friedel saw the night sky lit up by flares
(dropped from the lead planes to illuminate the targets) and by the fires
that were spreading in the city center.

Friedel's description of going into Essen a day later was even more har-
rowing and revealed a new reality: that a raid lasting little more than an
hour could destroy an entire city center.[9] Friedel approached the center
through smaller side streets that remained accessible. Up and down street
after street, she saw only ruins. Some buildings had collapsed, everything

inside them burned to the ground. Others had lost their outer walls, revealing strangely intact scenes within. She saw "on a rear wall, a shelf full of wine bottles carefully piled upon one another, or a row of bath tubs, or a meaningless notice that read, 'This land including all the buildings on it, is for sale' when not a building had been left standing." Big public buildings were gone. So were large inns, where kitchen stoves could still be seen in the rubble, twisted and glowing. So, too, were modern department stores. Only an indescribable confusion of joists, cables, and remnants of ironwork remained. In some streets, the air was so hot it was almost impossible to breathe. Halfway through the center of a city she had known since birth, Friedel lost her bearings.

As unearthly as the buildings were the people, walking silently through the devastated streets or raking through the ruins in search of loved ones. There were ghostly apparitions, such as the old woman Friedel saw tidying up under the eaves of a ruined house. Desperate figures dragged handcarts, rescuing a couple of pots and pans and half a piece of furniture from the rubble. Someone would stop and say, "The things I'm wearing are all I have left," and then start to laugh in a way that chilled Friedel to the bone. Someone stood on the square and repeated over and over again, *"Es ist gar nichts kaputt, nein gar nichts ist kaputt, nichts ist kaputt."* ("Nothing is broken, no, nothing at all.") Witnessing such scenes, she wrote, "a feeling of horror crawls over your skin." Having spent the night elsewhere, Friedel was worried that her own home had been destroyed. She was grateful that a friend (again, probably Sonja) had accompanied her there. In fact, her apartment had been miraculously unharmed, the only one in the building to survive unscathed. She could hardly take pleasure in her good fortune, however; it seemed so unjust. She reassured her sister that she was rarely in Essen at night and would soon be traveling back to Elberfeld—a plan that was far more ominous than she knew, since Elberfeld would be flattened by bombing on June 24. Friedel's Essen apartment would be destroyed in mid-July, though luckily she would be at a Bund outing in the Sauerland at the time.[10]

Sonja also wrote an account of her visit to the ruined city the day after the bombing. It was like chancing upon a battleground where the fight had been raging just minutes before, she said. She was driven on by the desire to find her sister Johanna, whose apartment and small shop were in the neighboring Pferdemarkt district. Every building on her sister's street was

flattened. Where her apartment had been, nothing but a black hole
remained. In front of the shop, the sign that had read "Schreiber" was
reduced to only the "Schrei" ("Cry"). There was not a soul to be seen. There
were no neighbors, because there were no houses. The walls of the Ger-
trudiskirche, the Church of Saint Gertrude, fell in while Sonja stood there.
The giant movie theater on the Viehofer Platz was the only building in the
area still standing. It had become a refuge for the homeless. Inside, there
was no power, just a dark mass of shadowy people. Sonja called out into
the murky throng within, peering toward the glimmers of light from the
occasional candle, and her sister emerged. In the tearful reunion that followed, Johanna told Sonja that she had lost everything.

The Essen raid was the beginning of a devastating bombing campaign.
By May 1943, major industrial centers had suffered countless assaults. The
Ruhr port of Duisburg had been attacked 161 times, and its population had
suffered 643 alarms. Because Essen had also become such a frequent target, the Jacobses moved their possessions to Wuppertal for safekeeping;
that smaller, less significant city had been largely spared by the air raids.
They also spent most nights in the Bund collective on Wuppertal's Ottostrasse. But then the British began to attack second-class targets, including
the cluster of smaller towns northeast of Cologne—Solingen, Remscheid,
and Wuppertal—in an effort to force the Germans to spread their air
defenses more thinly. And on the night of May 29, 1943, the Jacobses once
again found themselves taking cover.[11]

The Bund members learned what happened next from Artur and Ernst,
who wrote their own eyewitness accounts a day or two later. Artur had
taken some sleeping tablets just before the attack started and was so dazed
when the siren sounded that he did not manage even elementary precautions. Everything was left behind—his clothes, his watch, his wallet full of
money, his ID papers, some parts of his diary (his April entries have not
survived), and his briefcase. As he and Dore rushed down to the cellar,
barely dressed, the first bombs were already falling (luckily, by 1943 Dore
was reasonably mobile again). Just as they had descended the stairs, a phos-
phorus bomb fell into the stairwell, which was instantly ablaze. Had they
been even a few seconds slower, they would have been incinerated. Down
in the shelter, the other Bund members—there were eleven of them in all—
managed to scrape together enough clothes to get Artur dressed, using

trousers from his brother, Walter (but no suspenders, so he had to hold the waist up with his hands), and shoes from Erna. Above them, the building shook and rumbled as two more bombs carved out massive craters in front of the house and in the backyard; just a few feet closer and they would all have been buried under the rubble. To get away from the firestorm raging above, someone smashed through a basement wall so that the group could move into the shelter next door. As the fire continued to spread, the Bundists in the basement forced their way through the second shelter and into a third. Now they were among strangers, including children almost paralyzed with fear.[12]

Finally, they managed to crawl outside and run to safer ground—the wooded park on the hill across the street was spared from the bombing because there were no houses there. In the rush up the hill, it was impossible for the Bund members to keep track of one another. Only by calling out into the night did they find each other again. A few minutes later, they saw their house going up in flames. It was here in the park that the Bundists witnessed some of the worst scenes of misery and hardship they would encounter firsthand. Thousands of people spent the rest of the night in the cold, whistling wind. Some were half naked, their eyes swollen from smoke, their clothes scorched; some were barefoot. There were crying babies and small children, forlorn individuals ceaselessly wandering and plaintively calling out for missing family members, a frail woman in her seventies or eighties clawing her way up the hill.

A day or two later, it was Ernst's turn to write an account. In it, he described a walk through the town. The Wuppertal conurbation is a long strip running along the Wupper Valley, extending from Elberfeld, in the southwest, through Barmen, where the Bund had its house, to Oberbarmen, three miles northeast. From what Ernst could see, every house from Barmen through Oberbarmen had been destroyed. He reported, "To be taken literally: you can walk in this densely populated valley for one hour, without seeing a house standing."[13] In the area where the Bund's house had been, south of the river and somewhat removed from the town center, everything had burned down; in the center, the damage took a different form—there the houses had been demolished by high explosives. According to the Royal Air Force report, its 719 bombers had destroyed 80 percent of the buildings in Wuppertal-Barmen, and 3,380 people had been killed. It was the misfortune of Essen and now Wuppertal, the two centers of Bund activity, to have been the two sites where the Allies dramatically escalated the destructiveness of their bombing raids.[14]

Those who emerged from this night alive could not stop talking about what they had seen. In the maternity hospital, for example, twenty-eight women had died, the survivors escaping into the woods carrying their newborns. Ernst himself lost a sister-in-law and two nieces in the bombing; a third niece was saved. In general, the Bund members had been very lucky— since they lived opposite an undeveloped area, they had been able to escape the firestorm. Both of Ernst's daughters had been out of danger, though young Ursel, staying with Ernst's sister on the other side of town, had suffered terrible anxiety seeing the city on fire.[15]

After Ernst's walk, it began to sink in that everything was gone. "You think of some object you use every day," he wrote, "watch, glasses, pencil, wallet, handkerchief, etc.—and suddenly realize that you have nothing." He tried to take an optimistic view, claiming this was not so much a sad as an interesting experience. But he added that when Ellen had given him some things, "pencil, knife, comb, toothbrush, a shirt—every object was a source of happiness."[16] For Artur, too, the initial relief at having survived soon gave way to an increasing awareness of the "thousand things, from piano to toothbrush, from the bookshelves to the very last cup, from the beautiful dress to the ink pen, from the typewriter to one's last pencil, everything torn away, gone, destroyed, no longer there!" That was hard enough. The real challenge, however, was the loss of the irreplaceable:

> The writings above all, the many manuscripts of which there was only one copy, all my songs and music which were in the bookcase and which cannot be recovered. Burned too are the beautiful picture albums from the history of the family [i.e., the Bund], (Julie's beautiful Album, the folder of Eyhof pictures from Gert) all my birthday folders, ach, and so much more that is irretrievable.[17]

He had brought everything that was most precious to Wuppertal, believing it to be safer there. In reality, the Essen house would survive, and it was the Wuppertal house, along with all its contents, that was gone.

Three and a half weeks later, on June 24, a follow-up raid on Wuppertal-Elberfeld, to the southeast, flattened over 90 percent of the town's buildings. Artur and Walter's mother was killed; Walter almost lost his life trying to save her.[18]

Victims of Nazism, Victims of War

In late August, Artur was in the Sauerland, at one of the Bund's retreats, trying to find some solace and reconnect with nature. But his peace did not last for long. Lisa later recalled the "shattering news, never to be forgotten" that reached them as they returned from a long hike: Friedl had disappeared.[19] Artur's diary entry for August 25 records the moment. They had just descended from a high hill and returned to the farmhouse where they were staying to find an alarming note from Friedl's landlady in the Netherlands informing them that Friedl had, in fact, been missing for weeks:

> My heart stopped as I began to read, and I am still completely numb. What has happened? Where is he? Why is he gone? Voluntarily? Involuntarily? If voluntarily, he would have plenty of time to send us a message. So it must be involuntarily. Arrested, imprisoned. By whom and why?

Artur threw himself into reaching out to any and all authorities who might be able to assist: the German consulate in Amsterdam, the ordinary police in Amsterdam, and, with Ernst's help, some other contacts he did not name. A frantic search for a typewriter in the little village ensued, so that Artur could draft a letter to the authorities. But it was hard enough to get any information in Germany. How could he possibly find out what was happening in Holland? "Still," he affirmed, "I am not abandoning hope." The intensity of the writing, rewriting, and going over his letters once more before entrusting them to the mail remained indelibly inscribed on Lisa's memory decades later.[20]

This same day, August 25, Artur learned that southern Essen had been hit by an air raid and that the windows in the house on Dönhof Street had been blown in. As he noted in his diary, the housing question was much more serious for a couple in which one partner was Jewish than for "normal" citizens.[21] If they lost their own house, where would a mixed-race couple, even one in a "privileged marriage," be able to rent?

Four days later, just before the group split up to go home, Artur discovered what had happened to Friedl: he had been imprisoned on political grounds, though the details of the accusations against him remained unclear. Adversity could sometimes make a person stronger, Artur reflected, grasping for hope, but he also understood that under the present conditions, a human life was worth so little, and brutality and terrible suffering were a daily occurrence. He confided, "I am worried for the child and my heart is often full of fear."[22]

He was most troubled when he thought of Dore. She had not been with them in the Sauerland and was recovering from the exertions of their near-death ordeal in Wuppertal by staying with Hedwig in Göttingen. So, she was still unaware that her son was missing. Artur was determined that she should learn nothing until she was back in Essen, because otherwise she would suffer to no purpose. In early September, a postcard arrived from a neighbor suggesting that Friedl might be in the horrific Vught concentration camp, a piece of misinformation that triggered a new round of anxieties on his father's part. (In fact, Friedl was in the somewhat better conditions of the Police and Investigatory Prison in Haaren.)[23]

If a narrow escape from death, the loss of his house, the death of his mother, and Friedl's dire situation were not enough on Artur's plate, it was now, just a few days after Artur's return from the Sauerland, that Marianne Strauss turned up at the Blockhaus in Essen. Given all he was going through, Artur's warm welcome of Marianne is all the more impressive.[24] A week earlier, worrying about Friedl, Artur had cited in his diary a recent letter from Dore, written while she struggled with cares of her own but not yet with knowledge of Friedl's fate: "'Again, and again, I find that what creates calm in this unsettled life is performing constructive and much-needed deeds.' That is true! I feel it even in this unsettling situation."[25] Perhaps Marianne's arrival provided Artur with an opportunity to bring his own distress under control. In admiring Marianne's "undiminished spirit," he may also have been hoping that the same would be true of Friedl in captivity. It was only toward the end of October that Artur would have the "indescribable joy" of learning that his son had been set free.[26]

Artur's diary entries during the summer of 1943 move seamlessly from his experience of terrifying bombing raids through his worries about Friedl to his care for Marianne. Reading them, and the overlapping threats they describe, deepens our understanding of all that Artur and the group had to contend with. Nevertheless, by overlaying dangers of different provenance and moral import, the diary has also complicated our picture of the rescuers' struggle. The fear of Jewish persecution was something that Dore, Lisa, and Artur (on his wife's and son's behalf) shared with other Jews. Yet if the group's leaders were themselves victims of persecution, does that make the help they offered less selfless? In order to protect his loved ones, Artur had no choice but to fight the regime. It is because of this sense that there was no choice that Yad Vashem does not recognize Jews—and, for the most part, their non-Jewish spouses—as "righteous." On the other hand, we might see the Jacobs family's achievements as even more remarkable given the threats they faced. After all, Artur and Dore had managed not to be consumed by their own troubles and, in fact, had extended a helping hand to others.

Another complication relates to the bombing. Our sense of the Bundists' heroism is undoubtedly enhanced by our recognition that they succeeded in maintaining their activity despite the massive impact of the air raids. But then we remember that millions of their fellow Germans were dealing with the same calamities and also moving on with their lives. Of course, unlike them, Artur and his fellow Bund members remained committed to helping others. Yet there is something disconcerting about wanting to recognize the Bund for a struggle they faced along with Hitler's followers. It is no doubt partly because of these complexities that in the Bundists' postwar accounts, the focus is all on the Gestapo and its threat to the group as resistance fighters and as helpers of Jews, and the war virtually disappears.

The Life Raft

When the Wuppertal group was still in the basement, with incendiaries raining down from the sky, Artur was profoundly touched, almost shaken, by a gesture of Lisa's: she held her hands over his head, as if to protect him.[27] With the war literally hitting home, Bund members came to appreciate their group more than ever. After the raid on Wuppertal-Barmen was over, Ernst remarked that "the best thing about the experience" had been the role "of our friends."[28] And Artur wrote Friedl about the strength they derived from standing on such an unshakable set of values.[29]

Even in the midst of total war, the group remained full of life and activity. Until 1943, the Blockhaus and the Bund houses continued to be the center of action, and even after the "Barmen catastrophe," the house on Dönhof Street in Essen was home to a variety of Bund members. Ever since Dore had become incapacitated, there seems to have been—all gender equality to the contrary—an assumption among Bund members that Artur needed someone to keep house. Grete Ströter lived there with her children after Reinhold was called up in 1940. So, too, at different times did Hedwig, Karin Morgenstern from Braunschweig, Lisa, Änne Engels, and Erna Löhrke. For her part, Sonja remained in the Blockhaus until late 1944, joined at some point by another Bund member, Erich Nöcker, and later by the Schuberts. The Blockhaus basement was the center of Bund activity.[30]

Across the Ruhr, local groups met until very late into the war. In addition to the Wuppertal group, the chapter in Düsseldorf remained active, above all due to Else's presence; so did the chapters in Mülheim, where the Krahlisches and the Zenkers were the leading figures; in Remscheid, where the Briels and Grete Dreibholz continued to live and work; and, further afield, in Göttingen, where the gentle Georg Reuter had succeeded in recruiting a number of active and enthusiastic participants, including the Gehrkes and Hermann Schmalstieg. The Inner Circle seems to have continued to convene in Essen. At least some of the younger members, presided over by Lisa, were able to come together, too.[31]

Before the war, the most solemn event on the Bund's calendar had been the Verpflichtungstag, or Commitment Day, around Easter, when new members pledged themselves to the group and others renewed their vows. (In 1943, it was Ellen's turn to swear her oath to the Bund.) But in the dark years of the war, the Lichtfest, celebrated on Christmas Day and with many of the accoutrements of a German Christmas—such as decorations with pine twigs, ribbons, verses, and small gifts—came to seem most meaningful. Like everything else the Bund did, the celebrations were organized with much thought and attention to detail. Their houses were carefully decorated earlier in December. At the Bund house on Dönhof Street, for example, there were stockings on the wall, a wreath with a red candle in Artur's room, pine branches with fat cones, a big bag of baked cookies, lines of poetry by Lisa, and small gifts, each beautifully wrapped with red and gold ribbons.[32]

Over the years, the Bund's celebration took on its own style, embodying the way in which the Bund brought philosophy and everyday practical gestures together. In December 1942, for example, those able to attend the celebrations in the house on Dönhof Street read aloud a story by Tolstoy about two Russian pilgrims to Jerusalem. Then, in an upstairs room, they festively decorated three tables, exchanged gifts, played improvised games, and read out verses they had written, the best of them from Friedel Kette and Lisa. Above all, the Lichtfest was a time for Bund members to take stock. Whereas the Verpflichtungstag reminded the members of all the commitments they were unable to fulfill, Artur argued, the Lichtfest gave them a chance, during the shortest days of the year, to enjoy the metaphor of glimmers of light in the darkness, and to remind themselves of the underlying currents that promised better things in the coming year. For weeks in advance, like a parish vicar, Artur would be honing his "Lichtfest thoughts." For his listeners, Artur's address was a quasi-religious experience.[33]

Around Pentecost and again in the summer months, there were excursions into the hills. Whereas nature had always been a pleasure, during the war it felt nothing less than miraculous that the normal rhythms of life still continued there. Even at home, Artur could always find solace in the song of a thrush, or a stray poppy flower that suddenly surfaced in the garden, or a particular cast of light. Nature was ever ready with metaphors for the struggle of sustaining life and spirit in war—the violence of storms, the adversity of rain, or the obfuscation of fog. Sometimes in days of crisis, the "normality" of nature could appear disturbing or surreal. And yet a couple of days later, the countryside would work its magic, and Artur would claim to feel stronger than ever. Remarkably, these gatherings continued at least until the summer of 1944, and probably into the fall of that year. Afterward, the participants would disperse—to the Baltic Sea, to Lake Constance, to Göttingen, to the Ruhr. Discussions and conclusions were shared by mail with those who could not take part.[34]

Fellow Victims

Total war created a greater sense of mutual dependency among Bund members, but it also brought them closer to their neighbors. While this was partly due to the experience of negotiating the same dangers, glimpses of real humanity emerged in such extreme times. What they dubbed the "phraseology and superficiality" of conformist behavior under the Nazis dropped away. Neighbors and relatives from whom Bund members had felt alienated were suddenly helpful and supportive. Moreover, in the aftermath of major attacks, and particularly in August and September 1943, the Bund sensed a new critical mood in the air. While watching the flames destroy their Wuppertal home from the safety of the opposite hillside, Artur was struck by how outspoken those around them were in their critique of the regime.[35] Ernst, too, observed "much outrage at this madness." Cries had echoed through the night: "This is the total war that you wanted!"—a reference to Goebbels's infamous speech at the Berlin Sportpalast in which he had rhetorically asked the thousands of people in the audience if they wanted total war, and they had screamed back, "Yes!"[36]

Early in August, Artur was encouraged by a scene he witnessed at the Essen railway station:

> People are in an uproar like never before. At the station, in the train carriages, on platform benches, waiting for the train, they conduct frank conversations that were impossible a month ago.
>
> Such a storm of anger, indignation, horror. "We've had enough," "This can't go on," "Do we want to wait till everything is just a wasteland?" "This crazy war!"—one woman exclaimed quite loudly—she had lost her son on the Eastern Front and her husband in the latest air raid. . . .
>
> "We're getting paid back for our sins," another said, "what we did to others, who could not defend themselves, is now being done to us."[37]

A week later, Artur noted again with satisfaction that his fellow Germans were no longer stolidly bearing everything that was being done to them. No one believed the babble in the papers anymore.[38] Traveling

through Hanover, which had recently suffered a heavy bombing raid, Karlos wrote that many were beginning to see the light.[39]

Though undoubtedly too ready to declare that anger and opposition
were "fermenting," Bund members' sense that popular dissatisfaction and
unrest reached new heights in the autumn of 1943 was well founded. A
series of recent misfortunes both at home and on the battlefront was undermining confidence and raising new questions about Germany's leadership.
At home, there was the bombing in the Ruhr and the Hamburg firestorm.
Abroad, there was bad news from the eastern front, General Erwin Rommel's defeat in Tunisia earlier in May, the Allied conquest of Sicily in August,
and the invasion of Italy in September. Germany's alliance was crumbling:
Prime Minister Benito Mussolini fell in July, and Marshal Pietro Badoglio
announced the Italian armistice in early September. All of this left its mark.

The mood did not last, however. Luftwaffe successes against the bombers, containment of the Russian advance on the eastern front, the speedy
Wehrmacht occupation of mainland Italy, and hopeful rumors, as Artur also
observed, of a miracle weapon revived confidence that Germany's position
remained sound and stilled the protests.[40] In January 1944, Karlos, undergoing basic training, wrote to his wife, Karin, that his comrades were hang-
ing all their hopes on Goebbels's talk of the "revenge weapon."[41] Their
unwillingness to face reality drove him mad.[42] In the hospital with a broken leg, Ernst, too, saw little reason to expect much from his fellow patients,
particularly the younger ones.[43] A month later, Artur was traveling back
to the Ruhr and registered "not outrage so much as a resigned acceptance"
among his fellow passengers.[44] The notion that bombing might be revenge
for what the Germans had done to others did not last long, either. As confidence revived, talk of others' fates disappeared. Fear of reaping what one
had sown would become a topic of open discussion again only at the very
end of the war.[45]

The War and the Lessons of History

In April 1944, Artur upbraided his son, who was still living in Holland after
his release from prison. Despite repeated letters, Friedl had offered no reaction to his parents' brush with death in Wuppertal-Barmen almost a year

earlier. A week later, Friedl wrote both, confirming that he had indeed heard the news:

> I am surprised sometimes myself, how lightly I take such reports. It is probably because I myself have never experienced anything of the sort. The things that I have been through were indeed of a completely different nature. But I believe that they were worse, at least those in 1942 were.[46]

On one level, as Friedl recognized, proximity was everything. Writing to Erna Michels a couple of months before the destruction of the Wuppertal house, Dore acknowledged and at the same time bemoaned the fact that she found herself much more troubled by news of bombing when it came within sixty miles of home. It was impossible to survive psychologically without erecting this kind of protective wall of relative indifference to distant events, she observed, but at the same time one was shocked that this was so.[47]

On another level, by referring to the deportation and murder of his girlfriend in 1942, Friedl was suggesting something else: that the Holocaust had a different moral weight and engendered a different order of horror. In writing this to his father he was, in fact, preaching to the converted. What is so striking about the Bund members is that even as they were in the thick of the bombing, they remained from beginning to end acutely aware that there were fates far worse than theirs.[48] The day following the massive Essen bombing, as Sonja walked home after finding her sister in the bombed-out city center, she was shocked to see that in the wealthy and untouched Bredeney suburb, everyone was carrying on as though nothing had happened. It was emblematic, she wrote, of the way they were all oblivious. "What is this event in relation to Stalingrad, in relation to, well, I don't need to spell it out, you know what I mean."[49] The thing she didn't need to spell out was, of course, the persecution of Jews.

In the same vein, after the Wuppertal attack, Artur wrote that their own sacrifice was a paltry tribute compared with the far greater distress of those thrown out of their homeland, cast into the abyss, unacknowledged and friendless. Artur returned to this theme a few days after the bombing, when the Bund received a card from a "Trude B." (It's not clear if this is the same

Trude with whom Lisa had been communicating.) The writer had evidently been able to convey that she was about to be murdered. This message, Artur added, "darkened my mood more than the whole Barmen tragedy. (One is more like a natural catastrophe, the other reveals the whole abyss of human evil and the thousand-fold torture of the innocent and the defenseless.)"[50]

Friedl's and his father's moral scales were thus in many respects the same. After Hitler's defeat, this strong sense of the Holocaust's enormity was one reason why the impact of war is downplayed so much in the group's narrative. Yet Artur's irritation at Friedl's obliviousness in 1944 expressed something also important—namely, Artur's knowledge that they had been through an existential and tumultuous experience. In the contemporary accounts we can see how fear and the feeling of powerlessness tested the Bundists' physical and psychological fortitude to the hilt and, in fact, transformed the group's philosophy.

One concrete expression of the group's fears was Artur's idea of a *Vermächtnis*, or legacy. Recognizing that they might be killed at any time, he called for the group to produce a kind of philosophical tool kit. This was the *Vermächtnis*. The idea was to produce a usable set of documents capturing their philosophy, so that if the core membership were eliminated in the bombings, others would be able to carry on. No doubt Artur felt that this kind of task would also be psychologically beneficial, giving unsettled Bund members a sense of continuity and purpose. Intensive work on this project took place in the months following the Wuppertal bombing.[51]

On a deeper level, being exposed to the merciless forces of war had unexpected consequences for the Bund's philosophy. As optimistic Marxists, they had trusted in the dialectic of class struggle. As Kantians, they had believed that the categorical imperative would ultimately force humans to recognize that living in mutual respect was the only rational choice. In the earlier years of the regime, Nazism's extraordinary success at home and then its military victories abroad had represented a sharp challenge to this optimism. The wrong forces were winning, and the horrific character of Nazi policy suggested that those forces were more insidious than anyone had imagined. As the war turned, Bund members could start to believe that history was moving in the right direction after all, but the terror of the air raids made the quest for meaning and purpose, and for a new source of strength, all the more pressing.

In early July 1943, under the title "Words for Our Work," Artur began drafting an address for the next Sauerland retreat.[52] They had just emerged, he wrote, from days utterly dominated by worries about the most basic things in life, cares that had absorbed most of their energies and pursued them through the day like hunted animals. Besieged by terror, they had learned what it was like to be on the front line of total war. Now, here they were in the quiet world they knew so well. Clouds drifted across the sky, the trees whispered in the wind, the birds sang. Everything was familiar. But they could no longer be the same. The images of burning cities, of a world of horror and suffering, were indelibly inscribed on their souls. Their task was to understand these images for what they were: the battleground of a global transformation. What did this mean? As Artur saw it, the war was utterly transforming the organization of states and economies, creating a new world order, and pushing humanity toward new forms of cooperation, both at home and internationally.

Such a transformation could not be painless, Artur said. They did not have the luxury of watching from the sidelines. Since they themselves were caught up in the maelstrom, the only choice they had was between being uncomprehending, complaining victims, on the one hand, and engaging with the cataclysmic global forces that were leading toward a new and better world, on the other.[53]

This choice entailed a very different view of the Bund's role. In the Weimar era, the group had seen itself as a model and catalyst of change. To be sure, its radius of action was small, but nonetheless it had aspired to be an agent of social transformation. The massive scale of the war, however, brought home the enormity of the forces reshaping the globe, forces that dwarfed the national class struggle, which the Bund had once imagined would serve as the motor for change. Everything she had understood about history had been upended, Else said in an extensive address on Verpflichtungstag 1944.[54] Implicitly, the group's own role had been downgraded. The ordinary person, as Else put it, was no longer the agent of change but, rather, its servant. The group's sense of its own power was vastly diminished. What remained to them was an almost spiritual task: to genuflect with awe before the historical power reshaping the world.[55] "It's a strange feeling," Artur confided to his diary in February 1944. "On the one hand I become ever smaller and less important, but the thing that draws my life into its orbit, and that I am drawn to serve, becomes more and more significant, powerful, distant, unreachable, yes infinite."[56] For all their courage and their activism, the lesson Bund members were learning—on one level surprising, on another perhaps logical—was a new appreciation of their powerlessness. In the face of a conflict of such shocking, terrifying, awe-inspiring magnitude, their former hopes of changing the world looked like youthful folly.

The Bund in the Battlefield

While the Bund was rethinking historical necessity on the home front, we have few insights as to how the war may have influenced the thinking of its members in uniform, including Fritz Denks, Gustav Gehrke, Karl Heilwagen, Karlos Morgenstern, Albert Schürmann, August Schwab, and Reinhold Ströter. By the time I conducted interviews, only one of the veterans, Reinhold Ströter, was still living. Reinhold wanted to talk about the wonders of the Bund and said little about his military service other than offering the telling remark that he would not have believed beforehand how much it would change him. But for all this, letters from the front do survive, often in the versions that were copied in order to be circulated within the group, and sometimes as reproduced in Artur's diary.

Sensitive, thoughtful, teetotaling, pacifist, and left-wing, Bund members would have felt out of place and lonely in any modern conscript army. "Dear friend," Reinhold wrote to Artur in the late winter of 1942, a day or two after his unit had been pulled back from a murderous battlefront in the East, "how horribly sick I am of this life that is no life at all. How rigid and dull the people are! The tone of their interactions and the topics of conversation make me sick. Oh, if I could only find one friend among them!"[57] Karlos wrote home from his basic training in Toulouse in January 1944 that unless his fellow soldiers could get used to him not "taking part in their drinking parties," he would find himself in a very uncomfortable position.[58] Karlos was an awkward character; at one point or another in his life, he fell out with colleagues, employers, and even fellow Bund members.

Stuck with eighteen people in an improvised billet a few months later, he wrote, with a hint of wryness, that he would have found this hard enough with "our people," let alone these "increasingly unbearable men."[59]

In any case, this was not just any modern conscript army. The Wehrmacht was an increasingly Nazified institution waging, without restraint, a war that almost all the Bundists regarded as utterly unjust. Surrounded by many confirmed Nazis among the troops, the Bund friends had to watch what they said. Even many educated and thoughtful non-Nazis were supportive of the war, retreating behind the fatalistic stance that it was an unstoppable natural force.[60] In this climate, Reinhold, Karlos, and August cautiously tried to convince their fellow soldiers that they were caught up in a criminal enterprise. August wrote to Artur, for example, that he found points of contact with his comrades in many areas but that there always came a moment where a gulf opened up between them, and he felt thrown back on himself. In a recent conversation about "Ruth's *Kinder*" (i.e., "Ruth's children," a euphemism for the fate of the Jews), he wrote, he had abandoned his usual impassioned manner and presented his views in a matter-of-fact way and "with love." There was no response, though, and he ended up feeling isolated, consoled only by the thought of the Bund.[61] Karlos repeatedly groused about his comrades' delusions, though, like August, he occasionally enjoyed more meaningful conversations.[62]

Did some Bund members succumb to the pressure of opinions in the barracks? In an interview recorded in the 1980s, Gustav Zenker, who himself had been in essential war work and thus escaped the call-up, suggested that some Bund followers had been influenced by Nazi propaganda, specifically when it came to the Soviet Union.[63] But he did not name names, and in any case, he implied that these opinions had been short-lived. In a letter preserved in Artur's diary, Fritz Denks so uncritically identified with the battles of his beleaguered unit that we wonder whether his closing comment—"What I wish is that this sacrifice is not for nothing"—implied some validation of the German war effort.[64] But if Artur, too, wondered, he did not comment in his diary. He would have been conscious that poor Fritz had just made an all too real sacrifice of his own—he had lost a foot and, with it, his livelihood as a plasterer. Similar remarks crop up in letters from August, a fierce critic of the war. It was not possible to escape a feeling of utter waste as one saw one's comrades mowed down.[65]

For most Bund members in the military, it was the contact with their Bund friends back home that kept them sane. In February 1942, we find Reinhold writing of his efforts to hold on to the Bund's ideas. To him, those ideas were the real world, and the war was a brutal distraction. This may well be why Artur cites him more frequently than any other voice from the front. "I cannot tell you, Reinhold," Artur wrote that same month, "how much the way you are holding on to our life and retaining your trust in it helps us."[66] That February, Artur also copied out a letter sent from a military training camp; its author talked about the importance of his "inner yardstick"—a coded reference to the Bund values—which had protected him from the debilitating small-mindedness of his comrades.[67] For soldiers on leave, reunions with Bund friends were sometimes almost too much, only underlining the contrast between the brutality of the front and the comforting atmosphere at home. In February 1942, Gustav Gehrke, singing songs with the group, broke down in tears. And as we know, this happened to another front soldier in September, while Marianne Strauss held herself in check.[68]

In any case, contact with home could not protect the Bund soldiers from an increasingly desperate military situation. A number of them did manage to get assigned to noncombat roles. Reinhold, for example, was a medical orderly and Alfred Stürmer a member of the engineering corps. But others, including Gustav, Karlos, August, Fritz, Albert Schürmann, and many more, were caught up directly in the fighting. In any case, as Reinhold's letters show, even a medical orderly might find himself in situations of acute danger. Combat was enormously demanding even for the men who believed in the cause for which they were fighting. But for the Bund members who held on to their principles—and that seems to have been almost all of them—the stresses of war must have been doubly hard to bear. As his unit retreated before the U.S. Army, Karlos wrote one last letter before he was captured. He referred to the "terrible psychological situation" he and his comrades faced, almost all of whom were inexperienced and all keenly aware of their powerlessness. He was no coward, he wrote, but—and here he had to be cautious in a letter that would pass through the censor—"it is the whole ideological background which affects me so deeply."[69] In other words, fleeing in disarray before the overwhelming might of the U.S. Army was bad enough, but facing mortal danger for a cause one utterly rejected was intolerable.

Two Letters

Of course, the problem of serving in the Wehrmacht went beyond the challenge of mortal combat in an illegitimate war. As we know, the German army participated in countless criminal actions, from shooting Soviet commissars on sight and starving millions of Soviet prisoners of war to death to murderous anti-partisan actions all across occupied Europe and direct participation in the Holocaust. It is not clear to what extent Bund soldiers were implicated, but two letters from Karlos—or, rather, handwritten extracts from his letters that were circulated within the Bund—survive in his daughter's possession:

> Toulouse, May 17, 1944

> I was once more in Paris. Again, a transport. Whereas the earlier one was in a passenger train and took only 12 to 14 hours to reach its destination, this time it was in a freight train, and we were traveling for three days and two nights. One of the days was hot. You just have to imagine that. I cannot describe it to you. This and some other things I have to keep to myself until we next see each other.
>
> I am grateful for every day that goes by without something terrible and inhuman happening.[70]

Another letter, undated, also sent in May, either refers to yet another transport or, more likely, describes the one above in greater detail:

> Accompanied a second transport, larger than the earlier one and in freight cars. The guards were in the third class, there was even a first-class and second-class coach on the train. Again, Jews were on the transport. There was no ventilation and the wagons were sealed with thick wire. They remained

closed for the entire transport. The first day was hot. It must have been horrible in the freight cars. When the doors were opened, we saw the people now wearing just shirts and underpants, sweaty and dirty. They had had to relieve themselves in the wagon.

We left Toulouse on Friday and were in Paris on Sunday evening, Monday evening we were in Compiègne.[71]

The Red Cross treatment of the people varied.

I did not have much time in Paris but I had in any case lost all desire to see it. I kept seeing the train and thinking about the innocent people and the new worlds of suffering and misery they were about to enter. The children too. My thoughts returned again and again to a book from the last war. It was written by a German soldier about the deportation and extermination of the Armenians by the Turks.[72]

In the spring of 1944, German Security Police, together with local collaborators, mounted raid after raid on French provincial cities in the hunt for Jews. In May alone some fourteen hundred Jews from all over France were sent to the Drancy holding camp, in northeastern Paris. These included children from orphanages run by Jewish welfare organizations. Overall in 1944, almost fifteen thousand Jews were sent to Auschwitz from Drancy. Karlos's transport, however, clearly contained prisoners with different kinds of status, and each group, as he noted, was treated differently by the Red Cross. This transport thus was probably composed not only of Jews but also of people suspected of aiding the resistance or those who had evaded conscription to work in Germany. There is little doubt that the Jews among them were going to be sent on to be murdered.[73] Far more people would have been on this train than the Bund ever managed to rescue, perhaps more than they ever managed to help in any form.[74]

We know from recent research that perpetrators could also be helpers. Even confirmed Nazis or anti-Semites might allow ties of personal friendship to overrule their ideological commitment.[75] There are several recorded cases of Jews being warned by old friends now in the SS. In 1944, just such a tip sent Hanna Jordan's family into hiding.[76] We know other instances of Nazis who helped, motivated by the promise of money, or property, or sex.[77] This is all well established. We are less familiar, however, with the idea that those who made a strong and conscious moral decision to help Jews might also have been involved in their destruction. The two propositions—some perpetrators were rescuers, and some rescuers were perpetrators—might seem indistinguishable, but they carry different implications. The former reminds us that assistance for Jews was not necessarily the result of a moral calculus and that rescuers were often far from saints. But we are less accustomed to the idea that even those who assisted Jews out of moral principle may have been caught up in the killing process.[78]

Could and should Karlos have avoided involvement? It is a remarkable fact that, after the war, although many German defendants claimed to have acted under duress, no one was able to prove that refusing to carry out a criminal shooting had led to any kind of threat to life or limb.[79] This was because of a special dispensation given to those police and SS units directly involved in the mass murder of civilians. In the Wehrmacht, normal military orders were strictly enforced, however, and by 1944 the punishments for disobedience were becoming more severe. Firing squads were an increasingly common occurrence in the military; more than twenty thousand German soldiers were court-martialed and executed by the Wehrmacht (as compared with 150 or so death sentences carried out in the First World War). Ernst's son, Eberhard, was forced to participate in the shooting of a young man supposedly guilty of sabotage.[80] Military and police personnel who illegally assisted Jews were subject to punishment, and a number were killed.[81] Karlos thus must have faced an impossible situation. By the time of this transport, it surely would have been clear to him that the Jews were being taken to their deaths. But since this transport was part of a Wehrmacht operation, there would have been no dispensation for a soldier who disobeyed orders. Even postwar courts would treat such military orders as legal.[82]

The extracts from Karlos's letters are preserved in two forms: the handwritten copies and then another typewritten set containing shorter extracts, designed to be copied and distributed among Bund members. In the typed-up version, Karlos's second letter about transports is followed by some reflections about the life of the mind, and about how to deal with the imminent threat of death.[83] This kind of reflection on Geist and mortality is standard Bund fare, but its impact is rather different when it immediately follows an account of the murder of Jews. There is nothing in the Bund files to show how the letters were received.

There is no question that Karlos was profoundly disturbed by his mission. His reference to the Armenian genocide in correspondence that would be subject to censorship was also courageous. According to his daughter, on several occasions when as an adult she visited her father, Karlos would allude to having had to herd Jews together on a platform. Nightmares plagued him throughout his postwar life.[84]

Until now, Artur's comments about the Bund's "guilt" and "complicity" have appeared the mark of a generous conscience, acknowledging a shared responsibility that was more formal than real. The Bundists had in so many ways sought to reject and withdraw from every aspect of Nazi society. But they had concluded that if they did not want to die at the hands of the regime, they had to be willing to serve in Hitler's army, and that meant serving in a murderous war of annihilation. Only now do we see the full implication of that decision.[85] Still, what distinguished Bund members like Karlos from so many of their countrymen was their awareness that horrific injustice was being done and their efforts to do good where they could.

8

The Endgame

Calculated Risks: The Jacobses in a Time of Danger

In February 1944, Artur and Dore decided to flee from the Ruhr. On February 21 we find them "in a cold, drafty train carriage heading south." The preceding days, Artur noted, had been "unsettling and distracting. So much to think about and remember; so much going up and down stairs, so much opening and closing suitcases." But now he could sit in the train car and "study the world in people's faces."[1] Dore, always somewhat frail, was wrapped in a sleeping bag, trying to protect herself from the cold. A "friend"—Lisa Jacob, it turns out—joined them at Düsseldorf. After Offenburg they saw the first tree-lined mountains. Then they were racing through a wintry black forest. Arriving in Constance, they found that the rooms they had booked had been given to someone else, so they dragged themselves from hotel to hotel. Every establishment was full of soldiers on leave. At ten p.m., the streetlights were extinguished and the city fell into darkness, and still the Jacobses had no shelter. Finally, they managed to rouse the host of an inn in pitch darkness and secure a place for the night.

The following day, they made their way to Julie and Käthe's inn, Auf dem Fohrenberg, in Meersburg, on Lake Constance. Here Dore would spend the rest of the war, and Artur much of it, too.[2] This was far from the first time the couple had headed south to the inn. In the past, such visits had been an invaluable opportunity to recover from the stresses and strains of war-torn Essen, even if Artur always felt guilty for enjoying the peace and quiet. But this was different—now they and Lisa would be staying for an indefinite period.

Why leave the Ruhr now? For years, mixed-race individuals and Jews in mixed marriages had been living on a knife edge. Even if not directly targeted for deportation, they knew their exemption was precarious. Radical elements within the SS and the Nazi Party continually pressed for new rules that would deliver these groups up for extermination. Historians are still not sure why these radicals did not succeed. Probably Hitler remained just wary enough of unsettling morale during wartime. But rumors of impending doom persisted among the "mixed," and sometimes the rumors were borne out by the facts. In the fall of 1942, the gauleiter of Hessen-Nassau, Jakob Sprenger, whose fiefdom included Frankfurt, gave instructions for one hundred mixed-race Jews and Jews in mixed marriages to be deported each month. The arrest of Jewish male spouses in mixed marriages as part of the notorious "factory action" in Berlin in the spring of 1943 raised new alarms, even though those arrested were ultimately released. In January 1944, the Party Chancellery mounted a revived effort to force mixed-marriage couples to divorce, but Hitler rejected the proposal. Even so, some one thousand Jews from across Germany who had lost non-Jewish partners through death or divorce were sent to Theresienstadt, and from there, for the most part, on to Auschwitz.[3]

In the absence of a clear national line toward mixed-marriage couples, a number of regions took the initiative. In February 1944, Baden began deporting both partners to labor camps belonging to the Organization Todt (OT), the Nazi construction agency. This did not apply to the Ruhr (and, in fact, did to Meersburg), so it does not quite explain why the Jacobses decided to take flight. On or around February 13, 1944, someone Artur refers to in his diary as "J," perhaps Sonja's sister Julie, heard a rumor from her masseuse that Jewish partners in mixed marriages would be soon deported.[4] Artur and Dore spent some profoundly anxious hours processing the information. The rumors, however, soon proved to be "alarmist and exaggerated," at least as far as their own situation in the Ruhr was concerned. Artur did not scare easily, and even when nervous, he worked hard to contain his fears. Yet the couple still decided to leave.

Understandably, Artur did not confide all his thinking to his diary. A week after their escape, he wrote to Friedl that they had left just at the right moment to avoid a period of unrest and uncertainty, a comment that might have referred to the generally more hostile atmosphere toward mixed marriages or might have hinted at something more personal.[5] After the war, the issue of why they had left was, oddly enough, discussed in court. In the context of restitution proceedings to gain compensation for their time on the run, the Jacobses needed to prove that they had been objectively in danger. Their difficulty in doing so revealed that there had probably been no direct threat against them. But it also showed how hard it had been, even for a canny observer like Artur, to read the writing on the wall. Probably the rumors from Baden had indeed been sufficiently alarming that the couple felt they had to be in a place where they were not known.[6]

The postwar restitution depositions are also useful in helping us make sense of wartime maneuvers too sensitive to record at the time. We learn, for example, that Artur and Dore did not register their departure with the police. Artur did, however, log his departure (destination unknown) with the ration office, in the hope of being able to draw rations in Meersburg. With the help of his brother, Walter, in Barmen, in whose name the Wuppertal house had been registered, he was able to establish his status as a bombing victim. But the couple was reluctant to do the same with Dore's rations, wanting to avoid alerting the authorities to her departure. So her ration cards continued to be collected on her behalf by Bund friends, to maintain the fiction that she was in Essen. But as the cards were clearly marked with a "J," they were unable to redeem them. And without a ration card, Dore, like Lisa, had to depend on Artur and others to share their rations. We also learn that with help from Hedwig Gehrke in the summer of 1943, Dore had managed to get a postal pass—like the one Marianne Strauss had obtained—without the obligatory middle name Sara, and also using her maiden name, misspelled as "Markes," rather than Jacobs. It was not foolproof, however, and would not hold up under any real degree of scrutiny, so she kept herself hidden as much as possible. Even so, according to her postwar account, the pass saved her life during at least one encounter with the Constance Gestapo.[7]

Despite all these precautions, the couple's hideaway came very close to being exposed. In early August 1944 two women, a certain Hilde Hesse, who lived near the Blockhaus, and Gisela Lönne, a twenty-three-year-old League of German Girls functionary, who also lived in south Essen, came to the Gestapo with a strikingly well-informed denunciation. It turned out that Hilde Hesse had been one of the residents at the guesthouse in Meersburg but at some point had been ejected from the house.[8] The two women told the Gestapo that Artur Jacobs was often in Meersburg, in the pension "Haus auf dem Vohrenberg" (sic!), where he met with like-minded people, "who reject our current state." Among those people, the witnesses named Käthe Franke and Julie Schreiber, the pension's co-owners, along with Tilde Stürmer, Grete Ströter, and Artur's brother, Walter, who all spent extended stays there.

To reinforce the sense of a conspiracy, they also noted the fact that "in the holidays Dr. J is visited by his former followers from Essen and Elberfeld. Although he is not always present, these people have access to the house." Frau Lönne claimed that Artur and his friends were "exploiting the freedom allowed local inhabitants to cross the frontier in order to post letters in Switzerland, some of which are sent abroad, above all to America. As further proof, we note that inhabitants of the house with different views are removed by various diplomatic means, if not to say driven out." This had happened to Frau Hesse and, they claimed, to Sonja Schreiber's other sister, Johanna, who was "pro-Nazi and a member of the Nazi women's league." (We do not know why Frau Hesse had been a guest at the inn to begin with, but clearly there had been paying guests there with no particular allegiance to the Bund.)

Whether Artur got wind of the denunciation we do not know. No evidence remains of an interrogation, and in September the Gestapo said that monitoring his mail had produced no incriminating evidence.[9] Though strikingly accurate, the denunciation probably did not contain enough criminal activity to interest the Gestapo—and perhaps most fortunately for the Jacobses, it was made just before a decision was taken in the Rhineland to deport Jewish spouses. For in September, Rhineland and Westphalia (which together included the Ruhr) were moving further than other parts of Germany toward expelling Jews in mixed marriages. There is some evidence that, faced with the possibility that Allied troops might soon occupy parts of the area, Higher SS and Police Leader Karl Gutenberger ordered the shooting of all remaining Jews within his jurisdiction. Local security police chiefs did not carry out this command but did order a major deportation. Given that few records survive, we do not know exactly how many Jews were called up for transport, although it was probably several hundred. About half of those summoned reported for deportation. Their initial destinations were various OT labor camps; in January 1945, some were sent on to Theresienstadt. From elsewhere in Germany, February and March 1945 saw around twenty-six hundred Jewish partners in mixed marriages also dispatched to Theresienstadt.[10]

Whether they were aware of the denunciation, the Jacobses were continually gauging the temperature and calculating how to behave. It seems that at first Dore sometimes left the guesthouse for walks, but from autumn 1944 onward she no longer felt it safe to go into town. By contrast, in October 1944 Artur decided to risk registering himself (but not Dore) with the police in Meersburg, having learned that it was possible to do so without unregistering in Essen. There was a small risk, of course, that his name might be on some wanted list, though given the increasing number of checks in Meersburg itself, the potential benefits of being officially recorded seemed to outweigh the dangers. Dore remained undocumented for the time being; in February 1945, however, Artur and Dore decided that she, too, should register, obviously as an "Aryan," relying presumably on her postal ID and on the claim that she was a bombing victim whose papers had been destroyed. The immediate stimulus to take this further step, Artur later wrote, was the need to get Dore medical treatment in Constance. Here again the couple was successful, though the whole ordeal was enormously stressful. Artur and Dore's strategic moves relied on the fact that the growing number of bombing victims moving out of the big cities— and the disruption to postal communication between the various authorities—made it easier to play the system.[11]

On top of the threats to themselves, Artur and Dore were also increasingly worried about Friedl. Back in the spring of 1944, Jews of mixed race aged seventeen years or older had begun to be conscripted to the labor battalions of the Organization Todt. In May, Artur sent Friedl a coded warning, urging him to make sure he was registered as employed and to keep his eyes open for trouble. Trude Nöcker, who was living in the Block-haus with Sonja Schreiber, traveled to Holland and visited Friedl in July, presumably to caution him in person. (Evidently Friedl had resented this parental intrusion; we learn from an angry letter from his father that Friedl made no effort to look after Trude, leaving her to search for accommodations at night in a foreign city.) As anxieties grew, in August 1944 Artur sent his son a large sum of money, in case Friedl had to go underground.[12]

Sensing that danger might pounce at any time, Artur sent his most somber letter yet:

> I am doing all right, Mother not very well. The blows and turmoil of our times have left their mark. Hopefully the end is near. But perhaps the hardest time is yet to come. We'll adapt to whatever happens for as long as we can . . . worries about loved ones and friends weigh heavily. It is a time of highest tension. You have to take your courage in both hands.[13]

And after signing off with hopes for a speedy reunion from *"Vater und Mutter,"* Artur added, "Stay healthy for us, dear son!"

Lives in the Balance

For many Bund members, the loss of housing and personal possessions made sheltering others harder or impossible. And yet the last twelve months of the war were also the period in which the Bund rescued the largest number of individuals. Chaotic conditions were tearing holes in the Nazi dragnet. As defeat moved closer, radical groups were pushing harder to eliminate the remaining protected categories—such as mixed-race Jews or those in mixed marriages. But at the same time, the disruption to daily life and the growing number of refugees who had lost everything created opportunities to slip through the net. Moreover, because it seemed that the war might end sooner rather than later, the Bund found it easier to convince others to take the risk of offering help. German officials themselves seem to have been less consistent in their commitment to rounding up those in protected categories.[14] Hanna Jordan, the daughter of a mixed-race couple, was a beneficiary of the new possibilities. Her non-Jewish father was tipped off by a friendly SS man that her mother was about to be deported. With a little help from the Bund, and more from the Quakers, all the Jordans managed, with some difficulty, to find places where they could disappear for the rest of the war.[15]

The sources we have regarding this late phase of the war are fragmentary, offering us only glimpses of the Bund's activities. One case we know of is that of forty-five-year-old Grete Menningen, a Jewish woman in a mixed marriage and the sister of a nurse, Irma Ransenberg, who had worked alongside Marianne Strauss in the Essen community offices. Grete lived with her non-Jewish husband in Barmen and had helped Marianne more than once by hosting her for a few days.[16] Now, in September 1944, Grete herself was in need of help, having been assigned to the transport for Jews in mixed marriages. Marianne wrote after the war that through Else Bramesfeld's assistance, someone was eventually found who lived in an isolated house near Remscheid and was willing to hide Grete.[17] Other sources suggest that Grete's trajectory was more complex. Initially, through Marianne's intervention, she hid in the apartment of Emilie Busch, a former housekeeper to an aunt of Marianne's, and someone with whom Marianne herself had hidden on several occasions. Then, from October 1944 to March 1945, Grete did indeed stay in a small town in the Bergisches Land, a hilly region south of the Ruhr, with a teacher, Hedwig Clasen (not a Bund member), whom Else Bramesfeld had found to host her. Fears about the safety of the house led Grete to return to Emilie Busch in March 1945.[18] Here she lived out the last weeks of the war. The Gestapo records show that agents were monitoring Grete's ration card to make sure no one tried to use it. The Bund probably assisted in providing food.

Another glimpse of the Bund's involvement is offered by the denazification form that Sonja, as a former and would-be teacher, had to fill out after the war. In it she recorded having sheltered not only Marianne Strauss but also Else Güldenring for the last ten months of the war. This is another name that does not appear in any Bund publication. Else Güldenring was one of eight Jews living in Solingen in a mixed marriage, and the only one of the eight not to report when she was called for transport. She survived at least some of the remaining months of the war, and perhaps all, in the Blockhaus. Ellen Jungbluth told me, in fact, that there was always someone hiding in Sonja's apartment. At the beginning of November 1944, Sonja herself was sent by the education authorities to the Sudetenland to help look after Essen children who had been evacuated. She left behind Erich and Trude Nöcker, and the Schuberts also took refuge in Sonja's apartment after their house was destroyed. They may have assumed the role of sheltering Frau Güldenring.[19]

The most substantive, if cryptic, hint at the scale of the group's activity during this time can be found in a letter from Ernst paraphrased in Artur's diary in September 1944:

> "Much to think about and to do for the fate of the relatives who have now been so badly hit," writes Ernst. "How much one's commitment to help comes through in every act, even if it is only a tiny drop in the ocean. And what different perspective one gains—despite all the distress, there is so much uplifting humanity, so much beautiful courage, so much selfless activity, from both those who have been hit by fate and from the others."[20]

After the war, to remove any ambiguity, a Bund member crossed out "relatives" and wrote in "Jewish friends." Given the timing, it is clear that Ernst's letter refers to Bund efforts to help mixed couples avoid the September 1944 deportations. Ernst coordinated Bund actions in the Ruhr, a task that involved, as he wrote, not just arranging hiding places but also providing food. Marianne Strauss later remembered how important his role had been. It was Ernst who took her to Änne Schmitz in 1944 to ask for help. Ernst's postwar denazification file includes a résumé written in February 1946, describing his wartime activities. In addition to the three Jewish women (Dore, Lisa, and Marianne) protected by the Bund, he wrote that when the Nazis began pursuing those in mixed marriages, another five Jews were hidden and fed by the group.[21]

Years later, in an interview, Ernst's wife, Ellen, offered another glimpse. Sometime near the end of 1944 she came home, she said,

> And there sits a woman, a stranger, and says, "I was given your name by Hanna Jordan and I should turn to you. We have someone we need to hide—she's been living in a shed on a garden allotment and she's going crazy. She wants to turn herself in."

The woman continued: "The war will be over next year, we all know that—the Germans are finished. So could you help?" Of course, there was no question, you know.[22]

Whether this was one of the cases Ernst referred to in his postwar statement, we do not know. But here was another instance of "Jewish" self-help; just like Marianne, Hanna was making connections while herself on the run.

Could the group claim to have actually "rescued" those they helped in the fall of 1944? In retrospect, we know that the large majority of those deported to labor camps in the fall of 1944 and those sent on to Theresienstadt in January and February 1945 did not die. Thus, for example, the Jews in mixed marriages from Solingen who, unlike Else Güldenring, were unable to elude the deportations were not killed. There was, in fact, no systematic killing policy for these deportees. The conditions were rough but survivable. Thus, to be "rescued" from deportations seldom meant the difference between life and death. Even so, the authorities were not expecting the deportees to return, and conditions were brutal enough that some did not live to see the end of the war.[23] The deportees themselves certainly feared the worst. In Remscheid, a woman being deported called out to her daughter, "We're being done in."[24] Those who risked much to help had every reason to believe that they were involved in a mission to save lives.

The Front Moves Closer

The Bund was now even more dispersed across Germany than before, with some friends in the Ruhr, some in Göttingen, others on special duty for various agencies in different parts of Germany. As conditions in the Ruhr worsened, a growing number made their way down to Meersburg, including Artur's brother and sister-in-law, Walter and Gertrud Jacobs; Grete Ströter and her children; Tilde Stürmer and her son; Karl Heilwagen's wife, Medi; Else Bramesfeld; and more. By the end of the war, some eighteen people, all of them connected to the Bund, were in the overcrowded guesthouse. For those Bund members on the front, or who had loved ones on the front, the situation was growing increasingly desperate. In the first three years of the war, up to the end of 1942, Germany had lost around a million soldiers. In the last eighteen months of the war, it lost over three million, a figure that speaks to the increasingly suicidal and irrational German war effort. Reports from the eastern front like this one, probably from August Schwab, only deepened the anxiety of friends back home:

> Everything is so much more terrible and senseless than I could ever imagine. We are on sentry duty for twelve hours at a stretch, and we also have to build our own bunker and dig the trenches. We have to walk for 2 km at night to get supplies and food. We sleep on bare ground. There's no way to dry our wet things. At night, we have to keep all our senses at the highest level of alert. In front of me, directly in my line of view, lies a dead Russian. I'm always seeing his young face and his outstretched arm. Tonight, I will have to crawl out and bury him, he allows me no peace.[25]

Walter's son, Dieter, was now involved in heavy fighting in France. Liesel Speer's son, Friedl, had enjoyed relatively safe service for two years in an army food center in the Crimea, as a result of a Wehrmacht decree preventing only sons of fallen World War I heroes from being placed in danger. But in 1944, faced with massive losses, the Wehrmacht rescinded the decree, and after training with captured Russian weapons—since there weren't enough German weapons available—Friedl was transferred to the front. Within a few weeks he was reported as missing; a year later, his mother was still without news.[26] In late July or early August, Ernst's son, Eberhard, was killed on the eastern front. This death devastated the Bund. Tall, gentle, and philosophical, Eberhard had become their great hope to carry the Bund's mantle into the new generation. With typical lack of paternal tact, Artur wrote to his son that Eberhard had been the best of his generation. Marianne's diary entries and Karlos's letters show that the group really had seen Eberhard as a future leader.[27]

In August, Gustav Gehrke went missing near Melun, a town on the Seine River south of Paris. The army report said only that he had failed to return from a defensive action on August 24. In October, still without news, his wife, Hedwig, was beside herself. The evenings, she said, belonged to the radio, her thoughts, and the soldiers. Every evening she wrote a letter to her three brothers at the front. Her letters to Bund friends show a woman twisting and turning between conviction, hope, and despair.[28]

In September or October, Bund member Fritz Denks, thirty-three years old, was badly injured in action. Since the middle of July, he wrote to Artur, he had experienced days of horror unlike anything in his three years at the front.[29] At some point that fall August Schwab's letters to the Jacobses stopped coming, and by the end of the war he had become one of the many Bund members whose fates were still unknown. At the end of 1944, Änne Engels wrote to Liesel Speer in despair that her favorite brother had died as a result of complications from shrapnel wounds in his intestines. "He suffered badly," she wrote. "I was almost paralyzed by the news. It can't be true! This is the third of my brothers to go!"[30] Käthe Franke had no idea if her son, Hans Hermann, was alive. Albert Schürmann, a witty poet from Wuppertal, also disappeared.[31] And still the war ground on.

Conditions on the home front changed just as dramatically. The real turning point for the Ruhr came in the fall of 1944. By then the Luftwaffe had been significantly diminished. Allied progress in Italy and France gave the U.S. and British air forces bases from which to attack Germany. A new Allied directive on September 25, 1944, called for intense attacks on German industrial centers and populated areas. Over half the total tonnage of bombs dropped on Germany would rain down during the last eight months of the war. From August onward, the British and U.S. air forces were conducting both daylight attacks and nighttime raids on German targets. With good visibility and undefended skies, the fighter-bombers soon targeted not only major cities but also more specific targets like trains, marshaling yards, and bridges.[32]

In October, Bund members began to experience a level of unpredictability and disruption unlike anything they had encountered previously. Karin Morgenstern was traveling back to the Ruhr from Braunschweig when her train was strafed by fighter-bombers and the track ahead destroyed. She had to complete the last six miles of her journey on foot. On a lighter note, Else wrote that she was naked in the kitchen, about to wash herself in the sink, when a full alarm sounded in daytime and she had to flee, abandoning her precious bath. Ernst arrived in Essen to find not a single tram running in the entire area. His coded account implies that he had come for a Bund meeting. Everyone who eventually arrived at the meeting had an odyssey behind them. It was a relief to see them, Ernst wrote, but "a lot of planning is simply wasted," by which he probably meant that the meeting could not take place.[33] War was no longer something you heard about on the radio or in the newspaper, he added. Now danger, threat, and uncertainty accompanied every trip into the city, every day-time task.[34]

Mixed in with these fears, Bund members also experienced profound anxiety about what awaited them down the road. One wrote Artur fear-fully about the "shortages, homelessness, cold, wet, freezing and hunger" that were to come.[35] Artur, too, allowed himself an unusually pessimistic and fearful entry in his diary on October 20, after reading an article about how the final phase of the war was likely to play out on German soil: "A feeling of horror runs through you. You think you are prepared for the worst. But the reality is always one notch more terrible than you had expected." Battle was raging in the city of Aachen, just across the Rhine from the Ruhr area, Artur continued, and there were reports of house-to-house fighting. The city's proximity and familiarity to people living in the Rhineland made this news feel threatening and immediate in a way that previous reports had not.

Supposing the Bund did manage to survive to the end of the war: Would there be anything for them to do in the postwar wasteland beyond the struggle to survive? At that year's Lichtfest, held in Meersburg, rather than looking with expectation to the new light of the coming year, the group found itself worrying that the postwar recovery would take so long that they might not live to see it completed.[36] "The coming time will be hard," Artur wrote on January 20, 1945. "Many shortages, life reduced to its most primitive. No time, no energy, no possibility to engage in the many things that used to make life easy, comfortable and beautiful."[37] But he tried to see the positive side—the opportunity to throw unnecessary ballast overboard, and to remember what was most important in life.[38]

Others, particularly Ernst, were even more somber.[39] One of the Meers-burg group, probably Lisa, sent Ernst a letter of comfort and encourage-ment. Certainly, she wrote, there would be a transitional period with many burdens: "Separations, hunger, cold, no place to live, no energy and no time for the most important things, all one's strength used up in the struggle to eke out a bare existence."[40] But not everyone would be afflicted by all these problems, she pointed out—the Bund would provide solidarity, and in any case, transport and communications could not remain severed for very long. It was inevitable that solutions would soon be found, because people could not work if they had nothing to eat and nowhere to live. Whether Lisa believed her words (which were hardly encouraging), we don't know, but the whole exchange revealed how dismal their prospects of making a difference looked in the wake of so much destruction.

Bund members whom fate or official postings had sent to the East, even those with strong Communist sympathies, shared the fear of others in their region that they might be caught by the approaching Red Army. While Doris Braune waited in Finkenkrug, near Berlin, for the Russian advance, Guste Denks was in flight westward, on a trek in which she would lose her third child. Sonja was stranded in Czechoslovakia. In January 1945, Walter's wife, Gertrud, received the last note from her sisters, stuck in Allenstein, in East Prussia, ready to flee before the Russian advance. Of the horrors that awaited them, and the loss of her father, she would hear only months after the end of the war.[41]

Besieged

By mid-July 1944 at the latest, Lisa was living permanently in Meersburg, away from the bombing.[42] But Marianne Strauss was still traveling from address to address and, as such, had to deal with the increasing risks of train travel. In a bomb shelter in Braunschweig, Marianne wrote that she had the feeling that the war was coming closer every day: "How much it devours and how frighteningly small are the personal sacrifices we've made until now!"[43] In October, she was in Duisburg during one of the most concentrated air raids of the war, Operation Hurricane. On October 14 and 15, some eighteen hundred British aircraft pummeled Duisburg. In an attack that cost more than twenty-five hundred lives, nine thousand tons of explosives were unleashed on the city. "Attacks day and night," Marianne recorded. "Yesterday and last night Duisburg. The bombs just kept falling. One dies a thousand deaths. And people manage to put up with it!" In an obviously Bund-influenced passage, she wrote of trying to rise above

selfish concerns and daily cares so that she would be able to live properly—
and die properly. But it was hard to find composure.[44]

On another occasion, Marianne was at the Wuppertal-Vohwinkel station, waiting for a train to a Solingen suburb, where she planned to stay
with Reni Sadamgrotzky, an ally she had been directed to by Bund members. Suddenly the station came under direct attack. The following day,
by which time she was ensconced at Reni's, waves of bombers flew over
without warning while they were eating lunch; bombs exploded around
the house as they fled to the cellar. The house received a direct hit, and
the whole neighborhood was destroyed in minutes. Luckily, Reni and
Marianne emerged from the cellar unharmed.[45]

By late September, the Bund had managed to find refuges for five Jews
in mixed marriages. Lisa was comparatively protected in Meersburg. Why
was Marianne still on the move? The only answer can be that the Bund
did not think it wise to arrange a lengthy stay for her somewhere. She was
too striking, too unwilling to stay hidden, as Hermann Schmalstieg had
discovered, and probably even, in the Bund's view, too disruptive to join
those staying at the guesthouse in Meersburg. (She would have been
another mouth to feed, too.) This is speculation, but it is hard to see another
explanation. Even willing helpers were having to make fine calculations
about risk.

In February 1945, however, with the Allies close on the left bank of the
Rhine, Bund member Grete Dreibholz gave Marianne the name and address
of a friend, a grammar school teacher in Düsseldorf, with whom she would
be able to stay, presumably in the hope that this would be the final, brief
leg in Marianne's journey. At six in the morning, Marianne knocked on the
door of a woman she had never met. Marianne knew that her arrival would
mean new and serious risks for the stranger. It turned out she was lucky to
have arrived just then, as Hanni Ganzer was generally in the house for only
an hour or so in the early mornings and spent the rest of the day in the
air-raid shelter. Hanni read Grete's letter of introduction and said, without
hesitation, "Of course you can stay."[46]

While Marianne was on the run, Meta Kamp-Steinmann, in Göttingen,
embarked on a private rescue action of her own. In August 1944, conscription was expanded to include sixteen-year-olds, a call that was met with
great enthusiasm: 60 percent of this age cohort joined the army within a

few weeks. Meta's son Ernst, born in October 1928, turned sixteen in October, and sometime after his birthday he, too, was mobilized. At Lebus, in the state of Brandenburg, which is today on Germany's border with Poland, he was injured by Soviet fire. After four weeks in a military hospital, he was allowed home for two weeks to recuperate.

Meta did not want him to return to the front and hoped that some friends (these were, according to Ernst, the Gehrkes) might be able to hide him. The Gehrkes owned a plot of land nearby with a small wooden hut— Ernst remembered it as having been for beekeeping. Meta was unable to contact them (Gustav Gehrke was a prisoner of war by this time), but she had access to the key. With the help of her younger son, Walter, she hid foodstuffs near the shack and made it a little more weatherproof. Then she persuaded an initially shocked Ernst to hide there. After making the rounds of relatives and neighbors, telling them he was reporting to the front, Ernst went with his mother as far as the railway station, then doubled back and ran to the hut. Walter was there with bedding and civilian clothes. He spent the first night with his older brother, and in the days following, he made regular trips back, bringing food.[47]

Utopia on Two Wood Burners

The guesthouse Haus auf dem Fohrenberg, in Meersburg, was a relatively safe place, out of the bombers' sights and, as far as we can tell, not subject overmuch to the prying eyes of the Gestapo. Located on a hillside above Lake Constance, it should have been a place of comfort and solace, a place where Bund members could mull over their plans for the future, work out their ideas in writing, and, above all, practice their communal philosophy. But the group's records tell a different story. As soon as the Jacobses arrived, in February 1944, Artur began to complain about how difficult it was to get anything done. In April, his spirits actually rose as he sped north on a train back into the danger zone—to check on their house in Essen and make contact with Bund members in the Ruhr. Again and again, we find Bund accounts—even witty poems—returning to the difficulties of living and working in Meersburg. In her later memoirs, Dore tried to put a brave face on it. Yet even thirty years after the event, she still dwelled at length on the challenges of living and working there.[48]

For Artur, Lisa, and others, the small children running around, seemingly without supervision, were a major source of irritation. The children's noise was the first thing Artur noted in his diary after arriving.[49] (In later life, those children's recollections corroborated his account, only with a different slant: they were indeed almost completely neglected, but that neglect also gave them freedom.)[50] A couple of days later, Artur sought to resume work on the *Vermächtnis*, the comprehensive statement on Bund philosophy and practice, which had proceeded with such verve in Essen. But the housemates were not able to work with the same devotion that they had shown in the Dönhof Street kitchen. There were material difficulties—the house was small for the number of people it held. With the Jacobses' arrival, there were at least thirteen people in the guesthouse's eight little rooms, sharing one living room and one kitchen, which had just two wood burners for cooking and for heating. By the end of the war, there were eighteen people. A continual stream of visitors added to the crowding. Because wood shortages were a constant problem, the kitchen was the only heated room, and even then, it was heated only when the temperature fell below fifty degrees Fahrenheit. Walter Jacobs wrote a witty poem about the different styles of the house members as they arrived in the kitchen in the morning, each yearning for something they did not find—Julie Schreiber's sense of order colliding with Dore's more chaotic style, and so on. Lisa presented her housemates with a scathing set of recommendations full of rhetorical questions, such as "In the morning in the kitchen wouldn't it be better if people did not 'moan and groan'?"[51] The knowledge that they were much better off than so many only exacerbated their irritation.[52]

In March and again in November 1944, the group held long discussions about how to improve things. In May, Artur went so far as to suggest that members—even the mothers with small children—should take turns staying in the Ruhr, despite the danger, both to help improve the atmosphere in Meersburg and to provide solidarity with their beleaguered friends to the north. It is not clear if the group ever carried out this proposal. A letter Lisa sent to Sonja in November, reflecting on discussions in the house, makes clear some of the reasons for the difficulties. This was not a collective that had been created with an eye to constructive work on a program but an emergency community fleeing persecution and war. There was no one there to help clean and look after the place, Lisa continued, and they did not have the option of caring for the children separately from the adults, though toward the end of 1944 Medi Heilwagen did help to manage and watch over them. (It remains nonetheless surprising that the group found it so difficult to manage three or four children!) What Lisa did not say explicitly was that the power dynamic of the Meersburg group was strained because of the ownership of the guesthouse. In the Essen collective, by contrast, the house was owned by the Jacobses, which put them in a position of authority consistent with the group's hierarchy. In Meersburg, this was not the case. Their hosts were Käthe Franke and Julie Schreiber, but Käthe was ill for a while and in the hospital, and she seems to have been increasingly alienated from the others.[53]

All in all, the Meersburg episode was a sad story. It is true that the house remained a center of Bund life. Dore Jacobs organized body-training workshops there, and important Bund publications were written in the kitchen. But the daily irritations, the straitened circumstances, the anxiety about those at the front, and the improvised character of the community all undermined the group's core mission: its commitment to rehearsing the rules and practices of a better society. The members soon began cooking by family, rather than together, and communal life turned into what Else called a "bitter pill to swallow."[54] It was a dispiriting endnote for a group poised to celebrate its own survival and resistance.[55]

At Risk till the Bitter End

The war dragged on longer than anyone thought possible. Already in November 1944, Artur could hear artillery pounding from the battle zone near the French town of Belfort, 130 miles away. But it took the Allies five months to cover what is today a three-hour drive. French troops entered Meersburg only on April 29, 1945, as Waffen-SS forces retreated to their final holdout farther east in the Austrian Vorarlberg.[56]

Meanwhile, in Düsseldorf, Marianne Strauss and Hanni Ganzer were faring little better. The Bund had arranged for Marianne to stay there in February 1945, hoping that the war would be over in a few days, since the

Allies were already just across the Rhine. But the German forces put up a bitter defense, and it was more than two months before the two women's vigil was over. They were spending up to twenty-three hours of each day in the shelter. When she could, Marianne would slip out and order a ration-free meal from one of the inns that was still functioning. Outside, she faced a double danger: American shells and Gestapo controls. In the bunker, she was protected from the former but not the latter. The local Nazi branch offices were next door. One of Marianne's relatives heard from her after the war that she had been stopped on one occasion but let go. Some officials had become more lenient, already mindful of the need for an alibi after the war. Others were intensifying their commitment to the regime. "Almost every night there was a raid in search of deserters," Marianne wrote a few weeks after liberation. "I always had to reckon with the possibility of being caught at the last minute, after surviving so many other dangers."[57] Two days before liberation, a Jewish man was discovered nearby and publicly hanged.[58]

Marianne's notes from this time show her more conscious of this looming threat than ever before. "We live with a thousand fears," she wrote to Maria Briel, "with danger always just around the corner, with constant premonitions of death by one means or another." Throughout this period, she spent a great deal of time writing in her diary "like someone possessed, in order to keep a record of the crazy, dreamlike, unbelievable life of those days."[59] It was not until April 17 that the U.S. 97th Infantry entered Düsseldorf and Marianne was saved.

By that point, the tension in Meersburg was acute. Bund members listened to every radio broadcast, tracking the reported battle positions on their maps. In a diary entry from April 9, Dore tried to record the day's discussions, which focused on the question "Can I attain faith through an act of will?" Ironically and rather touchingly, she found herself unable to impose her will on her thoughts and continually circled around another question: "When will the end come?" She thought of the heavy bombers that flew overhead at night, on to their metropolitan targets, and the low-flying fighters during the day. "It's coming closer," she wrote—that much was clear. "Will it end soon?" she asked. So many victims were dying every day. Everyone knew the fighting was utterly pointless. People were talking more openly with one another, taking more risks. Still, no one knew what to expect in the days to come. "All we can do is wait," Dore noted. "Hopefully it won't be long." Trying to hold on to the promise of a better future, she concluded, "I know that we have to get through this last diffi- cult phase and then a new life will begin. We will be free of this diabolical power that has held us in thrall for so many years."[60]

Dore had another worry. Would they have to flee the house? There was no chance of traveling very far, but it seemed possible that they might have to hide in the forest or make their way to nearby Schiggendorf. It is not clear whether her fear was that their house on the hillside would be exposed to enemy fire or that German forces moving through the area would identify her or the group as undesirables and kill them on the spot. Her trepidation was not unwarranted, since Waffen-SS troops were sta- tioned in the area.[61]

On Sunday, April 29, the group gathered for a discussion in the sun- room, where they had, for once, indulged themselves by building a fire.[62] The topic was "forms of political life in the future." They had almost resigned themselves to the fact that the war would last at least another day when the siren sounded, indicating imminent attack. For the next fifteen minutes, they rushed to gather their "emergency packs," which contained not emergency rations but, rather, those "treasures, the intellectual ones and the material ones," that they did not want to abandon. Dore's account of what happened next, scrawled hurriedly perhaps later that day or the next, shows that she was still utterly immersed in the events of that "Sun- day we will never forget."

With their packs, they returned to their discussion in the sunroom. As the surrounding area was under aerial bombardment, and machine guns rattled away nearby, it was not easy to think. Then came artillery fire. Some 150 Waffen-SS men barreled out of the woods, running past their house and up a nearby hill. According to Dore, the Bundists heard the "farmers' boys" in Waffen-SS uniforms complaining that they did not want to get into the fight but had been forced to engage by their "fanatic lieutenant." Now their artillery was on the hill and aiming at the French tanks. Dore won- dered why no one was willing to "sacrifice"—i.e., shoot—the lieutenant to spare the *Heimat*, the homeland. Around eleven-thirty, there was a terrible crash, as something detonated outside their front door. As they rushed down to the guesthouse's two cellars, there were two more loud reports.

They stood in the cellars, Dore noted, "shaken but even more, distraught. We hadn't expected that—and also not deserved it." The Bund members must have concluded that the shells were from the French, trying to root out the Waffen-SS. Käthe, the co-owner of the house, "rushed determinedly upstairs and hung out a white sheet." Dore went on: "It's a game of roulette. If we don't hang it out, the French shoot at us, if we do, the SS."

Dore's animated entry offers not just a poignant vision of the Bund members trying valiantly to discuss postwar politics with the sound of machine guns and heavy artillery in the background but also a rare account of her uncensored thoughts in a moment of acute tension. It also reveals an unexpected belief in the nation's honor, one that is almost entirely absent in postwar accounts. What did it mean to say that "we had not deserved this"? Dore complained angrily that the Waffen-SS were "attacking their own *Volksgenossen*," or countrymen. She noted, too, that Nazis had been fleeing through the area with trucks full of possessions. It wouldn't do them any good, she observed, but "that does not diminish the shame in which they are wrapping themselves and their supposed ideals of people and fatherland and heroism and soldier's honor." All this suggested some disappointed expectation that Germany's leaders would act with honor, as well as a sense that they, the Bund members, were being let down as part of the German people. Germans' collective identity as a beleaguered nation (orchestrated by the Nazis but not simply a Nazi idea) was so powerful that it invaded the vision even of regime opponents like Dore.

Dore's report of the last hours before liberation is full of uncertainty. From eleven-thirty till two in the afternoon, the sounds of the battle moved closer. A phone call from a neighbor came in: for God's sake, get rid of the white flag, or the SS will flatten the house. But, Dore wrote, they "left it flying there." The Bund group again split up between the two cellars. Dore's group cleared a path to the windows and placed chairs underneath them, so that if necessary, they could climb out. Medi played board games with the children to distract them. Around five p.m., they learned that French troops were in the neighborhood, searching the houses for arms. The Waffen-SS forces retreated to their final holdout in the Austrian Vorarlberg.[63]

It is doubtless a sign of their utter exhaustion that Dore's report ends with no liberation, no relief, no sigh, just a single (rather German) sentiment: "And then we had to clear up."

9

Our Flock Has Grown Lonely

Liberation

Gathered around the radio on the evening of May 1, the Meersburg group heard a stunning announcement. "Hitler Dead!" Artur exclaimed in his diary. "Where and how, nobody knows. Not much more on the radio than this short report. Two days after Mussolini!" Once they heard the additional news that the Nazi administration in Baden (the area to which Meersburg belonged) had fallen, it began to sink in that they had been liberated. Other parts of Germany would have to endure a few more days before Germany's formal capitulation, but as Artur recorded in his diary disbelievingly, the Bund members could now venture outside without fear: "We can now be seen as what we are."[1] The change was almost impossible to take in, Dore wrote to a friend, fear had lodged itself so deeply. For the children, too, the sudden shift was hard to process. Eberhard Stürmer, just five years old at the time, recalled being terrified by the celebratory fireworks the French soldiers set off on May 8.[2] A few weeks later, one of the Ströter children shocked the group by greeting occupation forces with "Heil Hitler."[3]

Liberation also meant no more war—no longer facing the threat of bombs and artillery, no more disturbed nights, no more days spent running back and forth to the shelters, no more worrying for the safety of loved ones in battle. The reaction of most Germans in this moment was relief that they were alive, but for the Bund this was often eclipsed by amazement at being free. For the Meersburg group, who had been spared some or all of the Ruhr's intense experience of bombing, release from war ranked second to the end of persecution. At last they could go for walks again and roam the nearby fields and farms freely, marveled Else Bramesfeld; they could "live openly, be the Bund again. How wonderful!"[4]

The long years of opposing Hitler and helping persecuted Jews were over. Dore, Lisa, Marianne, Grete Menningen, Else Güldenring, and all the others the Bund had helped and sheltered were safe. What did this mean now for the group? How would it emerge out of the struggle against Nazism? Would it be able to play a part in rebuilding a new Germany? And would it be recognized for its struggle?

Ready for the Future

Earlier that same day, May 1, International Workers' Day, Artur had given a speech to the group.[5] "Today we celebrate the victory of the world over National Socialism," he began. "The only people who can understand what that means are those who lived under this terrible physical and spiritual pressure, always fending off attacks from the system and always in danger." Withstanding twelve long years of constant peril had been much harder than pulling off a single daredevil deed, he said. He reminded everyone of the threats that had been ever present under Nazi rule: job dismissals, house searches, Gestapo surveillance, imprisonment, and, of course, the horrific concentration camps. Harder still, though, had been to resist being co-opted by the system. When every sphere of life was claimed by the regime, maintaining their integrity had meant living as outcasts. They had been put in a position of wishing for the defeat of their own country, welcoming the bombing attacks that set their houses on fire, or cheering for the ground-attack aircraft that turned every rail journey into a high-risk adventure. It had been possible to remain resolute only by looking beyond self-interest to the needs of the German people and of humanity as a whole:

That we remained strong, that not a single one of us fell by the
wayside, even among those who lived far from us, that is a glo-
rious page in the Bund's history. And that we remained alive,
that we lived through this time <u>awake</u>, that we matured and
grew—we owe all that to the Bund.[6]

The group had shined a light into every corner, Artur said, and had
demonstrated beyond doubt that the Nazi system had not contained the
smallest space for human decency. But the Bund had never wanted to
engage in mere critique, and had lived by its own values. It had even reached
out to other Germans chafing under the system, educating and encouraging them. The Bund had been a source of life, work, politics, historical
research, philosophy, a new spirituality, celebration, and more. But all this
alone would not have prevented the group from feeling utterly marginalized, Artur continued. What saved them was their ability to discern the
underlying laws of history. The Bund had come to recognize not only
that the Nazi regime was doomed by its own hand but also that a new
and better era was inevitably on its way. "Today," he continued, "we are
witnessing more than victory. We are witnessing the dawning of a new
world."[7]

Their experience, and their vision of past and future, he concluded, this
"is our first of May."

Artur was an impassioned orator, and his reckoning with the Nazi years
would have electrified his listeners. Isolated in the primitive conditions of
their house on Lake Constance, blinking in the bright light of their newly
attained freedom, they must have felt not only powerfully vindicated but
also somehow transported from the margins to the center of history. Link-
ing, for the first time, the lessons of life under the Nazi past to the future,
Artur told the group that its hard-won insights had equipped it to lead.
He dubbed their experience *"erlittene Erkenntnis,"* an understanding won
through suffering. As a community modeling the good society through
daily practices, the Bund had always sought to provide a living, ethical
example for others to follow. But in this speech Artur recast everything
they had done up until 1933 as simply youthful experimentation. Only in
the struggle against Nazism had the group reached a mature understanding of the world.

Freedom's Frustrations

For all the joy at being free, the early days after the war contained tensions and uncertainties. Even if one regarded the occupying forces as liberators, how would they behave? In the Ruhr, Braunschweig, Göttingen, and Hamburg, Bund members were confronted, briefly, with American forces, and then the British Military Government. For Doris Braune, near Berlin, it was the Russians who were now in charge. Meersburg fell under the French military's jurisdiction, and in the days following liberation, there seemed a strong likelihood that the French authorities would seize the guesthouse to use for their personnel as well as a place to put up signal antennae. However, according to the diary of a local citizen, Ilse van Dyk, discussions with the new city commander, Major Quantin, successfully protected the house "in recognition of the Jewish fellow citizens who were hidden among us for years."[8] Meanwhile, in their respective locations near Berlin and in Göttingen, both Doris and Meta experienced protection or largesse from former forced laborers they had helped. These were small signs from the outside world that they had been on the right side, after all.

The Bund had never aspired to become a community withdrawn from the world; indeed, *Weltfremdheit*, unworldly utopianism, was anathema to their philosophy. In order to be a model, they understood, they would have to be seen and heard. During the Nazi period, the Bund's ability to reach beyond its own network had been severely circumscribed. Now, at war's end, Bund members were aching to be active and engage with others once more. But first they would have to endure months of restrictions and difficulty, as the occupying forces consolidated their rule.

Only a week after liberation, Artur was already grumbling about the everyday problems that put them at risk of forgetting the magnitude of what had just happened.[9] In the Ruhr, most Bund members had been bombed out of their homes and were trying to cope with their miserable makeshift accommodations. The Schuberts had lost their home and were living with Erich and Trude Nöcker in the Blockhaus. Strangers had been assigned to rooms in the Jacobses' Essen residence on Dönhof Street. The Meersburg group, though conscious of how much they had been spared, were busy contending with the problems of keeping warm, feeding all the occupants from a primitive and defective stove, collecting wood, growing

vegetables, and so on. In the immediate aftermath of German defeat, shortages and shuttered shops made obtaining food a daily struggle. Within a
couple of weeks of the end of war, they were again able to obtain basic
rations, but it took enterprise and endurance. The official rations were low,
and the stresses of the war had left all the older Bund members weakened
and vulnerable to illness. They were all fearful that in the coming years,
their material conditions would only be worse.[10]

Military occupation initially brought severe limitations on movement
and communication. Until June, the two Bund centers, in Meersburg and
the Ruhr, were completely disconnected. No one knew who was still alive
or where. Worrisome questions about the fate of the Bundists' friends in
the armed forces were always in the back of their minds. Georg Reuter
was missing, as were Albert Schürmann, Alfred Ströter, and August
Schwab, last reported in the Caucasus. So, too, were a number of Bund
sons who had been called up, including Friedl Speer, Dieter Jacobs, and
Hans Hermann Franke. Then there were the Bund friends and relatives
who had been fleeing from and possibly caught up by the Soviet advance
in the eastern territories: Guste Denks, Gertrud Jacobs's family, and Sonja,
who had been looking after Essen children evacuated to the Sudetenland.
There was no news from the émigrés in Holland—neither from Erna
Michels, hiding in Roermond, nor from Friedl. The Meersburg group did
not know who had survived in the Ruhr, which had undergone an intense
final phase of bombing and artillery attacks. Indeed, it was not until June
that they received word even from Karin Morgenstern, who was living
just a few miles down the road from Meersburg. The joy of liberation was
constantly tempered by fears about what might have befallen family and
comrades.[11]

There were some happy reunions. In June 1945, the doorbell at the
Meersburg guesthouse rang and everyone rushed down, wondering who
it would be. It turned out to be Reinhold Ströter, who had managed to make
his way back to Grete and the children by walking for four days from Stuttgart. Dore confessed that she could not suppress a tiny twinge of disappointment that it was not her beloved Sonja walking through the door. In
July, Walter's son, Dieter, returned. A few days later, another veteran, Alfred
Stürmer, whose wife, Tilde, and son, Eberhard, were among the Meersburg party, turned up at the house. "What joy rang out!" wrote Dore.[12] Yet

even three months after the end of the war, many fellow Bund members remained unaccounted for. It would be almost the end of the year before Dore had the deep pleasure of being reunited with Friedl and getting to know him as an adult, in some ways so familiar, and yet so different.[13]

As much as these trials and tribulations, however, one other factor that tested the Bund members' patience was the fact that they were being given no part in rebuilding the country. Many on the left had taken hope from Eisenhower's proclamation in a radio broadcast in December 1944 that German workers would be able to organize as soon as conditions allowed. But wary of radicalism on both the left and the right, the western Allies kept a tight lid on political revival. Most of the mayors that the military government put in office were conservative Christian figures, particularly where the left was weak, as in Meersburg. This was not the democratic renewal the Bund had yearned for.[14]

As a leading figure in the reviving Communist Party in Wuppertal, Ernst Jungbluth could at least take satisfaction in being part of a lively and emergent political scene. In Meersburg—that "little provincial morass," as Else called it—Bund members felt intensely frustrated at the lack of serious renewal.[15] "I don't understand you!" Artur wrote angrily to the local mayor, complaining that after twelve years of oppression, their first instinct should not be to call for "order and artificial harmony." The task was to create a new world, difficult as that might be.[16]

During these early months, the Bundists were able to engage with their fellow Germans only on a limited basis, often just one to one, much as they had during the Nazi years. Now, instead of trying to alert their neighbors to the evils of a depraved political system, the group found itself reminding them of Germany's responsibility for its current mess. Germans, they argued, should stop complaining, because they had deserved a great deal worse than they were getting. At different times, Artur and Else fumed with unaccustomed venom about neighbors who griped about their misfortunes, seemingly oblivious to what had been done to others in their name.[17] Sonja, unbeknownst to the rest of the Bund at the time, was undergoing a brutal eviction from Czechoslovakia and ended up in a refugee camp in Thuringia. Later, she described her efforts to make her fellow refugees understand their fate. We have only a crude English translation from a letter she wrote after her return to Essen:

How often times did these people ask when I stood in line with
them for hours waiting for a meager soup in a refugee's camp:
"with what did we deserve this?" Then, I showed the severe guilt,
told of the people sacrificed, the thousand who were tortured
to death without that we even looked at it, not to speak of something we did in order to prevent it or ease it.[18]

Sonja was playing the same courageous role in the food line as she had
in the ration office in Essen in 1939. In that case, the Gestapo had hauled
her in for questioning. Now there was no secret police to harass her. But
would her words have any more impact on her neighbors? "You cannot
believe," she wrote (this is from the same poor translation), "how deadly
sick these people are in whom the poisoning of years has wasted away and
destroyed all forces of life so that no will power remained to rid of the yoke
and no hope for new building and revival is alive."

Given the restrictions the military government continued to impose on
political activity, which compounded their frustrated hopes for the new
era, Bund members took to passionate letter writing. Dore's first missives
were written "wallowing in the illusory fantasy" that peace would enable
her immediately to reconnect to Wasja and Tove in the United States.[19]
This was also a time of intense conversation and energetic planning for the
moment when they hoped they'd be called on to act. Despite all the frus-
trations of communal living, the Meersburg group managed to spend two
hours a day working on new texts and pamphlets. Dore "discovered her
political side," and the group marveled at Artur's renewed energy. He
recorded events in his diary, developed topics for leaflets and pamphlets,
and wrote scripts for potential radio broadcasts. In early June, he read his
recently finished piece "Who Was Hitler?," which struck many of his companions as profound and incisive. Near the end of August, Dore wrote to
Bund friends abroad with a list of more than twenty pamphlets the group
had written about the recent past and the current situation, including *All
the Sacrifices! And All in Vain!*, *I Was Forced into the Party, I Could Not Help It*, and
The "Decent Nazis."[20]

In June, the military government eased some restrictions on movement.
The adventurous could begin thinking of traveling farther afield. Toward
the end of the month, Ernst's enterprising older daughter, Helga, came

down from the Ruhr on a freight train to help Lisa return home.[21] After a couple of months, Else followed them north. In a letter sent to Tove in October 1945, Else conveyed a sense of what train journeys were like then:

> I can tell you, travelling in Germany to-day is an adventure! A trip from Meersburg to Düsseldorf (400–500 miles) takes at least 3–5 days, on open coal trains, in wind and rain, day and night. If one is lucky the train keeps on moving steadily, if not one has to wait around at railroad stations. Once in a while one catches a passenger or even an express train for a few hours ride. Another problem is to procure food for so many days of travel in advance, and to obtain the travel permit to pass the "borders" between occupation zones. I waited for 6 weeks, and then took the risk to travel without—and succeeded![22]

That same month, the political passivity in Meersburg became too much for Artur. He resolved to return to the Ruhr, despite the continuing challenges of undertaking such a journey, and despite the fact that it meant leaving Dore behind. She was not well enough to cope with either the rigors of early postwar train travel or the very limited food supplies in the Ruhr.

Letters began pouring in from farther afield and even from overseas. The Meersburg group learned that Guste Denks's third child had died during their flight west, and that Gertrud Jacobs's father was lost, presumed to have perished while fleeing East Prussia. Her sisters had fallen into Soviet hands. "I don't know any further details," Gertrud wrote in December 1945, "only that they have suffered terribly. They can't bring themselves to write about it."[23] Dore, Else, and others learned now that Sonja, too, had endured a great deal. After living in the refugee camp in Thuringia, she had made it home only with great difficulty.[24]

Yet for all these tragedies, the Bund also learned that the war had been much kinder to the large majority of its members than they could have possibly hoped. No one in the Bund had been killed. The missing servicemen had either returned home—Albert Schürmann had managed to avoid falling into Soviet hands and had made his way, much of it on foot, back to Germany—or had been able to send word to their loved ones that they were in captivity. Karlos Morgenstern was in American hands; Gustav Gehrke was being held by the French.[25] Friedl Speer endured two brutal years mining uranium for the Soviets, and would eventually return to his mother in 1947, terribly thin but alive. Käthe Franke's son, Hans Hermann, was also a POW. The group hoped that they would soon hear from Erna Michels. "Our friends are alive and are heathy," Dore wrote, "doesn't that seem like a miracle?"[26]

The Chance of Renewal

The western Allies were somewhat more cautious than their Soviet counterparts when it came to allowing political groups to revive, but gradually they, too, began licensing political parties, first at the local level, then for the regions and the zones. Communists and Social Democrats quickly reorganized and for a while, at least, were determined to work together, mindful that divisions had weakened their opposition to the Nazis before 1933. A new party of the center, the Christian Democratic Union (CDU), was similarly conscious of the fragmentation of the pre-Nazi political scene—in this case aspiring to overcome the divisions between Protestant and Catholic parties in the Weimar era. Though it would soon move to the right, in the early postwar years, the CDU embraced many left-wing ideas.

Ordinary Germans, too, were initially receptive to calls for reform, not least because they were fearful that the German war crimes would lead to severe retribution, and they wanted to distance themselves from the former regime. With Germany divided between the occupying powers, it was not at all clear what its future shape would be—or even if there would be a future Germany. Though it was never really official U.S. policy, Germans were aware of the so-called Morgenthau Plan, drafted by U.S. treasury secretary Henry Morgenthau, which envisaged Germany's partition and partial deindustrialization, including dismantling all Ruhr industry not destroyed by bombs. Until 1947, there still seemed a chance that the four Allies would be able to agree on what to do with their occupied area, so the outcome was likely also to bear Stalin's imprint.

For the Bund, the revival of political life was an opportunity to lead. The group saw itself as having passed test after test in the brutal laboratory of Nazi rule and felt profoundly vindicated. The members also saw Hitler's fall as proof that history was on their side.[27] In December 1945, celebrating the Bund's first Lichtfest in freedom and reviewing the momentous changes the year had brought, Artur offered a powerful and emotional address, in which he argued that history had served as Hitler's judge and jury. In a world destined in the long run to embrace the inevitable logic of international cooperation, Hitler's ultranationalism had been counterhistorical. Hitler had, in fact, been so effective in mobilizing national energies that he had summoned an unprecedented global anti-German coalition into being. He had thus unwittingly accelerated the very long-term trends that were always going to be his undoing.

"Evil has done marvels," Artur proclaimed. "It has forged a fractured world together—not only for this fight, already that is a marvel, but for a shared rebuilding of the world."[28] The old divisions had broken down, the capitalist system had been shaken to its foundations, and everything was driving forward toward economic, social, cultural, and spiritual restructuring. Even the capitalist democracies, he believed, were increasingly moving in a socialist direction. The need to ensure international peace was drawing former ideological enemies together to create the foundations for enduring stability. In short, Artur's claim was that the underlying logic of historical development, by brutal and unexpected means, was proving them right. The faith the group had forged in the moment of its deepest terrors was now unbreakable.[29]

Though they were critical of their fellow Germans' acquiescence to the Nazis, Bund members showed remarkably little resentment toward neighbors whom just a year earlier they had feared as potential informants. Despite all they had been through, they had not lost their inveterate optimism in their ability to teach and others' ability to learn, once shown the truth. As Artur suggested in his Lichtfest speech, the disorientation of the immediate postwar period had made the German people unusually open to new ideas.[30] Perhaps circles the Bund had not been able to reach in the past might be open to their message now.[31]

Reinvigorated, the Bund returned to work with renewed enthusiasm. For Lisa, there was an additional question to weigh. Relatives abroad invited her to leave Germany. But, like many other survivors, she felt that "now that I have come through thanks to the help, the endless help, of my friends—I could never have done it alone—now I have to begin a new life, one that has value, and not just a safe retirement abroad."[32] Marianne, though not formally a Bund member, felt similarly inspired to commit to the cause and became a regular participant in meetings, an enthusiastic writer of affidavits on behalf of her former helpers, as well as a correspondent for the Communist newspaper *Die Freiheit*.[33]

Writing to Wasja in the fall of 1945—now that letters could be freely sent to the States—Dore marveled at how much Lisa, for one, was doing:

> She is in the thick of it! Work and more work. Women's Training College and Kindergarten Teaching College Elberfeld, Movement Choir of the Working Youth of Duisburg-Mülheim, Adult Education Classes, and writing all kinds of pieces.[34]

In November 1945, Lisa once again began to offer *Körperbildung*, or physical education training, at the Bund school. Meanwhile, as a Communist representative in the Wuppertal city administration, Ernst was tirelessly participating in committee after committee, particularly in education and youth policy, while seeking to extend the Bund's influence.[35] In the fall of 1945, Artur, Lisa, and others were able to resume teaching at adult education institutes, which had been such an important activity for them in the Weimar period. In March 1946, after the last lecture of the first semester was over, Artur wandered home full of optimism for the future and profoundly touched and moved by the students' response. "The soil has been tilled," he said. "Now we have to plant new seeds."[36]

By the fall of 1946, the Bund's Weimar palette of activities was being applied to the postwar canvas in bold strokes and vivid colors. There were the monthly meetings of all Bund members, as well as weekly meetings of local groups. Adult education courses were held in Wuppertal and Mülheim—and, before long, were expanded to Essen, Marl, and Krefeld. (By 1948, Bund members would be offering eight separate lecture series simultaneously in Wuppertal alone.) Overall, some twenty to thirty events a week were the norm. The Bund created a new "circle of friends," specifically aimed at interested non-members, which met on a monthly basis. The group held various political education meetings, some for the "friends" and some for core members. In October 1946, a new beginners class was inau-

gurated at the Bundesschule für Körperbildung und rhythmische Erziehung, and on November 1, the first group moved into its second year. Lisa
was teaching gymnastics for kindergarten teachers at a women's training
college in Wuppertal and offering a class on physiotherapy for children.
In 1947, the Bund offered no fewer than four different summer camps and
excursions for different groups, including mothers, youths, the participants
in their adult education courses, and the pupils at the Bundesschule. It also
intensified its outreach to other youth organizations, arranging presenta-
tions to the Communist Free German Youth (FDJ), the Naturfreunde, a
youth conference organized by the International Fellowship of Reconciliation, and others.[37] Despite the emerging tensions of the Cold War, on the
ground Communists and Social Democrats were still committed to working together.[38]

All in all, this was a striking testament to the Bund's energy and commitment, especially considering how difficult material conditions were. For
any members not on a pension, there was the pressing task of earning a
living. Many, like Alfred Stürmer, had seen their careers disrupted by the
global depression and the war—and now they had to find a way to put
food on the table once again. Some, like Fritz Denks, had suffered permanent injury and could not resume their former careers. Others, like Tilde
Stürmer and Grete Dreibholz, had been fired from promising office jobs
for political reasons in the 1930s and now struggled to find their way back.

In late 1946 and 1947, the food supply in the British Zone, which
included the Ruhr, dropped to such disastrously low levels that Britain felt
obliged to introduce bread rationing at home in order to keep their former
enemy alive. Though they never succumbed to self-pity, Bund members'
private correspondence was full of the food crisis. The massive shortages
and destruction made every group activity difficult. Travel remained complicated and unpredictable. There was a paucity of suitable venues for
meetings. Because the Catholic church had taken over the Blockhaus and
continued to offer services there, the Bund did not regain access to its
meeting hall until the spring of 1948. Even when a gathering place could
be found, infrastructure and supplies were lacking. A Bund meeting in a
youth hostel in 1947 depended on members bringing not only ration cards,
foodstuffs, and blankets but also lightbulbs.[39]

Under these conditions, the Bund's émigré members were an important source of material and moral support. Amid the bitter shortages of the postwar years, Wasja and Tove, in the States, proved to be indefatigable suppliers of gym shoes, women's clothing, socks, slippers, a scarf, figs, nuts, chocolate, and much more. Pages of letters from Else, Erna in Holland, and others overflow with thanks and appreciation for all the wonderful parcels sent from America. After the deutsche mark was introduced, everything was available in the shops—but only if you had money, and many Bund members had little to spare. As late as October 1949, a report on a meeting of the Bund in Düsseldorf still made special mention of the "coffee from America" that made a real coffee break possible.[40]

Creating a Public Record of Resistance and Rescue

In the late 1920s and early 1930s, the Bund had produced a series of publications (books and journals printed under the Bund imprint) designed to introduce the Bund and spread its message to the wider world.[41] Censorship and paper shortages in the early postwar period made it impossible for the group to do the same. It received a print license only after the currency reform and the introduction of the deutsche mark in June 1948, by which time paper was freely available, but the costs were prohibitive.[42] At that point, there were only two pamphlets the Bund felt warranted the expense of printing: the second and third of a three-part statement of purpose termed "Letters Abroad."[43]

The "Second Letter," which was formally titled "From the Illegal Work of the Bund" and completed in late 1946 or 1947, began with a brief introduction to the Bund's history before 1933, then focused on the group's illegal activities under Nazi rule. The "Third Letter," completed later in 1947 or perhaps even early 1948 and titled "Illegal Life," analyzed how and why the group had managed to survive and act under the Nazis.

The designation "Letters Abroad" reminds us how significant the international community was in shaping Germany's future. The "First Letter," written in 1946 (which the group probably felt was no longer relevant by the time they got their print license in 1948), explicitly addressed the citizens of the Allied countries. The letter was sent to the Bund's émigré members, and the Bund clearly hoped they would act as conduits to influential Allied figures.[44] By 1948, the Bund was thinking more of domestic recipients of its message, but it retained the subtitle "Letters Abroad" probably to indicate that the group had international strong connections— still an important claim in an occupied Germany so dependent on Allied decisions.[45]

These pamphlets offer the Bund's first public reckoning with its Nazi past. They show that Bund members saw their Nazi record not just as an enormously testing experience now behind them but also as vital political capital. This had been evident already in Artur's remarks at the end of the war, and a couple of weeks later in May 1945 when Ernst Jungbluth submitted an appeal (in English) to the local military authorities:

> The Allied Occupation Authority has marked as her most important task the extermination of fascism and militarism in Germany. To this purpose it is necessary to crush the fascistic and militaristic power-apparatus as well as to do a deep-going and radical cleaning of the world of ideas and feelings of our people. The latter is a long-range task which can be solved only with the assistance of the German people. It will consist essentially of educational and enlightening work in word and script, and can be done by people only who have not been affected by all these years of national-socialistic poisoning because they firmly had been anchored in a spiritually and morally sound life.
>
> My friends and I have the strong desire to assist in this work. We believe that we do have the qualifications on account of our life during the last 20 years in Germany.
>
> I belong to a movement which continuously before and after 1933 has fought this system with all possible means. To this movement belong college graduates, teachers, middle class men and women, workers, Jews and Gentiles, who have been active in various cities in Germany, especially in the industrial district of the Ruhr. Until lately we had contact with emigrated friends in USA, Sweden and Holland.
>
> Especially we took care of the Jews. We hid and fed our own Jewish friends, helped the half-Jews since Sept 1944 in the same

way, and organized a package service for the deported Jews in
Poland and Theresienstadt.[46]

The "First Letter" made the point even more forcefully that the group's
Nazi record equipped it to lead. It argued that for a postwar Germany desperately needing a new direction, only those who had endured a life of
trial and danger under Nazi rule, and above all those who had learned the
right lessons from their painful experience, were in a position to provide
guidance. The final sentence of the "First Letter" concluded:

> One could almost say that the whole structure, the whole
> makeup of the Bund . . . and its illegal work during the twelve
> years of darkness, were all simply a prelude, in which we worked
> toward and readied ourselves for this historical moment.[47]

Of course, the idea that the Nazi period was simply a "prelude" was one
that could be voiced only in retrospect. Back in the 1930s, the Bund had
been devastated by the realization that it no longer had a mission. Having
to conduct its activities in secret, it could not be a model for others. But in
the group's postwar narrative, it was this lonely struggle that had given its
members their new insights into the workings of history and prepared them
for future leadership. Nazi tyranny and all the hardship thus remained in
view, but something significant was no longer visible: the group's despair
at the time that it had become pointless. Here was the delicate irony. If
there was one key word for the Bund in staking its claim in the postwar
period, it was that it had continued to "live" in Nazi Germany—that is, it
had gained vibrant, meaningful, lived experience. Yet the more the group
marshaled its memories to establish its postwar fitness to lead, the more
the complexity of lived experience—with its despair, fears, and more—
slipped out of view.

For anyone seeking to learn about the group's Nazi years, the "Second"
and "Third" letters nevertheless provide a natural starting point, offering
a vivid account of the group's actions and wise insights into the reasons
for its success. Yet the picture that emerges from the "Letters" is subtly different to the one provided by the wartime sources. In part, as the remark

about the prelude shows, this is the logical result of looking back with hind-sight. Other exclusions seem more deliberate.

In the "Letters Abroad," the war, for example, is strikingly absent. There is just one brief reference to the bombing, and then only to affirm that lively conversations had continued during the raids.[48] When we recall all that the war had wrought—separations, combat, bombing raids, the general dis-ruption of ordinary life—the absence of reference to its terrors is note-worthy. One reason for minimizing the war's place in the narrative was that Bund members were shocked by their neighbors' ability to forget what had been unleashed on the world in Germany's name. "Everything is judged only from today's perspective," argued the "First Letter," "as though there had been no past, no provocation of war, no Lidices, no extermination camps, no Night and Fog decrees, no millions murdered."[49] (Lidice was the Czech town whose population was massacred in reprisal for the assassina-tion of Reinhard Heydrich, and the Night and Fog decrees had delivered many foreign citizens in the occupied territories to the concentration camps.) Confronted with such forgetfulness, the Bund felt a duty not to foreground Germany's wartime suffering.[50] The Bund's decision to focus its narrative squarely on Nazi terror was reinforced by the obvious point that having endured total war was not something that differentiated Bund members from their German neighbors. Highlighting the group's distinc-tive stance meant foregrounding opposition and persecution.

The "Letters Abroad" also play down—indeed, ignore—the Jewish connections and milieu that had once been such an important part of the Bund's social fabric. This is at its clearest in another postwar pamphlet, the group's *Report on the Help Operation for Jews by the "Bund" Community for Socialist Life*, written in 1946 or 1947.[51] Though not widely disseminated (again, pre-sumably because of restrictions), it offers the most comprehensive account of the actions the group had undertaken for Jews. It ascribes those actions not to "cheap empathy" but, rather, to the group's sense of responsibility for injustice wherever it occurred. Just as in earlier periods Bundists had spoken out in public on behalf of workers, women, black people, colonial peoples, minorities, and other oppressed, the report said, now the Bund had had to intervene on behalf of Jews, and for the Jews above all, as the group hardest hit by persecution. Far from acting on the basis of arbitrary human sympathy, it claimed, they had in fact felt obliged to help those whose way of life was alien.[52] It seems that to establish the group's credentials, the Bund felt it essential to emphasize the ethical roots of its activities. German Jews and the Bund thus appear as separate entities. The Bund's prewar and wartime Jewish connections, connections that were so important in creating bonds with the persecuted, remain invisible.

None of these omissions were the result of loss of memory or forgetting; none were made out of malice. But they do show how the postwar vantage point, the needs of the moment and a sense of what the wider world was looking for, colored the picture of the past. In places, the Bund also felt under pressure to use vague and grandiose language that implied that it had operated on a far larger scale than it had or indeed could have done. As we will see, this would come back to haunt the group in later years.

Grappling with Change

Would the Bund's political message continue to resonate and grow in postwar Germany? Any would-be activists faced not only mountains of rubble but also a society transformed. Even before the Ruhr's cities were flattened by Allied bombs, the Bund's natural habitat had been pulverized by Nazi terror. The Ruhr's left-wing milieu had been shattered, and the left-liberal Jewish circles on which the Bund had also drawn had been murdered or were in exile. For more than twelve years, the group had had few opportunities to recruit new members. The Bund knew that it could not simply pick up where it had left off.

The biggest challenge was connecting to young people. During the war, Artur, Dore, Ernst, and others had worried that the younger generation— including the Bund children—had succumbed to the regime's ideas. Even when not mouthing Nazi slogans, the young seemed cynical and unreachable. The Bund was not alone in such apprehensions; in fact, the early postwar years saw an explosion of commentators bemoaning a youth "crisis." Some feared that it would be hard to reverse the Nazi indoctrination. Others—and this was the predominant concern—worried that young people had lost their moral compass. There was no lack of hypocrisy here, as older generations consciously or unconsciously used these scare stories about immoral youths to forget their own complicity in Nazi crimes.[53]

This charge could not be leveled at the Bund. Dore's lengthy "Appeal to Youth," written in 1946, began with a forthright preface "to the older generation." Dore noted, "The young mistrust us—and they have reason to do so."[54] Postwar Germany, she went on, should be absolutely uncompromising in eradicating those forces that exerted a negative influence on the young—but it needed to approach young people themselves with solidarity and forbearance. At the same time, Dore argued, young people were in desperate need of guidance.[55] Before and after the First World War, the older generation's task in the Bund had been simply to let young people develop under their own self-guidance. But now the young had to be led.

Her approach was understandable, and yet not without irony. Certainly, growing up under Nazism was not a healthy preparation for becoming a democrat. But was the antidote more "leadership"? Moreover, one cannot avoid a wry smile, noticing how the Bund's distinction mirrored its own aging from one generation to another. In the 1920s, the Bund had been a very young group, with most of its members in their early twenties and Artur, the youthful forty-year-old, as their guru. Now the Bund's core members were in their forties, and both Artur and Ernst had reached retirement age, sprightly though they remained. The Bund was no longer a group *of* youth but one of middle-aged people seeking to speak *to* youths. Of all the changes wrought by twelve years of Nazi rule, this was perhaps the most fundamental.

To lead, one had to be understood, and the young, according to Dore, no longer recognized the language of their elders. One of the striking features of her "Appeal to Youth" is thus its strange mixture of tones. Much of it could have been lifted verbatim from a Bund pamphlet of the 1920s: the virtues of the youth movement, the necessity of socialism, and much more. But we also find talk of *Volk*, heroism, sacrifice, and nation, language that had previously been the purview of the nationalist right. No one, the Bund now assured young people, wanted to rob them of their love for the fatherland (even though the very notion of a fatherland had been anathema for this internationally minded group). Instead, young people should relearn what "fatherland" really meant. Germany was great not because of its efforts to dominate its neighbors but because of the intellectual giants who had shaped its tradition of ideas. Bund speakers were now at pains to acknowledge the self-sacrifice and idealism with which young people had devoted themselves to the national cause, and the pure spirit of camaraderie that many had experienced under the Nazi banner. Those very values and commitments, Dore argued, were now more necessary than ever.[56]

In general, the postwar Bund talked less about the proletariat and socialism and more about national renewal. It recognized that though aggressive nationalism had been discredited, the language of *Volk* and nation had become second nature for much of the population. As Dore's scribbled diary entry about the *"Volksgenossen"* in the last frightening hours before their liberation suggests, Bund members themselves had been dragged onto this terrain almost without realizing it. Perhaps more than before 1933, the Bund felt able to express pride in Germany's intellectual culture, extolling a tradition of *Geist* embodied by Kant, Goethe, Schiller, and Beethoven.[57] The Bund was also prompted to speak more explicitly about the German nation by dint of its own internationalism. With the fatherland brought so low and its future so uncertain, the Bund felt itself to be a privileged mediator, paving the way for Germany's return to the fellowship of nations.[58] For a few years in the late 1940s, the Bundists, along with many of their countrymen, hoped that because Germany was the joint object of western and Soviet deliberations, it might somehow be the key to achieving future peace and international cooperation.[59]

On the day the war officially ended, Artur recorded some prescient reflections in his journal. A people could bear the physical misfortune of having lost a war without humiliation, he wrote. But just a few days earlier, he had been overcome by shock and dismay as revelations about Nazi horrors poured in via the BBC, atrocities that far exceeded even his ample knowledge. To have committed such offenses against all the people of Europe, and against every human value, he continued, left such a freight of shame and humiliation as to burden the soul. Artur knew firsthand that some brave citizens had opposed the Nazis. He was unsure if people of other nations would have behaved any better. But the fact remained that all adult Germans had to take responsibility for the crimes committed in their name. The bitter paradox, as Artur saw it, was that it was the internationalists of the Bund's stamp, the *Weltbürger* (citizens of the world), who were most willing to assume this burden. Over the next decades, guilt, reparations, and, increasingly, Israel would seldom move from the top of the group's agenda. Members were quick to write letters of protest whenever a public statement was made that did not acknowledge Germany's historic responsibility. Even as the prewar Jewish milieu disappeared, the Bund became philo-Semitic in a way this once fiercely anti-religious group had never been.[60]

The group also placed far more emphasis on faith, in the sense of a belief in a kind of universal global plan. This was above all because of that overwhelming sense they had gained amid the bombing that history was proceeding according to long-term, objective, rational laws. But the new emphasis on *Glauben*—faith—also had another source. Artur recognized that Nazi crimes raised new kinds of questions about humanity.[61] Reeling from reports about the Nuremberg Trials, he recognized that the people who had committed unspeakable crimes in the concentration camps with no sign of horror, empathy, or any other natural human reaction "were at the same time good family men, fathers, helpful neighbors and upright citizens."[62] The question posed by the "abyss" the Nazis had revealed in man was whether some countervailing force could prevent humanity from falling into it again. For Artur, the only answer was a deep, objectively founded, and yet religious faith in the historical forces working toward a better world.[63] Like nothing else, Artur's appeal to "objective faith" showed the strange mixture of continuity and change in Bund thought. The emphasis on the "abyss" was the Bund's concession to Auschwitz. The underlying belief in progress remained.

Where Are the Young People in the Bund?

Glancing back over their shoulders, however, the Bund's members soon realized how few were marching along behind. The "First Letter Abroad" bemoaned the fact that "our flock has grown small. Often we feel lonely. We are going against the flow just as we did during the 12 years."[64] Despite the Bund's frenetic activity in 1947 and 1948, its leaders bemoaned the fact that there were "far too few" motivated participants.[65]

These were years of dramatic economic and political change in Germany. U.S. and British aid and the revival of some domestic production meant that in the second half of 1947, the worst of the shortages began to be overcome. The announcement of the Marshall Plan in June 1947 had reassured West Germans that the United States was committed to German economic revival. Though the currency reform a year later left many citizens very short of money, the full shop windows promised improvements to come. By then, the failure of the Allies to come up with a common plan for Germany's future made it clear that a separate West German state was going to emerge, integrated into a western alliance. The Federal Republic of Germany and its East German counterpart, the German Democratic Republic, came into being in 1949.

During these tumultuous years, Bund members were engaged in a persistent campaign to win over young people, attending numerous youth conferences and building relationships wherever they could. Bund members who taught adult education courses cultivated personal connections with the young adults in their classes. Bund newsletters reflected on what the "youth of today" wanted. Echoing a concern in postwar Germany, Ernst spoke at seminars on "why youth rejects politics."[66] The group's view was that young people may well have rejected party politics—but they were far from uninterested in political issues per se. Fritz Denks, for example, argued that young people saw through the hypocrisy of teachers who lamented youth's follies while refusing to acknowledge their own complicity in the Third Reich. He felt that the Bund could offer more honest guidance.

But by 1950, the young people's lack of response to the Bund's outreach efforts had become so obvious that a round of soul-searching ensued. In a letter to Dore in 1950, Ellen admitted that the problem was pursuing her into her dreams. She wondered whether the Bund should try to create a separate youth organization, an idea that led to a series of conferences for young people in Wuppertal from November of that year through at least October 1951. These meetings did indeed generate a circle of as many as fifty regular participants, some of whom, decades later, would remain appreciative of everything they had learned from the Bund. But after a year or two, they withdrew from Bund meetings and formed their own circle.[67]

It is tempting to assume that youngsters were repelled by the Bund's call to own up to Germany's crimes. Certainly, an early postwar willingness to confront the past rapidly disappeared.[68] The years of shortages and hardship had left many Germans feeling sorry for themselves. The Cold War let many feel they were now on the right side of history, against the Communists, and that the past could be put to rest. Yet the Bund's willingness to openly discuss the Nazi era without demonizing the young people who had been drawn to Nazism was actually one of its attractions.

Ellen found it particularly worthy of note that Friedl Jacobs's new girlfriend, Gisela Lenders, had become an enthusiastic participant in Bund events. Gisela had been an ambitious member and, eventually, a leader of the Nazi girls' movement. Her father, Peter Lenders, had been a highranking SA officer. Gisela's journey toward the Bund had begun in Ellen's gymnastics classes, which she had taken as part of a training program for kindergarten teachers. Thanks to Gisela, her brother, Helmut, also began attending Bund meetings. Impressed by Artur, he would also be a participant in the Wuppertal youth meetings in the early 1950s. He went on to be a delegate in the West German national parliament, the Bundestag, and a senior national figure in the German Social Democratic Party. For him, the Bund was the turning point in his political education. Another participant in this group, Kurt Schmidt, had also been an enthusiastic Hitler Youth member, and his mother and brothers ardent Hitler supporters. Schmidt had already undergone something of a political reeducation after the war while doing an apprenticeship in Leipzig. He, too, welcomed the chance to engage with the Nazi past that the Bund offered. Ernst was particularly effective at connecting with such youngsters, acknowledging the higher motives that had drawn them to Nazism in the first place, and steering them toward recognizing what had gone wrong with Germany.[69]

Dore's "Appeal to Youth" had hinted at her hope that the Bund could now redirect the idealism the Nazis had so successfully mobilized. The Bund and the Hitler Youth, after all, drew on the common roots of the *bündisch* youth movement, and both emphasized voluntary obedience to a freely chosen charismatic leader. While the Bund was committed to democracy in the wider realm, it believed that an organic community required a clear hierarchy, as long as the chosen leader was worthy. In short, Dore clearly felt that for all its opposition to Nazi goals, the Bund's structure and philosophy was potentially well placed to appeal to those who had learned the meaning of subordinating themselves to a higher cause.[70]

But, in fact, it was the Bund's hierarchical character and discipline that proved to be the major deterrent in recruiting new younger members. Just a couple of years after the end of the war, Ernst was already noting that the young representatives he met rejected every kind of compulsion.[71] Änne Schmitz recalled that after the war Dore's gymnastics lessons did appeal to young women from the League of German Girls, but "they did not want to accept obligations and firm rules."[72] Kurt Schmidt burst out laughing when he remembered, after having participated in a couple of the Wuppertal group weekends, being taken to Ernst's apartment to meet some of the "grown-ups" in the Bund. What tickled him in retrospect was the memory of having to sit at Artur's feet. Literally? I asked. Well, he said, he wasn't sure, but it seemed in memory that Artur was on some kind of raised stage. The sense of being allowed in only on condition of good behavior, along with the awe everyone felt toward Artur, made it impossible for him to utter a word.[73]

As alienating for youngsters as the hierarchy was the solemn emphasis on quasi-religious ceremony. Friedl Speer, who was around eighty years old when I interviewed him, recalled that in 1948, not long after they had met, his girlfriend, Margaret (whom he later married), had been invited along to the Bund's annual Lichtfest. While I was interviewing Friedl, Margaret was listening in, and at this point she interrupted us to emphasize just how off-putting it had been to witness the group's self-invented ceremonies. For her as a young woman, seeing all these "adults" engaging in such a strange ritual had been downright disturbing.[74] The situation was thus the reverse of what the Bund hoped for. Rather than allowing them to repurpose the idealism of Nazi followers for a good cause, it was precisely the similarity with the Nazi youth movement style that proved repellent.

The Bund had always hoped that their own children would become the group's future. During the war, as concerns had grown about the political estrangement between the generations, many had invested their hopes in Eberhard Jungbluth as a potential new leader, and his death on the front was met with intense grief. Eberhard's younger sister Ursula told me, however, that in her view he would never have fulfilled this role.

After the war, Bund members were delighted by the reflectiveness and maturity they found in Friedl Jacobs when he returned from Holland.[75] Friedl joined the Bund in a ceremonial event during a summer excursion to the Sauerland in August 1948, a fact that gave his father much pleasure.[76]

Friedl's relationship to the organization, however, remained ambivalent. He did not swear the *Verpflichtung*, which had been the threshold for core membership in the pre-Nazi period. And his involvement with the Bund on any level appears to have been unusual. None of the group's other children joined. Some were deeply alienated by the recurrent childhood experience of seeing the Bund claim priority in their parents' lives, a priority that, they felt, put them in second place. Others simply believed that the group was not for them.

In later life, surviving Bund members reflected openly on the challenges they faced in finding new members after 1945. What did not emerge from interviews, however, was that by 1948 the old practices were no longer working for many of the existing members, either. Contemporary documents hint at tensions and challenges. During his address at the Verpflichtungstag in March 1948, Artur was blunt. He was troubled that no one new was being sworn into commitment but also that some of those who had formerly done so were not honoring it. He warned they would have to be excluded.[77] The group's initial bout of activity in the immediate postwar period had, he complained, been followed by "impassivity, lack of courage, and fatigue." The group had to relearn what it meant to commit to the Bund before all else, and to practice what it was to be an order again. He followed up with a circular distributed to all the local chapters, asking members if they were really committed to the Bund. Repeated exhortations to the members followed.[78]

When, in July 1948, Liesel Speer sent out a circular encouraging local groups to take on responsibility for the next Bund summer camp, there was no doubt a certain levity in her comment that "today people object to 'following orders' even when assigned the nicest of tasks."[79] But the reluctance to accept the old hierarchy was real. Tensions boiled over in the following year when Karlos and Karin sent an open letter to all Bund members, protesting Karlos's exclusion from the circle of the *Verpflichteten* (it may be that Artur's comment from the previous year in fact related to Karlos) and complaining about a lack of democracy. This letter, in turn, provoked angry and shocked responses from other Bund members who considered it a fundamental assault on the group's core principle of putting the collective before the individual.[80]

There were many reasons why the group lost its élan, quite apart from growing old. Some members, like Alfred Stürmer, were probably alienated by the new emphasis on faith. For others, the Cold War split between the Communists and the Social Democrats drew a wedge between members. Some Bund members remained close to the Communists, but while the group refrained from demonizing the Soviet Union, it increasingly operated on the terrain of German social democracy. Ernst, for instance, left the Wuppertal Communist Party in 1949 in a very public confrontation. The worsening Cold War not only ended the Bund's dream of being a bridge between the leftist parties but also rendered the prospect of an imminent global framework for peace ever more implausible. The group's "objective historical faith" seemed more and more fanciful. Finally, its unflinching support for Israel later troubled at least some members concerned about the Palestinian cause.[81]

Recognizing the trends, and mindful of new requirements the Bund had to meet for state funding, Lisa steered Dore's school toward a more professional approach and pushed to separate it from the group as a whole. Bund members were kept informed about the school's progress, and Dore, Ellen, and others were intimately involved in its management and teaching. But the school pupils and newly recruited staff members were not made aware of the Bund's existence. Dore's postwar approach to *Körperbildung* continued to be holistic in one sense: it still drew on the whole person, mind and body. But it no longer made body training the kernel of social and cultural renewal, as it had in the 1920s.[82]

Meanwhile, other Bund members were moving into promising new careers. The Bund had given working-class participants with little formal education the confidence, knowledge, and motivation either to enter politics or to move into some form of education. Rudi Heiland, who had been a regular participant in Bund meetings before 1933, became mayor of the Ruhr town of Marl and a member of the Bundestag. Willi Zimbehl, one of the young working-class men for whom Artur's lectures had opened new horizons, became the first labor director under the new codetermination laws, which created a role for labor representatives in management. In 1952, four Bund members—Änne Engels, Marta Börkenkrüger, Hermann Krahlisch, and Fritz Denks—were elected to city assemblies. Fritz would later become an SPD deputy in the North Rhine–Westphalian parliament and mayor of Mülheim. Several members moved into education or youth work, including Karl Heilwagen, formerly a baker, Hermann Schmalstieg, and Reinhold Ströter. Fritz was active in rebuilding the Falken, the SPD's youth wing, and Karlos became a teacher at a vocational school. Both he and his wife, Karin, in particular, were heavily engaged in educational work in the Falken. She went to England for congresses on reeducation and was often at Falken conferences and executive meetings. She also became a magistrate, presiding over, among other things, a trial of former Nazis. Ernst remained active in adult education into the 1960s. Several of the youngsters whose lives the Bund had touched in the postwar era were also inspired to take up new careers, such as Helmut Lenders, who, as noted, became an SPD member of parliament.

The Bund could take pride in these achievements. Its commitment to education, welfare, and social justice had lasting consequences all across the region. But this yet unknown future could not allay worries about where the group was headed in the late 1940s and early 1950s. At the Verpflich-tungstag in 1951, there was open acknowledgment that the Bund was not what it had been. Artur said definitively that they were no longer an order. Over the next year or two, the group would experiment in self-definition. In truth, however, it was evolving into a circle of morally upright and politi-cally minded friends, many of whom would continue to meet until their deaths.[83] But the life of its members, as Ernst acknowledged to Artur, "no longer belonged to the Bund." Members' career choices, their approach to bringing up their children, and their work for other organizations were no longer determined by the group.[84] In 1960, reflecting on all they had achieved, Ernst wrote wistfully to Artur that they would not be able to pass on the "energy and enthusiasm, the heightened sense of life" to the next generation.[85] "The postwar experience was hard and bitter for the old Bundists," said Tove, looking back. "They thought, now our time has come and things would blossom. . . . Not a bit of it."[86] Instead of being the pre-lude to their leadership in postwar society, the Nazi era turned out to have been the Bund's finest hour.

10

Beyond Recognition

Back in June 1946, Artur had filled out a questionnaire to establish his status as a victim of persecution. If his request was approved, he would receive supplementary rations, the reinstatement of his pre-Nazi pension, and the return of books taken by the Gestapo. In the end, he was successful—but only after a struggle, and only after making claims that rather stretched the truth of what he and the Bund had done. Artur's struggle for recognition was one of the first indications that translating the Bund's wartime experience into categories the postwar world would accept would not be easy.

Neither the Bund nor Artur sought glory. They hoped to be influential and, failing that, expected justice. Yet over the following decades, the Bund would suffer disappointments and, indeed, some humiliation as authorities, scholars, and even Yad Vashem called their achievements into question. Those evaluating the Bund's wartime record seldom undertook their own investigations. Rather, they read what Bund members wrote or listened to what they said about their Nazi experiences. In collective texts like the "Letters Abroad" or in applications for support like Artur's questionnaire, Bund members tried hard to describe their trajectory through the Third Reich in ways that would resonate with their listeners. By exploring the "conversation" between the Bund and the wider world, we can understand why the Bund's record failed to resonate and how and why public recognition of rescue and resistance was so selective.

Bund Members, Official Assistance, and Compensation

Efforts to assist those the Nazis had persecuted began as soon as Germany was defeated. However, the Allies initially focused their energies on foreign displaced persons and left it to local German administrations to help their compatriots. The results were extremely patchy. For the British Zone (which included the Ruhr), it was not until December 1945 that Zonal Policy Instruction No. 20 established a common framework for short-term help for victims. Victims were now entitled to extra rations, priority in the allocation of jobs and housing, and rent support for a transitional period. Initially restricted to concentration camp survivors, within a few weeks the policy was de facto extended to others who could claim to have suffered equivalent hardship. The policy was intended not just to provide help but also to explicitly demonstrate to the German public that opponents of the Nazi regime were being given appropriate recognition.[1] It was now that Artur submitted his request for support.

In seeking short-term help in 1946, Bund members were in many ways in a favorable position. The local welfare committees that made recommendations to the military government as to who should receive benefits were staffed by members of the left-wing political networks to which the Bund had extensive ties. Ernst worked in a variety of Wuppertal committees and was able to provide supportive affidavits for applications elsewhere. The challenge Bund members faced was in persuading Communists and Social Democrats who had spent lengthy periods in Nazi prisons and camps that the Bund had engaged in serious opposition to the regime, and that its members had endured conditions worthy of compensation.

Artur's claim in June 1946 provides revealing insight as to how he believed he needed to present his experience in order to meet the welfare committee's expectations. He wrote that he had been the head of an illegal organization "that had actively fought against National Socialism." He noted that as the leader of an "antifascist fighting organization" and as someone married to a Jew, he had been subject to Nazi persecution and had been forced to live underground (the terminology at the time was "illegally") before the summer of 1934 and toward the end of the war in Meersburg.[2]

Though recognizing Artur as a victim of persecution, the district welfare committee declined to approve him for supplementary rations on the grounds that he had not been incarcerated. Artur appealed, arguing that the deprivation he had suffered was just as severe as that of those who had been.[3] He was probably motivated as much by a desire to see his wartime record vindicated as by the promise of any palpable benefits, although in the dire postwar conditions, the prospect of receiving supplementary rations was no small thing. In the appeal, Artur described at length all that he had endured: house searches, Gestapo persecution, the loss of all income, and fears for his wife and son. He again cited his early months on the run, claiming that he had been wandering without a home for years.[4] He also stated that as a result of persecution, he had suffered serious consequences to his health. In short, he claimed, he was someone "who had made real sacrifices for his beliefs, and who lived illegally for years in a dangerous battle with National Socialism." It was only a matter of luck that he had avoided prison. During the twelve years of Nazi rule, he argued, the Bund had "worked tirelessly to expose the true nature of the Nazi regime and enlighten people." It had also helped many who were persecuted by the Gestapo and had rescued some Jewish people from certain death by sheltering them with friends.[5] He attached supportive letters from Ernst, then serving as head of the denazification committee of Wuppertal teachers, and from Lisa and Marianne, as rescued Jews.

Artur's appeal was successful, and he did receive the supplementary rations.[6] But he had been forced to work hard to establish his bona fides and would have to do so again. He also had to mount a rather complex case, one that mingled the initial experience of persecution, the moral claim of having been the leader of a resistance group, and the stress and suffering he had endured as a husband and father of a wife and son subject to racial persecution. In several important ways, he stretched the truth. His depiction of the group as a "fighting organization," for example, implied an aggressive resistance that had not been the group's strategy. And his suggestion that he had been forced to live illegally for years also did not exactly correspond with the facts.

Other Bund members submitted similar applications. From 1947 onward, new legislation expanded the range of compensation for Nazi victims, including modest pensions for those whose health had been affected or who were over sixty-five. A 1949 regional law provided fixed sums of financial compensation for periods of imprisonment and explicitly recognized illegal life as equivalent to life in jail.[7] Although the range and value of potential benefits was growing, the authorities (by now most matters were back in the hands of German bodies) were also becoming more restrictive in awarding them. With the introduction of the deutsche mark, public money became extremely tight, and every administration had to manage its funds carefully. In March 1948, anticipating the financial constraints the currency reform would bring, the Social Ministry of North Rhine–Westphalia ordered a review of everyone who had been recognized as a victim. After receiving an inquiry dated March 4 asking for proof of her status, Lisa Jacob sent a caustic response. The ministry's question was "easily answered," she said, noting that she had disobeyed the Gestapo order to report for resettlement to the East and had thus lived illegally from April 1942 on. "It is news to me," she added, "that full Jews without ration cards (an inquiry at the local ration office will confirm this), without any financial resources, living for three years under permanent threat to their life, fleeing from one place to the next, now have to prove that during the period of National Socialist rule they lived in worse conditions than the rest of the German population."[8]

For Jewish Bund members like Lisa or Dore, having to prove their right to compensation was distressing. It suggested that they were impostors or that German officialdom was feigning ignorance of the monstrous deeds recently carried out by the German state. However, once Lisa and Dore swallowed their anger and filled out the forms, achieving formal recognition as victims of racial persecution was relatively straightforward.

For Artur, the situation was more complicated. A day after receiving notification that his status was under review, Artur responded with a passionate account, single-spaced, detailing the suffering he had endured for his political views, the periods he had lived illegally at the beginning and the end of the Nazi regime, and all the terrors of the time in between. He attached a new set of supporting letters.[9] Yet two years later, despite repeated entreaties and more affidavits, the authorities were still reluctant to confirm his status as a victim of persecution.[10] One challenge facing claimants such as Artur was that oversight of their cases had progressively shifted from local welfare committees to civil servants in the regional ministries, many of whom had served under the Nazis, and who often proved less sympathetic.[11]

Artur did eventually prevail, but to do so, he again had to exaggerate. He continued to claim that he had lived illegally until the summer of 1934 because a warrant was out for his arrest. It's possible that such a warrant did exist, but Artur was never able to produce evidence of it.[12] His correspondence with Friedl confirms that in the spring of 1933 he was indeed on the run, spending a very uncomfortable few weeks tramping through the Sauerland. He clearly felt himself a wanted man. But by June of that year, he was apparently in correspondence with the Essen authorities; this indicates that however endangered he considered himself, it was not enough to dissuade him from making his presence known.[13] In a statement made under oath, Liesel Speer said that he had stayed with her (i.e., in the Bund's Wuppertal apartment) until April 1934, though during a period of particular danger he had spent some weeks in the Sauerland, and some with other Bund friends.[14] Her testimony thus confirms the fact that Artur was on the run for just a few weeks. Artur's claims about living illegally toward the end of the war were misleading, too, and also more inconsistent. At one point in 1948, he claimed that his period on the run had begun as early as the end of 1943, and he referred to time spent in Göttingen and Braunschweig.[15] Here he must have meant his visits to Dore while she was staying with the Gehrkes and the Morgensterns—but Artur was neither under cover nor on the run at that time. It is understandable that he would make these assertions, since he had, in fact, felt threatened for twelve long years. Why shouldn't he be compensated? But to convince the state, he was having to stretch the truth.

Inscribed on the Body

Accounts submitted by older Bund members to the restitution authorities often described the consequences of their travails in terms of their health.[16] Ernst wrote about the appalling conditions in the Bendahl prison in 1933, where he had been held in a small cell along with six to eight other men, some of whom had tuberculosis. He himself suffered from a serious gastrointestinal disorder, which would worsen under the stresses of persecution and force him to take early retirement at the end of 1943.[17] The first entry in Dore's restitution file is a lengthy account of her illnesses, including nervous ailments brought on by anxiety and persecution.[18] Lisa, too, recorded her health issues, specifically rheumatism, which had been brought on by stress and poor diet.[19]

After 1949, when it became possible to obtain a pension on the grounds of having suffered ill health as a result of persecution, such accounts were framed specifically to obtain state support, and in that sense they were making an "argument" that the authorities would understand. Yet there was no doubt that for the older generation of Bund members, in particular, the stresses of persecution left lasting scars. Because this was something too private to be written about very much elsewhere—if at all—these accounts offer an authentic, if fragmentary, glimpse of a distinct kind of memory of the past, one etched painfully on the nervous and digestive systems, on sinews and the gastrointestinal tract.

The authorities, however, were not sympathetic listeners. Dore's ailments were, true enough, recognized as a function of the stresses of persecution, but she was declared only 30 percent incapacitated and thus entitled to only a fraction of the already modest pension. Dore responded angrily, refuting the judgment—after all, she had been completely unable to leave her bed for several lengthy periods of time.[20] Her response made no difference. Ernst was even more unfortunate. In July 1949, the district welfare office in Wuppertal recognized the long-term health effects he had suffered as a result of persecution.[21] However, the final decision about whether he would be eligible for benefits was determined by the Labor Ministry. In April 1950, the ministry informed Ernst that, based on a new medical opinion, it now considered his condition to be unrelated to persecution; as a result, he would not receive a pension.[22] Despite the passing of new compensation laws in 1953 and 1956, Ernst was never able to have this judgment overturned.

One difficulty for claimants like Dore and Ernst is that they were not permitted to enlist their own medical experts to challenge official findings.[23] A survey of similar claims in Düsseldorf over this period suggests that one in three applicants was rejected—and this rate would get even worse over the following years.[24] The outcome did more than deprive the claimants of much-needed resources. When we read the letter in which Ernst responded angrily to the rejection, we also hear his bitterness at being denied recognition of what he had suffered.[25]

Taking Liberties

Claims for health issues were contentious because it was difficult to determine the etiology of any given disorder. Claims for having been deprived of one's liberty on political or racial grounds were more straightforward—or, at least, they were for those who had endured actual imprisonment. In those cases, a simple mathematical formula would determine how large a payment a person would receive. As long as they had spent at least six months in jail or a concentration camp, they received a one-time sum of DM 150 for each month of internment. This was very modest compensation for the suffering incurred (though equivalent to workers' average monthly earnings), but for the most part it was relatively easy to substantiate and obtain. Proving eligibility became more difficult when the applicants had not suffered actual imprisonment and were claiming a life of hardship equivalent to time spent in jail. Here, the jurisprudence became increasingly restrictive. A number of Bund members engaged in protracted disputes with the authorities, disputes that not only had negative financial implications but, again, challenged the integrity of their experience.[26]

A problem for both Artur and Dore was that they wanted to claim on the basis of the specific predicament of having been targeted both as left-wingers and as a part-Jewish family. Yet the law treated racial and political persecution as distinct categories. When, in 1954, Artur submitted an application for compensation according to the new Federal Compensation Law of 1953, the form asked whether he had been persecuted because of his political beliefs or for reasons of race. He crossed out "or," wrote in "and," and added to "political beliefs" the "race of my Jewish wife."[27] True, the law did make provision for people who were targeted for multiple reasons—for example, a left-wing radical who had been incarcerated at first on political grounds and then later sent to Auschwitz as a Jew. Were the person in

STEFAN BRANDT

Trude and Georg Brandt in happier times

ALTE SYNAGOGE, ESSEN

One of the Bund sons, Eberhard Jungbluth,
in Wehrmacht uniform with his sisters, 1940

The community in the Meersburg guesthouse, c. 1943. From left: Käte Franke, unknown, Walter Jacobs, Julie Schreiber, unknown, unknown, Gertrud Jacobs, Lene Krahlisch, Tilde Stürmer

Gina (Regina Gaenzel), a friend of Friedl's, in 1941, a year before her deportation and murder

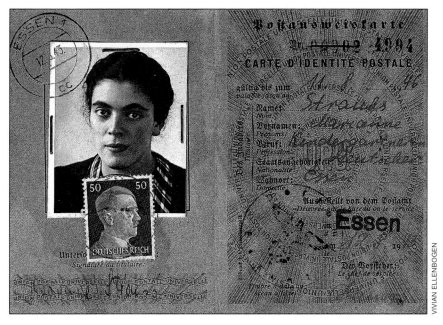

Lisa Jacob's authentic ID card, identifying her as a Jew

Marianne Strauss's postal pass, which did not identify her as Jewish

Marianne Strauss posing as
an aunt with Wolfgang Briel

A panorama of the destroyed center of Essen taken in 1944 from the roof of the synagogue burned out on Kristallnacht. The numbers identify various churches (2, 3, and 6), the town hall (4) and other notable buildings

A makeshift kitchen photographed on March 12, 1945, a day after the last major bombing of Essen. In the background, the main railway station

A thriving black market on Essen's Kastanienallee, c. 1947

Dore in 1947

Artur still active in his 70s

Dore and Artur Jacobs leading a Bund excursion in the 1950s

The Blockhaus in 2010 with Karin Gerhard, Lisa Jacob's successor as director of the Dore Jacobs school

question lucky enough to survive, he or she could claim compensation for loss of liberty on both counts. But as Artur and Dore saw it, what they had suffered was not sequential persecution but an especially acute sense of vulnerability that had arisen from political and racial threats taken together—and this was *not* something the law recognized.

In 1949, when Dore applied for compensation for loss of liberty, she implicitly acknowledged that her case might fall between categories.[28] She had been, she wrote, not only racially persecuted but "long before that already politically persecuted." In her application, she included time she spent living in the Bund house in Wuppertal after leaving the hospital in 1939. This extended period living away from home proved, Dore said, that as a left-wing Jew she had felt particularly exposed to potential persecution. She made the same claim about the period she spent in Göttingen with Hedwig Gehrke in 1943 and her year and a half in Meersburg. In December 1950, the committee adjudicating damages to liberty agreed to the full period Dore was claiming—and awarded the DM 150 rate for the full sixty months.[29] This was an excellent result, but a short-lived one.

In 1951, the Interior Ministry in Düsseldorf challenged Dore's account of the period from 1939 to 1943. It was prepared to recognize the sixteen months spent in Meersburg as a period of loss of liberty, but not the rest. Dore employed a lawyer, Paul Grundmann, to refute the challenge.[30] His central argument was that in 1939, the Bund had been subject to Gestapo searches and interrogations, and that given her fragile state of health, this was too stressful for Dore to endure. Therefore, the group had spirited her away to Wuppertal.

The ministry was still not convinced that the move to Wuppertal could be viewed as the result of duress analogous to imprisonment. In December 1952, Dore and her lawyer appeared in a special hearing before a restitution tribunal within the ministry. Lisa, Else, Sonja, and Liesel Speer also attended as witnesses. During the hearing, the ministry's representative grew more aggressive.[31] The interaction revealed how the brutal reality of the past was being diluted into pale legal categories. At one point, the representative argued that the "persecution of Jewish partners in mixed marriages had begun only in fall 1944." True enough, that was when deportations had started, but harassment and threats against Jews in mixed marriages had been commonplace long before. Given the deportations, the representative continued, "it is thoroughly understandable that the husband became illegal in 1944" and conceded graciously that there would also be "no objections" to the contention that the applicant herself became illegal at this time.[32] Rebutting the idea that Jews in mixed marriages had been under threat beginning only in September 1944, Dore's lawyer emphasized her subjective perception, arguing that one could not ask of a person who had been persecuted for six years to calibrate the danger with such precision. Anyone in her position, he said, would have reacted the same way.[33]

In subsequent hearings in Essen and Düsseldorf, the state representatives grew even more obdurate. "Generally, in this case," one official maintained, "we have heard repeatedly about illegal political work. But there has never been any concrete evidence that this was the case." The ministry's representatives now even claimed that there was no evidence from the Gestapo that agents had been pursuing Dore and Artur—a barely credible conclusion, given the number of investigations and interrogations the files reveal. The officials went further, arguing that Dore would have to prove that other members of the group had been imprisoned if she wanted to establish that she, too, had really been in danger. In short, Dore's entire experience of life in Nazi Germany was being delegitimized before her eyes.

The ministry thus persisted in denying her claim except for the part involving the final phase of the war. Dore appealed the decision, and the ministry agreed, without conceding the claim, to a compromise of an additional one-time sum of DM 3,375—in effect, splitting the difference between what it had previously conceded and the original award it had rejected.[34] Despite Dore's partial success in financial terms, the stinging lack of recognition remained.

For Ernst, the outcome was even more disappointing. In November 1950, his claim for loss of liberty was rejected outright, and an appeal met with no success.[35] The jurisprudence was clearly defining ever more rigidly what constituted "prison-like conditions."

This was grotesquely evident in the different outcomes of Lisa's and Marianne's claims for loss of liberty. Both women had lived underground in very similar circumstances. Lisa's application, made early in 1950, was awarded the full amount—DM 5,550—for the period in which she had been on the run, between April 1942 and the end of the war. Under later

Federal Compensation legislation, the time when Jews had been forced to wear the yellow star was recognized as equivalent to time spent in prison, and so Lisa was awarded additional compensation for the brief period between when the star was introduced in September 1941 and when she went underground in April 1942.[36]

Marianne's case was not dealt with until much later.[37] Because the Federal Compensation Law of 1956—which treated claimants more fairly than the 1953 law had—had taken effect by that time, she had no problem getting recognition for the period when she had worn the yellow star (though she was outraged that she had to prove that she had done so, given the severe consequences meted out at the time to any Jew found without the demeaning symbol attached to their clothing).[38] But this was insignificant compared with what followed. Marianne's lawyer wrote to her in June 1957 that the official in Düsseldorf was skeptical of her claims concerning the time after August 31, 1943, the day Marianne fled from her parents' house and disappeared underground. Given recent court decisions on other cases, the lawyer informed her, the official had "concluded that it would not be correct to say that you had lived under inhuman conditions after August 31, 1943! He did want to approve the compensation, however, if you had worn the Jewish star after August 31, 1943."[39] This was legal reasoning at its most fantastical. Had Marianne worn a yellow star while on the run, which would certainly have resulted in her capture and murder, she would now be entitled to the compensation. In a powerful reply to her lawyer, she wondered whether the official could imagine himself at all in her position,

> being pursued and hunted by the Gestapo and the criminal police, without ration cards or sufficient food, dependent on the goodwill of strangers, confined to very restricted living space; unable to leave the apartment during the day for fear of being found and inevitably shot by the Gestapo, and at night unable to leave the apartment even to seek protection in a cellar from the persistent bombing attacks; forced to change my residence constantly under threat—and being always aware of this danger, always dependent on unknown people, having to trust them with my very life; being always on the wanted list, and without

false papers or fake ID; with no access to medical treatment
when ill, and, though constantly malnourished, forced to meet
these demands physically, spiritually, and morally, knowing that
this was the only way to survive the horror.[40]

Still the ministry was unmoved, justifying its rejection by pointing out
that Marianne had had a circle of friends during this time and had been
able to obtain ration cards by selling artificial flowers she had made from
felt. All of this suggested, according to the ministry, that her living situation had not been comparable to the living conditions of a prisoner, the
requirement for compensation stipulated by the law. In the end, as in Dore's
case, Marianne hammered out a compromise, but she, too, believed that
the state was bluntly disregarding the terror and uncertainty she had experienced. In other words, everything the Bund had invested to enable Marianne to survive and to feel that she was part of a community while on the
run now formed the basis of the state's denial that she had suffered enough
to merit compensation.

Of course, there were also more general reasons for the difficulties
Dore, Ernst, and Artur experienced in getting recompense. They faced a
complex legal-bureaucratic process run by a state seeking to limit its financial exposure, using chronically understaffed administrators of widely
varying quality.[41] Failure to obtain benefits was common. As far as the Bund
was concerned, however, we should not speak of outright failure. By the
end of the 1950s, Artur, Dore, Lisa, Marianne, the Gersons, the Enochs,
the Stürmers (albeit with a case that dragged into the 1960s), and a few
others, though not the luckless Ernst, had ended up with sums sufficient
to improve their quality of life, in some cases substantially. In addition to
the categories mentioned above, for example, some, such as Tilde Stürmer,
were able to claim compensation for professional damages, either as capital sums or as pensions.[42]

The fact remains that this whole process constituted a most painful
chapter for the Bund's leading members. Their sense of having engaged in
active resistance and their experiences of duress, risk, and fear were being
belittled—or ignored. Their plentiful correspondence, as well as the testy
exchanges in their hearings, vividly conveys their exasperation and hurt.
For Artur, Dore, and Ernst, it was probably the first and certainly the most

sustained context in which outsiders (in this case, state representatives) challenged their account of their past.

A Footnote in History

A thickening fog of amnesty and amnesia in the late 1940s and early 1950s stifled discussion of opposition to Nazi rule. When the Federal Republic of Germany came into being in 1949, many disapproved even of those who had participated in the military resistance to Hitler in 1944, believing it was treasonous for army officers to turn against the national leadership in a time of war. One telling indicator of attitudes at the time was that the widow of a leading general lost her military pension in 1951 because her husband had been convicted by the Nazis of high treason for his involvement in the plot to kill Hitler.[43] True, a sizable minority within the population was dealing more critically with the Nazi era. As we have seen, individuals responded positively to Bund meetings and adult education classes. In 1960, Ernst Jungbluth could look back with some pride on more than a decade of teaching and outreach on the theme of the "unmastered past."[44] But the mainstream was hostile or silent.[45]

The only opposition that could genuinely be celebrated in the late 1940s and early 1950s was religious. While the Confessing Church (a group within Protestantism that had not ostentatiously embraced the regime, unlike the Nazi-aligned German Christians) had engaged in resistance, those efforts were now inflated, and doctrinal disputes were retrospectively cast as principled opposition to the Reich. In the Cold War climate, left-wingers who had courageously fought the Nazis were viewed with suspicion. Indeed, there was a general unease about political activism of any sort—an unease the Bund itself encountered among the young people "scarred" (the German term was "burned children") by their experience under the Nazis. In recognition of this apolitical mood, Inge Scholl, for example, deliberately depoliticized the courageous stance of her siblings, Hans and Sophie Scholl, and emphasized their humanity and religiosity, rather than the clear political opposition to the Nazis that had led to them being sentenced to death and executed by guillotine.[46]

The rare exception to the general trend of silence about opposition, and particularly left-wing opposition, was Günther Weisenborn's 1953 study *Der lautlose Aufstand* ("The Silent Uprising"). *Der lautlose Aufstand* celebrated grassroots political opposition from left-wing and other groups, offering brief accounts of a large number of organizations and circles that had opposed Hitler. Evidently, Weisenborn, a writer and an affiliate of the Red Orchestra resistance circle who had himself faced the death penalty in 1942, had carried out the research for the book in the 1940s. In May 1947, the Bund learned of his endeavor and wrote to his publisher in Munich.[47] Keen to ensure recognition of their anti-Nazi activities, the Bundists submitted copies of two of the reports they had produced about their resistance to the regime and how they had helped Jews, as well as an additional summary of their actions. Weisenborn included the group among the unsung heroes listed in his volume and seems to have quoted directly from Bund publications. Given the general climate, this was as much as the Bund could hope for.[48]

As is well known, the political mood in postwar West Germany began to liberalize markedly toward the end of the 1950s and particularly during the 1960s. By the end of the 1950s, the idea that the army had opposed Hitler had become respectable. During the 1960s, student unrest and the revival of interest in Marxist thought in West German universities created a new willingness to recover the heroism of left-wing opponents to the Nazis. In 1969, two major well-researched books heralded what would become a flood of publications and local celebrations uncovering resistance and opposition at the grassroots level. The most important was Hans-Josef Steinberg's history of resistance, which focused on Essen, the Bund's heartland. Steinberg's account remains the most substantial and thoroughly researched narrative of political resistance to the Nazis in the city and, indeed, one of the best local studies on resistance anywhere in Germany. The book represented the Bundists' best chance to achieve recognition for their actions in what would soon be the burgeoning historiography of grassroots anti-Nazism.[49]

But they would be sorely disappointed. Steinberg did indeed mention the Bund—but just once, in an early footnote. The footnote comes after a passage discussing which sources were most reliable. Steinberg asked whether testimony from surviving victims was accurate enough to correct and complement the files produced by their persecutors. In the 1960s, oral history was still not widely accepted, and so it is not surprising that Steinberg was cautious about victims' testimony and mindful of the problems inherent in interviewing. Time had passed, he observed; memories had been lost and facts muddled. He added, "It should also be briefly noted that it can be problematic when those involved misconstrue their own role or retroactively inflate their own relatively minor involvement." And now comes the footnote:

> Thus Weisenborn writes for example . . . of a resistance group in Essen, "the Bund," which according to his text carried out unbelievably effective illegal work, and continued to do so despite house searches and imprisonment. The Bund is said to have aided suffering victims, above all deported Jews, with "thousands of parcels." How members of the Bund could "wander around illegally for years" will remain a mystery to everyone who knows the situation under the Nazi regime. A written inquiry to Weisenborn about who his sources were in the case of the Bund was unfortunately not answered. My own research established that he is referring to the Adult Education circle "Bund," operating under the leadership of Artur Jacobs, whose members did indeed stick together during the Third Reich, protected Jewish fellow citizens from the clutches of the Gestapo, and provided rations to foreign workers. That was the limit of what was possible for such a group to do under Nazi rule and it speaks for the moral constitution of its members that they did what was possible. Transparent exaggerations can only discredit such efforts.[50]

And that was that. Surviving members of the Bund never mentioned the book to me, and there is no direct trace of it in the group's files. They cannot have been unaware of it, however. When the book appeared, they must surely have had much higher expectations, and they would certainly not have anticipated that their organization's name would appear solely as an example (and as the sole example) of the perils of exaggeration.[51]

Several considerations predisposed Steinberg to dismissing the Bund or acknowledging it only cursorily. He was rightly conscious that the celebrations of moral and spiritual resistance in the early postwar decades had often blurred the line between fairly low-risk nonconformity or oppositional thinking, on the one hand, and actions that risked life and limb, on the other. It is not surprising, then, that he focused on actions likely to arouse the wrath of the regime. Fully one-quarter of his book, over one hundred pages, consists of an appendix listing all the trials in which the Nazis prosecuted resistance fighters and other oppositional groups from Essen. Steinberg also had a narrow political-party focus. This, again, was an understandable reaction to the earlier postwar writing. He argued that for those who took up the fight against the regime, politics, not abstract ethical principles, had been the decisive motivating factor. But as a result, he focused almost exclusively on the main left-wing political parties (with a few pages devoted to Jehovah's Witnesses). Finally, as he freely admitted, the persecution of Jews barely figured in his book. He was, in effect, guided by a model of political action that privileged efforts to bring down the regime—ineffective though they all proved to be—over other acts of moral courage. The saving of lives through concealment barely figured, but every anti-Nazi poster that prompted a Gestapo interrogation was honorably mentioned.

This was just one book, and it would be easy to deem it a simple matter of bad luck that the chronicler of the Bund's home city was someone so skeptical. But Steinberg's work reflected broader trends. The Bund did not fit the emerging notion of what resistance groups looked like. The group's early decision to refrain from what it saw as foolhardy, ineffective actions like leafleting; its consequent lack of martyrs; and the fact that its most courageous actions had consisted in helping individual Jews and saving lives excluded it from the realm of the heroic political opposition.

Who Were the Righteous?

In the early postwar years, help for Jews occupied an ambivalent place in public consciousness. Such actions did not carry the same connotations of disloyalty to the war effort as outright resistance. Overblown or invented stories of helping Jews became a widespread, if short-lived, aspect of postwar culture (a fact that no doubt helped fuel Steinberg's skepticism).[52] Not a few former Nazis negotiated the denazification process by attesting that they had Jewish acquaintances whom they had helped. However, such stories were rapidly displaced by the consensus that Germans had been as powerless to assist Jews as they had been ignorant of their fate.[53] Rescue was largely banished from view, not because it was considered a disloyal act but because it was seen as an impossibility. It was thus not surprising that the Bund's actions did not resonate—they offered unwelcome evidence of what had been possible.

During the 1950s, only one individual received the Federal German Grand Cross (*Grosses Verdienstkreuz*) for assisting Jews, the Heidelberg priest Hermann Maas.[54] When the German Jewish émigré Kurt Grossmann compiled his collection of rescuer accounts in a volume titled *Die unbesungenen Helden* ("The Unsung Heroes"), it was only thanks to the author's unusual efforts and some institutional support from American Jewish organizations that he was able to publish a first edition of three thousand copies.[55] The most significant development at the time was the Berlin Jewish Community's decision in 1958 to create a prize for the "unsung heroes" who had helped the Jewish community during the Nazi years. But this initiative, which lasted until 1966, considered only West Berliners.

Both the trial of Adolf Eichmann in Jerusalem (which began in April 1961) and the Frankfurt Auschwitz trial (which began in 1963) were accompanied by campaigns in the German press intended to counterbalance the bad news by honoring good Germans who had gone against the grain. A few small compendia of rescuers were published, and some German helpers were recognized with the *Verdienstkreuz*. The 1970s saw more efforts at recognition. But these initiatives remained limited and fragmentary until virtually all of the Bund's founders had died. The Bund's failure to find public recognition in Germany thus said less about its members as a group and more about the prevailing attitudes toward rescue at the time. In part to correct this oversight, Lisa Jacob and Marianne Ellenbogen made a concerted effort in the 1980s to have the Bund honored in Israel as part of the international program of the righteous, housed at Yad Vashem. Much to their chagrin, they, too, were unsuccessful.

Israel's program had roots that went back to before the creation of the state. During the war, Jewish representatives from around the world had called for the helpers to be honored.[56] In Palestine, Mordechai Shenhabi proposed a monument to victims that would include the "righteous of the nations." For Shenhabi, the motive was diplomatic: honoring rescuers would reinforce ties between a future Hebrew nation and other sovereign states. The idea of the "righteous" harked back to the rabbinic notion of *hasidei umot ha-olam*, the righteous in the world, a reference to the small number of gentiles who recognized God and befriended the Jewish people. The label rapidly became the common currency of postwar proposals in Palestine/Israel, though what people understood it to mean varied considerably. During the key debate on the matter in the Israeli Knesset in 1953, those on the left favored collective recognition for political groups or nations whom they judged to have assisted Jews. Those on the right tended to favor the concept that eventually won out: restricting the label of "righteous" to individuals.

Though the basic legal framework for the honor was established in 1953, little was done during the following decade. There were disagreements about the form and location of a memorial, and in any case, Yad Vashem's top priority was collecting documentation concerning the Nazis' program of extermination. Many at Yad Vashem wanted to foreground the heroism and resistance of Jews themselves, rather than those who had assisted them.[57] After the Eichmann trial, the government took more concrete steps to commemorate non-Jews who had saved Jewish lives. At this point, the purpose was almost entirely diplomatic, a means of managing the fallout from the trial. After a scandal ensued over Oskar Schindler's recognition (since Schindler had been both a profiteer during the Nazi era and far from blameless in the postwar period), a special commission was created to vet and select future honorees. The Commission for the Designation of the Righteous Among the Nations met for the first time on February 1, 1963, and thus was born the procedure for recognizing rescuers that continues to this day.

We do not know why it was only in 1984, well after both Artur and Dore had died, that Lisa sought recognition for the Bund at Yad Vashem. She may have begun to feel, at eighty-five, that her own time was running out. Interest in rescue narratives was growing, and Inge Deutschkron's memoir of living underground, later published in English as *Outcast: A Jewish Girl in Wartime Berlin*, had recently enjoyed enormous resonance in Germany.[58] Marianne supported Lisa's application and added the names of her own helpers who were not on Lisa's list. Both women published short pieces about their experiences in an Essen journal. But the application failed. In the early 1990s, after Lisa had died, Marianne visited Jerusalem and made another attempt, again with the same outcome.

Yad Vashem had not, however, ignored the requests. In 1985, the director of Yad Vashem had met with a senior member of the Social Democratic Party, Heinz Putzrath, to ask him about the Bund. Putzrath had never heard of the group. He wrote to Gustav Streich, a longtime Social Democratic functionary in Essen and the author of a short history of social democracy in his hometown, to see if there was more to be learned. In his letter, Putzrath noted that the Israeli embassy in Bonn had sent him a series of Bund publications (which Lisa had presumably submitted with her application), adding that he had at first assumed that the Bund was part of the ISK, the group founded by Leonard Nelson, before realizing his error.[59] "Much speaks against what is claimed in these reports," he continued. "Also the ISK people know of no one who carried out this kind of work."[60] Putzrath asked Streich if he or anyone else might have information about the Bund. Streich's reply is not recorded, but it seems that the SPD sent a skeptical answer back to Yad Vashem. Moreover, as the then director of Yad Vashem, Mordecai Paldiel, indicated to me later in an interview, Yad Vashem had an additional problem in that, as he put it, "here, we discriminate against Jews."[61] The Righteous Among Nations program recognized only non-Jews, and the Israelis were unsure which Bund members had been Jewish. Yad Vashem was in any case not inclined to recognize collective activity, since its defining image of the rescuer was that of the righteous individual. Now the committee members were being asked to recognize a whole group, but they had to examine each individual carefully. So, explained Paldiel, the case "schlepped and schlepped for years."[62]

It is nonetheless striking that the Bund, which demonstrably had saved the lives of several Jews and had offered wide-ranging help to many others, should have failed to gain recognition here. Once again, the issue was partly the blurring of boundaries between resistance and rescue. Because Lisa and Marianne described the Bund as a left-wing group, Yad Vashem vetted them through contacts in the SPD, and the West German Social Democratic milieu once again acted as skeptical gatekeeper. The representatives might have consulted Steinberg's book and, like him, found the Bund's accounts implausible. In any case, as a politically motivated group, and one containing gentiles and Jews, the Bund did not easily fit the mold of those Yad Vashem honored. According to Paldiel, if just a couple of names had been put forward, it would have been easier. But this, of course, would not have reflected the communal effort Lisa and Marianne had experienced. In terms of the Bund's self-perception, it would have been a travesty.

Changed Beyond Recognition?

Given what we know about the Bund's achievements (and probably the members did more than we will ever know), it is a frustrating and, indeed, distressing experience observing the postwar world's failure to recognize the group's actions. And yet Hans-Josef Steinberg's footnote does raise a troubling issue. When Steinberg wondered how Bund members could claim that they had been "illegally wandering for years," he was citing Weisenborn, but Weisenborn was, in fact, merely repeating the Bund's own words. Steinberg's skepticism reminds us that Artur's restitution application contained exaggerated claims about his time on the run. To what extent, then, had the Bund distorted or obfuscated what it had done? Had it doctored its own experience beyond recognition, as it were?

Artur's speeches and writings produced just a couple of days after liberation were restrained in their claims of outright resistance. Artur dwelled instead on the group's ability to hold firm, stick to its values, and resist being sucked into the Nazi system.[63] But Artur and Ernst soon became aware that to persuade outsiders of their relevance and fitness to lead, they would have to emphasize not only resilience and learning but also their actions on behalf of others.[64] As the efforts to get themselves into Weisenborn's book show, they knew they had to promote their record.[65]

Although much of the *Report on the Help Operation for Jews by the "Bund" Community for Socialist Life*, written in the fall of 1946 or the spring of 1947, is informative, it is impossible to tell if, for example, the "systematically organized parcel service" that the Bund orchestrated was helping only a few lucky recipients or hundreds of people.[66] The report claimed that it had organized fake IDs for *"einige"* (several) people, but in fact, so far as we can tell, this meant only two—Dore and Lisa. While the report, echoing a sentiment from Artur's diary, freely acknowledged that any assistance could only be a drop of water in the ocean of suffering, it still managed to implicitly suggest that the Bund was working on a grander scale than we know was possible.[67]

The "Second Letter Abroad," drafted around the same time, is where the group made its most hyperbolic claims about having undertaken illegal actions during the war. At times we find the same vague expansiveness as in the report on help for Jews, including the claim that the Bund's "illegal activity" "did not stop for an instant" and, in fact, became "livelier and more comprehensive over time." We also read:

> Through its fighting cells, its secret meetings disguised as birthday celebrations, physical education conferences, conversations in factories, on the train, through leaflets etc. countless people had their backs straightened and were enlightened about National Socialism and its evil acts.

The same implicit exaggeration can be found in claims about the threats faced by Bund members:

> Key people able to avoid KZ [concentration camps] and worse only by going on the run. Many in prison, others illegally wandering for years. Almost all pursued, threatened, pressured, and robbed by the Gestapo. Continual house searches. Our Bund house in Essen immediately surrounded, protected from confiscation only by playing the police . . . against the Party. Confiscation of writings, typewriters, monitoring of our post etc etc.

"Key people . . . on the run" almost certainly means Artur, unless the Bund was counting Jews fleeing the regime; but if so, threats to the Bund are getting entangled with persecution that had nothing to do with the group per se. "Many in prison" must refer to those members briefly incarcerated in the 1930s for illegally helping the Communists. The others "illegally wandering for years" must mean Artur again, since no one else at the time or later claimed that they had been on the run, unless the Bund is here again including those targeted as Jews.

In writing its postwar accounts, the Bund had no interest in being recognized as saviors or rescuers per se and, in fact, never named those it
helped to avoid suggesting any demeaning sense of dependency. If it
exaggerated, then it did so because political pressures in the postwar
period made its leaders worry that simply describing their actions would
not be enough to generate the attention and following they believed they
merited. The group was also drawing on a rhetorical register that it had
previously deployed in the 1920s. Back then, as a small group with aspirations to be a model for society, it had had to talk big in a similar way. For
the myriad splinter groups of Weimar's left and alternative scene, this was
the standard register.

But the implied picture of sustained, substantial battle may indeed have
given observers like Steinberg good reason to doubt the group's veracity.
The Bund's efforts to align itself with early postwar left-wing expectations
had actually made it look less impressive, not more. Steinberg's skepticism
is less warranted when he challenges the Bund's claim of having sent "thousands of parcels." Yet this, too, was partly engendered by the Bund's
vagueness about the extent of its enterprise. The kind of industrial-scale
dispatch operation implied would have been impossible—though the
Bund's helpers probably did send more than a thousand small packages.

For Yad Vashem, the problem was a little different. One of the challenges its investigators faced, as we know, was determining who in the Bund
was Jewish. The "Letters Abroad" and other information available to Yad
Vashem were not helpful in this respect. It was both clear to the investigators and yet not properly stated in the Bund literature that its leading couple
was in a mixed marriage. For Yad Vashem, because Artur was a non-Jew
married to a Jew, any assistance he offered could be ascribed to personal
motivation rather than noble commitment. Probably most significant for
Yad Vashem was the fact that their trusted informants in Germany could
not corroborate the Bund's accounts.

A Spiritual Journey

When Artur died in 1968, at the age of eighty-eight, his role as the
Bund's leader had been much reduced since an illness he'd suffered in

1956; nevertheless his death was still a major milestone for the group. (He was spared being confronted by Steinberg's book, which came out a year after his death.) During the 1970s, as Dore herself approached eighty, Bund friends talked about the need to record their history and memorialize Artur while memories of the early days were still present. With the help of surviving members of the old guard such as Else, Doris Braune, and Sonja, Dore produced an impressive 232-page manuscript, titled "Gelebte Utopie: Geschichte einer Gemeinschaft" ("Lived Utopia: The History of a Community").[68] She finished it sometime between 1975 and 1977, a couple of years before her death, and saw it distributed among the members.[69]

"Gelebte Utopie" follows the Bund from its beginnings until its latter years. Each chapter is composed of a brief introduction accompanied by an extended set of original texts, letters, poems, and more from the Bund's past. Because many of the documents no longer exist outside the manuscript, it is a wonderful source. But as an act of remembrance, it places the Bund's experience in a new light. For one thing, Dore and her fellow compilers were clearly writing a paean to Artur. Their account of the Nazi years drew attention to Artur's realism, courage, and wisdom. What had been presented in the "Third Letter Abroad" as group insights were here offered as his guidance. Presumably such overt celebration had not appeared seemly in early postwar public texts, when the group was emphasizing its collective strengths, and when Artur himself had a strong hand in the writing. Now, after his death, it felt only right.

The "conversation" between the Bund and the outside world continued to evolve. As in the earlier postwar texts, the Nazi years continued to be the heart of the story, but it is clear that Steinberg's book had had a major impact. The word "resistance" does not appear once in "Gelebte Utopie," and despite offering an almost comprehensive collection of Bund texts, the "Letters Abroad" are not included. The focus now is far more spiritual. Artur's magnum opus, *Die Zukunft des Glaubens: Die Entscheidungsfrage unserer Zeit* ("The Future of Belief: The Decisive Question of Our Times"), had appeared posthumously just a few years earlier.[70] In it, Artur had developed his views on man's need for a new kind of faith. He argued that a belief rooted in appreciation of the underlying logic of history would provide the ethical foundation for a secure and morally committed life.

In "Gelebte Utopie," Dore presented the Bund's story as one of growing awareness that its quest was at core religious—though not in the traditional sense. Rather, she meant that they were collectively learning to genuflect before the "objective spiritual force" guiding historical development. The Nazi period, she argued, played the crucial role in this awakening.[71] Thus, many of the texts reproduced in the chapter on the Nazi years contain vivid imagery of light in the darkness and descriptions of the solace that a new kind of religious belief brings. The following chapter is titled "The Religious Core of Commitment." After a eulogy to Artur, the volume closes with a section called "Commitment Today," which ends with the sentence *"Das Endziel bleibt"* ("The ultimate goal remains").[72] From Dore and her colleagues' vantage point, then, the Nazi period appeared above all as a time of transformation and maturation, in which under the greatest stresses the Bund learned a new kind of faith.

This is the most explicitly "religious" version of the Bund's history the group produced. In 1990, after both Dore and Lisa had died, a group of surviving Bundists, including Else, Doris, Tove, Ellen, and Berthold Levy, managed to see a version of Dore's manuscript into print. This *Gelebte Utopie* was a different work again.[73] The impetus for publication came from outside, thanks to the interest of younger friends of the Bund, above all the director of what was by then called the Dore Jacobs School, Karin Gerhard. Her input and that of other outsider advisors meant that the revised version of the book was as much attuned to the interests of a new younger German readership as it was driven by the Bund's own mission.[74] The spiritual undercurrent in Dore's account was largely gone. The term "resistance," which by this period had become somewhat fashionable, made a modest comeback, including on the book's back cover. One of the "Letters Abroad" was now included. Equally significantly, for the first time in a postwar Bund history, the Third Reich was no longer the linchpin of the narrative. Instead, the Weimar years received greater emphasis, appearing as a harbinger of the alternative culture that was then blossoming in West Germany. As in the earlier versions, the Bund's close links to a left-wing Jewish scene were largely absent, as were the trials of war.

Unrecognizable Pasts

In 2004, after the publication of *A Past in Hiding*, in which I recounted Marianne Strauss's story, I and others made renewed requests to Yad Vashem to in some way acknowledge the Bund's achievement.[75] A number of people named in the original applications were at last honored in Jerusalem.[76] All those named—and the people they helped—had long since died, but some of their children witnessed the ceremony that took place at the Israeli embassy in Berlin on September 15, 2005.[77] Local events commemorating the role of particular individuals followed, including a commemoration of Meta Kamp-Steinmann and Hedwig Gehrke in Göttingen in November 2005, and of Hanni Ganzer in Düsseldorf in January 2006.[78] But while Yad Vashem's narrative indeed mentioned the Bund, those honored were of course recognized not as a group but as individuals. Many who had played key roles in the rescue effort were left out.[79] Neither Artur nor Ernst were recognized, though their support and leadership had been central. Many others who have figured in these pages were also missing. At the same time, the list of those honored included Marianne's aunt's former housekeeper Emilie Busch, who had nothing to do with the Bund. Her inclusion was entirely warranted, but it only added to the sense that the real story of the Bund—its achievements, its motivations, and the qualities that had enabled it to act—was lost from view.[80]

Conclusion

The Rescue of History

The Bund's Achievement

Whoever saves a life saves the world, and the Bund had a hand in saving at least eight. Scholars have reckoned that on average it took seven, eight, or more people to save just one life in Nazi Germany. Survival trajectories have been recorded in which fifty to sixty helpers played a role in a single rescue.[1] Saving even a single individual involved sacrifice, risks, and fear—sometimes over the course of many years. As a result, very few people managed to survive in hiding. In 1941, some ten thousand Jews were still living in each of the big cities of Frankfurt and Cologne; only a couple hundred made it through the Holocaust. In Munich, out of the 3,500 Jews present before the major deportations, just 77 have been documented as having successfully hidden in the city until the end of the war.[2] In Berlin, where the anonymity of the metropolis offered certain advantages, only a quarter of those who sought to evade deportations by hiding were successful—around 1,700 saw liberation.[3]

The Bund's aid, in any case, extended well beyond its rescue actions. In their readiness to enter destroyed Jewish homes after Kristallnacht, to venture into Jewish organizations and Jewish barracks in the era of deportations, to line up in the post office with packages for Theresienstadt, or to brave a visit to the cells in a local police station with a message for imprisoned Jews, Bund members showed enormous courage. Their aid also had a keen moral and psychological dimension. Mindful of the spiritual predicament of the beneficiaries, they took pains not to undermine their dignity. However stark the differences were between the objective situation of the helpers and of those they were helping, Bund members tried to convey a sense of reciprocity. They were brave, they were thoughtful, and they were generous.

We marvel, too, at the energy and activity they were able to sustain amid persecution, denunciations, and total war. They talked, they argued, they hiked, they celebrated. They maintained contact with members stationed at the front, with Friedl and Erna in Holland, and with exiled friends in Scandinavia and the United States. They traveled to Holland and Switzerland, looked after friends and relatives subject to persecution. They disseminated information about Jewish persecution, and at least one of their letters found its way to a dissident military officer in Berlin. They followed the news, analyzed the regime, produced manuscripts, and prayed for their country to lose the war, even as they waited anxiously for news from loved ones engaged in the fighting. Despite all this courage, they knew they were compromised just by being members of German society: some Bundists were, after all, fighting for the army of a murderous regime. Yet their ethical radar remained intact—as their awareness of being compromised only proves. Their lives and deeds deserve to be remembered, commemorated—and understood.

Motives and Means

Every Bund member I spoke with offered a lucky escape story. There was the time when documents, hidden in an umbrella, went flying down the street, because someone (no one told me who) forgot they were there and opened the umbrella against the rain. And there was the time Mathilde Zenker was able to escape from the Jewish barracks in Duisburg, where she had been smuggling in clothing and food, after a bombing raid scared away the guards. The Bund understood that it had been lucky, and because there were so few groups like it, it is difficult to say whether luck, in the end, was the decisive ingredient for its success. We know there were other rescue networks, like the Kaufmann Group in Berlin, that were destroyed by a denunciation. But though the Bund suffered numerous denunciations, none quite stuck.[4]

If luck was important, it was far from the whole story. Looking back, Bund members themselves had a sophisticated sense of the advantages that had helped them survive. The "Third Letter Abroad" drew attention, for example, to the fact that the Bund owned a number of buildings and thus had access to more or less protected living and meeting spaces. It also pointed out how important *Körperbildung*'s role had been as a central activity, offering camouflage for get-togethers and meetings. To outsiders and authorities, the classes did not look like nefarious political meetings but seemed to be focused on a harmless pastime—not least because similar movements of dance and gymnastics had been drawn into the regime's orbit. Even when the Gestapo discovered literature on *Körperbildung* during house searches, the agents did not immediately assume that the group was involved in subversive activity.[5] Most remarkably, as we have seen, *Körperbildung* classes became a safe space in which potential new recruits could be covertly sounded out. In one sense, *Körperbildung* was an "accidental" advantage, since Dore had conceived of it not as a means of hiding the Bund's political character but as a political and philosophical project. On another level, it showed something systematic—namely, the virtue of having political networks that were organized around a lifestyle choice. The same was true of the Internationaler Sozialistischer Kampfbund (ISK), whose vegetarian restaurants provided perfect meeting places.[6]

Another such "accidental" advantage enjoyed by the Bund was its large number of female members. During the 1920s and early 1930s, as we know, many had come into the Bund's orbit because of the training and professional opportunities offered by Dore's school. Others had been drawn by Artur's erudite and spiritual version of socialism. After 1939, women's significance increased rapidly as men were called up to the front. We know that when it came to helping Jews in Germany, broadly speaking, women played a disproportionate role. Nationally, approximately two-thirds of German rescuers were women.[7] Apart from the fact that so many men were serving in the armed forces, the regime took women less seriously as political actors (though substantial risks remained). Women also tended—even in the Bund, with its progressive attitudes—to be in charge of managing the household. The tasks of hosting, hiding, and feeding all fell within their realm. Notwithstanding the importance of Ernst Jungbluth, of couples like the Briels and the Zenkers, and of the rare solo male host like Hermann Schmalstieg, it is fair to say that the Bund's rescue work was very much a woman's business.

The Bund's "Third Letter Abroad" drew attention to another of the group's features that proved advantageous in a dictatorship: its hybridity and lack of official structures. The Bund had emerged organically from Artur's adult education classes without the trappings of a party, and without being formally registered as an association. This did not, of course, make it invisible. During the pre-Nazi period, the group *wanted* to be known. As a result, it was targeted by the local pro-Nazi press, and in September 1933, after the police confiscated trunks containing incriminating records at Martin Schubert's house, it was banned. But the absence of formal status as political party or registered association, and a concomitant lack of membership lists or financial records, meant that the full scope of the group's activity was difficult for the authorities to discern. After 1933, the Bund rapidly built on this advantage by vigilant self-policing and the destruction of incriminating records. This was key—when the Kaufmann network in Berlin was fatally compromised in 1943, the disaster was less the denunciation per se than a notebook discovered in Franz Kaufmann's possession containing the names of fifty helpers.[8]

If the group's camouflage was largely unplanned, what was integral to its identity and vision was the forging of such haphazard arrangements into bonds of steel. The Bund's fierce bonds of solidarity depended in part on "Weimar" resources—the habit of loyalty and deference to the charismatic leader and of self-sacrifice for the group. They also drew on the Bund's particular philosophy, its notion that an ethical life, free from arbitrary whim, could be attained only through voluntary subordination to collective needs. Hidden within this philosophy were sometimes older, religious impulses, above all pietistic notions of struggling for holy life, that appeared in the ostensibly secular guise of working for the good socialist society.

Whatever their precise nature, the bonds that held the group together gave it the cohesion to engage in collective action and overrode individuals' personal fears. Just as important in enabling action—and, again, probably influenced by inherited religious influences—was the group's embrace of both the macro and the micro. Its goal had always been vast and ambitious: to create a just, socialist society. But the means were small-scale, day-to-day decisions, commitments, and practices. At times this created a strange disconnect. For example, the group proffered grandiose rhetoric in the early 1930s about uniting the working-class parties in a time of crisis but offered as a vision of the way forward only its incremental, long-term model of a living and learning community. After the Nazis' ascent to power, Bund members adjusted to the idea that they could no longer be a model to the outside world, and their strategy of gradual progress gave them a means of taking action in meaningful, if limited, ways. Their political reflexes had primed them to take small-scale action seriously and to devote themselves to attaining the possible.

Resistance and Resilience

During the 1950s, as we saw, "resistance" (*Widerstand*) was understood rather narrowly in West Germany to mean activity aimed at toppling the regime, and for many observers the only resistance that counted was organized military opposition.[9] Once the Nazis had consolidated their rule, the German army had indeed been the only institution left with the autonomy and firepower to challenge them. However, the postwar focus on the plot of July 1944 ignored the sizable groups on the left that had organized against the Nazis from the very beginning. Since the 1960s, serious accounts of resistance have included the actions of the Communists, the Social Democrats, and the various small splinter parties. Should the Bund's achievements stand alongside theirs?

With some important exceptions, the Bund never participated in a direct effort to bring down the regime. It did not collect arms and it did little leafleting, though some Bund members did protect other leftists on the run.[10] It is worth noting, however, that a great deal of the "resistance" work by other left-wing groups—maintaining the network, keeping themselves informed, and so on—was not so different from the Bund's. Most of these groups only occasionally took steps designed to challenge the Nazis' power openly. When they did take part in leafleting, scrawling slogans in public places, or trying to influence factory council votes, the result was often disastrous. The apparent distinction between the Bund and these parties, so evident to Hans-Josef Steinberg, is thus in reality often not so clear-cut. And unlike many of its counterparts, the Bund was successful in gaining several trustworthy new members during the Nazi years.

In the 1970s and 1980s, historians of German resistance widened their scope to include groups whose actions fell short of trying to topple the regime but in some way opposed Nazi efforts to bring them into line.[11] As a result of this shift, Social Democrats who continued to meet and maintain some kind of community, for example, were now deemed to have offered resistance. Socialist pensioners' regular gatherings in local inns, the historians reasoned, offered a more realistic, robust challenge to the Nazis' control over society than foolhardy dissemination of poorly printed pamphlets.[12] It is certainly true that in a society so effectively mobilized by the regime, even the simple act of maintaining political independence and integrity was an achievement. In his 1945 May Day speech, reminding his Meersburg friends of all they had been through, Artur said that the biggest challenge they had faced had not been the Gestapo or the concentration camps, terrifying though they were. Instead, it was the risk of succumbing to what he called the regime's "inner embrace."[13] When almost every aspect of life had been co-opted by the regime, it was the temptation to fit in that had represented the greatest threat to the group's integrity. What the idea of the pensioners' group as a source of resistance gets wrong, however, is the inference that such clandestine gatherings might have burgeoned into a broad oppositional culture. Even in formerly socialist strongholds, working-class milieus did not remain intact. Denunciations undercut easy sociability and made even casual grumbling risky business. Against that background, isolated voices had little chance of joining up to create a groundswell of opposition, as the Bund's profound sense of isolation makes clear.[14]

In the postwar years, the Bund itself was inconsistent in the way it talked about resistance. Its members never doubted that they had constituted "a strong resistance group,"[15] and, as we know, the group sought to enhance its postwar resonance with at times inflated language about its "battle" against the Nazis. For the most part, however, it used the term *Widerstand*, "resistance" as a synonym for "resilience"—for example, in referring to Bund members' "inner powers of resistance"[16] or their ability "to resist twelve terrible years unbroken."[17] At the same time, they would have balked at being placed into the same category of passive endurance as, say, the socialist pensioners' groups mentioned above. The most interesting distinction postwar Bund texts made is, in fact, not so much between actively fighting the regime and passively withstanding it but between living engaged with the world and living withdrawn from it. The terms "illegal work" and "illegal life" recur throughout the "Letters Abroad," and the word "life" is often set in bold to indicate something far more than mere existence—something buoyant, rich, and purposeful. This was the group's pre-Nazi distinction between a disengaged romantic utopianism, which it despised, and a committed life pursued in the heart of an industrial region, now reappearing in a new form. In the words of the "Third Letter Abroad":

> Not a life alongside the system, not a life withdrawn, and certainly not the "happiness of the niche," as it were, a respite from the horrors of real life, but instead a life amid these horrors, permanently contending with the system, in the struggle and through struggle, through the shocks, suffering and uncertainties which it brings.[18]

The Bund was making an important distinction here. Its efforts at sustaining an ethical life and its commitment to dismantling every aspect of the regime's philosophy did represent something more significant than get-togethers with other skeptics in the neighborhood pub. This is partly a question of motive and partly one of risk and effort. Its members found themselves having to make hard choices on a daily basis, choices that put them constantly at risk of denunciation and interrogation. It is interesting to note that the Nazis took efforts to maintain and develop illicit learning communities very seriously. Consider the example of an underground resistance group of young Jewish Communists, often referred to as the Herbert Baum Group. When they were captured after a now famous attack on an anti-Soviet exhibition in 1942, the official indictment explicitly identified the holding of Communist school sessions as one of the most serious offenses.[19] The more historians have uncovered the degree of support the regime was able to elicit in its "dictatorship by acclamation," the more impressive the Bund's ability to maintain its separate life becomes. Perhaps we do not quite have a category that fits this intense, self-conscious cultivation of a communal shared space. It was more than mere nonconformity, but less than active combat against the regime.[20]

What also distinguished the Bund from many oppositionally minded circles, of course, is that the Bund saved lives. Until a few years ago, none of the attempts at defining resistance—whether in Germany or the occupied countries—took help for Jews particularly seriously. In the historiography of the French resistance, rescue had long been marginalized, since it did not have the same liberatory goals as armed opposition to the occupiers. Those who sought to help Jews for the most part did not assail the regime or seek actively to bring it down, though there were participants in active resistance who also assisted Jews. However, as definitions of resistance broadened to include refusal to submit, then all Jews who did not accept death were engaged in it, as indeed were all who worked to help them survive. The Holocaust survivor and historian Arno Lustiger coined the term *Rettungswiderstand*,[21] or "rescue-resistance," which is now commonly used in the German historiography of rescue. In the French case, rescue, instead of being on the margins, is increasingly treated as the archetype of resistance.[22] Even if we may feel that these moves risk blurring important distinctions, we can certainly agree that rescuers hoped to throw a small spanner into the machinery of destruction. The idea of "humanitarian resistance" tries to capture this.[23]

Rescue, Help, and Self-Help

Debates about the nature and limits of nonconformity, dissent, and opposition to Nazi rule have made clear that there are many ways of defining resistance. When it comes to "rescue," however, the paradigms that thwarted Lisa and Marianne's efforts to get the Bund recognized continue to exercise a powerful hold on our thinking.[24] The most recent study on Germany carries the subtitle "individuals versus the Nazi system."[25] In the popular imagination, the individual, unpolitical rescuer, motivated by goodness of heart, remains the dominant archetype.

Only very recently has scholarship begun to upend our assumptions.

We are now learning how often money, property, cheap labor, sexual favors, or religious conversion were the price of help.[26] This was clearly not true for the Bund, for whom the deed was its own reward. Yet the Bund differs markedly from the expected model of the "righteous gentile," not least because of the way it functioned as a network. We do not know how many other groups with a strong political or philosophical basis acted to help Jews. It seems not many. But if we extend our definition of groups to include more loosely defined networks, then it is the individual rescue that begins to look more like the outlier. The majority of German rescues may have been initiated by individuals, but most required support from a network of social relationships.[27] At their most passive, those might be mere audiences of complicity, groups of acquaintances and neighbors who were in the know and willing not to inform the authorities.[28] For Berlin, where by far the largest number of Jews survived, research has shown that many rescues depended on more active social networks—whether to provide new places to stay when existing ones became compromised or helpers lost their nerve, or to help with food, money, documents, and moral support. Of course, such networks were fragile and often failed to sustain assistance long enough to ensure survival.[29] Even the Bund was sometimes left with no other option than to hand those it was helping on to others.

When help is collective, can we still justify the central emphasis scholars have placed on the individual rescuer's personality? Ever since Samuel Oliner and Pearl Oliner's foundational work on the "altruistic personality" in the 1980s, psychologists and ethicists have characterized rescuers as having a high degree of empathy, or what the Oliners called "extensivity."[30] Other influential analyses have seen the rescuers as exhibiting a distinctive degree of personal autonomy, enabling them to think independently and form judgments unaffected by prevailing views.[31] Clearly, some Bund members possessed these qualities. But does the individual's capacity for empathy or any type of individual personality really account for such a coordinated campaign of action? In its postwar *Report on the Help Operation for Jews*, the Bund attributed its commitment, as we saw, not to "cheap empathy" but to principle. Indeed, it argued that principle had driven it to act on behalf of people for whose bourgeois lifestyle they felt more antipathy than sympathy.[32]

Yet if individuals' ability to empathize seems a poor way of understanding how the Bund worked, the Bund's own postwar depiction of itself does not convince, either. Certainly, the Bund's ethical philosophy was a vital resource that nourished its members' commitment to one another and to the persecuted. Artur was eminently justified in seeing their actions as the expression of their principles. But we have also learned that personal connections were crucial. Above all, these ties created awareness of Jewish persecution. Reconstructing the Bund's experience, rather than relying on its postwar self-account, corroborates existing scholarship suggesting that rescue, like other forms of collective action, is very rarely the result of principle alone, even when conducted by highly politically or religiously motivated groups.[33] Group dynamics, internal pressures, and leadership all have a part to play. The Bund's forthright assertion that it was motivated by principle rather than empathy is therefore probably just as misleading as explaining the group's actions in terms of individual psychologies. For different members of the group, varying degrees of idealism, group loyalty and friendships, empathy with the victims, potential shame at letting others down, and so on combined to impel them to act.[34]

Michael Gross's work on Le Chambon-sur-Lignon, a French village that sheltered thousands of Jews from the Nazis, suggests that the personality of the leader of a group or network was crucial. Artur was a charismatic man, and his self-confidence and sense of conviction were infectious. His decisive role is probably more attributable to classic leadership qualities than to qualities of empathy. As far as empathizing is concerned, what likely made the suffering of the Jewish world so evident to him was the fact that he was in a mixed marriage. As leader, he was then able to transform this direct experience into a group mission.

We might add an intriguing twist to this discussion in that the Bund, like other bündisch groups in the 1920s, had emphasized the personality of the natural leader as an important part of what gave the group structure and coherence. What seems at least as significant as Artur's particular qualities, therefore, is the shared "ideology" of personality, so strong in the 1920s, an ideology on which the Nazis also drew. In other words, the widely shared assumption that there should be a natural leader fostered a readiness among members to follow a particular individual, and to do what that leader asked. That, in turn, helped furnish the group with the cohesion, loyalty, and trust essential for acting against the regime.

Mixed-marriage couples like the Jacobses played a leading role in other networks of help. In Munich, such couples could be found at the center of many rescue actions. In Berlin, Otto Weidt, the owner of a work-shop for the blind and deaf who saved a number of Jews, was supported by the "Aryan" wife of a Jewish doctor. Converts, too, bridged gentile and non-gentile worlds, and they also are overrepresented in informal net-works, such as the Kaufmann Group in Berlin. In Holland, rescue and survival rates were higher in areas where there were more converted Jews. Converts and Jews in mixed marriages brought together those affected by Nazi policy and those in a position to assist. The role of mixed couples was strengthened in Germany not least because in 1933 there had been some 35,000 Jews in mixed marriages (or about 7 percent of the Jewish population), and even by December 1942 there were still 16,760 such couples left in the country. Moreover (and no doubt because of the size and influence of this group), there was the fact that the Nazis had, with regional variations, long exempted persons in mixed marriages from deportation.[35]

This leads to one other facet of the Bund's story. Our search for selfless rescuers has often overshadowed the role of Jewish "self-help." The type of rescuer that our accounts have honored most is one who not only helped but did not *have* to help, since he or she was not in the firing line. The rec-ognition of the righteous at Yad Vashem explicitly excludes Jews, presum-ing that Jewish help was self-interested and thus does not carry the same moral weight. In the Bund's case, however, we saw at every stage that the distinction between helper and helped, Jews and non-Jews, is more ambig-uous than we might expect. The Jacobs family were "victims" as well as helpers, and Lisa Jacob and Marianne Strauss were far from being passive recipients of aid. Scholars are beginning to pay greater attention to Jewish "self-help," whether in actively participating in resistance, organizing and providing resources to assist rescue actions, initiating their own rescue, or showing great enterprise in evading capture. So much of Lisa's and Marianne's survival hinged on their initiative, self-possession, and courage. Even while in hiding, they continued to help others. Lisa maintained extensive correspondence and sent parcels to deportees in Theresienstadt. Marianne, too, continued to send parcels to her loved ones in Theresien-stadt, as surviving friends were able to acknowledge after the war, and even arranged assistance for an endangered friend—just as Hanna Jordan had done when she was on the run.[36]

Rescue, Experience, and Memory

A recurrent theme of this book has been the sometimes subtle, sometimes stark contrast between the Bund's experience during the Third Reich and its later memories. By contrast, in her magisterial study of rescue based on interviews conducted decades after the war, Nechama Tec wrote that rescuers' memories of the dramatic events in which they were engaged are too powerful to become clouded over time.[37] Certainly, many episodes of the Bund's wartime life emerge vividly in later narratives or interviews. Even the exaggerations in the "Letters Abroad" are often rhetorical overreach rather than outright errors of fact. Yet subtle shifts in the framing, along with new emphases and exclusions, means that the group's postwar texts tell a different story from the one that unfolds from the wartime records.[38]

Such differences were evident even in the immediate aftermath of liberation, when the Nazi "present" had only just become the past. Freed of uncertainty as to whether they would survive and if the regime would fall, Bund members now viewed their past hopes and fears in a new light. New knowledge about the Holocaust flooded in, overwhelming even a previously well-informed observer like Artur. It also put much that one had thought and feared into a new perspective. Life under Nazi rule had, in any case, been at once so extraordinary and yet often so mundane that it was hard to grasp even at the time, and it rapidly became ever more elusive. In a letter penned to Wasja just a week after liberation, Dore was already doubting that she would ever be able to convey what they had lived through.[39]

Adding to the problems of translation into a postwar idiom were the new political pressures of the postwar era. The group wanted to use its Nazi record to appeal to a postwar audience and establish its fitness to lead. But even if it had not sought to do so, it would still have found many of the choices, dilemmas, perceptions, and even the language from its days under Nazi rule no longer appropriate to the postwar era. Artur's hope, in the late 1930s and early 1940s, that Jews might be cured of materialism by their sufferings, for example, was in light of Auschwitz now unthinkable. As the generations sought to find one another again after 1945, the wedge the Nazis had driven between some Bund members and their children, as another example, was similarly too uncomfortable to articulate.

Often such omissions reflect conscious choices about what was relevant or seemly. But the persistent absence, in the postwar writings, of the terrifying and transformative experience of air raids, for example, feels like more than a simple narrative choice.[40] In an insightful, if controversial, lecture given at the University of Zurich in 1997 and later published as a book, the writer W. G. Sebald argued that the postwar period was characterized by a striking inability to engage with the real terror of the bombings.[41] Local publications in many German cities diligently documented the extent of the destruction, yet these accounts were always couched in pious and formulaic language that buried the real experience deeper under the rubble.[42] Perhaps because Bund members felt it would contradict the image of vigor and promise they wished to present, perhaps because of their rather old-fashioned understanding of the psyche, perhaps because of a deeper trauma, in the collective texts that survive from the postwar period, the Bundists never wrote about their fears and their vulnerability—except where doing so reinforced the idea that the group had been stronger together than each individual could have been alone.

Some of the contrasts between wartime experience and postwar accounts were no doubt peculiar to the Bund. Some arose because the Bund's "memory" was being produced collectively for a purpose, and not narrated privately to a curious interviewer.[43] But the very real difficulty of recapturing dilemmas faced, choices made, perceptions noted, and traumas experienced under Nazi rule is far from unique. These tensions between experience and memory are not limited to rescue, but they feel particularly relevant for rethinking rescue, because so much of what we want to find out about the rescuer relates to the rescuer's mental world and decisions at the time.[44] Discovering the ways in which the Bund came to remember its past, and also the many ways it failed to achieve recognition, makes us realize how unwittingly retrospective our approach to rescue has been.

It was the postwar search for appropriate heroes, after all, that created frame and canvas for our image of the rescuer and, in the process, denied some a place in the picture. Yad Vashem's model of the "righteous," much as it responded to a deeply felt need to honor those who had helped, was not dictated by history per se; rather, it was the result of postwar diplomatic, political, and religious considerations.[45] In Europe, in recent decades, public interest in rescue has grown, driven, above all, by hope of gleaning useful lessons for civil society and perhaps even training the Good Samaritans of the future.[46] Yad Vashem's model of the "righteous" has shaped other countries' approaches to public commemoration of the rescuer, even beyond the Holocaust (for example, in Rwanda).[47]

The model has also decisively influenced scholars' treatment of the subject. Many have not only followed Yad Vashem's definition of who counts as a rescuer but have restricted their analysis to individuals recognized by Yad Vashem.[48] And it has probably colored the rescuers' memories themselves. Most scholarship on the subject, after all, has relied almost exclusively on interviews recorded decades after the fall of Nazism. Given that Yad Vashem and other commemorations created a framework of public recognition for "rescue" that simply did not exist at the time when the lauded acts occurred, it is hard to believe that this does not have an impact on the self-concept and memory of those now (quite rightly) praised as rescuers.[49]

All this is not to discount the value of retrospective accounts. Later reflections and memories on the part of rescuer and rescued are in many cases all we have to go on. The way the women and men who took such risks under the Nazis come to interpret their actions as they grow older is often interesting and, indeed, moving in its own right. Yet it is surprising how often we have assumed that postwar accounts give us direct access to wartime selves, and how little effort has been made to understand the rescuer's thoughts and perceptions in the moment. Perhaps we need to reverse Kierkegaard's famous dictum "Life can only be understood backwards; but it must be lived forwards." History can only be viewed backward, true enough, but if we want to truly comprehend the rescuer's actions and trajectory, we have to try to be with the rescuer in the moment—to reclaim their lives, as they were being lived.

In light of the Bund's experience, we wonder, in fact, if the notion of rescue itself is not too retrospective. Does it really capture the myriad of choices, motives, and actions at the time? After the event, once it is clear that lives have been saved, it may make sense as a concept. But helpers often did not know what the extent and duration of their support would be. Even after the event, "rescue" may be misleading, because it implies that Jews' survival was the direct result of an intent to save them, whereas most survival trajectories were more complicated. In the Bund's case, acts of solidarity with no immediate prospect of saving anyone seem at least as impressive as those that we know contributed to saving a life. Walking through a hostile crowd to present flowers to the Heinemanns after Kristallnacht was never going to lead to a "rescue." After the war, once the full scale of the Holocaust was known, such acts perhaps looked less meaningful. But viewed from the conditions of the time, Tove's march through a baying mob or Grete's visit to the prison to reassure the Strausses seem gestures as splendid and courageous as any.

Lives Reclaimed

The Bund's postwar intellectual trajectory is full of bitter ironies. The group talked up its game to the point of provoking detractors. It hid how fragile it had felt at times during the Nazi era and the war, making it harder for us to see its true heroism. The lessons it drew from the past did not match the ones contemporaries wanted to hear. The Nazis had discredited the very traditions from which the Bund drew its strength. As a result, the reflexes of postwar generations were different. After the war, even some of the Bund's own members found the discipline of the "order" unpalatable. Many of the former servicemen soon withdrew their involvement. The Bund's belief in the logic of history, a belief that had helped it maintain its bearing despite the brutal challenges of Nazism and total war, also did not make sense to others. Probably others could understand the Bund's view, as indeed we can, that some kind of faith might be essential for the future of humanity, encouraging humility, and creating a shared perspective beyond the narrow needs and drives of the self. But neither they nor we are convinced that the Bund had found the "objective spiritual force" or the underlying logic of history. The failure to convey this faith—or, to put it another way, the obsolescence of its Kantian belief in progress—was another part of the group's postwar disappointment.

The Bund nevertheless deserves recognition. We may think of Artur and Dore, Walter and Gertrud, Ernst, Ellen, Lisa, Sonja, Else, Fritz and

Maria, Änne and August, Gustav and Mathilde, Reinhold and Grete, Alfred
and Tilde, Liesel, Karlos and Karin, Karl, Doris, Meta, Grete, Hedwig and
Gustav, Hermann, and all the others as righteous individuals. A few of them
have now been recognized as such. But it was, in the end, the group—or,
as Bund members would say, *die Sache*, "the cause"—that had triumphed.
For all our distance from their beliefs, and their habits of obedience and
obeisance, still there remains in the Bund's achievement a hint of something more universal. The intensity of their focus on the here and now
meant that every gesture counted. That translated into flowers, parcels, a
shared couch, saved lives. Yet all the while the group's eyes were cast "heav-
enward," toward the great goals of human freedom and ethical responsibility.

SOURCES

Primary Sources

Public Archives

Alte Synagoge, Essen (ASE)

Archiv der Akademie der Künste, Berlin (AAK)

Gedenkstätte des deutschen Widerstand, Berlin

Landesarchiv Nordrhein-Westfalen (LAN)

Landeshauptarchiv Koblenz (LHAK)

Schlesinger Library, Radcliffe Institute of Advanced Study, Harvard University (SLC)

Stadtarchiv Essen (StAE)

Stadtarchiv Remscheid (StAR)

Stadtarchiv Wuppertal (StAW)

Private Collections

Bund archive, housed in the former home of the Dore Jacobs School, Essen (BAE)

Papers consulted when in the possession of Vivian Ellenbogen, Liverpool, from his mother, Marianne Ellenbogen, née Strauss. They are now held in the Parkes Archive, Hartley Library, University of Southampton, File MS 301 (EP)

Papers formerly in the possession of Ursula Jungbluth, Wuppertal, for her father, Ernst Jungbluth, and from Ellen Jungbluth, now among the Bund papers in Essen (JP)

Papers in the possession of Stefan Brandt, Berlin—these are letters his grand-
mother Trude Brandt, in Poland, sent to Bund members (SBP)
Papers in the possession of Wolfgang Briel, Barsinghausen, from his parents,
Fritz and Maria Briel (WBP)
Papers in the possession of Barbara Martin, Marl, from her parents, Karlos and
Karin Morgenstern, kindly made available by Norbert Reichling (BMP)
Papers in the possession of Annette Speer, Wuppertal, from her father, Friedl
Speer, son of Bund member Liesel Speer (SP)
Papers in the possession of Alfred Stürmer, Munich, from his parents, Alfred
and Tilde Stürmer (ASP)

Printed Primary Sources

Anstadt, Milo. *De verdachte oorboog: Autobiografische Roman* [in Dutch]. Amster-
dam: Contact, 1996.
Behrend-Rosenfeld, Else R., Erich Kasberger, and Marita Krauss. *Leben in zwei
Welten: Tagebücher eines jüdischen Paares in Deutschland und im Exil*. München: Volk
Verlag, 2011.
Boor, Lisa de. *Tagebuchblätter aus den Jahren 1938–1945*. München: Biederstein
Verlag, 1963.
Brandt, Heinz. *Ein Traum, der nicht entführbar ist: Mein Weg zwischen Ost und West*.
München: List, 1967.
Cohen, Susi. "My First Ninety Years." Unpublished manuscript, 2011.
Cohn, Willy. *Kein Recht, Nirgends: Tagebuch vom Untergang des Breslauer Judentums,
1933–1941*. Köln: Böhlau, 2006.
Deutschkron, Inge. *Ich trug den gelben Stern*. Köln: Verlag Wissenschaft und Poli-
tik, 1978; published in English as *Outcast: A Jewish Girl in Wartime Berlin*.
Translated by Jean Steinberg. New York: Fromm International, c. 1989.
Dore Jacobs Schule, ed. *Für Dore Jacobs, 1894–1994*. Essen, 1994.
Ellenbogen, Marianne. "Flucht und illegales Leben während der Nazi-
Verfolgungsjahre 1943–1945." *Das Münster am Hellweg* 37 (1984): 135–42.
Freund, Elizabeth, and Carola Sachse. *Als Zwangsarbeiterin 1941 in Berlin: Die
Aufzeichnungen der Volkswirtin Elisabeth Freund*. Selbstzeugnisse der Neuzeit. Ber-
lin: Akademie, 1996.
Funk, Rainer. "Erleben von Ohnmacht im Dritten Reich: Das Schicksal der
Jüdischen Verwandtschaft Erich Fromms aufgezeigt Anhand von Doku-
menten und Briefen auf dem Weg in die Vernichtung." *Fromm-Forum* 9
(2005): 35–79.
Herz, Yitzhak Sophoni. *Meine Erinnerung an Bad Homburg und seine 600 Jährige
jüdische Gemeinde (1335–1942)*. Rechovoth, Israel: S. Herz, 1981.
Jacob, Lisa. "'Der Bund': Gemeinschaft für Sozialistisches Leben und Meine
Rettung vor der Deportation." *Das Münster am Hellweg* 37 (1984): 105–34.

————. "'Der Bund': Gemeinschaft für sozialistisches Leben und meine Errettung vor der Deportation; Ein Brief geschrieben nach Kriegsende an meine im Ausland lebenden Geschwister." Bund Archive, Essen, no date.

Jacobs, Artur. *Über Wesen und Ziele einer Volkshochschule: Ein Entwurf zu einer Neuen Volkserziehung; der proletarischen Jugend gewidmet.* Essen: Freier Ausschuss für Volksbildung in Essen, 1919.

————. *Die Zukunft des Glaubens: Die Entscheidungsfrage unserer Zeit.* Frankfurt am Main: Europäische Verlagsanstalt, 1971.

Jacobs, Dore. "Erinnerungen." In Dore Jacobs Schule, *Für Dore Jacobs, 1894–1994*, 3–6.

————. "Gelebte Utopie." Unpublished manuscript, c. 1975–77.

————. "Das Ringen der Zeit um körperseelische Erneuerung." *Die Tat* (1922): 1–20.

————. "Werdegang der Schule." In Dore Jacobs Schule, *Für Dore Jacobs, 1894–1994*, 7–15.

————. "Zur Frage der Kollektiventscheidung." In *Sozialistische Jugend und ihre Erziehungsaufgaben: Bundgedanken zur politischen Erziehung*, ed. Der Bund. Essen: Der Bund [1928], 12–14.

Jacobs, Dore, Else Bramesfeld, et al. *Gelebte Utopie: Aus dem Leben einer Gemeinschaft.* Essen: Klartext, 1990.

Kamp, Meta. *Auf der anderen Seite stehen.* Göttingen: printed by the author, 1987.

Victor Klemperer. *I Will Bear Witness: A Diary of the Nazi Years, 1933–1941* (New York: Modern Library, 1998).

Victor Klemperer. *I Will Bear Witness: A Diary of the Nazi Years, 1942–1945* (New York: Modern Library, 2001).

Matthäus, Jürgen, and Mark Roseman. *Jewish Responses to Persecution.* Vol. 1: *1933–1938.* Documenting Life and Destruction: Holocaust Sources in Context. Lanham, Md.: AltaMira Press in association with the United States Holocaust Memorial Museum, 2010.

Noack-Mosse, Eva. *Journey into Darkness: Theresienstadt Diary, January–July 1945.* Madison: University of Wisconsin Press, 2018.

Reese, Willy Peter, and Stefan Schmitz. *A Stranger to Myself: The Inhumanity of War: Russia, 1941–1944.* New York: Farrar, Straus and Giroux, 2005.

Reichmann, Hans, and Michael Wildt. *Deutscher Bürger und verfolgter Jude: Novemberpogrom und KZ Sachsenhausen 1937 bis 1939.* Biographische Quellen zur Zeitgeschichte. München: R. Oldenbourg, 1998.

Seligmann, Eva, and Heide Henk. *Erinnerungen einer streitbaren Pädagogin.* Bremen: Edition Temmen, 2000.

Simon, Marie Jalowicz, Irene Stratenwerth, and Hermann Simon. *Untergetaucht: Eine junge Frau überlebt in Berlin 1940–1945.* Bonn: Bundeszentrale für Politische Bildung, 2014.

Simon, Marie, and Anthea Bell. *Underground in Berlin: A Young Woman's Extraordi-nary Tale of Survival in the Heart of Nazi Germany.* New York: Little, Brown, 2016.
Sozialdemokratische Partei Deutschlands and Klaus Behnken, *Deutschland-Berichte der Sopade 1934–1940,* 7 vols. Salzhausen: Verlag Petra Nettelbeck; Frankfurt am Main: Zweitausendeins, 1980.
Stenbock-Fermor, Alexander. *Deutschland von Unten: Reise durch die proletarische Provinz.* Stuttgart: J. Engelhorns nachf., 1931.
———. *Meine Erlebnisse als Bergarbeiter.* Lebendige Welt Erzählungen und Beken-ntnisse. Stuttgart: J. Engelhorn, 1928.

Interviews

(All interviews are with Mark Roseman unless otherwise stated.)

Individual Interviews and Conversations

Eric Alexander, Stamford, Conn., July 16, 1998

Karien Anstadt, telephone interview, March 2011

Huberte Arnsmann, Essen, October 2015

Doris Braune, October 1991 (conducted by Heidi Behrens-Cobet)

Fritz Briel, Remscheid, telephone interview, January 1997

Maria Briel, Remscheid, November 1990 (video interview conducted by Jochen Bilstein)

Wolfgang Briel, Barsinghausen, April 2006

Susi Cohen, Essen, September 1996 (conducted by Judith Hess)

Marianne Ellenbogen, Liverpool, October 1989, July 1996, October 1996

Elisabeth Feldman, June 2004 (conducted by Norbert Reichling)

Karin Gerhard, Essen, May 1999

Tove Gerson, talk given to Handelsschule Essen 1988 (audio recording in pos-session of the author)

Tove Gerson, Essen, January 1997

Hanna Jordan, Wuppertal, July 1997

Ellen Jungbluth, Wuppertal, July 1997 and March 2000

Ursula Jungbluth, Wuppertal, May and June 1999

Helmut Lenders, Düsseldorf, June 1999

Berthold Levy, Essen, December 1985 (conducted by Angela Genger)

Barbara Martin, Lüdinghausen, June 2004 (conducted by Norbert Reichling)

Elfriede Nenanovic, Göttingen, April 2006

Mordecai Paldiel, Jerusalem, July 1998

Kurt and Jenni Schmidt, Wuppertal, July 1999

Änne Schmitz, Wuppertal, January 1997

Armgard Schubert, Seeheim-Jugenheim, June 1999

Friedl Speer, Wuppertal, April 2000

Ernst Steinmann, telephone conversation, January 1997; interview, May 2006

Reinhold Ströter, Mettmann, November 1998

Alfred Stürmer, Innsbruck, June 2011

Eberhard Stürmer, telephone conversation, October 2011

Gustav Zenker, Mülheim, February 1988 (conducted by Monika Grüter)

Group Conversations

Sonja Schreiber and Else Bramesfeld, 1986 (conducted by Heidi Behrens-Cobet)

Else Bramesfeld, Doris Braune, Tove Gerson, Ellen Jungbluth, and Reinhold Ströter, March 1988 (conducted by Heidi Behrens-Cobet)

Hermann Schmalstieg, Ellen Jungbluth, Reinhold Ströter, and others, Bund retreat, summer 1999

Radio Broadcasts and Online Interviews

Fritz Denks, *Mülheimer Zeitzeugen*, https://www.youtube.com/watch?v=rnr0n7 IZmG0&t=94s.

"Lebenserfahrungen," Tove Gerson interviews, Südfunk II, Stuttgart, six installments, beginning August 4, 1987.

"Sie wussten was sie tun: Von Menschen, die der nazistischen Unmenschlichkeit widerstanden," Ruth Kotik, WDR 1, July 1, 1983.

"Ein Vorläufer alternativer Lebensformen: Der Bund—Gemeinschaft für sozialistisches Leben," Ruth Kotik, WDR 3, November 16, 1984.

Gustav Zenker, *Mülheimer Zeitzeugen*, https://www.youtube.com/watch?v=HdyA0oCK5J8.

Secondary Literature

Abelshauser, Werner, Wolfgang Köllmann, and Franz-Josef Brüggemeier. *Das Ruhrgebiet im Industriezeitalter: Geschichte und Entwicklung*. 2 vols. Düsseldorf: Schwann im Patmos Verlag, 1990.

Ahrens, Rüdiger. *Bündische Jugend: Eine neue Geschichte, 1918–1933*. Göttingen: Wallstein Verlag, 2015; doi:9783835317581.

Allen, William Sheridan. "Die deutsche Öffentlichkeit und die 'Reichskristallnacht': Konflikte zwischen Werthierarchie und Propaganda im Dritten Reich." In *Die Reihen Fast Geschlossen: Beiträge zur Geschichte des Alltags unterm*

Nationalsozialismus, ed. Detlev Peukert, Jürgen Reulecke, and Adelheid Castell Rüdenhausen. Wuppertal: Hammer, 1981, 397–411.

———. "Die Sozialdemokratische Untergrundbewegung: Zur Kontinuität der subkulturellen Werte." In *Der Widerstand gegen den Nationalsozialismus: Die deutsche Gesellschaft und der Widerstand gegen Hitler*, ed. Jürgen Schmädeke and Peter Steinbach. Publikationen der Historischen Kommission zu Berlin. München: R. Piper, 1985, 849–66.

Andresen, Knud. *Widerspruch als Lebensprinzip: Der undogmatische Sozialist Heinz Brandt (1909–1986)*. Reihe Politik und Gesellschaftsgeschichte. Bonn: Dietz, 2007.

Bajohr, Frank. "Die Zustimmungsdiktatur: Grundzüge nationalsozialistischer Herrschaft in Hamburg." In *Hamburg im "Dritten Reich,"* ed. Josef Schmid. Göttingen: Wallstein, 2005, 69–131.

Bajohr, Frank, and Michael Wildt. *Volksgemeinschaft: Neue Forschungen zur Gesellschaft des Nationalsozialismus*. Die Zeit des Nationalsozialismus. Original ed. Frankfurt am Main: Fischer Taschenbuch Verlag, 2009.

Banke, Cecilie, Felicia Stokholm, Anders Jerichow, and Paul Larkin. *Civil Society and the Holocaust: International Perspectives on Resistance and Rescue*. New York: Humanity in Action Press, 2013.

Baron, Lawrence. "Restoring Faith in Humankind." *Sh'ma* 14, no. 276 (1984): 124–28.

Barth, Emmy. *An Embassy Besieged: The Story of a Christian Community in Nazi Germany*. Eugene, Ore.: Cascade Books; Rifton, N.Y.: Plough, 2010.

Beaulieu, François de. *Mein Vater, Hitler und Ich*. Bremen: Donat Verlag, 2013.

———. *Mon père, Hitler et moi*. Rennes: Ouest-France, 2008.

Beer, Suzanne. "Aid Offered Jews in Nazi Germany: Research Approaches, Methods, and Problems." Violence de masse et Résistance—Réseau de recherche, https://www.sciencespo.fr/mass-violence-war-massacre-resistance /en/document/aid-offered-jews-nazi-germany-research-approaches -methods-and-problems.

Behrens, Heidi, and Norbert Reichling. "'Umbau des Ganzen Lebens': Frauenbildung und Geschlechterfragen in der sozialistischen Bildungsgemeinschaft 'Bund' seit 1919." In *Zwischen Emanzipation und 'besonderer Kulturaufgabe der Frau': Frauenbildung in der Geschichte der Erwachsenenbildung*, ed. Paul Ciupke and Karin Derichs-Kunstmann. Essen: Klartext, 2001, 149–66.

Benz, Wolfgang. "Solidarität mit Juden Während der NS-Zeit." In *Solidarität und Hilfe für Juden während der NS-Zeit*. Vol. 5, *Überleben im Untergrund: Hilfe für Juden in Deutschland*, ed. Beate Kosmala and Claudia Schoppmann. Reihe Solidarität und Hilfe 9–16. Berlin: Metropol, 2002.

Berschel, Holger. *Bürokratie und Terror: Das Judenreferat der Gestapo Düsseldorf 1935–1945*. Düsseldorfer Schriften zur Neueren Landesgeschichte und zur Geschichte Nordrhein-Westfalens. Essen: Klartext, 2001.

Bilstein, Jochen, and Frieder Backhaus. *Geschichte der Remscheider Juden*. Remscheid: Verlag der Buchh. Hackenberg Wermelskirchen W. Dreyer-Erben, 1992.

Bludau, Kuno. *Gestapo, Geheim! Widerstand und Verfolgung in Duisburg, 1933–1945*. Schriftenreihe des Forschungsinstituts der Friedrich-Ebert-Stiftung. Bonn–Bad Godesberg: Verlag Neue Gesellschaft, 1973.

Bonavita, Petra. *Mit falschem Pass und Zyankali: Retter und Gerettete aus Frankfurt am Main in der NS-Zeit*. Stuttgart: Schmetterling Verlag, 2009.

Borgstedt, Angela. "'Bruderring' und 'Lucknerkreis': Rettung im Deutschen Sudwesten." In Kosmala and Schoppmann, *Solidarität und Hilfe für Juden Während der NS-Zeit*, 191–204.

———. "Hilfe für Verfolgte: Judenretter und Judenhelfer." In Steinbach and Tuchel, *Widerstand gegen die Nationalsozialistische Diktatur*, 307–21.

Breyvogel, Wilfried. "Jugendliche Widerstandsformen: Vom organisierten Widerstand zur jugendlichen Alltagsopposition." In *Widerstand gegen den Nationalsozialismus*, ed. Peter Steinbach and Johannes Tuchel. Bonn: Bundeszentrale für Politische Bildung, 1994, 426–42.

Brocke, Michael, and Nathana Hüttenmeister. *Der jüdische Friedhof in Solingen: Eine Dokumentation in Wort und Bild*. Solingen: Stadtarchiv, 1996.

Broszat, Martin. "Resistenz und Widerstand: Eine Zwischenbilanz des Forschungsprojektes." In Broszat, Frölich, and Wiesemann, *Bayern in der NS-Zeit*, vol. 4, 691–709.

Broszat, Martin, Elke Fröhlich, and Falk Wiesemann. *Bayern in der NS-Zeit*. 6 vols. München: Oldenbourg, 1977–83.

Caldwell, J. Timothy. *Expressive Singing: Dalcroze Eurythmics for Voice*. Englewood Cliffs, N.J.: Prentice Hall, 1995.

Caplan, Jane. "'Ausweis Bitte!' Identity and Identification in Nazi Germany." In *Identification and Registration Practices in Transnational Perspective: People, Papers and Practices*, ed. Ilsen About, James Brown, and Gayle Lonergan. St. Antony's Series. New York: Palgrave Macmillan, 2013.

Cesarani, David. *Final Solution: The Fate of the Jews, 1933–1949*. New York: St. Martin's, 2016.

Cox, John M. *Circles of Resistance: Jewish, Leftist, and Youth Dissidence in Nazi Germany*. Studies in Modern European History. New York: Peter Lang, 2009.

Crew, David F. *Bodies and Ruins: Imagining the Bombing of Germany, 1945 to the Present*. Social History, Popular Culture, and Politics in Germany. Ann Arbor: University of Michigan Press, 2017.

Croes, Marnix. "The Holocaust in the Netherlands and the Rate of Jewish Survival." *Holocaust and Genocide Studies* 20, no. 3 (2006): 474–99.

Croes, Marnix, and Beate Kosmala. "Facing Deportation in Germany and the Netherlands: Survival in Hiding." In *Facing the Catastrophe: Jews and Non-Jews in Europe During World War II,* ed. Beate Kosmala and Georgi Verbeeck. Occupation in Europe. New York: Berg, 2011, 97–158.

Degen, Michael. *Nicht alle waren Mörder: Eine Kindheit in Berlin.* München: Econ, 1999.

Delius, Friedrich Christian. *Mein Jahr als Mörder: Roman.* 2nd ed. Berlin: Rowohlt, 2004.

Dickinson, Edward Ross. *Dancing in the Blood: Modern Dance and European Culture on the Eve of the First World War.* Cambridge: Cambridge University Press, 2017.

Dörner, Bernward. *Die Deutschen und der Holocaust: Was niemand wissen wollte, aber jeder wissen konnte.* Berlin: Propyläen, 2007.

———. "NS-Herrschaft und Denunziation: Anmerkungen zu Defiziten in der Denunziationsforschung." *Historical Social Research / Historische Sozialforschung* 26, nos. 2–3 (2001): 55–69.

Dostoyevsky, Fyodor. *The Brothers Karamazov: A Novel in Four Parts and an Epilogue.* Translated by David McDuff. London: Penguin, 2003.

Düring, Marten. *Verdeckte soziale Netzwerke im Nationalsozialismus: Die Entstehung und Arbeitsweise von Berliner Hilfsnetzwerken für verfolgte Juden.* Berlin: De Gruyter Oldenbourg, 2015.

Dutt, Carsten. *Die Schuldfrage: Untersuchungen zur geistigen Situation der Nachkriegszeit.* Heidelberg: Manutius Verlag, 2010.

Echternkamp, Jörg. "Von Opfern, Helden und Verbrechern—Anmerkungen zur Bedeutung des Zweiten Weltkrieges in den Erinnerungskulturen der Deutschen, 1945–1955." In *Kriegsende 1945 in Deutschland,* ed. Jörg Hillmann and John Zimmermann. Munich: R. Oldenbourg Verlag, 2002, 301–18.

Ellger-Rüttgardt, Sieglind. "Das Israelitische Waisenhaus Dinslaken." In *Juden im Ruhrgebiet: Vom Zeitalter der Aufklärung bis in die Gegenwart,* ed. Jan-Pieter Barbian, Michael Brocke, and Ludger Heid. Essen: Klartext, 1999, 503–22.

Evans, Richard J. *The Coming of the Third Reich.* New York: Penguin Press, 2004.

———. *The Third Reich at War.* New York: Penguin Press, 2009.

———. *The Third Reich in Power, 1933–1939.* New York: Penguin Press, 2005.

Finkel, Evgeny. *Ordinary Jews: Choice and Survival During the Holocaust.* Princeton: Princeton University Press, 2017.

Fischer-Hübner, Hermann. "Zur Geschichte der Entschädigungsmaßnahmen für Opfer nationalsozialistischen Unrechtes." In *Die Kehrseite der "Wiedergutmachung": Das Leiden von NS-Verfolgten in den Entschädigungsverfahren,* ed. Helga Fischer-Hübner and Hermann Fischer-Hübner. Gerlingen: Bleicher, 1990, 9–42.

Florath, Bernd. "Die Europäische Union." In *Der vergessene Widerstand: Zu Realgeschichte und Wahrnehmung des Kampfes gegen die NS-Diktatur,* ed. Johannes Tuchel. Dachauer Symposien zur Zeitgeschichte. Göttingen: Wallstein, 2005, 114–39.

Fogelman, Eva. *Conscience and Courage: The Rescuers of the Jews During the Holocaust.* New York: Anchor Books, 1994.

Frei, Norbert. "'Volksgemeinschaft.'" In *1945 und wir: Das Dritte Reich im Bewusstsein der Deutschen,* ed. Norbert Frei. München: C. H. Beck, 2005, 121–42.

Frey, Heinrich, and Museumsverein Meersburg. *Meersburg unterm Hakenkreuz, 1933–1945.* Friedrichshafen: Robert Gessler; Meersburg: Museumsverein Meersburg, 2011.

Fritzsche, Peter. *Life and Death in the Third Reich.* Cambridge, Mass.: Belknap Press of Harvard University Press, 2008.

Gellately, Robert. *Backing Hitler: Consent and Coercion in Nazi Germany.* Oxford: Oxford University Press, 2001.

———. *The Gestapo and German Society: Enforcing Racial Policy, 1933–1945.* New York: Oxford University Press, 1990.

Gensburger, Sarah. "From Jerusalem to Paris: The Institutionalization of the Category of 'Righteous of France.'" *French Politics, Culture & Society* 30, no. 2 (2012): 150–71.

———. "La création du titre de Juste parmi les nations." *Bulletin du Centre de Recherche Français à Jérusalem* 15 (2004): 15–37.

———. "L'émergence de la catégorie de Juste parmi les nations comme paradigme mémoriel: Réflexions contemporaines sur le rôle socialement dévolu à la mémoire." In *Culture et mémoire,* ed. Carola Hähnel-Mesnard, Marie Liénard-Yeterian, and Cristina Marinas. Paris: Éditions de l'École Polytechnique, 2008, 25–32.

———. *Les Justes de France: Politiques publiques de la mémoire.* Gouvernances. Paris: Presses de Sciences Po, 2010.

Gleisner, Martin. "Tanzvergnügen und Tanzfeier." *Leib und Seele: Monatszeitschrift für deutsche Leibesübungen* 5 (1929): 114.

Grabowski, Jan. *Rescue for Money: Paid Helpers in Poland, 1939–1945.* Includes a summary in Hebrew. Search and Research, Lectures and Papers. Jerusalem: Yad Vashem, 2008.

Greenberg, Udi. *The Weimar Century: German Émigrés and the Ideological Foundations of the Cold War.* Princeton: Princeton University Press, 2014.

Gross, Michael L. *Ethics and Activism: The Theory and Practice of Political Morality.* Cambridge: Cambridge University Press, 1997.

Großbröhmer, Rainer. "Dore Jacobs—ein Leben in Bewegung." In *Für Dore Jacobs 1894–1994,* ed. Dore Jacobs Schule, 45–50.

Großbröhmer, Rainer, and Karin Kirch. *Von Bildungsbakterien und Volkshochschulepidemien: Ein Beitrag zur Geschichte der Volkshochschule Essen, 1919–1974.* Essen: Klartext-Verlag, 1994.

Grossmann, Atina. *Jews, Germans, and Allies: Close Encounters in Occupied Germany.* Princeton: Princeton University Press, 2007.

Grossmann, Kurt Richard. *Die unbesungenen Helden: Menschen in Deutschlands dunklen Tagen.* Berlin: Arani Verlags-GmbH, 1957.

Gruner, Wolf. *Widerstand in der Rosenstrasse: Die Fabrik-Aktion und die Verfolgung der "Mischehen" 1943.* Die Zeit des Nationalsozialismus. Frankfurt am Main: Fischer Taschenbuch Verlag, 2005.

Grüter, Monika. "Der 'Bund für ein sozialistisches Leben': Seine Entwicklung in den 20er Jahren und seine Widerständigkeit unter dem Nationalsozialismus." MA dissertation. University of Essen, 1988.

Gudehus, Christian. "Helping the Persecuted: Heuristics and Perspectives (Exemplified by the Holocaust)." In *Online Encyclopedia of Mass Violence* (2016), https://www.sciencespo.fr/mass-violence-war-massacre-resistance/fr/node/3269.

Haase, Norbert, and Wolfram Wette. *Retter in Uniform: Handlungsspielräume im Vernichtungskrieg der Wehrmacht.* Zeit des Nationalsozialismus. Frankfurt am Main: Fischer Taschenbuch Verlag, 2002.

Haffner, Sebastian. *The Meaning of Hitler.* London: Weidenfeld and Nicolson, 1979.

Halle, Anna Sabine. *Thoughts Are Free: A Quaker Youth Group in Nazi Germany.* Pendle Hill Pamphlet. Wallingford, Pa.: Pendle Hill Publications, 1985.

Hardt, Yvonne. "Ausdruckstanz und Bewegungschor im Nationalsozialismus: Zur politischen Dimension des Körperlichen und Räumlichen im modernen Tanz." In *Körper im Nationalsozialismus: Bilder und Praxen,* ed. Paula Diehl. Paderborn: Schöningh, 2006, 173–89.

Henke, Klaus-Dietmar. *Die amerikanische Besetzung Deutschlands.* Quellen und Darstellungen zur Zeitgeschichte. München: R. Oldenbourg, 1995.

Hetkamp, Jutta. *Die jüdische Jugendbewegung in Deutschland von 1913–1933: Anpassung, Selbstbehauptung, Widerstand.* Münster: Lit, 1994.

Hikel, Christine. "Erinnerung als Partizipation: Inge Scholl und die 'Weisse Rose' in der Bundesrepublik." In *Lieschen Müller wird politisch: Geschlecht, Staat und Partizipation im 20. Jahrhundert,* ed. Christine Hikel, Nicole Kramer, and Elisabeth Zellmer. München: Oldenbourg, 2009, 105–14.

Hoffmann, Stefan-Ludwig. "Besiegte, Besatzer, Beobachter: Das Kriegsende im Tagebuch." In *Demokratie im Schatten der Gewalt: Geschichten des Privaten im deutschen Nachkrieg,* ed. Daniel Fulda, Dagmar Herzog, Stefan-Ludwig Hoffmann, and Till van Rahden. Göttingen: Wallstein, 2010, 25–55.

———. "Germans into Allies. Writing a Diary in 1945." In *Seeking Peace in the Wake of War. Europe, 1943–1947,* ed. Stefan-Ludwig Hoffmann, Sandrine Kott, Peter Romijn, and Olivier Wieviorka. Amsterdam: Amsterdam University Press, 2015, 63–90.

Homberg, Frank. "Retterwiderstand in Wuppertal während des Nationalsozialismus." PhD Dissertation, University of Düsseldorf, 2008.

Hüttenberger, Peter. *Düsseldorf: Geschichte von den Ursprüngen bis ins 20. Jahrhundert*. Vol. 3, *Die Industrie und Verwaltungsstadt (20. Jahrhundert)*. Düsseldorf: Schwann, 1989.

Jäger, Herbert. *Verbrechen unter totalitärer Herrschaft: Studien zur Nationalsozialistischen Gewaltkriminalität*. Texte und Dokumente zur Zeitgeschichte. Frankfurt am Main: Suhrkamp, 1982.

Jerouschek, Günter, Inge Marssolek, and Hedwig Röckelein. *Denunziation: Historische, juristische und psychologische Aspekte*. Forum Psychohistorie. Tübingen: Edition Diskord, 1997.

Jungbluth, Ernst. "Unbewältigte Vergangenheit in der Praxis der Erwachsenenbildung." *Volkshochschule im Westen* 11, nos. 11–12 (1960): 346–48.

Kabalek, Kobi. "The Commemoration Before the Commemoration: Yad Vashem and the Righteous Among the Nations (1945–1963)." *Yad Vashem Studies* 39, no. 1 (2011): 169–211.

———. "The Rescue of Jews and the Memory of Nazism in Germany, from the Third Reich to the Present." PhD diss., University of Virginia, 2013.

Kardorff, Ursula von, and Peter Hartl. *Berliner Aufzeichnungen, 1942–1945*. München: C. H. Beck, 1992.

Karina, Lilian, and Marion Kant. *Hitler's Dancers: German Modern Dance and the Third Reich*. Trans. Jonathan Steinberg. New York: Berghahn Books, 2003.

———. *Tanz unterm Hakenkreuz: Eine Dokumentation*. Berlin: Henschel Verlag, 1996.

Kershaw, Ian. *The Nazi Dictatorship: Problems and Perspectives of Interpretation*. 4th ed. New York: Oxford University Press, 2000.

Kingreen, Monica. "Die Aktion zur kalten Erledigung der Mischehen: Die reichsweit singuläre systematische Verschleppung und Ermordung jüdischer Mischehepartner im NSDAP-Gau Hessen-Nassau 1942–1943." In *NS-Gewaltherrschaft: Beiträge zur historischen Forschung und juristischen Aufarbeitung*, ed. Alfred Gottwaldt, Norbert Kampe, and Peter Klein. Berlin: Edition Hentrich, 2005, 187–201.

Kitchen, Martin. *Nazi Germany at War*. New York: Longman, 1995.

Klär, Karl-Heinz. "Zwei Nelson-Bünde: Internationaler Jugend-Bund (IJB) und internationaler sozialistischer Kampf-Bund (ISK) im Licht neuer Quellen." *Internationale wissenschaftliche Korrespondenz zur Geschichte der deutschen Arbeiterbewegung* 18, no. 3 (1982): 310–59.

Klatt, Marlene. "Die Entschädigungspraxis im Regierungsbezirk Arnsberg und die Reaktion jüdischer Verfolgter." In *"Arisierung" und "Wiedergutmachung" in deutschen Städten*, ed. Christiane Fritsche and Johannes Paulmann. Köln: Böhlau Verlag, 2014, 363–86.

Klemperer, Victor, and Roderick H. Watt. *An Annotated Edition of Victor Klemperer's LTI, Notizbuch eines Philologen*. Text in German; preface in English.

Studies in German Thought and History. Lewiston, N.Y.: E. Mellen Press, 1997.

Klotzbach, Kurt. *Gegen den Nationalsozialismus: Widerstand und Verfolgung in Dortmund, 1930–1945; eine historisch-politische Studie.* Schriftenreihe des Forschungsinstituts der Friedrich-Ebert-Stiftung B: Historisch-Politische Schriften. Hannover: Verlag für Literatur und Zeitgeschehen, 1969.

Kock, Gerhard. *"Der Führer sorgt für unsere Kinder . . .": Die Kinderlandverschickung im Zweiten Weltkrieg.* Paderborn: F. Schöningh, 1997.

Kolakowski, Leszek. *Main Currents of Marxism: The Founders, the Golden Age, the Breakdown.* New York: W. W. Norton, 2005.

Kosmala, Beate. "Mißglückte Hilfe und ihre Folgen: Die Ahndung der 'Judenbegünstigung' durch NS-Verfolgungsbehörden." In Kosmala and Schoppmann, *Solidarität und Hilfe für Juden während der NS-Zeit*, 205–21.

———. "Überlebensstrategien jüdischer Frauen in Berlin: Flucht vor der Deportation (1941–1943)." In *Alltag im Holocaust: Jüdisches Leben im grossdeutschen Reich, 1941–1945*, ed. Andrea Löw, Doris L. Bergen, and Anna Hájková. Schriftenreihe der Vierteljahrshefte für Zeitgeschichte. München: Oldenbourg, 2013, 29–47.

Kosmala, Beate, and Claudia Schoppmann, eds. *Solidarität und Hilfe für Juden während der NS-Zeit.* Vol. 5, *Überleben im Untergrund: Hilfe für Juden in Deutschland.* Berlin: Metropol, 2002.

———. "Überleben im Untergrund: Zwischenbilanz eines Forschungsprojekts." In Kosmala and Schoppmann, *Solidarität und Hilfe für Juden während der NS-Zeit*, 17–32.

Krüger, Norbert. "Die Zerstörung Wuppertals: Ein Überblick über die Luftangriffe im Sommer 1943." In *Wuppertal in der Zeit des Nationalsozialismus*, ed. Klaus Goebel. Wuppertal: P. Hammer, 1984, 163–78.

Kühne, Thomas. *Belonging and Genocide: Hitler's Community, 1918–1945.* New Haven: Yale University Press, 2010.

Kulka, Otto Dov. "'Public Opinion' in Nazi Germany and the Jewish Question." *Jerusalem Quarterly* 25 (1982): 121–44.

———. "'Public Opinion' in Nazi Germany and the Jewish Question." *Jerusalem Quarterly* 26 (1983): 34–45.

Kwiet, Konrad, and Helmut Eschwege. *Selbstbehauptung und Widerstand: Deutsche Juden im Kampf um Existenz und Menschenwürde, 1933–1945.* Hamburger Beiträge zur Sozial und Zeitgeschichte. Hamburg: Christians, 1984.

Laqueur, Walter. *The Terrible Secret: Suppression of the Truth About Hitler's "Final Solution."* Boston: Little, Brown, 1980.

Lazare, Lucien. *Rescue as Resistance: How Jewish Organizations Fought the Holocaust in France.* New York: Columbia University Press, 1996.

Liman von Sanders, Otto Viktor Karl. *Fünf Jahre Türkei.* Berlin: A. Scherl, 1920.

Link, Werner. *Die Geschichte des internationalen Jugend-Bundes (IJB) und des Internationalen sozialistischen Kampf-Bundes (ISK): Ein Beitrag zur Geschichte der Arbeiterbewegung in der Weimarer Republik und im Dritten Reich.* Marburger Abhandlungen zur politischen Wissenschaft, vol. 1. Meisenheim am Glan: A. Hain, 1964.

Linse, Ulrich. *Die entschiedene Jugend, 1919–1921: Deutschlands erste revolutionäre Schüler—und Studentenbewegung.* Quellen und Beiträge zur Geschichte der Jugendbewegung, vol. 23. Frankfurt am Main: Dipa-Verlag, 1981.

Linsel, Anne. *Weltentwürfe: Die Bühnenbildnerin Hanna Jordan.* Essen: Klartext, 2006.

Longerich, Peter. *"Davon haben wir nichts gewusst!": Die Deutschen und die Judenverfolgung, 1933–1945.* München: Siedler, 2006.

Löw, Andrea, Doris L. Bergen, and Anna Hájková. *Alltag im Holocaust: Jüdisches Leben im grossdeutschen Reich, 1941–1945.* Schriftenreihe der Vierteljahrshefte für Zeitgeschichte. München: Oldenbourg, 2013.

Lustiger, Arno. *Rettungswiderstand: Über die Judenretter in Europa während der NS-Zeit.* Göttingen: Wallstein, 2011.

Lutjens, Richard. "Jews in Hiding in Nazi Berlin, 1941–1945: A Demographic Survey." *Holocaust and Genocide Studies* 31, no. 2 (2017): 268–97.

———"Vom Untertauchen: 'U-Boote' und der Berliner Alltag, 1941–1945." In *Alltag im Holocaust: Jüdisches Leben im grossdeutschen Reich, 1941–1945,* ed. Andrea Löw, Doris L. Bergen, and Anna Hájková. Schriftenreihe der Vierteljahrshefte für Zeitgeschichte. München: Oldenbourg, 2013, 49–63.

Mariot, Nicolas, and Claire Zalc. "Reconstructing Trajectories of Persecution: Reflections on a Prosopography of Holocaust Victims." In *Microhistories of the Holocaust,* ed. Claire Zalc and Tal Bruttmann. New York: Berghahn, 2017, 85–112.

Marszolek, Inge. "Denunziation im Dritten Reich: Kommunikationsformen und Verhaltensweisen." In *Solidarität und Hilfe für Juden während der NS-Zeit.* Vol. 5, *Überleben im Untergrund: Hilfe für Juden in Deutschland,* ed. Beate Kosmala and Claudia Schoppman. Berlin: Metropol, 2002, 89–107.

Mehringer, Hartmut. "Die Bayerische Sozialdemokratie bis zum Ende des NS-Regimes. Vorgeschichte, Verfolgung und Widerstand." In *Bayern in der NS-Zeit, vol. 5, Die Parteien KPD, SPD, BVP in Verfolgung und Widerstand,* ed. Hartmut Mehringer and Martin Broszat. München: Oldenbourg, 1983, 237–432.

Meyer, Ahlrich. *Die deutsche Besatzung in Frankreich, 1940–1944: Widerstandsbekämpfung und Judenverfolgung.* Darmstadt: Wissenschaftliche Buchgesellschaft, 2000.

Meyer, Beate. *A Fatal Balancing Act: The Dilemma of the Reich Association of Jews in Germany, 1939–1945.* New York: Berghahn Books, 2013.

———. *"Jüdische Mischlinge": Rassenpolitik und Verfolgungserfahrung, 1933–1945.* Studien zur Jüdischen Geschichte. Hamburg: Dölling und Galitz, 1999.

Meyer, Kristina, and Boris Spernol. "Wiedergutmachung in Düsseldorf: Eine statistische Bilanz." In *Die Praxis der Wiedergutmachung: Geschichte, Erfahrung und Wirkung in Deutschland und Israel*, ed. Norbert Frei, José Brunner, and Constantin Goschler. Göttingen: Wallstein, 2009, 690–727.

Meyer, Winfried. *Unternehmen Sieben: Eine Rettungsaktion für vom Holocaust bedrohte aus dem Amt Ausland/Abwehr im Oberkommando der Wehrmacht*. Frankfurt am Main: Hain, 1993.

Möckel, Benjamin. *Erfahrungsbruch und Generationsbehauptung: Die "Kriegsjugend-generation" in den beiden deutschen Nachkriegsgesellschaften*. Göttinger Studien zur Generationsforschung. Göttingen: Wallstein Verlag, 2014.

Moeller, Robert G. *War Stories: The Search for a Usable Past in the Federal Republic of Germany*. Berkeley: University of California Press, 2001.

Monroe, Kristen R. *The Hand of Compassion: Portraits of Moral Choice During the Holocaust*. Princeton: Princeton University Press, 2004.

———. *The Heart of Altruism: Perceptions of a Common Humanity*. Princeton: Princeton University Press, 1998.

Moore, Bob. "The Rescue of Jews from Nazi Persecution: A Western European Perspective." *Journal of Genocide Research* 4, no. 3 (2003): 293–308.

———. "The Rescue of Jews in Nazi-Occupied Belgium, France and the Netherlands." *Australian Journal of Politics & History* 50, no. 3 (2004): 385–95.

———. *Survivors: Jewish Self-Help and Rescue in Nazi-Occupied Western Europe*. Oxford: Oxford University Press, 2010.

Müller, Willi, ed. *Demokratie vor Ort: Ein Lesebuch zur Geschichte der Sozialdemokratischen Partei Deutschlands in Mülheim an der Ruhr*. Mülheim: Vor Ort Verlag, 1979.

Niven, William John. *Germans as Victims: Remembering the Past in Contemporary Germany*. New York: Palgrave Macmillan, 2006.

Oliner, Samuel P., and Pearl Oliner. *The Altruistic Personality: Rescuers of Jews in Nazi Europe*. New York: Free Press, 1988.

Paldiel, Mordecai. *German Rescuers of Jews*. London: Vallentine Mitchell, 2017.

Paul, Gerhard, and Klaus-Michael Mallmann. *Milieus und Widerstand: Eine Verhaltensgeschichte der Gesellschaft im Nationalsozialismus*. Widerstand und Verweigerung im Saarland, 1935–1945. Bonn: J.H.W. Dietz, 1995.

Paulsson, Gunnar S. *Secret City: The Hidden Jews of Warsaw, 1940–1945*. New Haven: Yale University Press, 2002.

Peukert, Detlev. *Inside Nazi Germany: Conformity, Opposition, and Racism in Everyday Life*. New Haven: Yale University Press, 1987.

Pietsch, Hartmut. "Militärregierung und kommunale Politik." In *Zwischen Gestern und Morgen: Kriegsende und Wiederaufbau im Ruhrgebiet*, ed. Jan-Pieter Barbian and Ludger Heid. Essen: Klartext, 1995, 44–73.

Poznanski, Renée. "Rescue of the Jews and the Resistance in France: From History to Historiography." *French Politics, Culture & Society* 30, no. 2 (2012): 8–32.

Reichling, Norbert. "Der 'Bund': Jugendbewegte Bildungsarbeit und Lebensreform im Ruhrgebiet." In *Jugendbewegung und Erwachsenenbildung. Historische Jugendforschung: Jahrbuch des Archivs der deutschen Jugendbewegung*, ed. Paul Ciupke, Franz-Josef Jelich, Alfons Kenkmann, and Barbara Stambolis. Jahrbuch des Archivs der Deutschen Jugendbewegung. Schwalbach/Ts: Wochenschau Verlag, 2011, 61–76.

———. "Mit Kant gegen die Nazis: Der 'Bund' und sein vergessenes 'Judenhilfswerk' im Rhein-Ruhr-Gebiet." In *Rettungswiderstand: Über die Judenretter in Europa während der NS-Zeit*, ed. Arno Lustiger. Göttingen: Wallstein, 2011, 59–63.

Renaud, Terence Ray. "Restarting Socialism: The New Beginning Group and the Problem of Renewal on the German Left, 1930–1970." PhD diss., University of California, Berkeley, 2015.

Riffel, Dennis. *Unbesungene Helden: Die Ehrungsinitiative des Berliner Senats 1958 bis 1966*. Reihe Dokumente, Texte, Materialien. Berlin: Metropol, 2007.

Roseman, Mark. "Ein Mensch in Bewegung: Dore Jacobs, 1894–1978." *Essener Beiträge: Beiträge zur Geschichte von Stadt und Stift Essen* 114 (2002): 73–109.

———. *A Past in Hiding: Memory and Survival in Nazi Germany*. New York: Metropolitan Books, 2001.

———. "Surviving Memory: Truth and Inaccuracy in Holocaust Testimony." *Journal of Holocaust Education* 8, no. 1 (1999): 1–20.

Ross, Chad. *Naked Germany: Health, Race and the Nation*. New York: Berg, 2005.

Rothbart, Daniel, and Jessica Cooley. "Hutus Aiding Tutsis During the Rwandan Genocide: Motives, Meanings, and Morals." *Genocide Studies & Prevention* 10, no. 2 (2016): 76.

Rothfels, Hans. *Die deutsche Opposition gegen Hitler: Eine Würdigung*. Bücher des Wissens. Rev. ed., Frankfurt am Main: Fischer, 1958.

———. *The German Opposition to Hitler: An Assessment*. London: O. Wolff, 1961.

Rudolph, Katrin. *Hilfe beim Sprung ins Nichts: Franz Kaufmann und die Rettung von Juden und "Nichtarischen" Christen*. Reihe Dokumente, Texte, Materialien. Berlin: Metropol, 2005.

Salomon, Ernst von. *Der Fragebogen*. Hamburg: Rowohlt, 1951.

Schieb, Barbara. "Die Gemeinschaft für Frieden und Aufbau." In *Der vergessene Widerstand: Zu Realgeschichte und Wahrnehmung des Kampfes gegen die NS-Diktatur*, ed. Johannes Tuchel. Dachauer Symposien zur Zeitgeschichte. Göttingen: Wallstein, 2005, 97–113.

Schiller, Friedrich. *Don Carlos, Infante of Spain*. New York: F. Ungar, 1974.

Schmalenbach, Hermann. "Die soziologische Kategorie des Bundes." *Die Dioskuren: Jahrbuch für Geisteswissenschaften* 1 (1922): 35–105.

Scholtyseck, Joachim. "'Mit alten Kräften und im alten Stile'? Die Überlebenden des deutschen Widerstandes gegen Hitler und der politische Neubeginn in der Bundesrepublik." In *Die Überlebenden des deutschen Widerstandes und ihre Bedeutung für Nachkriegsdeutschland,* ed. Joachim Scholtyseck and Stephen Schröder. Münster: Lit, 2005, 11–32.

Schoppmann, Claudia. "Rettung von Juden: Ein kaum beachteter Widerstand von Frauen." In *Solidarität und Hilfe für Juden während der NS-Zeit.* Vol. 5, *Überleben im Untergrund: Hilfe für Juden in Deutschland,* ed. Beate Kosmala and Claudia Schoppmann. Reihe Solidarität und Hilfe, 7 vols. Berlin: Metropol, 2002, 109–26.

Schrafstetter, Susanna. *Flucht und Versteck: Untergetauchte Juden in München: Verfolgungserfahrung und Nachkriegsalltag.* Göttingen: Wallstein Verlag, 2015.

———. "Von der Soforthilfe zur Wiedergutmachung: Die Umsetzung der Zonal Policy Instruction Nr 20 in der britischen Besatzungszone." In *"Arisierung" und "Wiedergutmachung" in deutschen Städten,* ed. Christiane Fritsche and Johannes Paulmann. Köln: Böhlau Verlag, 2014, 309–34.

Schröter, Hermann. *Geschichte und Schicksal der Essener Juden: Gedenkbuch für die jüdischen Mitbürger der Stadt Essen.* Essen: Stadt Essen, 1980.

Sebald, W. G. *On the Natural History of Destruction.* New York: Random House, 2003.

Sokolow, Reha, and Al Sokolow. *Ruth und Maria: Eine Freundschaft auf Leben und Tod: Berlin, 1942–1945.* Berlin: Metropol, 2006.

Spector, Irwin. *Rhythm and Life: The Work of Emile Jaques-Dalcroze.* Dance and Music Series. Stuyvesant, N.Y.: Pendragon Press, 1990.

Spector, Shmuel, and Geoffrey Wigoder, eds. *The Encyclopedia of Jewish Life Before and During the Holocaust.* Jerusalem: Yad Vashem, 2001.

Stargardt, Nicholas. *The German War: A Nation Under Arms, 1939–1945: Citizens and Soldiers.* New York: Basic Books, 2015.

———. "The Troubled Patriot: German Innerlichkeit in World War 2." *German History* 28, no. 3 (2010): 326–42.

Steber, Martina, and Bernhard Gotto. *Visions of Community in Nazi Germany: Social Engineering and Private Lives.* New York: Oxford University Press, 2014.

Steinbach, Peter, and Johannes Tuchel. *Widerstand gegen die nationalsozialistische Diktatur, 1933–1945.* Berlin: Lukas, 2004.

———. *Widerstand in Deutschland, 1933–1945: Ein historisches Lesebuch.* München: C. H. Beck, 1994.

Steinberg, Hans-Josef. *Widerstand und Verfolgung in Essen, 1933–1945.* Hannover: Verlag fur Literatur und Zeitgeschehen, 1969.

Steinweis, Alan E. *Kristallnacht 1938.* Cambridge, Mass.: Belknap Press of Harvard University Press, 2009.

Stern, Frank, and Vidal Sassoon International Center for the Study of Antisemitism (Universiṭah ha-ʿIvrit bi-Yerushalayim). *The Whitewashing of the Yellow Badge: Antisemitism and Philosemitism in Postwar Germany.* Studies in Antisemitism.

New York: Published for the Vidal Sassoon International Center for the Study of Antisemitism (SICSA), the Hebrew University of Jerusalem, by Pergamon Press, 1992.

Steuwer, Janosch. *"Ein Drittes Reich, wie ich es auffasse": Politik, Gesellschaft und privates Leben in Tagebüchern, 1933–1939.* Göttingen: Wallstein Verlag, 2017.

Stoltzfus, Nathan. *Resistance of the Heart: Intermarriage and the Rosenstrasse Protest in Nazi Germany.* New York: W. W. Norton, 1996.

Strnad, Maximilian. "The Fortune of Survival: Intermarried German Jews in the Dying Breath of the 'Thousand-Year Reich.'" *Dapim: Studies on the Holocaust* 29, no. 3 (2015): 173–96.

Suedfeld, Peter, and Stefanie de Best. "Value Hierarchies of Holocaust Rescuers and Resistance Fighters." *Genocide Studies and Prevention* 3, no. 1 (2008): 31–42.

Sznaider, Natan. "Zwischen Liebe zur Welt und politischer Verantwortung: Das Neinsagen in der Diktatur." In "Helfer, Retter und Netzwerker des Widerstands. 3. Internationale Konferenz zur Holocaustforschung / Praxisforum: Zivilcourage lernen." Berlin, 2011.

Tec, Nechama. *In the Lion's Den: The Life of Oswald Rufeisen.* New York: Oxford University Press, 1990.

———. *Resilience and Courage: Women, Men, and the Holocaust.* New Haven: Yale University Press, 2004.

———. "Righteous Christians in Poland." *International Social Science Review* 58, no. 1 (1983): 12–19.

———. "Toward a Theory of Rescue." In *Making a Difference: Rescue and Assistance During the Holocaust; Essays in Honor of Marion Pritchard,* ed. David Scrase, Wolfgang Mieder, and Katherine Quimby Johnson. Burlington: Center for Holocaust Studies at the University of Vermont, 2004, 21–48.

———. *When Light Pierced the Darkness: Christian Rescue of Jews in Nazi-Occupied Poland.* New York: Oxford University Press, 1986.

Tuchel, Johannes. "Vergessen, Verdrängt, Ignoriert: Überlegungen zur Rezeptionsgeschichte des Widerstandes gegen den Nationalsozialismus im Nachkriegsdeutschland." In Tuchel, *Der Vergessene Widerstand,* 7–38.

———. *Der vergessene Widerstand: Zu Realgeschichte und Wahrnehmung des Kampfes gegen die NS-Diktatur.* Dachauer Symposien zur Zeitgeschichte. Göttingen: Wallstein, 2005.

Volmer-Naumann, Julia. "'Betrifft: Wiedergutmachung': Entschädigung als Verwaltungsakt am Beispiel Nordrhein-Westfalen." In *"Arisierung" und "Wiedergutmachung" in deutschen Städten,* ed. Christiane Fritsche and Johannes Paulmann. Köln: Böhlau Verlag, 2014, 335–62.

Vorholt, Udo. *Die politische Theorie Leonard Nelsons: Eine Fallstudie zum Verhältnis von philosophisch-politischer Theorie und konkret-politischer Praxis.* Baden-Baden: Nomos, 1998.

Wachsmann, Nikolaus. *KL: A History of the Nazi Concentration Camps*. New York: Farrar, Straus and Giroux, 2015.

Walk, Joseph. *Das Sonderrecht für die Juden im NS-Staat: Eine Sammlung der gesetzlichen Massnahmen und Richtlinien, Inhalt und Bedeutung*. Uni-Taschenbücher 2nd ed. Heidelberg: C. F. Müller Verlag, 1996.

Weisenborn, Günther. *Der lautlose Aufstand: Bericht über die Widerstandsbewegung des deutschen Volkes, 1933–1945*. Hamburg: Rowohlt, 1953.

Wette, Wolfram. *Feldwebel Anton Schmid: Ein Held der Humanität*. Die Zeit des Nationalsozialismus. Frankfurt am Main: S. Fischer, 2013.

———, ed. *Zivil Courage: Empörte, Helfer und Retter aus Wehrmacht, Polizei und SS*. Die Zeit des Nationalsozialismus. Frankfurt: Fischer Taschenbuch Verlag, 2003.

Wickert, Christl. "Frauen zischen Dissens und Widerstand." In *Lexikon des Deutschen Widerstandes*, ed. Wolfgang Benz and Walter H. Pehle. Frankfurt am Main: S. Fischer, 1994, 141–56.

Wildt, Michael. *Volksgemeinschaft als Selbstermächtigung: Gewalt gegen Juden in der deutschen Provinz 1919 bis 1939*. Hamburg: Hamburger Edition, 2007.

Wolfson, Manfred. "Der Widerstand gegen Hitler: Soziologische Skizze über Retter (Rescuers) von Juden in Deutschland." *Aus Politik und Zeitgeschichte* 15 (1971): 32–39

Wollasch, Hans-Josef. *Gertrud Luckner: "Botschafterin der Menschlichkeit."* Freiburg im Breisgau: Herder, 2005.

ABBREVIATIONS

AAK	Archiv der Akademie der Künste, Berlin
AB1, AB2, AB3	The "Auslandsbriefe," or "Letters Abroad," written by the Bund after the war. Copies in the BAE.
AJ	Artur Jacobs
AJD	Artur Jacobs's diary. Unless otherwise stated, the copies are to be found in the Jacobs Nachlaß in the Stadtarchiv Essen. But some are in the BAE.
ASE	Alte Synagoge, Essen
ASP	Papers of Alfred Stürmer (private papers of Alfred and Tilde Stürmer, his parents), Munich
AStE	Aussenstelle Essen (the Gestapo branch office)
BAE	Bund archive, in the Blockhaus, Leveringstrasse, Essen
BMP	Papers of Barbara Martin, Marl
DJ	Dore Jacobs
DJGU	Dore Jacobs, "Gelebte Utopie"
EB	Else Bramesfeld
EJ	Ernst Jungbluth
EP	Ellenbogen Papers
GJ	Gottfried (Friedl) Jacobs
JP	Jungbluth Papers

KfH	Kammer für Haftentschädigung (restitution court for loss of liberty)
LAN	Landesarchiv Nordrhein-Westfalen, Düsseldorf (formerly Hauptstaatsarchiv Düsseldorf)
LHAK	Landeshauptarchiv Koblenz
LJ	Lisa Jacob
ME	Marianne Ellenbogen, née Strauss
NGJ	Alte Synagoge, Essen, Bestand 45-2AS, Nachlaß Gottfried Jacobs
NJ	Stadtarchiv Essen Bestand 626, Nachlaß Jacobs
NRW	Nordrhein-Westfalen
SBP	Papers of Stefan Brandt, Berlin
SLC	Schlesinger Library, Radcliffe Institute of Advanced Study, Harvard University, Cambridge, Massachusetts
SP	Speer Papers, Wuppertal
SSch	Sonja Schreiber
StAE	Stadtarchiv Essen
StapoD	Staatsleitpolizeistelle Düsseldorf
StAR	Stadtarchiv Remscheid
StAW	Stadtarchiv Wuppertal
WBP	Papers of Wolfgang Briel, Barsinghausen
WG	Wiedergutmachung
WGA	Wiedergutmachungsamt
WE	Wasja Enoch
WJ	Walter Jacobs

NOTES

Introduction

1. There is some scholarship on the Bund. The first serious study was an MA dissertation, Monika Grüter, "Der 'Bund für ein sozialistisches Leben': Seine Entwicklung in den 20er Jahren und seine Widerständigkeit unter dem Nationalsozialismus" (University of Essen, 1988). The group first attracted wider public notice in my account of the survival of Marianne Strauss: *A Past in Hiding: Memory and Survival in Nazi Germany* (New York: Metropolitan Books, 2001). The other historian to have worked seriously on the group is Norbert Reichling. See Heidi Behrens and Norbert Reichling, "'Umbau des ganzen Lebens': Frauenbildung und Geschlechterfragen in der sozialistischen Bildungsgemeinschaft 'Bund' seit 1919," in *Zwischen Emanzipation und 'besonderer Kulturaufgabe der Frau': Frauenbildung in der Geschichte der Erwachsenenbildung*, ed. Paul Ciupke and Karin Derichs-Kunstmann (Essen, 2001), 149–66; Norbert Reichling, "Der 'Bund': Jugendbewegte Bildungsarbeit und Lebensreform im Ruhrgebiet," in *Jugendbewegung und Erwachsenenbildung: Historische Jugendforschung; Jahrbuch des Archivs der deutschen Jugendbewegung*, ed. Paul Ciupke et al. (Schwalbach am Taunus: Wochenschau Verlag, 2011), 61–76; and Norbert Reichling, "Mit Kant gegen die Nazis: Der 'Bund' und sein vergessenes 'Judenhilfswerk' im Rhein-Ruhr-Gebiet," in *Rettungswiderstand: Über die Judenretter in Europa während der NS-Zeit*, ed. Arno Lustiger (Göttingen, 2011), 59–63.

2. Martin Broszat, Elke Fröhlich, and Falk Wiesemann, *Bayern in der NS-Zeit*, 6 vols. (München: Oldenbourg, 1977–83); Martin Broszat, "Resistenz und Widerstand: Eine Zwischenbilanz des Forschungsprojektes," in Broszat, Fröhlich, and Wiesemann, *Bayern in der NS-Zeit*, vol. 4 (München: Oldenbourg, 1981), 691–709; Detlev Peukert, *Inside Nazi Germany: Conformity, Opposition, and Racism in Everyday Life* (New Haven: Yale University Press, 1987); Ian Kershaw, *The Nazi Dictatorship: Problems and Perspectives of Interpretation*, 4th ed. (New York: Oxford University Press, 2000); Peter Steinbach and Johannes Tuchel, *Widerstand in Deutschland, 1933–1945: Ein historisches Lesebuch* (München: C. H. Beck, 1994); Peter Steinbach and Johannes Tuchel, *Widerstand gegen die nationalsozialistische Diktatur, 1933–1945* (Berlin: Lukas, 2004); Johannes Tuchel, *Der vergessene Widerstand: Zu Realgeschichte und Wahrnehmung des Kampfes gegen die NS-Diktatur*, Dachauer Symposien zur Zeitgeschichte (Göttingen: Wallstein, 2005). On swing youth, see Wilfried Breyvogel, "Jugendliche Widerstandsformen: Vom organisierten Widerstand zur jugendlichen Alltagsopposition," in *Widerstand gegen den Nationalsozialismus*, ed. Peter Steinbach and Johannes Tuchel (Bonn: Bundeszentrale für Politische Bildung, 1994), 426–42.
3. Frank Bajohr, "Die Zustimmungsdiktatur: Grundzüge nationalsozialistischer Herrschaft in Hamburg," in *Hamburg im "Dritten Reich,"* ed. Josef Schmid (Göttingen: Wallstein, 2005), 69–131; Frank Bajohr and Michael Wildt, *Volksgemeinschaft: Neue Forschungen zur Gesellschaft des Nationalsozialismus*, Die Zeit des Nationalsozialismus (Frankfurt am Main: Fischer Taschenbuch Verlag, 2009); Peter Fritzsche, *Life and Death in the Third Reich* (Cambridge, Mass.: Belknap Press of Harvard University Press, 2008); Martina Steber and Bernhard Gotto, *Visions of Community in Nazi Germany: Social Engineering and Private Lives* (New York: Oxford University Press, 2014).
4. Denunciations: Robert Gellately, *The Gestapo and German Society: Enforcing Racial Policy, 1933–1945* (New York: Oxford University Press, 1990); Günter Jerouschek, Inge Marssolek, and Hedwig Röckelein, *Denunziation: Historische, juristische und psychologische Aspekte*, Forum Psychohistorie (Tübingen: Edition Diskord, 1997); Robert Gellately, *Backing Hitler: Consent and Coercion in Nazi Germany* (Oxford: Oxford University Press, 2001). Knowledge of and attitudes to the Holocaust: Peter Longerich, *"Davon haben wir nichts gewusst!": Die Deutschen und die Judenverfolgung, 1933–1945* (München: Siedler, 2006); Bernward Dörner, *Die Deutschen und der Holocaust: Was niemand wissen wollte, aber jeder wissen konnte* (Berlin: Propyläen, 2007); Michael Wildt, *Volksgemeinschaft als Selbstermächtigung: Gewalt gegen Juden in der deutschen Provinz 1919 bis 1939* (Hamburg: Hamburger Edition, 2007); Thomas Kühne, *Belonging and Genocide: Hitler's Community, 1918–1945* (New Haven: Yale University Press,

2010). On emphasizing coercion more than consensus, see Richard J. Evans's trilogy *The Coming of the Third Reich* (New York: Penguin Press, 2004); Richard J. Evans, *The Third Reich in Power, 1933–1939* (New York: Penguin Press, 2005); and Richard J. Evans, *The Third Reich at War* (New York: Penguin Press, 2009).

5. For a discussion of the relationship between rescue and resistance, see the Conclusion, especially the section titled "Resistance and Resilience."

6. Much of the influential work in the 1980s and 1990s was done by psychologists and ethicists. See Samuel P. Oliner and Pearl Oliner, *The Altruistic Personality: Rescuers of Jews in Nazi Europe* (New York: Free Press, 1988); Eva Fogelman, *Conscience and Courage: The Rescuers of the Jews During the Holocaust* (New York: Anchor Books, 1994); Kristen R. Monroe, *The Heart of Altruism: Perceptions of a Common Humanity* (Princeton: Princeton University Press, 1998); Kristen R. Monroe, *The Hand of Compassion: Portraits of Moral Choice During the Holocaust* (Princeton: Princeton University Press, 2004). It is worth noting that the best earlier scholars on rescue—for example, the Oliners—were well aware of the importance of environmental and other historically specific conditions. At the time, they saw themselves as pushing against an overemphasis on environment. Oliner and Oliner, *The Altruistic Personality*, 8. Although also emphasizing psychological dispositions, Nechama Tec offered a more sociological framework in her landmark study *When Light Pierced the Darkness: Christian Rescue of Jews in Nazi-Occupied Poland* (New York: Oxford University Press, 1986). See also Nechama Tec, "Righteous Christians in Poland," *International Social Science Review* 58, no. 1 (1983): 12–19; Nechama Tec, *Resilience and Courage: Women, Men, and the Holocaust* (New Haven: Yale University Press, 2004); and Nechama Tec, "Toward a Theory of Rescue," in *Making a Difference: Rescue and Assistance During the Holocaust; Essays in Honor of Marion Pritchard*, ed. David Scrase, Wolfgang Mieder, and Katherine Quimby Johnson (Burlington: Center for Holocaust Studies at the University of Vermont, 2004), 21–48.

7. Among many others, Gunnar S. Paulsson, *Secret City: The Hidden Jews of Warsaw, 1940–1945* (New Haven: Yale University Press, 2002); Jan Grabowski, *Rescue for Money: Paid Helpers in Poland, 1939–1945*, Search and Research, Lectures and Papers (Jerusalem: Yad Vashem, 2008); Evgeny Finkel, *Ordinary Jews: Choice and Survival During the Holocaust* (Princeton; Oxford: Princeton University Press, 2017). A wonderful autobiographical account that exemplifies this is Marie Jalowicz Simon, Irene Stratenwerth, and Hermann Simon, *Untergetaucht: Eine junge Frau überlebt in Berlin 1940–1945*, Schriftenreihe vol. 1532 (Bonn: Bundeszentrale für Politische Bildung, 2015); the English version is Marie Simon and Anthea Bell, *Underground in*

Berlin: A Young Woman's Extraordinary Tale of Survival in the Heart of Nazi Germany (New York: Little, Brown, 2016). The most significant comparative project remains Wolfgang Benz and Juliane Wetzel, *Solidarität und Hilfe für Juden während der NS-Zeit*, Reihe Solidarität und Hilfe, 7 vols. (Berlin: Metropol, 1996). See also Bob Moore, "The Rescue of Jews from Nazi Persecution: A Western European Perspective," *Journal of Genocide Research* 4, no. 3 (2003): 293–308; Bob Moore, "The Rescue of Jews in Nazi-Occupied Belgium, France and the Netherlands," *Australian Journal of Politics & History* 50, no. 3 (2004): 385–95; and Bob Moore, *Survivors: Jewish Self-Help and Rescue in Nazi-Occupied Western Europe* (Oxford: Oxford University Press, 2010). For an excellent regional study about hiding in Germany that also looks comparatively at other regions, see Susanna Schrafstetter, *Flucht und Versteck: Untergetauchte Juden in München: Verfolgungserfahrung und Nachkriegsalltag* (Göttingen: Wallstein Verlag, 2015). On rescue in the region in which the Bund operated, see Frank Homberg, "Retterwiderstand in Wuppertal während des Nationalsozialismus" (PhD diss., University of Düsseldorf, 2008). See also Marnix Croes and Beate Kosmala, "Facing Deportation in Germany and the Netherlands: Survival in Hiding," in *Facing the Catastrophe: Jews and Non-Jews in Europe During World War II*, ed. Beate Kosmala and Georgi Verbeeck (New York: Berg, 2011), 97–158; Suzanne Beer, "Aid Offered Jews in Nazi Germany: Research Approaches, Methods, and Problems," Violence de masse et Résistance—Réseau de recherche, https://www.sciencespo.fr/mass-violence-war-massacre -resistance/en/document/aid-offered-jews-nazi-germany-research -approaches-methods-and-problems; and Marten Düring, *Verdeckte soziale Netzwerke im Nationalsozialismus: Die Entstehung und Arbeitsweise von Berliner Hilfsnetzwerken für verfolgte Juden* (Berlin: De Gruyter Oldenbourg, 2015). On particular groupings, see Angela Borgstedt, "'Bruderring' und 'Lucknerkreis': Rettung im deutschen Sudwesten," in *Solidarität und Hilfe für Juden während der NS-Zeit*, vol. 5, *Überleben im Untergrund: Hilfe für Juden in Deutschland*, ed. Beate Kosmala and Claudia Schoppmann (Berlin: Metropol, 2002), 191–204; Bernd Florath, "Die Europäische Union," in *Der vergessene Widerstand: Zu Realgeschichte und Wahrnehmung des Kampfes gegen die NS-Diktatur*, ed. Johannes Tuchel (Göttingen: Wallstein, 2005), 114–39; and Katrin Rudolph, *Hilfe beim Sprung ins Nichts: Franz Kaufmann und die Rettung von Juden und "nichtarischen" Christen*, Reihe Dokumente, Texte, Materialien (Berlin: Metropol, 2005). A work of fiction that is nonetheless most insightful on the "Europäische Union" is Friedrich Christian Delius, *Mein Jahr als Mörder: Roman*, 2nd ed. (Berlin: Rowohlt, 2004). On the role of women, see Claudia Schoppmann, "Rettung von Juden: Ein kaum beachteter Widerstand von Frauen," in Kosmala and Schoppmann, *Solidarität und Hilfe für Juden während der NS-Zeit*, vol. 5, 109–26. Finally, on the important role of Jewish self-help, see Konrad Kwiet and Helmut Eschwege, *Selbstbehauptung und Widerstand: Deutsche Juden im Kampf um Existenz und Menschenwürde, 1933–1945*, Hamburger Beiträge zur Sozial und Zeitgeschichte (Hamburg: Christians, 1984), and Moore, *Survivors: Jewish Self-Help and Rescue in Nazi-Occupied Western Europe*.

8. The book also draws on interviews with a further ten Bund members, friends, or children conducted by others.

9. On hindsight in the Holocaust, see Nicolas Mariot and Claire Zalc, "Reconstructing Trajectories of Persecution: Reflections on a Prosopography of Holocaust Victims," in Claire Zalc and Tal Bruttmann, eds., *Microhistories of the Holocaust* (New York: Berghahn, 2017), 85–112. See also Jürgen Matthäus and Mark Roseman, *Jewish Responses to Persecution*, vol. 1, *1933–1938* (Lanham, Md. AltaMira Press in association with the United States Holocaust Memorial Museum, 2010), xv–xvii.

10. This is pursued above all in chapter 10 and the Conclusion. For the historiography of resistance, see the references in Tuchel, "Vergessen," and chapter 10. The best surveys of rescue's postwar reception in Germany are Dennis Riffel, *Unbesungene Helden: Die Ehrungsinitiative des Berliner Senats 1958 bis 1966*, Reihe Dokumente, Texte, Materialien (Berlin: Metropol, 2007), and Kobi Kabalek, "The Rescue of Jews and the Memory of Nazism in Germany, from the Third Reich to the Present" (PhD diss., University of Virginia, 2013).

1. Years of Innocence

1. Dore Jacobs, Else Bramesfeld, et al., *Gelebte Utopie: Aus dem Leben einer Gemeinschaft* (Essen: Klartext, 1990), 11. LHAK 405A-3879, letter from Steinecke in response to Artur Jacobs's effort to skip the probationary year, February 12, 1906. On the barn, see the anonymous letter sent to the Königliches Provinzschulkollegium, July 14, 1909; Direktor der städt. Gymnasiums in Entw., Essen, October 7, 1905; LHAK 405A-3879; 405A—1290, Report on "Beschwerde gegen Jacobs" at Realgymnasium Essen, signed Steinecke, April 24, 1911.

2. Ulrich Linse, *Die Entschiedene Jugend, 1919–1921: Deutschlands erste revolutionäre, Schüler—und Studentenbewegung*, Quellen und Beiträge zur Geschichte der Jugendbewegung, vol. 23 (Frankfurt am Main: Dipa-Verlag, 1981).

3. Ibid., 18; LHAK 405A, 1290, Städtisches Realgymnasium Essen to Provinzialschulkollegium, Coblenz, September 16, 1919; LHAK, Schreiben des Städtischen Gymnasiums und Realgymnasiums Essen-Rüttenscheid an das Lehrerkollegium des Städtischen Realgymnasiums Essen in the

manuscript Norbert Krüger, "Der Zweite Weltkrieg im Spiegel von Feld-postbriefen, Tagebüchern, und Erinnerungen" (2011).

4. Rainer Großbröhmer and Karin Kirch, *Von Bildungsbakterien und Volkshoch-schulepidemien: Ein Beitrag zur Geschichte der Volkshochschule Essen, 1919–1974* (Essen: Klartext-Verlag, 1994), 23–25. Artur Jacobs, *Über Wesen und Ziele einer Volks-hochschule: Ein Entwurf zu einer neuen Volkserziehung, der proletarischen Jugend gewid-met* (Essen: Freier Ausschuss für Volksbildung in Essen, 1919).

5. The 1924 Bund was preceded by a short-lived organization created in 1923—the Bund für Proletarian Education. BAE, DJGU, 27. The gender balance is based on Norbert Reichling's and my reconstruction of who made up the group's Inner Circle. Jacobs, Bramesfeld, et al., *Gelebte Utopie*, 13. In addition to the Bund's own sources, see Behrens and Reichling, "'Umbau des ganzen Lebens': Frauenbildung und Geschlechterfragen in der sozialistischen Bildungsgemeinschaft 'Bund' seit 1919"; Reichling, "Der 'Bund': Jugendbewegte Bildungsarbeit und Lebensreform im Ruhrge-biet"; and Reichling, "Mit Kant gegen die Nazis: Der 'Bund' und sein verges-senes 'Judenhilfswerk' im Rhein-Ruhr-Gebiet."

6. Alexander Stenbock-Fermor, *Meine Erlebnisse als Bergarbeiter*, Lebendige Welt Erzählungen und Bekenntnisse (Stuttgart: J. Engelhorn, 1928), and Alex-ander Stenbock-Fermor, *Deutschland von Unten: Reise durch die proletarische Provinz* (Stuttgart: J. Engelhorns nachf., 1931).

7. Werner Abelshauser, Wolfgang Köllmann, and Franz-Josef Brüggemeier, *Das Ruhrgebiet im Industriezeitalter: Geschichte und Entwicklung*, 2 vols. (Düssel-dorf: Schwann im Patmos Verlag, 1990).

8. Anyone familiar with the Weimar political scene will recognize, for exam-ple, many similarities between the Bund and an organization that was bet-ter known at the time, the Internationaler Sozialistischer Kampfbund—also known as the ISK or the "Nelson-Bund"—which was led by the philoso-pher Leonard Nelson. Werner Link, *Die Geschichte des internationalen Jugend-Bundes (IJB) und des internationalen sozialistischen Kampf-Bundes (ISK): Ein Beitrag zur Geschichte der Arbeiterbewegung in der Weimarer Republik und im Dritten Reich*, Marburger Abhandlungen zur politischen Wissenschaft, vol. 1 (Meisenheim am Glan: A. Hain, 1964); Karl-Heinz Klär, "Zwei Nelson-Bünde: Interna-tionaler Jugend-Bund (IJB) und internationaler sozialistischer Kampf-Bund (ISK) im Licht neuer Quellen," *Internationale wissenschaftliche Korrespondenz zur Geschichte der deutschen Arbeiterbewegung* 18, no. 3 (1982): 310–59; and Udo Vorholt, *Die politische Theorie Leonard Nelsons: Eine Fallstudie zum Verhältnis von philosophisch-politischer Theorie und konkret-politischer Praxis* (Baden-Baden: Nomos, 1998).

9. Hermann Schmalenbach, "Die soziologische Kategorie des Bundes," *Die Dioskuren: Jahrbuch für Geisteswissenschaften* 1 (1922): 35–105, and Rüdiger

Ahrens, *Bündische Jugend: Eine neue Geschichte, 1918–1933,* Moderne Zeit (Göttingen: Wallstein Verlag, 2015).

10. From the pamphlet *Der Bund: Eine sozialistische Lebens und Kampfgemeinschaft im Industriegebiet* (no place, no date); in the BAE.

11. Ibid.

12. *Der Bund: Gestalt und Ziel,* Essen, 1929, 51.

13. BAE, Notebook "Gesetze" (no date).

14. Else Goldreich, see BAE folder "Nachrufe," typescript, "Else Goldreich zum Gedächtnis," no author, no date. Tove Gerson, interview with the author, January 8, 1997, and Meta Kamp, telephone interviews with author, January 24, 1997, and September 11, 1998. For analogous issues in the Nelson Bund, see Klär, "Zwei Nelson-Bünde," 319n340.

15. Mülheim members included Fritz and Guste Denks, Helmut and Lene Krahlisch, Fritz Strothmann, and Gustav and Mathilde Zenker. In Wuppertal, Ernst Jungbluth was the leading spirit, alongside Artur's brother, Walter, and Walter's wife, Gertrud, Erna Michels, Liesel Speer, and others. Remscheid's leading lights included Fritz and Maria Briel and Grete Dreibholz. On Bund activities, see Jacobs, Bramesfeld, et al., *Gelebte Utopie* and the Bund leaflet *Internationaler sozialistischer Orden Bund,* in appendix to LAN, BR 007 30646f, Polizeipräsident in Düssseldorf to Herrn Reg-Präsidenten in Düsseldorf, November 19, 1931, re Internationaler Sozialistischer Orden: "Bund" (ISO). BAE, blue folder "Gruppenberichte."

16. In addition to *Gelebte Utopie,* the BAE contains many of the group's publications from the late 1920s and early 1930s. It also contains a pencil-written list of the adult education lecture topics from 1919 to 1931.

17. On convention, see, e.g., BAE folder "Nachrufe," typescript, "Else Goldreich zum Gedächtnis," no author, no date. On Marx and Kant, see Leszek Kolakowski, *Main Currents of Marxism: The Founders, the Golden Age, the Breakdown* (New York: W. W. Norton, 2005), 554–61. On Quakers, see Anna Sabine Halle, *Thoughts Are Free: A Quaker Youth Group in Nazi Germany,* Pendle Hill pamphlet (Wallingford, Pa.: Pendle Hill Publications, 1985), 13.

18. Dore Jacobs, "Zur Frage der Kollektiventscheidung," in Der Bund, ed., *Sozialistische Jugend und ihre Erziehungsaufgaben: Bundgedanken zur politischen Erziehung* (Essen: Der Bund, [1928]), 12–14.

19. This is certainly true of the ISK. See the sources in chapter 1, note 8.

20. The Bund destroyed records that would allow us to recover with certainty exactly who was in the Inner Circle (IK), but from surviving minutes from the end of the 1920s and other Bund records, we know that it included Artur, Dore, Lisa, Ernst, Käthe, Sonja (often referred to in the minutes as Emmi), Elsa Goldreich until her death in February 1928, Else Bramesfeld,

Berthold Levy, and Maria Fuhrmann. In the 1930s, until her 1938 emigration, Wasja Enoch (WE) was also part of the IK.

21. On Neo-Kantians and Marxism, see Kolakowski, *Main Currents of Marxism,* especially 554–56. On the way the Bund lived with its contradictions, see the remark by Gerda Hajek-Simons on living with the contradictions in DJGU, 215. On similarities with the ISK, see Klär, "Zwei Nelson-Bünde," and Link, *Die Geschichte des Internationalen Jugend-Bundes (IJB) und des Internationalen Sozialistischen Kampf-Bundes (ISK).*

22. Leo Baeck Institute, New York, AR 4322 C.1719, Ernst Marcus to Frau Henf, Essen, April 10, 1914; BAE, unpublished manuscript, Dore Jacobs, "Aus meiner Kindheit; Erinnerungen von Dore Jacobs geb. Marcus" in Hermann Schröter, *Geschichte und Schicksal der Essener Juden: Gedenkbuch für die jüdischen Mitbürger der Stadt Essen* (Essen: Stadt Essen, 1980), 189.

23. Chad Ross, *Naked Germany: Health, Race and the Nation* (New York: Berg, 2005); Edward Ross Dickinson, *Dancing in the Blood: Modern Dance and European Culture on the Eve of the First World War* (Cambridge: Cambridge University Press, 2017); J. Timothy Caldwell, *Expressive Singing: Dalcroze Eurythmics for Voice* (Englewood Cliffs, N.J.: Prentice Hall, 1995), 12ff.; Irwin Spector, *Rhythm and Life: the Work of Emile Jaques-Dalcroze,* Dance and Music Series (Stuyvesant, N.Y.: Pendragon Press, 1990), 149; Rainer Großbröhmer,"Dore Jacobs—ein Leben in Bewegung," in *Für Dore Jacobs, 1894–1994,* ed. Dore Jacobs Schule (Essen, 1994), 45–50; and Dore Jacobs, "Das Ringen der Zeit um körperseelische Erneuerung," *Die Tat.* Special Impression (1922): 1–20.

24. Lilian Karina and Marion Kant, *Tanz unterm Hakenkreuz: Eine Dokumentation* (Berlin: Henschel Verlag, 1996), 28–31; Dore Jacobs, "Erinnerungen," in *Für Dore Jacobs, 1894–1994,* ed. Dore Jacobs Schule, 3–6; and Dore Jacobs, "Werdegang der Schule," in *Für Dore Jacobs 1894–1994,* ed. Dore Jacobs Schule, 7–15.

25. Interview with Ursula Jungbluth, Wuppertal, May 1999; BAE "Zum Gedenken an Sonja Schreiber," no date (1987); online interview with Gustav Zenker, *Mülheimer Zeitzeugen;* interview with Gustav Zenker, Mülheim, February 1988 (conducted by Monika Grüter); and interview with Tove Gerson, Essen, January 1997.

26. Interview with Tove Gerson, Essen, January 1997.

27. Jutta Hetkamp, *Die jüdische Jugendbewegung in Deutschland von 1913–1933,* Anpassung, Selbstbehauptung, Widerstand (Münster: Lit, 1994), 53–58. Information about memories of the basement are from an interview with Friedl Speer, Wuppertal, April 2000. Susi Cohen, in an interview in Essen, September 1996 (conducted by Judith Hess) and in her unpublished manuscript "My First Ninety Years" (2011), kindly provided to me by the

author, describes her Eastern European Jewish mother's encounter with the Bund. Further information is from an interview with Ursula Jungbluth, Wuppertal, May 1999; Jacobs, "Erinnerungen"; Ellen Jungbluth, "Leben und Lernen mit Lisa Jacob," in BAE, unpublished photocopied booklet produced by the Bund on the occasion of Lisa's death, "Für Lisa Jacob," no date [1989].

28. Interview with Änne Schmitz, Wuppertal, January 1997.
29. Maria Briel, Remscheid, November 1990 (video interview conducted by Jochen Bilstein).
30. DJGU, 125.
31. StAE Bestand 626, Nachlaß Jacobs, folder "Geschichte A," Unpublished text, Artur Jacobs, "Völkische Hochschule oder Volkshochschule," Essen (1919).
32. Hans-Josef Steinberg, *Widerstand und Verfolgung in Essen, 1933–1945* (Hannover: Verlag für Literatur und Zeitgeschehen, 1969), 27.
33. LAN, BR 007 30646f, Essen, Police President to District President, Düsseldorf, October 10, 1931, re Internationaler Sozialistischer Orden: Bund (ISO), Arbeitskreis Essen; online interview with Gustav Zenker, *Mülheimer Zeitzeugen*; Grüter, "Der 'Bund für ein sozialistisches Leben,'" 37; and LAN, BR 007 30646f, Düsseldorf Police President to District President, Düsseldorf, November 19, 1931, re Internationaler Sozialistischer Orden: Bund (ISO).
34. LAN, BR 007 30646f, Essen, Police President to District President, Düsseldorf, October 10, 1931, re Internationaler Sozialistischer Orden: Bund (ISO), Arbeitskreis Essen; Bund leaflet *Internationaler Sozialistischer Orden Bund*, in annex to LAN, BR 007 30646f, Düsseldorf Police President to District President, Düsseldorf, November 19, 1931, re Internationaler Sozialistischer Orden: Bund (ISO). If documents the Gestapo later captured and attributed to the group really are authentic, the IK was sufficiently alarmed by conditions to wonder what its stance should be if armed civil war were to break out. See LHAK 405A-3216, Confiscated document headed "Politischer Schulungsabend," March 19, 1931. However, these notes are in a different hand and are structured differently from other IK notes. Some phrases suggest that they were written by Communists or a Communist oppositional group, perhaps the Rote Gewerkschaftsopposition.

2. The Assault

1. Steinberg, *Widerstand und Verfolgung in Essen, 1933–1945*, 38; Nikolaus Wachsmann, *KL: A History of the Nazi Concentration Camps* (New York: Farrar, Straus and Giroux, 2015), 32, 37.

2. LHAK 405A-3216, Annex to Oberbürgermeister der Stadt Essen to Oberpräsident der Rheinlandprovinz, March 13, 1934. Annex Abschrift "Verhandelt," Essen, March 1, 1934; BAE, Unpublished report (probably spring 1947), "Aus der illegalen Arbeit des Bundes. 2. Auslandsbericht" (Henceforth AB2; this is the "Second Letter Abroad"), 6; StAE, Wiedergutmachungsakte Dr. Jacobs, Erklärung Karl Heilwagen, September, 23 1949; and Grüter, "Der 'Bund für ein sozialistisches Leben,'" 76.

3. LHAK 405A-3216, Annex to Oberbürgermeister der Stadt Essen to Oberpräsident der Rheinlandprovinz, March 13, 1934. Annex Abschrift "Verhandelt," Essen, March 1, 1934.

4. Volkshochschule Essen, Kanzlei to Studienrat Dr. Jacobs, February 27, 1933, reproduced in LHAK 405A-3216, Dr. Jacobs Essen-Stadtwald an den städtischen Kommissar für Schulangelegenheiten, Herrn Dr. Bubenzer, June 16, 1933; NGJ, DJ to GJ, June 6, 1933; NJ, Box 1, Draft, Dore Jacobs to Hildegard Tauscher, August 28, 1935.

5. BAE "Vernehmung am 7.IV.33," undated, unsigned memo clearly from Dore Jacobs; LHAK, 405/3216 Entwurf Oberpräsident der Rheinprovinz, Abt für höheres Schulwesen an den Minister für W, K u V in Berlin, August 25, 1933, Betr. Anwendung des §a des Gesetzes zur Widerherstellung des Berufsbeamtentums auf den Studienrat i.R. Dr. Arthur Jacobs; BAE, Martin Schubert to Dore Jacobs, August 30, 1933; LHAK, 405A-3216 Draft, Oberpräsident der Rheinprovinz Abt für höheres Schulwesen, August 20, 1933, Anwendung des §4 des Gesetzes zur Wiederherstellung des Berufsbeamtentums auf den Studienrat i.R, Artur Jacobs, and following letter from August 25, 1933; BAE, Police President Essen, September 14, 1933; BAE, copy E. Schreiber to Herrn Polizeipräsidenten, September 24, 1933; BAE, copy Dore Jacobs to Police President, September 26, 1933.

6. StAW, Wiedergutmachungsakte, Jungbluth Ernst 115, 24, Jungbluth, Fragebogen, Wuppertal, March 20, 1946; BAE, copy, Georg Reuter to Essen Police, September 12, 1933; Schröter, *Geschichte und Schicksal der Essener Juden*, 201–03; BAE, "Gretas Leben" [sic! Grete seems to have spelled her name both ways], in unpublished photocopied booklet produced by the Bund on the occasion of Grete Dreibholz's death, no date (1984), 1–2; and LAN, BR 3000, 76, Tilde Stürmer to Regierungspräsident, September 29, 1964, and subsequent correspondence.

7. Karlos Morgenstern and Georg Reuter went to Göttingen, Karl Heilwagen and Reinhold Ströter to Hamburg. Doris Braune headed down to Meersburg. BAE, "Zum Gedenken an Karl Heilwagen," in *Mitteilungen* (Bund newsletter), vol. 3 (1985), 9. LAN, RW58 19223, StapoD, Ast Oberhausen-Mülheim a.d. Ruhr to AstE, August 27, 1936; RW58 1808, Personalbogen; interview with Doris Braune by Heidi Behrens-Cobet,

October 24, 1991; NGJ, GJ to AJ, March 27, 1933; and NJ, Box 1, Draft, Dore Jacobs to Hildegard Tauscher, August 8, 1935.

8. LHAK, 405A-3216, Oberbürgermeister der Stadt Essen to Oberpräsidenten Koblenz, March 13, 1934, signed Bubenzer, Beigeordnete; Schröter, *Geschichte und Schicksal der Essener Juden*, 201–3.

9. BAE, DJ to Police President, Essen, September 26, 1933, and LHAK, 405A-3216 annexes to Bubenzer to Oberbürgermeister Essen, March 13, 1934.

10. Declarations by Georg Reuter, Karl Heilwagen, Doris Braune, and Anne Klein in June and July 1933, in BAE.

11. BAE, Martin Schubert to DJ, August 30, 1933.

12. BAE, Police President in Essen to DJ, October 28, 1933; BAE, Martin Schubert to DJ, November 6, 1933, and February 26, 1933; LHAK, 405/3216 Draft, Oberpräsident der Rheinprovinz Abt für höheres Schulwesen, August 20, 1933, Anwendung des §4 des Gesetzes zur Wiederherstellung des Berufsbeamtentums auf den Studienrat i.R, Artur Jacobs, and following letter from August 25, 1933; NJ, Box 1, copy, DJ to Herrn Schulrat Zellmer, December 26, 1933, DJ to Herrn Schulrat Zellmer, May 16, 1934, Präsident der Reichsmusikkammer to DJ, August 22, 1935. BAE Schulrat Essen IV to DJ, April 6, 1934; LHAK, 405/3216 Dr. Jacobs Essen-Stadtwald an den städtischen Kommissar für Schulangelegenheiten, Herrn Dr. Bubenzer, June 16, 1933; StAE, Bestand 141, ES an den Dezernenten für das Schulwesen der Stadt Essen, Herrn Beigeordneten Studientrat Dr. Bubenzer, durch Herrn Schulrat Schieffer, Essen, October 7, 1933; LAN, NW 1005 G33 1048 Denazification file Emmi Schreiber; Denunciation from Hilde Hesse née Rode and Gisela Lönne, born September 3, 1921, Goethestrasse 54, August 6, 1944, in LAN, RW 58 71703; ASE, IN 086 interview with Berthold Levy, December 17, 1985 (conducted by Angela Genger).

13. Transcript of interview with Doris Braune by Heidi Behrens-Cobet, October 24, 1991.

14. NGJ, GJ to AJ, March 27, 1933; undated letter GJ to AJ [from Hamburg, probably March or April]; GJ to AJ, May 8, 1933; GJ to AJ, "early June"; and DJ to GJ, July 3, 1933.

15. NGJ, AJ to GJ, May 18, 1933.

16. NGJ, GJ to AJ, "Anfang Juni," 1933.

17. Maria Briel, Remscheid, November 1990 (video interview conducted by Jochen Bilstein).

18. "Margarete," who was very critical of the Bund, preferred to remain anonymous.

19. Sebastian Haffner, *The Meaning of Hitler* (Cambridge, Mass.: Harvard University Press, 1983), 27.

20. LAN, RW58 19223, StapoD "Aussenstelle Wuppertal" to AstE, June 23, 1939. Imprisoned: Ernst Jungbluth, 1933; Ilse Bender, 1936; Paula Sauer, 1936–37; August Schmitz, 1938. With thanks to Dieter Nelles for providing the information from a University of Wuppertal database. Interview Änne Schmitz, Wuppertal, January 1997. Maria Briel, Remscheid, November 1990 (video interview conducted by Jochen Bilstein).

21. AB3.

22. Grüter, "Der "Bund für ein sozialistisches Leben,'" 51; BAE, unpublished transcript, Ruth Kotik, "Ein Vorläufer alternativer Lebensformen: Der Bund—Gemeinschaft für sozialistisches Leben," broadcast November 16, 1984, WDR3, 15 (Henceforth, Kotik, "Vorläufer"); interview with Friedl Speer, Wuppertal, April 2000.

23. LAN, RW58 19223, copy, Ortsgruppenleiter Biedemann to Kreisleitung, June 22, 1937.

24. LAN, RW58 19223, copy, re Zusammenkünfte in der kath. Notkirche Essen-Stadtwald, signed Max Fross, August 17, 1937.

25. Interview, Änne Schmitz, Wuppertal, January 1997.

26. Gerhard Paul and Klaus-Michael Mallmann, *Milieus und Widerstand: Eine Verhaltensgeschichte der Gesellschaft im Nationalsozialismus,* Widerstand und Verweigerung im Saarland 1935–1945 (Bonn: J.H.W. Dietz, 1995), 415–16 and 532ff.; Bernward Dörner, "NS-Herrschaft und Denunziation: Anmerkungen zu Defiziten in der Denunziationsforschung," *Historical Social Research / Historische Sozialforschung* 26, nos. 2–3 (2001): 55–69, specifically 62; Gellately, *The Gestapo and German Society;* Gellately, *Backing Hitler;* Inge Marszolek, "Denunziation im Dritten Reich: Kommunikationsformen und Verhaltensweisen," in Kosmala and Schoppman, *Solidarität und Hilfe für Juden während der NS-Zeit,* vol. 5, 89–107.

27. Interview with Ellen Jungbluth, July 29, 1997; Ellen in Kotik, "Vorläufer," 17.

28. Interview with Tove Gerson, Essen, January 1997; interview with Barbara Martin, Lüdinghausen, June 2004 (conducted by Norbert Reichling).

29. Maria Briel, Remscheid, November 1990 (video interview conducted by Jochen Bilstein).

30. AB3, 5.

31. AB1.

32. Artur Jacobs, "Unser Verpflichtungstag," Meersburg, 1944, reprinted in DJGU, 155. Also see chapter 9, the section "Creating a Public Record."

33. Artur Jacobs, "Ansprache zum Verpflichtungstag 1945," reprinted in DJGU, 3–6.

3. From Vanguard to Refuge

1. *"Einem ungemein raschen und starken Faschisierungsprozeß der Gesellschaft."* Cited in Norbert Frei, "'Volksgemeinschaft,'" in *1945 und wir: Das Dritte Reich im Bewusstsein der Deutschen,* ed. Norbert Frei (München: C. H. Beck, 2005), 121–42, specifically 126. The emphasis is in the original source.
2. Willy Cohn, *Kein Recht, nirgends: Tagebuch vom Untergang des Breslauer Judentums, 1933–1941* (Köln: Böhlau, 2006), vol. 1, 524, and Paul and Mallmann, *Milieus und Widerstand,* 532.
3. BAE, AB3, 11, and Artur Jacobs, "Unser Verpflichtungstag," Meersburg, 1944, reprinted in DJGU, 155.
4. Artur Jacobs, "Ansprache zum Verpflichtungstag 1945," reprinted in DJGU, 36.
5. Testimony of Reinhold Ströter, 1984, in Kotik, "Vorläufer," 16, and interview with Friedl Speer, April 3, 2000.
6. The group did not keep membership lists during the Nazi years, and it destroyed the ones it had held beforehand, so these figures are of necessity speculative, based on the names that recur in communications at the time, as well as later reminiscences. There were undoubtedly several individuals involved of whom we have no record.
7. Online interview with Fritz Denks, in the series *Mülheimer Zeitzeugen,* 1980, accessed June 26, 2017.
8. Interview with Ursula Jungbluth, May 19, 1999.
9. AB3, 7.
10. AB3, 8.
11. Ibid.
12. Lisa Jacob, "Zum Gedenken an Artur Jacobs" and interview with Ellen Jungbluth, Wuppertal, July 1997. On the interrogation of Bund members, see Gestapo files in LAN, RW58 1808 (Erna Michels), Grenzpolizei-Kommissariat Herzogenrat an Stapo Aachen September 21, 1938; RW58 19223 (Artur Jacobs) polizeiliche Untersuchungen 1933, 1936, 1937, 1939, 1940.
13. Kotik, "Vorläufer," 15.
14. Interview with Ellen Jungbluth, Wuppertal, July 1997.
15. AB3, 7.
16. Lisa Jacob, "'Der Bund': Gemeinschaft für sozialistisches Leben und meine Rettung vor der Deportation," *Das Münster am Hellweg* 37 (1984): 105–34. Unpublished version: Lisa Jacob, "'Der Bund': Gemeinschaft für sozialistisches Leben und meine Errettung vor der Deportation; Ein Brief geschrieben nach Kriegsende an meine im Ausland lebenden Geschwister" (Bund Archive, Essen, no date).
17. BAE, Lisa Jacob, "Zum Gedenken an Artur Jacobs," 13.

18. See the section "Rock Bottom" in chapter 4 for the context.

19. Jacob, "Der Bund," 5.

20. Victor Klemperer and Roderick H. Watt, *An Annotated Edition of Victor Klemperer's LTI, Notizbuch eines Philologen*, Studies in German Thought and History (Lewiston, N.Y.: E. Mellen Press, 1997), and AB3, 14.

21. AB3, 17.

22. Artur Jacobs, "Ansprache zur Maifaier," reprinted in DJGU, 176.

23. Ernst Jungbluth, "Ein Brief zur politischen Dunkelheit," reprinted in DJGU, 141. The letter is undated, but the contents make clear that it was written thirty years later than the original analysis, so it must be the early to mid-1960s.

24. Stadtarchiv Remscheid N41-7, typed manuscript, "Gedenkstunden für Walter," February 15, 1969.

25. Ibid.

26. BAE, DJGU, vol. 2, "Ansprache zur Maifeier," 175. See also BAE, type-written extract, "Aus einem Brief von Dore an Wasja von 22 Mai 1945, 'Was bedeutet für uns, für den Bund, die endgültige Niederschlagung des National-Sozialismus?'"

27. The letter was written in English because Ernst was addressing the British Military Government after the war. SLC, MC 447, Box 2-46, Ernst Jungbluth to the military government, May 1945.

28. See Sozialdemokratische Partei Deutschlands and Klaus Behnken, *Deutschland-Berichte der Sopade 1934–1940*, vol. 1 (Salzhausen: Verlag Petra Nettelbeck; Frankfurt am Main: Zweitausendeins, 1980).

29. Nicholas Stargardt, *The German War: A Nation Under Arms, 1939–1945: Citizens and Soldiers* (New York: Basic Books, 2015).

30. Willi Müller, ed., *Demokratie vor Ort: Ein Lesebuch zur Geschichte der Sozialdemokratischen Partei Deutschlands in Mülheim an der Ruhr* (Mülheim: Vor Ort Verlag, 1979), 184–85.

31. Institut für Zeitgeschichte, Munich, ED 106/97, undated report (probably late 1946), "Bericht über das Judenhilfswerk des 'Bundes' Gemeinschaft für sozialistisches Leben."

32. Maria Briel, Remscheid, November 1990 (video interview conducted by Jochen Bilstein).

33. It should be noted that the version of the Bund laws for the Nazi period that survives in the group's archive was clearly typed up after the fall of the regime, though we have no reason to distrust its accuracy. BAE, Box Bundschriften 5, folder "Gesetze des Bundes," typewritten page, "Während der zwölf Jahre," no date. The title "During the Twelve Years" makes obvious that this was typed after the regime had fallen. The full text runs:

    i. It is my aim to make responsibility for the fate of our mission the

central task of my life, above and beyond of all other goals and interests, and to commit myself to it with my best ability.

ii. I am ready to subject my daily actions to more serious and careful
scrutiny in order not to fall foul of the particular danger of our time,
namely, of denying my true beliefs and living as a private individual
rather than as a carrier of the mission.

iii. It is my firm will not to allow unacknowledged worries about my livelihood to push me to acts of omission and commission that I cannot
condone. I am ready continually to test my courage on small tasks, so
as not to succumb to the general cowardice and lack of character.

iv. It is my intention to keep my conscience alert despite the prevailing
pressures, and not to deceive myself with ostensibly "objective"
excuses into evading attainable demands and tasks.

v. It is my intention not to become habituated to lies, pernicious ideas
and injustice or to allow my conscience to become dulled by enforced
or routine fellow traveling.

vi. I will try to become more aware of the world around me, to seek connections to it rather than to avoid it, and everywhere to seek new
possibilities for action.

34. Lisa Jacob, "'Der Bund': Gemeinschaft für sozialistisches Leben und meine
Errettung vor der Deportation," 6.

35. Maria Briel made a rather striking and unironic quotation from Heine's
"Die Grenadiere" to this effect, in the interview with Jochen Bilstein,
November 1990.

36. Comments of Ellen Jungbluth in Kotik, "Vorläufer," 17.

37. William Sheridan Allen, "Die sozialdemokratische Untergrundbewegung:
Zur Kontinuität der subkulturellen Werte," in *Der Widerstand gegen den Nationalsozialismus: Die deutsche Gesellschaft und der Widerstand gegen Hitler; Publikationen
der Historischen Kommission zu Berlin*, ed. Jürgen Schmädeke and Peter Steinbach (München: R. Piper, 1985), 849–66, specifically 853.

38. Steinberg, *Widerstand und Verfolgung in Essen, 1933–1945*, 99–109.

39. Ibid., 855.

40. Paul and Mallmann, *Milieus und Widerstand*, 420–21.

41. Kurt Klotzbach, *Gegen den Nationalsozialismus: Widerstand und Verfolgung in
Dortmund, 1930–1945; Eine historisch-politische Studie*, Schriftenreihe des For-
schungsinstituts der Friedrich-Ebert-Stiftung B: Historisch-politische
Schriften (Hannover: Verlag für Literatur und Zeitgeschehen, 1969):
208–09. On a parallel set of arrests in Essen, see Steinberg, *Widerstand und
Verfolgung in Essen, 1933–1945*, 123–26.

42. Neu Beginnen reached the same conclusions. Terence Ray Renaud, "Restarting Socialism: The New Beginning Group and the Problem of Renewal on

the German Left, 1930–1970" (PhD diss., University of California, Berkeley, 2015), 51.

43. Emmy Barth, *An Embassy Besieged: The Story of a Christian Community in Nazi Germany* (Eugene, Ore.: Cascade Books; Rifton, N.Y.: Plough, 2010).

44. Interview with Friedl Speer, Wuppertal, April 2000.

45. Interview with Tove Gerson, Essen, January 1997.

46. Kershaw, *The Nazi Dictatorship*, 184.

47. LAN, RW58 1595, statement by Ernst Jungbluth, January 14, 1939. SD Oberabschnitt West, Unterabschnitt Düsseldorf to Gestapo, Düsseldorf, June 5, 1939, re "Ästhetischer Bund."

48. LAN, RW58-41452, copy of report, NSDAP Kreisgruppe Rellinghausen to Kreisleitung der NSDAP, Personalamt, Essen, December 22, 1939; StapoD, AstE, "Verantwortliche Vernehmung eines Beschuldigten. Verhandelt Essen," March 8, 1940.

49. LAN, NW 1022-5 11804, Luise Speer. Interview with Friedl Speer, Wuppertal, April 2000.

50. This is discussed further in the section "Rock Bottom" in chapter 4.

51. Papers in possession of Annette Speer, Wuppertal (SP), draft letter to the Evangelische Kirchengemeinde, Schellsitz bei Großjena, November 4, 1938, signed Liesel Speer. Karlos Morgenstern's marriage to Karin was delayed by the difficulty of getting the proof of Aryan status from church records from eastern Germany, for example. Interview with Barbara Martin (née Morgenstern) in Lüdinghausen by Norbert Reichling, June 2004.

52. Interview with Änne Schmitz, Wuppertal, January 1997.

53. See chapter 4.

54. Kotik, "Vorläufer," 17.

55. Paul and Mallmann, *Milieus und Widerstand*, 235.

56. Conversation between Mark Roseman and Reinhold Ströter and Hermann Schmalstieg, Haus an der Rüspe, May 2000.

57. Interview with Reinhold Ströter, Mettmann, March 2000.

58. LAN, RW58 47025, Grete Ströter, copy of undated letter from Tilde to Grete Ströter; copy of letter from Alfred Stürmer to Grete Ströter, April 7, 1940.

59. Renaud, "Restarting Socialism," 49.

60. Kotik, "Vorläufer," 16.

61. Interview with Tove Gerson, January 9, 1997.

62. AB3, 16.

63. See chapter 6.

64. As in note 56.

65. Sonja Schreiber, "Zum Gedenken an Artur Jacobs," March 1968, reprinted in DJGU, 218–21, particularly 220.

66. Papers in the possesion of Alfred Stürmer (ASP), notebook without author [Lisa Jacob] or date [1942]; NJ, AJD, June 27, 1942. Also see chapter 6.

67. See also AJD, June 27, 1942.

68. AJD, June 25, 1942.

69. Grüter, "Der 'Bund für ein sozialistisches Leben,'" 51.

70. Schreiber, "Zum Gedenken an Artur Jacobs," March 1968, reprinted in DJGU, 218–21, especially 220.

71. Poem "Wisst Ihr Noch?" in StAR, N41-7.

72. The diary seems to have been written by Lisa, dating from the time when she was living illegally, adding all the more power and pathos to her observations. See chapter 6.

73. AB2, 11.

74. Interview with Ellen Jungbluth, Wuppertal, July 1997.

75. Ibid.

76. "Lebenslauf" in BAE folder "Nachrufe," Nachruf für Wasja Enoch. (The account says that she joined the Bund in 1937. This seems too late, and since the next sentence talks about her having spent thirty-seven years in the United States, it seems likely that some mix-up over numbers has taken place. But we cannot be sure.)

77. Meta Kamp, *Auf der anderen Seite stehen* (Göttingen: Printed by the author, 1987), 34.

78. Video interview conducted with Maria Briel by Jochen Bilstein, Remscheid, November 1990.

79. Lilian Karina and Marion Kant, *Hitler's Dancers: German Modern Dance and the Third Reich* (New York: Berghahn Books, 2003).

80. SLC, MC 447, Tove Gerson, Box 1, Folder 17, "Education Boston University." The title is unfortunately illegible, but this was a paper submitted on relevant experiences for her postwar training as a social worker.

81. Ibid.

82. Yvonne Hardt, "Ausdruckstanz und Bewegungschor im Nationalsozialismus: Zur politischen Dimension des Körperlichen und Räumlichen im modernen Tanz," in *Körper im Nationalsozialismus: Bilder und Praxe*, ed. Paula Diehl (Paderborn: Schöningh, 2006), 173–89, specifically 173; Dickinson, *Dancing in the Blood*, 240–50.

83. Hardt, "Ausdruckstanz," 174–84, especially 179; Sonja Schreiber, "Aus der Körperbildungsfreizeit des Bundes 1936 in Mühlental: Ein Brief," reprinted in DJGU, 90–91. See also Martin Gleisner, "Tanzvergnügen und Tanzfeier," *Leib und Seele: Monatszeitschrift für deutsche Leibesübungen* 5 (1929): 114.

84. Tove Gerson, in Kotik, "Vorläufer," 14–15.

4. Calls to Arms

1. Information contained in LAN, Denazification files, NW 1022-5 11804, Luise Speer; NW1022 J 24280, Ernst Jungbluth; NW 1022, J 31069, Gertrud Jacobs; NW 1005 G33 1048, Emmi Schreiber.

2. LAN, BR 3000, Nr. 71 (Wiedergutmachung, Gottfried Jacobs), Gottfried Jacobs, "Eidestattliche Versicherung," June 9, 1955; "Eidestattliche Versicherung," Gelsenkirchen, September 7, 1955; Helmut Kalthaus, "Eidestattliche Versicherung," June 11, 1955.

3. BAE, Box "Bund 2," handwritten and typewritten report headed "Else, January 1986"; extract from letter to Artur Jacobs on the occasion of his eightieth birthday from Gerda Hajek Simons, reprinted in DJGU, 215; BAE, "Zum Gedenken an Gerda Hajek Simons," Essen, January 1984; and Eva Seligmann and Heide Henk, *Erinnerungen einer streitbaren Pädagogin* (Bremen: Ed. Temmen, 2000). It is another sign that some outreach was possible that Gerda Simons's connection with the Bund was established at a group retreat only in 1934.

4. LAN, RW 58-58105 Jacob, Elisabeth Sara, Interrogation, March 1, 1940.

5. Institut für Zeitgeschichte, Munich, ED 106/97, undated report [late 1946], "Bericht über das Judenhilfswerk des 'Bundes' Gemeinschaft für sozialistisches Leben," 6.

6. Inge Olesch, "Widerstand in Mülheim an der Ruhr," diplomarbeit, specifically 332, note 319.

7. Alan E. Steinweis, *Kristallnacht 1938* (Cambridge, Mass.: Belknap Press of Harvard University Press, 2009); William Sheridan Allen, "Die deutsche Öffentlichkeit und die 'Reichskristallnacht': Konflikte zwischen Werthierarchie und Propaganda im Dritten Reich," in *Die Reihen fast geschlossen: Beiträge zur Geschichte des Alltags unterm Nationalsozialismus*, ed. Detlev Peukert, Jürgen Reulecke, and Adelheid Castell Rüdenhausen (Wuppertal: Hammer, 1981), 397–411; Otto Dov Kulka, "'Public Opinion' in Nazi Germany and the Jewish Question," *Jerusalem Quarterly* 25 (1982): 121–44; and Otto Dov Kulka, "'Public Opinion' in Nazi Germany and the Jewish Question," *Jerusalem Quarterly* 26 (1983): 34–45.

8. The official death toll of ninety-one on November 9 and 10 is too low. It probably runs into the hundreds. Evans, *The Third Reich in Power*, 580–611.

9. Interview with Tove Gerson, Essen, January 1997.

10. Ibid.

11. NGJ, AJ to GJ, November 12, 1938.

12. NGJ, AJ to GJ, February 3, 1939.

13. SLC, MC447 Box 2, Folder 31, manuscript titled "Adult Group in First Christian Church," May 10, 1942.
14. Interview with Tove Gerson, Essen, January 1997. The remarks following the quote also draw on an interview Gerson gave to an Essen trade school in 1988, the tape recording of which can be found in the BAE.
15. See, e.g., Hans Reichmann and Michael Wildt, *Deutscher Bürger und verfolgter Jude: Novemberpogrom und KZ Sachsenhausen 1937 bis 1939*, Biographische Quellen zur Zeitgeschichte (München: R. Oldenbourg, 1998).
16. SLC, MC 447, Tove Gerson, Tape T-213, tape 1, side 1, recorded 1987.
17. Olesch, "Widerstand in Mülheim an der Ruhr," 331.
18. Sieglind Ellger-Rüttgardt, "Das Israelitische Waisenhaus Dinslaken," in *Juden im Ruhrgebiet: vom Zeitalter der Aufklärung bis in die Gegenwart*, ed. Jan-Pieter Barbian, Michael Brocke, and Ludger Heid (Essen: Klartext, 1999), 503–22.
19. Yitzhak Sophoni Herz, *Meine Erinnerung an Bad Homburg und seine 600 jährige jüdische Gemeinde (1335–1942)* (Rechovoth, Israel: S. Herz, 1981).
20. BAE, partial transcript of an interview recorded in an Essener Berufsschule, 1988.
21. Ibid.
22. Ellger-Rüttgardt, "Das israelitische Waisenhaus Dinslaken," 511–21; Herz, *Meine Erinnerung an Bad Homburg und seine 600 jährige jüdische Gemeinde (1335–1942)*.
23. Jochen Bilstein and Frieder Backhaus, *Geschichte der Remscheider Juden* (Remscheid: Verlag der Buchh. Hackenberg Wermelskirchen W. Dreyer-Erben, 1992), 133.
24. Olesch, "Widerstand in Mülheim an der Ruhr," 331–32.
25. SLC, MC447 Box 1, Folder, 16, autobiographical statement with Boston University.
26. BAE, handwritten and typewritten report headed "Else, January 1986."
27. NGJ, AJ to GJ, January 21, 1939.
28. NJ, folder "Geschichte C," Artur Jacobs, "Von der Geschichte gerichtet: Hitlers Erscheinung und Schicksal," 26.
29. In his perceptive study *The Whitewashing of the Yellow Badge*, Frank Stern has shown how in the postwar period the West German population telescoped onto Kristallnacht what had been a much longer history of anti-Jewish measures, and thereby hid its own acceptance or tolerance of a much longer, more gradual process. See Frank Stern and Vidal Sassoon International Center for the Study of Antisemitism (Universitah ha-'Ivrit bi-Yerushalayim), *The Whitewashing of the Yellow Badge: Antisemitism and Philosemitism in Postwar Germany*, Studies in Antisemitism (New York: Published for the Vidal Sassoon International Center for the Study of Antisemitism (SICSA), the Hebrew University of Jerusalem, by Pergamon Press,

1992). But in the Bund's case, the contemporary evidence suggests that it really was Kristallnacht that decisively pushed it into action.

30. SLC, MC447 Box 1, Folder, 16, autobiographical statement with Boston University.
31. Information on the correspondence in the Alte Synagoge provided by Susi Cohen. E-mail from Susi Cohen to Mark Roseman, July 31, 2011.
32. NGJ, AJ to GJ, January 21, 1939.
33. SLC, MC447 Box 2, Folder 31, manuscript titled "Rede vor der American Association of University Women. Bartlesville," March 9, 1942.
34. AJD, October 4, 1944.
35. NGJ, AJ to GJ, July 20, 1938.
36. DJ, "Brief an eine emigrierte Genossin (1938)," in DJGU, 129.
37. NGJ, DJ to GJ, August 21, 1938.
38. NGJ, AJ to GJ, February 21, 1939. Although the letter refers only to the Herzfelds, the information matches that for Salomon Herzfeld, Robert Marcus's father-in-law. See Schröter, *Geschichte und Schicksal der Essener Juden,* 581.
39. NGJ, AJ to GJ, September 6, 1938.
40. Ibid.; and AJ to GJ, February 21, 1939.
41. DJ, "Brief an eine emigrierte Genossin (1938)," in DJGU, 129.
42. NGJ, Karlos Morgenstern to AJ, January 10, 1940.
43. NGJ, DJ to "Anna," November 18, 1938; AJ to GJ, February 21, 1939; AJ to GJ, April 8, 1939; and AJ to GJ, June 30, 1939.
44. NGJ, AJ to GJ, June 30, 1939.
45. NGJ, AJ to GJ, January 21, 1939.
46. NGJ, AJ to GJ, February 21, 1939; AJ to GJ, March 30, 1939; LAN, RW58 19223, AJ to Gestapo, March 16, 1940.
47. NGJ, AJ to GJ, September 28, 1940, and October 28, 1940. Bund records sometimes still refer to the house as the Eyhof, using the name of the street before 1931.
48. NGJ, AJ to GJ, July 10, 1939.
49. NGJ, AJ to GJ, letters April 22, May 5, May 8, May 11, and May 20, 1939. Lisa Jacob to GJ, July 14, 1939; AJ to GJ, 4 April 1941; and AJD, June 27, 1942.
50. Joseph Walk, *Das Sonderrecht für die Juden im NS-Staat: Eine Sammlung der gesetzlichen Massnahmen und Richtlinien, Inhalt und Bedeutung,* 2nd ed., Uni-Taschenbücher (Heidelberg; Karlsruhe: C. F. Müller Verlag, 1996), 312, 314, 328; Elizabeth Freund and Carola Sachse, *Als Zwangsarbeiterin 1941 in Berlin: Die Aufzeichnungen der Volkswirtin Elisabeth Freund,* Selbstzeugnisse der Neuzeit (Berlin: Akademie, 1996), 123.
51. NGJ, DJ to her sister, Eva von der Dunk, April 20, 1940.

52. NGJ, AJ to GJ, January 3, 1940. The letter says "im Felde," so presumably Poland is meant. On call-up and U.K. status, see denazification files in LAN, NW 1035 6444; 1013—I/I 121; 1013 I/ PP 45; 1013 I/ DN 10; NW 1013 II/ ED 9990; and NW 1002—AD 268.

53. AB3.

54. NGJ, AJ to GJ, January 8, 1940.

55. SLC, MC 447, Box 1, Folder 30, Oklahoma correspondence re speeches, Tove Gerson to WE, April 15, 1942.

56. NGJ, GJ to EJ, October 2, 1942. Only in 1944 did Artur offer clear but cautious evidence that Ursula had been rethinking her relationship to the regime.

57. NGJ, AJ to GJ, April 16, 1940. Interview with Friedl Speer, Wuppertal, April 2000.

58. NGJ, DJ to GJ, October 10, 1938, and November 3, 1938.

59. Ibid.

60. NGJ, AJ to GJ, December 15, 1938. See also NGJ, DJ to GJ, February 6, 1939, and February 18, 1939; AJ to GJ, February 18, 1939.

61. See the letters from Artur and Dore to GJ on July 13, 17, 20, and 23, 1938 and April 20, 1939.

62. "Het Vrije Denken" in Milo Anstadt, *De verdachte oorboog: Autobiografische roman* (Amsterdam: Contact, 1996); see, in particular, 239.

63. Ibid., 241.

64. ASE, IN. 614, Susi Cohen interview with Judith Hess, September 5, 1996; Karien Anstadt to author, March 29, 2011.

65. NGJ, Erna Michels to Dore, June 1, 1939. Anstadt, *De verdachte oorboog*; e-mail to the author from Karien Anstadt, March 29, 2011; ASE, IN. 614, Susi Cohen interview with Judith Hess, September 5, 1996.

66. NGJ, AJ to GJ, June 29, 1940.

67. NGJ, AJ to GJ, February 8, 1943, and GJ to AJ, February 2, 1943. See Friedl's later marginalia in a letter from his father sent on October 4, 1942.

68. NGJ, Karlos Morgenstern to AJ, January 10, 1940.

69. NGJ, LJ to GJ, July 10, 1939; WJ to GJ, January 23, 1941; and EJ to AJ, October 8, 1942.

70. NGJ, AJ to GJ, April 2, 1940.

71. NGJ, WJ to GJ, January 23, 1941.

72. NGJ, WJ to GJ, June 16, 1941.

73. NGJ, AJ to GJ, October 3, 1938, and AJ to GJ, November 12, 1941.

74. AJD, March 17, 1942.

75. AJD, October 23, 1942.

76. AJD, October 26, 1942.

77. AJD, September 13, 1943.

78. LAN, RW 58-41452, undated transcript, Friedrich Gross, Riesweg 64 (Eingang December 9, 1939) and subsequent documents; memorandum, StapoD, AStE, March 6, 1940, signed Kosthorst.

79. LAN, NW 1005 G33 1048, Emmi Schreiber, "Lebenslauf (ab 1930)," no date [November 1945], and RW 58-41452, Regierungspräsident to Gestapo Düsseldorf, May 6, 1940.

80. LAN, RW58 580105, statement by Anna Gellingshausen, Essen, February 28, 1940.

81. LAN, RW58, 19223, StapoD, AStE,Vermerk, Essen, March 7, 1940.

82. LAN, 3000, 72, Dore Jacobs, "Sitzung of the Amtsgericht Essen," February 27, 1953.

83. NGJ, AJ to GJ, April 16, 1940.

84. BAE, "Aus Ferienbriefen von Artur Jacobs—Sommer 1940," undated typewritten compilation.

5. Lifelines

1. AJD, October 14, 1942.

2. According to Jacob, "'Der Bund': Gemeinschaft für sozialistisches Leben und meine Rettung vor der Deportation," 116, 127, the originals of the surviving letters are in Kibbutz Hazorea, the only kibbutz to be founded by the German youth movement. The copies I saw were in the possession of Trude's grandson Stefan Brandt, Berlin; reproduced in DJGU; and in Rainer Funk, "Erleben von Ohnmacht im Dritten Reich: Das Schicksal der jüdischen Verwandtschaft Erich Fromms aufgezeigt anhand von Dokumenten und Briefen auf dem Weg in die Vernichtung," Fromm-Forum 9 (2005): 35–79.

3. On the copy of Trude Brandt to Frau Bruchsal, January 29, 1941, in SBP, someone, presumably a Bund member after the war, has corrected "Bruchsal" to "Jordan." Hanna was the twenty-year-old daughter of a left-wing Wuppertal couple, a "mixed-race" Jew who would become a celebrated stage designer after the war.

4. SBP, Trude Brandt to "Frau Mitzi," July 13, 1941; Trude Brandt to "Frau Bruchsal," January 29, 1941; and Trude Brandt to "Frau Mitzi," September 17, 1941. In a small publication of letters from Trude Brandt, the author Rainer Funk has simply assumed that "Mitzi" was Lisa Jacob and, using this guesswork, has altered the name of the recipient accordingly; see Funk, "Erleben von Ohnmacht im Dritten Reich."

5. Andresen, Widerspruch als Lebensprinzip: Der undogmatische Sozialist Heinz Brandt (1909–1986), Reihe Politik und Gesellschaftsgeschichte (Bonn: Dietz, 2007), 107.

6. Figures are from a 1983 German radio program celebrating the Bund's wartime achievements and, in particular, the Lisa Jacob–Trude Brandt connection. See "Sie wussten was sie tun: Von Menschen die der nazistischen Unmenschlichkeit widerstanden," a program written by Ruth Kotik and produced by Carola Stern, broadcast Friday, July 1, 1983, on WDR/NDR 1. Transcript and tapes in BAE. At the time, Lisa must have been in possession of copies of Brandt's letters, extracts of which were read aloud in the broadcast itself. They were followed on the broadcast by the reaction of Trude Brandt's clearly moved son, Heinz Brandt. Brandt himself was a well-known political voice in the Federal Republic of Germany. Lisa's letters to Trude are not preserved. On Heinz Brandt, see Knud Andresen, *Widerspruch als Lebensprinzip*, and Heinz Brandt, *Ein Traum, der nicht entführbar ist: Mein Weg zwischen Ost und West* (Munich: List, 1967). I am grateful to Larry Friedman for the information about Fromm's role and for alerting me to Andresen's biography, and to Stefan Brandt for permission to see the copies of the letters in his possession.

7. SBP, Trude Brandt to "Frau Mitzi," September 17, 1941.

8. Trude is quoting the well-known folk song "Wenn ich ein Vöglein wär"— "If I Were a Little Bird."

9. SBP, Trude Brandt to "Frau Mitzi," September 17, 1941.

10. SBP, Trude Brandt to "Frau Bruchsal," January 29, 1941. In reproducing the letter in his article, Rainer Funk has changed the text so that the letter is addressed to "Meine Liebe und sehr werte Frau Jacob," but the letter is actually addressed to "Meine Liebe und sehr werte Frau Bruchsal," which, as indicated above, seems to have been code for Hanna Jordan. Funk, "Erleben von Ohnmacht im Dritten Reich."

11. Reproduced in Jacobs, Bramesfeld et al., *Gelebte Utopie*, 124. Rainer Funk dates the same letter to February 1943. I did not have the original to ascertain who was correct. See Funk, "Erleben von Ohnmacht im Dritten Reich," 46–7.

12. Andresen, *Widerspruch als Lebensprinzip*, 38, 41–42, 51.

13. SBP, Trude Brandt to "Frau Bruchsal," January 29, 1941. See also ibid., 68.

14. SBP, Trude Brandt to "Frau Bruchsal," January 29, 1941.

15. BAE, undated, unsigned note in Lisa Jacob's handwriting, beginning "Trude Brandt war einer der ersten." The note wrongly places Trude among deportees from Stettin in 1941.

16. I was lucky to stumble across the copy of Trude's letter, which was a copy of the one sent to "Frau Bruchsal" on January 29, 1941. It was only briefly on the Internet on a blog post of de Beaulieu's son and biographer, François de Beaulieu, accessed September 30, 2011. The son speculates that the letter was returned to his father by colleagues after the war. See François

de Beaulieu, *Mon père, Hitler et moi* (Rennes: Ouest-France, 2008). It might be that this letter is what is mistakenly referred to in legal materials connected to de Beaulieu's case as "letters from Theresienstadt." The legal reference to Theresienstadt can be found in an official letter from Oberstaatsanwalt Bremen, September 24, 1996, reference AR 69/96-'V, affirming that the conviction of de Beaulieu had been overturned. I assume that the reference to Theresienstadt is drawn from the original accusations. The letter was kindly made available by Johannes Tuchel, director of the Gedenkstätte Deutscher Widerstand, Berlin.

17. For example, one anonymized copy can be found among the Morgenstern papers in BMP.

18. Interview with Hanna Jordan, July 29, 1997. On Quaker circles, see François de Beaulieu, *Mein Vater, Hitler und ich* (Bremen: Donat Verlag, 2013), 92–93. E-mail from de Beaulieu to the author, August 21, 2011.

19. BAE, *Chronik*, January 1953, no author, "Ein Brief über die Bundestagung vom Jan 25 1953," Essen Stadtwald, January 26, 1953. On the Luckner circle, see Borgstedt, "'Bruderring' und 'Lucknerkreis': Rettung im deutschen Sudwesten," and Hans-Josef Wollasch, *Gertrud Luckner: "Botschafterin der Menschlichkeit"* (Freiburg im Breisgau: Herder, 2005). Luckner, though Quaker, was employed as a welfare officer in the Freiburg office of the Catholic Caritas.

20. BAE, undated, unsigned typewritten letter. The extant page begins "Ich schrieb Ihnen."

21. The consensus among German Jews was that the deportations would be survivable for the tough and healthy. Croes and Kosmala, "Facing Deportation in Germany and the Netherlands," 107.

22. LAN, RW58 71703, AStE to StapoD (Ratingen), September 13, 1944. This is pursued in more detail in the section "Calculated Risks" in chapter 8.

23. SLC, MC447 Box 2, Folder 35, Oklahoma, clips used in Tove Gerson's speeches, 1942–43.

24. SLC, MC447 Box 1, Folder 11, Tove Gerson to "Eugen," July 2, 1988. The reference is to Walter Laqueur, *The Terrible Secret: Suppression of the Truth About Hitler's "Final Solution"* (Boston: Little, Brown, 1980).

25. "Lebenslauf," in BAE, folder "Nachrufe," untitled memorial for Wasja Enoch, 5.

26. Archiv des Institut für Zeitgeschichte, Munich, ED 106/97, "Bericht über das Judenhilfswerk des 'Bundes' Gemeinschaft für sozialistisches Leben," no date, 7.

27. AJD, November 10, 1941. Other helpers in Germany similarly seem to have tried to offer deportees advice. Wollasch, *Gertrud Luckner*, 27.

28. Walk, *Das Sonderrecht für die Juden im NS-Staat*, 353.

29. Longerich, *"Davon haben wir nichts gewusst!,"* 160.

30. Beate Kosmala, "Mißglückte Hilfe und ihre Folgen: Die Ahndung der "Judenbegünstigung" durch NS-Verfolgungsbehörden," in Kosmala and Schoppmann, *Solidarität und Hilfe für Juden während der NS-Zeit*, vol. 5, 205–21.

31. Anne Linsel, *Weltentwürfe: Die Bühnenbildnerin Hanna Jordan* (Essen: Klartext, 2006), 23.

32. Archiv des Institut für Zeitgeschichte, Munich, ED 106/97, "Bericht über das Judenhilfswerk des 'Bundes' Gemeinschaft für sozialistisches Leben," no date, 4.

33. AJD, November 8, 1941.

34. Archiv des Institut für Zeitgeschichte, Munich, ED 106/97, "Bericht über das Judenhilfswerk des 'Bundes' Gemeinschaft für sozialistisches Leben," no date, 5.

35. BAE, Kotik, "Sie wussten was sie tun," 4.

36. "Brief in der Nazizeit (1942)," in DJGU, 146.

37. AJD, May 5, 1942.

38. BAE, Else Bramesfeld, handwritten and typewritten "Lebensbericht," January 1986.

39. Grüter, "Der 'Bund für ein sozialistisches Leben,'" 55.

40. AJD, March 27, 1942, and April 7, 1942.

41. AJD, June 13, 2011.

42. See the page "Dore schreibt" included in the extracts from Artur's June 1942 diary contained in BAE.

43. AJD, June 14, 1942.

44. NGJ, DJ to GJ, November 12, 1941.

45. Jacob, "'Der Bund': Gemeinschaft für sozialistisches Leben und meine Rettung vor der Deportation," 107.

46. Ibid.; the chapter "Love Letters in the Holocaust" in Roseman, *Past in Hiding*; Grüter, "Der 'Bund für ein sozialistisches Leben,'" 54; and EP, Ernst Krombach to Marianne Strauss, May 31, 1942.

47. AJD, entry headed "Im Juli," following July 9, 1942.

48. For the Krombachs' letters, knowledge, and fate, see Roseman, *Past in Hiding*, 182–218.

49. AJD, July 24 and 25, 1942; NGJ, GJ to AJ and DJ, July 17, 1942, and October 1, 1942.

50. NGJ, GJ to AJ and DJ, September 30, 1942.

51. NGJ, GJ to AJ and DJ, September 30, 1942, and October 1, 1942. Friedl himself writes in a kind of code, but the meaning emerges from his parents' response. It seems that Regina was indeed murdered in September 1942.

Her mother, however, survived, and immigrated to the US in 1951. See entry "Regina Gaenzel," in the Dutch registry Joods Monument, https://www.joodsmonument.nl/en/page/40971/regina-gaenzel, accessed January 20, 2019.

52. NGJ, DJ to Otto, May 16, 1942; AJ to GJ, August 9, 1942; BAE, AJD, December 14, 1942; NGJ, AJ to GJ, January 1, 1943, and December 23, 1943; and GJ to AJ, July 17, September 30, and October 1, 1942.

53. NGJ, EJ to AJ, October 8, 1942.

54. NGJ, DJ to GJ, October 12, 1942, and AJ to GJ, February 8, 1943; and information about Regina Gaenzel from note 51 above.

55. Jacob, "Der Bund"; Archiv des Institut für Zeitgeschichte, Munich, ED 106/97, "Bericht über das Judenhilfswerk des 'Bundes' Gemeinschaft für sozialistisches Leben," no date, 8.

56. NGJ, AJ to FJ, August 25, 1942.

57. AJD, February 19, 1944.

58. Appendix to StAE, Wiedergutmachung Bestand 158, J103 Artur Jacobs, AJ to Militärregierung Fürsorgeamt für politische Opfer, July 22, 1946.

59. Meta Kamp, *Auf der anderen Seite stehen*, 41.

60. Interview with Ernst Steinmann, May 2006.

61. BAE, *Chronik*, October 1954, "Kleine Mitteilungen."

62. Interview, Wolfgang Briel, Barsinghausen, June 1999.

63. Transcript of an interview with Doris Braune by Heidi Behrens-Cobet, October 24, 1991.

64. The letter is reproduced as an appendix to Jacob, "'Der Bund': Gemeinschaft für sozialistisches Leben und meine Rettung vor der Deportation," 131–34. A copy of the letter can be found in the BAE.

65. Information about Isa Herrmanns is from Angela Genger, Düsseldorf, and Frau Gabriele Werde, Stolperstein Bonn.

6. In Plain Sight

1. NGJ, DJ to GJ, November 12, 1941.

2. Jacob, "'Der Bund.'"

3. Ellen Jungbluth, "Leben und Lernen mit Lisa Jacob," in BAE, unpublished photocopied booklet produced by the Bund on the occasion of Lisa's death, "Für Lisa Jacob," no date [1989].

4. Jacob, "'Der Bund.'"

5. Ibid.

6. Reproduced in Grüter, "Der 'Bund für ein sozialistisches Leben,'" 82. Grüter assumes that the letter expresses Lisa's genuine emotion at the time.

7. Though reproduced in Grüter, it was no longer among the materials I found in the BAE.

8. Jacob, "'Der Bund.'"

9. SLC MC447 Box 2, Folder 48, Erna Michels to Tove Gerson, August 1, 1945.

10. NGJ, GJ to AJ, April 27, 1942.

11. Grüter, "Der 'Bund für ein sozialistisches Leben,'" 57, citing typed booklet produced on the death of AJ, "Zum Gedenken an Artur Jacobs," Essen, no date [March 1968], in BAE.

12. Conversation with Huberte Arnsmann, Essen, October 2015.

13. StAE, Wiedergutmachung Lisa Jacob, Antrag auf WG, July 18, 1945.

14. BMP, unsigned typed letter (clearly written by Lisa Jacob) to the commandant of the POW Camp Greeley, December 23, 1945.

15. Cited in Grüter, "Der 'Bund für ein sozialistisches Leben,'" 56.

16. Jacob,"' Der Bund,'" 112.

17. Interview with Ellen Jungbluth, Wuppertal, July 1997.

18. Interview with Friedl Speer, Wuppertal, April 2000.

19. According to Grüter, "Der 'Bund für ein sozialistisches Leben,'" 57.

20. See chapter 8.

21. Jacob,"' Der Bund,'" 113.

22. The importance of such emotional and symbolic support is affirmed by a recent analysis of testimonies of Berlin Jews who survived underground. Richard Lutjens, "Vom Untertauchen: 'U-Boote' und der Berliner Alltag, 1941–1945," in Alltag im Holocaust: Jüdisches Leben im Grossdeutschen Reich, 1941–1945, ed. Andrea Löw, Doris L. Bergen, and Anna Hájková (München: Oldenbourg, 2013), 49–63, specifically 62–63.

23. ASP, anonymous notebook.

24. Ibid., 12.

25. Ibid., 1.

26. NGJ, AJ to GJ, May 16, 1942.

27. BMP, EB to LJ, June 8, 1942.

28. ASP, anonymous notebook, 3.

29. Ibid., 10.

30. Jacob, "'Der Bund,'" 114.

31. Ellen Jungbluth, "Leben und Lernen mit Lisa Jacob," in BAE, unpublished photocopied booklet produced by the Bund on the occasion of Lisa's death, "Für Lisa Jacob," no date [1989].

32. Rainer Funk, "Erleben von Ohnmacht im Dritten Reich," 35–80, specifically 46–47.

33. Ellen Jungbluth, "Leben und Lernen."

34. On the Strauss family and the Abwehr, see Roseman, *Past in Hiding*, 118–45.
35. Interview with ME, September 10, 1996.
36. Above this phrase in Arthur's diary, someone has inserted in pencil "for deported Jews."
37. AJD, August 10, 1942.
38. On the role of Christian Arras in making a connection to Izbica, see Roseman, *Past in Hiding*, 182–210.
39. AJD, September 22, 1942.
40. AJD, November 20; EP, Marianne Strauss private diary entries, November 17 and November 23, 1942.
41. AJD, December 31, 1942.
42. Interview with ME, September 10, 1996.
43. The nurse, Sister Tamara (herself not Jewish and thus not threatened with deportation), with whom Marianne was in correspondence, expressed her pleasure in the spring of 1943 at learning that Marianne had found a regular sanctuary at the Blockhaus in Essen. EP, Schwester Tamara to Marianne Strauss, June 23, 1943.
44. Interview with Tove Gerson, Essen, January 1997.
45. All of this is documented in Roseman, *Past in Hiding*, 248–63.
46. Ibid., 260ff.
47. Ibid., 264.
48. EP, extract reproduced in a letter from Dore Jacobs to ME, September 24, 1973. The diary entries for September 1943 are missing in NJ. In the BAE, September is present but it contains most but not all of this quotation.
49. Else R. Behrend-Rosenfeld, Erich Kasberger, and Marita Krauss, *Leben in zwei Welten: Tagebücher eines jüdischen Paares in Deutschland und im Exil* (München: Volk Verlag München, 2011), 226–27; Jane Caplan, "'Ausweis Bitte!' Identity and Identification in Nazi Germany," in *Identification and Registration Practices in Transnational Perspective: People, Papers and Practices*, ed. Ilsen About, James Brown, and Gayle Lonergan (New York: Palgrave Macmillan, 2013), 224–42. I am grateful to Susanna Schraftetter for alerting me to Behrend-Rosenfeld's experience.
50. EP, ME, "Eidesstattliche Erklärung," May 22, 1957; copy Carl Hermann to Oberstadtdirektor, Essen, June 4, 1957.
51. Interview with ME, July 1996.
52. Interview, Lew and Trudy Schloß (née Ullmann), Teaneck, N.J., August 11, 1998.
53. Kamp, *Auf der anderen Seite stehen*; telephone conversation with Meta Kamp, January 24, 1997; and telephone conversation with Ernst Steinmann, Achim, January 24, 1997.

54. Telephone conversation with Meta Kamp, January 1997.
55. Maria Briel, Remscheid, November 1990 (video interview conducted by Jochen Bilstein).
56. Linsel, *Weltentwürfe*, 26.
57. Maria Briel, Remscheid, November 1990 (video interview conducted by Jochen Bilstein).
58. EP, copy, ME to Carl Hermann, February 3, 1958, annex: Declaration under oath.
59. EP, diary, June 2, 1944, "at the levee."
60. EP, diary, July 13, 1944.
61. Letter from Hermann Schmalstieg to the author, April 2, 1998.
62. EP, letter folded into diary, dated September 23, 1944.
63. The following information derives from a telephone conversation with Hermann Schmalstieg, January 24, 1997; subsequent letters from Schmalstieg to the author on May 4, 1997, April 2, 1998, and October 10, 1998; and an interview on August 25, 1999.
64. Letter from Hermann Schmalstieg to the author, May 4, 1997.
65. Telephone conversation with Hermann Schmalstieg, January 24, 1997.

7. The Test of Total War

1. AJD, November 18, 1941.
2. For example, NGJ, DJ to GJ, January 12, 1942.
3. AJD, December 2, 1941.
4. AJD, February 15, 1942; "Advice for unsettled nights," after entry for September 7, 1942.
5. AJD, June 4, 1943.
6. AJD, June 27, 1943.
7. Norbert Krüger, "Die Zerstörung Wuppertals: Ein Überblick über die Luftangriffe im Sommer 1943," in *Wuppertal in der Zeit des Nationalsozialismus*, ed. Klaus Goebel (Wuppertal: P. Hammer, 1984), 163–78, and Stargardt, *German War*.
8. NJ, Box 6, "Gedenkstunden an August Schwab 1960."
9. ASP, typed copy of a letter, handwritten note "from Friedel Kette to her sister in Vienna" [March 1943].
10. AJD, July 13, 1943.
11. Krüger, "Die Zerstörung Wuppertals," 164, and Martin Kitchen, *Nazi Germany at War* (New York: Longman, 1995), 90.
12. ASP, typed, undated, unsigned report "Ihr Lieben," handwritten note "Von Artur."
13. ASP, typed report, "Zwei Tage nach der Katastrophe," June 2, 1943.

14. Stargardt, *German War*, 347, and Lisa de Boor, *Tagebuchblätter aus den Jahren 1938–1945* (München: Biederstein Verlag, 1963), 144.
15. ASP, typed report, "Zwei Tage nach der Katastrophe," June 2, 1943.
16. Ibid.
17. ASP, typed, undated, unsigned report "Ihr Lieben," handwritten note "Von Artur."
18. NGJ, AJ to GJ, October 25, 1943.
19. Lisa Jacob's remarks in the typed booklet the Bund put together following the death of AJ, BAE, "Zum Gedenken an Artur Jacobs," Essen, no date [March 1968], 14.
20. Ibid.
21. AJD, August 25, 1943.
22. AJD, August 29, 1943.
23. AJD, September 7, 1943. Though as would later emerge, Friedl suffered psychologically from being incarcerated with two murderers, a situation that improved a little after he was transferred to solitary confinement. StAE, Widergutmachung J116a, Gottfried Jacobs, copy. Society of Friends, July 3, 1945, signed M. J. van Edingen; filled-out form "Der Landrat. Amt für Wiedergutmachung und Betreuung der Opfer des Faschismus. Stadt und Landkreis Neustadt an der Haardt," January 7, 1948; Karien Anstadt, telephone interview, March 2011.
24. AJD, September 5, 1943; see also chapter 6.
25. AJD, August 29, 1943.
26. NGJ, AJ to GJ, October 25, 1943.
27. ASP, typed, undated, unsigned report "Ihr Lieben," handwritten note "Von Artur."
28. ASP, typed report "Zwei Tage nach der Katastrophe," June 2, 1943.
29. NGJ, AJ to GJ, October 25, 1943.
30. ASP, copy, letter "Ihr Lieben! (von Artur)"; NGJ, AJ letters to GJ, January 21, February 3, and November 15, 1939; April 16, 1940; and September 6, 1938; LAN, RW58 19223, Vermerk, Essen, October 22, 1937; RW 58 58105, memorandum, February 27, 1940.
31. BAE, Lisa Jacob, "'Der Bund.'"
32. Interview with Ellen Jungbluth, Wuppertal, July 1997; DJGU; 133; and BAE, AJD, December 10, 1942.
33. BAE, AJD, December 26, 1942, and "Antwort an den Freund," attached to the entry. The Tolstoy story, "Two Old Men," was published in 1885; it can be read at https://lifeworkleadershipjax.org/wp-content/uploads/Two-Old-Men.pdf; DJGU, 155ff., Artur Jacobs, "Unser Verpflichtungstag," Meersburg, 1944.

34. DJGU, p. 138, "Selbst die Natur scheint nicht zufrieden mit der Welt." On fog as a metaphor, see Lisa Jacob, reprinted in DJGU, 142; AJD, entries June 1943 and July 18, 1943; PAS, MS 324, ME diary, Whitsun [May 28–29] 1944 and June 2, 1944.
35. ASP, copy, letter "Ihr Lieben! (von Artur)."
36. ASP, typed report "Zwei Tage nach der Katastrophe," June 2, 1943.
37. AJD, August 5, 1943.
38. AJD, August 12, 1943.
39. BMP, copy, Karlos Morgenstern to Karin Morgenstern, October 11, 1943.
40. Stargardt, *German War*, 381, and AJD, August 12, 1943.
41. BMP, handwritten extract, Karlos to Karin, Toulouse, January 25, 1944.
42. BMP, handwritten extract, Karlos to Karin, Toulouse, March 15, 1944.
43. Cited in AJD, March 6, 1944, "aus einem Krankenhaus."
44. AJD, April 26, 1944.
45. Stargardt, *German War*, 416ff.; Stefan-Ludwig Hoffmann, "Besiegte, Besatzer, Beobachter: Das Kriegsende im Tagebuch," in *Demokratie im Schatten der Gewalt: Geschichten des Privaten im deutschen Nachkrieg*, ed. Daniel Fulda et al. (Göttingen: Wallstein, 2010), 25–55. See also "The Chance of Renewal" in chapter 9.
46. NGJ, GJ to AJ, May 9, 1944.
47. NGJ, DJ to Erna Michels, April 6, 1943.
48. ASP, typewritten copy, letter "Lieber Alfred," June 14, 1943, and handwritten note, "von Maria."
49. ASP, typewritten copy of letter with handwritten heading "Essen Sonja, März 43 1.Angriff auf E."
50. AJD, June 7, 1943.
51. BAE, typed manuscript "Verpflichtungstag 1944. Ansprache von Else," and AJD, entries for March 1944.
52. AJD, after July 6, 1943.
53. Ibid.
54. BAE, typed manuscript "Verpflichtungstag 1944. Ansprache von Else." See also NJ, AJD, section headed "Blutopfer der Soldaten," one of several thought pieces following an entry for August 15, 1943. BMP, undated letter from Karlos Morgenstern; letter from Karlos to Karin, Hildesheim, January 1943.
55. AJD, December 4, 1943, August 8, 1943, and following "Aufriss zu einer neuen Schrift: Objektive Mächte als Helfer zum wahren Leben."
56. AJD, February 10, 1944.
57. Cited in AJD, March 1, 1942.
58. BMP, handwritten extract from Karlos to Karin, Toulouse, January 27, 1944.

59. BMP, handwritten extract from Karlos to Karin, September 19, 1944.
60. Nicholas Stargardt, "The Troubled Patriot: German Innerlichkeit in World War 2," *German History* 28, no. 3 (2010): 326–42, and Willy Peter Reese and Stefan Schmitz, *A Stranger to Myself: The Inhumanity of War: Russia, 1941–1944* (New York: Farrar, Straus and Giroux, 2005).
61. Cited in NJ, Box 6, "Gedenkstunde an August Schwab 1960."
62. BMP extracts from Karlos Morgenstern letters, January 25, 1944, March 15, 1944, September 21, 1944.
63. Interview with Gustav Zenker, Mülheim, February 1988 (with Monika Grüter).
64. Cited in AJD, October 19, 1944.
65. See excerpts from August's letters, NJ, Box 6, "Gedenkstunden an August Schwab 1960."
66. AJD, February 25, 1942.
67. AJD, February 17, 1942, "Aus einem Ausbildungslager."
68. AJD, entries, February 1942 and September 1942. Gustav's tears on February 21, and the evening with Marianne, September 22, 1942.
69. BMP, typewritten copy "Aus einem Brief von Karlos," September 28, 1944, "Letzter Brief."
70. BMP, folder "Aus Soldatenbriefen."
71. The copyist misread Karlos's handwriting and wrote "Konziègne."
72. There were several such books; one of the best known is Otto Viktor Karl Liman von Sanders, *Fünf Jahre Türkei* (Berlin: A. Scherl, 1920). With thanks to Donald Bloxham.
73. In the notorious Brehmer action in April, the army murdered Jewish men on the spot, and only their family members were sent to Drancy and then on to Auschwitz.
74. David Cesarani, *Final Solution: The Fate of the Jews, 1933–1949* (New York: St. Martin's Press, 2016), 724–27; and Ahlrich Meyer, *Die deutsche Besatzung in Frankreich, 1940–1944: Widerstandsbekämpfung und Judenverfolgung* (Darmstadt: Wissenschaftliche Buchgesellschaft, 2000), 134–41.
75. The executioner Johann Reichhart gave persistent help to a Jewish friend of the family, for example. See Schrafstetter, *Flucht und Versteck*, 243. Michael Degen wrote of the "crazy SS man" who helped his family: Michael Degen, *Nicht alle waren Mörder: Eine Kindheit in Berlin* (München: Econ, 1999). On anti-Semites as rescuers, see Tec, *When Light Pierced the Darkness*, 99–112.
76. See chapter 8 and Linsel, *Weltentwürfe*, 26.
77. See the section "Nazis as Rescuers" in Moore, *Survivors: Jewish Self-Help and Rescue in Nazi-Occupied Western Europe*, 330ff. On rescue for sex, see, for an example, Moore, "The Rescue of Jews in Nazi-Occupied Belgium, France and the Netherlands," 394.

78. This is obviously implicit in accounts of Wehrmacht soldiers and policemen who made a point of assisting Jews, since it is inevitable that, despite
their courage and good intentions, on other occasions they were enlisted
in persecutory measures. Wolfram Wette, ed., *Zivil courage: Empörte, Helfer
und Retter aus Wehrmacht, Polizei und SS*, Die Zeit des Nationalsozialismus
(Frankfurt: Fischer Taschenbuch Verlag, 2003); Norbert Haase and Wolfram Wette, *Retter in Uniform: Handlungsspielräume im Vernichtungskrieg der Wehrmacht*, Zeit des Nationalsozialismus (Frankfurt am Main: Fischer
Taschenbuch Verlag, 2002); and Wolfram Wette, *Feldwebel Anton Schmid:
Ein Held der Humanität*, Die Zeit des Nationalsozialismus (Frankfurt am
Main: S. Fischer, 2013).

79. Herbert Jäger, *Verbrechen unter totalitärer Herrschaft: Studien zur nationalsozialistischen Gewaltkriminalität*, Texte und Dokumente zur Zeitgeschichte (Frankfurt am Main: Suhrkamp, 1982), 156.

80. BMP, handwritten, undated extract "Aus einem Brief von Eberhard."

81. See, for example, Wette, *Feldwebel Anton Schmid*. In August 1942, Artur
recorded the fate of the husband of a close political colleague from Essen
who had told the army that religious convictions (he probably meant
political ones) prevented him from shooting other human beings. The
outcome had been detention, trial, and then being sent to the front, where
he died. AJD, August 23, 1942.

82. I am grateful to Jürgen Matthäus for this information.

83. BMP, typewritten extract dated August 1, 1944.

84. Interview with Barbara Martin, Lüdinghausen, June 2004 (conducted by
Norbert Reichling).

85. It also leaves us in the uncomfortable position of wondering whether we
should extend the same dispensation to the rest of the Wehrmacht's conscripts. This is not the first time the contemporary experience of the Bund
members, as credible and creditable Germans, has unsettled our moral
narrative about the German experience at war.

8. The Endgame

1. AJD, February 21, 1944.

2. See, e.g., StAE, Wiedergutmachung (WG), Artur Jacobs folder, AJ to
Wiedergutmachungsamt (WGA) January 1950.

3. Beate Meyer, *"Jüdische Mischlinge": Rassenpolitik und Verfolgungserfahrung
1933–1945*, Studien zur jüdischen Geschichte (Hamburg: Dölling und
Galitz, 1999), 11–12, 51; Monica Kingreen, "Die Aktion zur kalten Erledigung der Mischehen: Die reichsweit singuläre systematische Verschleppung und Ermordung jüdischer Mischehepartner im NSDAP-Gau

Hessen-Nassau 1942–1943," in *NS-Gewaltherrschaft Beiträge zur historischen Forschung und juristischen Aufarbeitung*, ed. Alfred Gottwaldt, Norbert Kampe, and Peter Klein (Berlin: Edition Hentrich, 2005), 187–201; Petra Bonavita, *Mit falschem Pass und Zyankali: Retter und Gerettete aus Frankfurt am Main in der NS-Zeit* (Stuttgart: Schmetterling Verlag, 2009), 9; Nathan Stoltzfus, *Resistance of the Heart: Intermarriage and the Rosenstrasse Protest in Nazi Germany* (New York: W. W. Norton, 1996); Wolf Gruner, *Widerstand in der Rosenstrasse: Die Fabrik-Aktion und die Verfolgung der "Mischehen" 1943*, Die Zeit des Nationalsozialismus (Frankfurt am Main: Fischer Taschenbuch Verlag, 2005); and Maximilian Strnad, "The Fortune of Survival: Intermarried German Jews in the Dying Breath of the 'Thousand-Year Reich,'" *Dapim: Studies on the Holocaust* 29, no. 3 (2015): 173–96.

4. AJD, February 13, 1944.

5. NGJ, AJ to GJ, March 4, 1944. Here he wrongly writes "January," but the diary makes clear it was February.

6. StAE, J153 WG, Dore Jacobs, "Begründung meines Antrags," received December 20, 1949. Unsigned affidavit from Dore; StAE, WG, Artur Jacobs, AJ to WGA, September 25, 1949; AB3, 5; SLC, MC 447, Dore to Tove Gerson, Meersburg, August 28, 1945.

7. StAE, WG file Artur Jacobs, AJ to WGA, August 18, 1949; StAE, J153 WG file Dore Jacobs, DJ, "Begründung meines Antrags," received December 20, 1949. Unsigned affidavit from DJ.

8. LAN, RW58 71703, Declaration Hilde Hesse nee Rode, Essen, Wittekindstrasse 21, and Gisela Lönne, Press and Propaganda Leader of the Hitler Youth, born September 3, 1921, Goethestrasse 54, August 6, 1944.

9. LAN, RW58 71703, AStE to StapoD (Ratingen), September 13, 1944.

10. Holger Berschel, *Bürokratie und Terror: Das Judenreferat der Gestapo Düsseldorf 1935–1945*, Düsseldorfer Schriften zur neueren Landesgeschichte und zur Geschichte Nordrhein-Westfalens (Essen: Klartext, 2001), 364; and Homberg, "Retterwiderstand in Wuppertal während des Nationalsozialismus," 155.

11. BAE, copy, DJ to WE, Meersburg, May 8, 1945; StAE, WG File Artur Jacobs, AJ to WGA, January 1950, received February 9, 1950, "Bestätigung unserer Anerkennung als politisch Geschädigte"; NGJ, AJ to GJ, April 29, 1944, and AJ to GJ, September 12, 1944.

12. Beate Meyer, *A Fatal Balancing Act: The Dilemma of the Reich Association of Jews in Germany, 1939–1945* (New York: Berghahn Books, 2013), 346; NGJ, AJ to GJ, May 31, 1944; StAE, WG file Gottfried Jacobs, Eidesst. Versicherung, signed S. M. Anstatt and M. Grünberg, Kaufmann, August 15, 1949; see

AJ to GJ, June 28, July 30, and August 25, 1944, and DJ to GJ, June 29, 1944.

13. NGJ, AJ to GJ, August 28, 1944.

14. Though there are plenty of examples in 1944 of brutal treatment of the "Aryan" spouse where the Jewish partner had gone into hiding: rations were withdrawn, physical violence was used, and threats of transfer to a concentration camp were issued, and sometimes even carried out. Berschel, *Bürokratie und Terror*, 383.

15. The suggestion that the Bund helped came from Hanna Jordan in an interview; see also Linsel, *Weltentwürfe*, 23. Homberg, "Retterwiderstand in Wuppertal während des Nationalsozialismus," 95–100; Yad Vashem Righteous Among the Nations online database, http://db.yadvashem.org/righteous/righteousName.html?language=en&itemId=5776697, consulted June 18, 2014.

16. Born Margarete Ransenberg, September 27, 1881; Schröter, *Geschichte und Schicksal*, 686.

17. Ellenbogen, "Flucht und illegales Leben," 139; and EP, diary, Mülheim, September 31, 1944, letter to Meta folded into diary.

18. Homberg, "Retterwiderstand in Wuppertal während des Nationalsozialismus," 130.

19. Günther van Norden, Review of *Die Dorper Kirche: Ein Symbol des bergischen Protestantismus im Aufbruch*. Herausgegeben v. Förderkreis "Initiative Rettung Dorper Kirche," in *Monatshefte für Evangelische Kirchengeschichte des Rheinlandes*, vol. 57 (2008): 307–9, especially 309. Michael Brocke and Nathana Hüttenmeister, *Der jüdische Friedhof in Solingen: Eine Dokumentation in Wort und Bild* (Solingen: Stadtarchiv, 1996), 17. LAN, NW 1005 G33 1048 Emmi Schreiber, 57 (2008). StAE, Bestand 141 Personalakten, 2326: Emmi Sonja Schreiber, Lebenslauf, October 10, 1953.

20. It carries the heading of "Anfang Oktober" and is entered before Artur's entry for October 1.

21. AJD, "Anfang Oktober"; LAN, NW1022 J 24280 Jungbluth, Lebenslauf, February 4, 1946; StAW, WG, Jungbluth Ernst 115, 24, affidavit, Marianne Strauss, Düsseldorf, August 24, 1945. This suggests that eight people were hidden by the group. The same figure was offered years after the war by Lisa Jacob in an interview and in the Bund's publication *Gelebte Utopie*. However, the way they arrived at the figure makes no sense. For example, Lisa said that among that number were seven Jewish Bund members. See Grüter, "Der 'Bund für ein sozialistisches Leben,'" 53. Since we know when the Bund's Jewish members left, we can say that five of these "rescued" must have emigrated before the war—and thus were not "saved" by the group.

What seems to have happened is that Lisa and the other authors of *Gelebte Utopie*, all by then in their eighties, had retained the number in memory but no longer recalled how it was calculated. The reason for this will have been the Bund's own reticence in publicly naming others as its beneficiaries.

22. Interview with Ellen Jungbluth, Wuppertal, July 1997.
23. Shmuel Spector and Geoffrey Wigoder, "The Encyclopedia of Jewish Life Before and During the Holocaust," ed. Shmuel Spector and Geoffrey Wigoder (Jerusalem: Yad Vashem, 2001). On these last deportations, see Eva Noack-Mosse, *Journey into Darkness: Theresienstadt Diary, January–July 1945* (Madison: University of Wisconsin Press, 2018).
24. Bilstein and Backhaus, *Geschichte der Remscheider Juden*, 159.
25. AJD, May 1944.
26. NGJ, AJ to GJ June 6, 1944; SLC, MC 447, Dore Jacobs to Tove Gerson, Meersburg, August 28, 1945.
27. "But such pain, such sadness, is always present in a place at the bottom of one's heart. . . . It is as if in the midst of everything else a hidden force keeps calling his name to you. And each time the tone is different: sometimes anger and no! no!—sometimes quiet sadness and raw pain, sometimes horror at everything that was destroyed with this shot—sometimes happiness in feeling everything beautiful that was connected to this young life, and—and that is the best—in feeling the connection with 'what remains' from his life." Ernst cited in NGJ, AJ to GJ, August 25, 1944. BMP, Karlos to Karin, September 18, 1944; EP, diary, Braunschweig, August 29–30, 1944; AJD, October 5, 1944, and January 24, 1945.
28. Cited in AJD, October 19, 1944.
29. AJD, October 19, 1944.
30. BAE, letter attached to AJD, January 1945, full version in papers provided by Renate Rohleder.
31. On fates, see SLC, MC 447, Dore Jacobs to Tove Gerson, Meersburg, August 28, 1945.
32. Stargardt, *German War*, 469.
33. All these accounts are from AJD, October 5, 1944.
34. See Grete Ströter's epic description of what should have been a short journey from Meersburg to Stuttgart in AJD, October 31, 1944.
35. Cited in AJD, October 20, 1944.
36. JP, "Brief an Ernst, February 4, 1945."
37. AJD, January 20, 1945.
38. BAE, AJD, January 20, 1945.
39. BAE, AJD, January 3, 1945—this is from the full version provided by Renate Rohleder.
40. JP, "Brief an Ernst, February 4, 1945."

41. On Doris Braune, see the interview with Doris Braune on October 24, 1991, conducted by Heidi Behrens-Cobet; a copy of the transcript is in the, author's possession. On Sonja Schreiber, see StAE, Bestand 141 Personalakten, 2326: Emmi Sonja Schreiber, Lebenslauf, October 10, 1953; SLC, MC 47 Box 2-46, "Translated from German, from a letter from Mrs. Sonja Schreiber," January 12, 1946. On Guste Denks, see SLC, MC447 Box 2, Folder 46, DJ to Tove Gerson, August 28, 1945. For a reference to the chaotic evacuation conditions of the KLV camps in formerly German territories, see Gerhard Kock, *Der Führer sorgt für unsere Kinder—: Die Kinderlandverschickung im Zweiten Weltkrieg* (Paderborn: F. Schöningh, 1997), 233. Some children took years to make it back home. On Gertrud's sisters, see BAE, Gertrud Jacobs to Sonja Schreiber, December 11, 1945.

42. StAE, WG file Elisabeth Jacob, affidavit from Julia Schreiber, June 1949.

43. EP, Marianne Strauss diary, Braunschweig, August 29–30, 1944.

44. Marianne Strauss diary, October 15–16, 1944.

45. ME, "Flucht," 139.

46. Ibid., 141.

47. Information from Kamp, *Auf der anderen Seite stehen*, 46–50; interview with Ernst Steinmann, Achim, September 2006.

48. AJD, February 22, February 27, March 5, March 7, and March 9, 1944; BAE, AJD, May 1944; AJD, October 14, 1944, and November 24, 1944; JP, letter to Sonja, November 14, 1944; undated copy of memorandum "Wie kann man dem Kräfteverschleiss entgegenwirken," written by "Gert"; StAR, NW41-7, "In der Küche"; SLC, MC447 Box 2, Folder 46, DJ to Tove Gerson, August 28, 1945; BAE, copy, DJ to WE, Meersburg, May 8, 1945—second part of letter undated, probably August or September 1945; DJGU, 88–89.

49. AJD, February 22, 1944.

50. A 2011 conversation with Eberhard Stürmer, born in 1940, produced positive memories of Meersburg. Barbara Martin, born in the same year, when interviewed on June 14, 2004, by Norbert Reichling, who was there for only a few weeks, was more critical.

51. JP, letter to Sonja, November 14, 1944, and undated copy of memorandum "Wie kann man dem Kräfteverschleiss entgegenwirken," written by "Gert."

52. Ibid. and AJD, February 27 and October 28, 1944.

53. AJD, entries for March 7 and 9, 1944; JP, letter to Sonja, November 14, 1944; AJD, May 1944; WBP, "Aus einem Brief von Medi, Lichtfest 1944"; JP, undated copy of memorandum "Wie kann man dem Kräfteverschleiss entgegenwirken," written by "Gert," annex, copy of letter of November 7, 1944, to "meine liebe Julie."

54. BAE, copy, DJ to Wasja Enoch, Meersburg, May 8, 1945—second part of letter undated, probably August or September 1945; BAE, undated letter from EB to Grete Dreibholz (June 1, 1945, and following days).

55. StAE, Bestand 141 8688 Emmi Schreiber, Emmi Schreiber to Fräulein Fisher, Essen, July 22, 1944; Emmi (Sonya) says she is going on vacation to visit her sister in Meersburg Bodensee, Haus auf dem Fohrenberg. Signed with "Heil Hitler"; DJGU, 89.

56. Heinrich Frey and Museumsverein Meersburg, *Meersburg unterm Hakenkreuz 1933–1945* (Friedrichshafen: Robert Gessler; Meersburg: Museumsverein Meersburg, 2011).

57. EP, in diary, copy Marianne Strauss to Meta, Hedwig, Elli, and Hermann, May 30, 1945.

58. Peter Hüttenberger, *Düsseldorf: Geschichte von den Ursprüngen bis ins 20. Jahrhundert*, vol. 3, *Die Industrie-und Verwaltungsstadt (20. Jahrhundert)* (Düsseldorf: Schwann, 1989), 631, 648.

59. EP, in diary, copy Marianne Strauss to Meta, Hedwig, Elli, and Hermann, May 30, 1945.

60. BAE, pencil-written text, "Vom ichhaften u horchenden Willen," April 9, 1945.

61. Ibid.

62. BAE, entry in Dore's handwriting, April 29, 1945, "Tagebuch."

63. Frey and Museumsverein Meersburg, *Meersburg unterm Hakenkreuz, 1933–1945*.

9. Our Flock Has Grown Lonely

1. AJD, entry. Handwritten on it, "Anfang Mai 1945 Meersburg." All the postwar diary entries are copies and extracts from missing originals. In this entry, next to the initials "D" and "L," which Artur used—no doubt still being cautious when the regime had not yet fallen—for Dore and Lisa, someone has typed in here "Juden," making it clear that this extract was being retyped for posterity or for circulation.

2. BAE, copy, DJ to WE Meersburg, May 8, 1945, and telephone interview with Eberhard Stürmer, October 2011.

3. BAE, undated typed notes "Gespräch in der Meersburger Hausgemeinde." Someone has handwritten on it "1944/1945," but obviously it is from the early postwar period.

4. BAE, EB to Ellen, May 27, 1945; AJD, May 8, 1945; and Hoffmann, "Besiegte," 36, 38.

5. AJ, "Ansprache zur Maifaier 1945," reprinted in DJGU, 176.

6. Ibid.

7. Ibid.

8. Frey and Museumsverein Meersburg, *Meersburg unterm Hakenkreuz, 1933–1945,* 440.

9. StAR, Nachlass Gertrud Jacobs, N41, 3; AJD, "Mai 1945. II Teil."

10. BAE, EB to Ellen, May 26, 1945; EB to SSch, June 16, 1945; undated letter from EB to Grete Dreibholz [June 1, 1945, and the following days], here June 11; AJD, "Ende Mai 1945"; for Ernst's weight, see LAN, NW1022 J 24280 Jungbluth.

11. BAE, AJD, "Aus Artur Jacobs Tagebuch 1945" entry, which appears under one for Meersburg "den 4. Mai"; copy, DJ to WE, Meersburg, May 8, 1945—second part of letter undated, probably August/September 1945; EB to SSCH, June 16, 1945; EB to Ellen, May 26 1945; DJ to SSCH, July 23, 1945.

12. Sources here are BAE EB to SSCH, June 16, 1945; DJ to SSCH, July 23, 1945.

13. BAE, copy, DJ to WE, Meersburg, May 8, 1945—second part of letter undated, probably August or September 1945; typed sheet, "Aus einem Brief von Dore," no date.

14. Klaus-Dietmar Henke, *Die amerikanische Besetzung Deutschlands,* Quellen und Darstellungen zur Zeitgeschichte (München: R. Oldenbourg, 1995), 591, 650ff.; Hartmut Pietsch, "Militärregierung und kommunale Politik," in Jan-Pieter Barbian and Ludger Heid, eds., *Zwischen gestern und morgen: Kriegsende und Wiederaufbau im Ruhrgebiet* (Essen: Klartext, 1995), 44–73, specifically 48–51.

15. BAE, undated letter from EB to Grete Dreibholz [June 1, 1945, and the following days]; EB to SSch, June 16, 1945, continued on October 11, 1945.

16. Letter from Artur Jacobs, May 1945, reprinted in Jacobs, Bramesfeld, et al., *Gelebte Utopie,* 139.

17. BAE, EB to Ellen, May 27, 1945; StAR, Nachlass Gertrud Jacobs, N41, 3, AJD "April 1945."

18. SLC, MC 47, Box 2-46 "Translated from German, from a letter from Mrs. Sonja Schreiber," January 12, 1946.

19. BAE copy, DJ to WE, Meersburg, May 8, 1945. The phrase comes from text added in October, when the letter could finally be sent.

20. BAE, DJ to SSch, November 21, 1945; EB to Ellen, May 27, 1945; EB to SSCH, June 16, 1945; undated letter from EB to Grete Dreibholz [June 1, 1945, and the following days]; Gertrud Jacobs to SSch, December 11, 1945; SLC, MC 47, Box 2-46, translated extract of letter from "Meersburg," dated August 28, 1945.

21. BAE, DJ to SSCH, July 23, 1945.

22. SLC, MC 447, Box 2-46, translated excerpt from EB to Tove Gerson, October 11, 1945. (The actual distance from Meersburg to Düsseldorf is a little over 350 miles.)

23. BAE, Gertrud Jacobs to SSch, December 11, 1945.

24. "I could have cried," Gertud responded, "when I learned from Friedl's let-ter how you got home." Ibid.; StAE, Bestand 141 Personalakten, 2326: Emmi Sonja Schreiber, Lebenslauf, October 10, 1953.

25. Interview with Barbara Martin, June 14, 2004 (conducted by Norbert Reichling).

26. Cited in BAE, copy, DJ to WE, Meersburg, May 8, 1945—the second part of the letter is undated, probably August or September 1945; interview with Friedl Speer, Wuppertal, April 2000; SP, Gerda Simon-Hayek to Liesel Speer, May 1947; and BAE, *Mitteilungen*, July 1947.

27. See also the two versions of "Wer war Hitler" in the Bund's own papers, as well as a longer version still, "Hitler: Von der Geschichte gerichtet," in NJ, folder "Geschichte C."

28. BAE, folder "Lichtfeste,"copy of undated typewritten memorandum "Lichtfest 1945. (Ausgeführte Disposition.)"

29. See also NGJ, Dore Jacobs to Carl Cohen, August 5, 1946.

30. Hoffmann, "Besiegte"; Stefan-Ludwig Hoffmann, "Germans into Allies: Writing a Diary in 1945," in *Seeking Peace in the Wake of War: Europe, 1943–1947*, ed. Stefan-Ludwig Hoffmann et al. (Amsterdam: Amsterdam University Press, 2015), 63–90.

31. The nationalist camp, which had been the Bund's natural enemy in Wei-mar, had certainly lost legitimacy. In this early period, only the revival of conservative church circles was a persistent source of concern. BAE, AJD, September 28, 1945; EB to EJ, April 19, 1947; and Bund, *Mitteilungen*, I/48, 20–21.

32. Lisa Jacob, in "Sie wussten was sie tun: Von Menschen, die der nazis-tischen Unmenschlichkeit widerstanden" WDR, July 1, 1983.

33. Roseman, *Past in Hiding*, 339–67.

34. BAE, copy, DJ to WE, Meersburg, May 8, 1945.

35. BAE, EB to SSch, June 16, 1945, continuation October 11, 1945, and EJ to Spieher, November 4, 1945.

36. BAE, AJD, March 27, 1946.

37. Ibid.; NGJ, Dore Jacobs to Carl Cohen, August 5, 1946; "Neues Wirken," in DJGU, 170; BAE, "Der Bund: Veranstaltungen in der Zeit vom 1. Sep-tember bis Ende des Jahres 1946"; "Der Bund Gemeinschaft für sozialis-tisches Leben. Arbeitskalender Sommerhalbjahr 1947" and for 1948.

38. BAE, undated, unsigned typewritten document, from the paper clearly early postwar, "Unsere Arbeit in den politischen Parteien."

39. LAN, BR 3000, Nr 76, Tilde Stürmer to Regierungspresidenten, August 15, 1965, and testimony from Alfred Stürmer, Krefeld, May 20, 1969; BAE, Rundschreiben re 1947 event in Haltern.

40. SLC, MC447, Box 2, Folder 48, Erna Michels to Tove and Wasja, October 11, 1945; various letters in Folder 49; BAE, Rundschreiben September 5, 1947; BAE, EB postcard to DJ, September 25, 1946; LAN, BR 3000, 76, Tilde Ströter to Regierungspräsident, August 15, 1965; and BAE, folder Postwar, "Bericht ueber das Treffen der Freunde des Bundes," October 16, 1949.

41. Printed for and distributed by the Bund's in-house press, without being formally published. These included *The Idea of the Bund, Bund: Form and Goals, Cultural Organism and Political Combat League* (all three were reproduced in one large volume called *The Bund: Order for Socialist Politics and Life Reform*), *Man and Woman as Comrades in the Struggle*, and a series of other publications on gender-related themes. Copies in BAE and in possession of the author.

42. BAE, EB to SSch, Meersburg, June 16, 1945, added to October 1945 folder "Rundschreiben 1947–48," circular from Essen-Stadtwald, "an alle Gruppen," dated September 9, 1948.

43. AB1; AB2; AB3.

44. AB1, 18. The translated texts in Tove Gerson's possession also indicate the importance the Bund placed in getting the word out through her and Wasja.

45. On the function of the letters abroad in Germany, see BAE, EB to SSch, Meersburg, June 16, added to October 1945; folder "Rundschreiben 1947–48," circular from Essen-Stadtwald, "an alle Gruppen," dated September 9, 1948. Even in 1950, the Bund was still using its ability to influence international opinion as an argument for official support. LAN, NW 17, 172–3, "Bericht über die Pfingstfreizeit des Bundes vom 26 Mai bis 5 Juni 1950 in Oberhundem (Sauerland)," and "Der Bund: Gemeinschaft für sozialistisches Leben (Bericht über unsere internationale Arbeit)," (1950).

46. An English-language copy survives in SLC, MC 447, Box 2-46, Ernst Jungbluth to the military government, May 1945.

47. AB1, 17.

48. AB3, 14. The May speech from 1945 similarly referred to the war only to make the point that the Bund had had to welcome Germany's destruction.

49. Ibid.

50. On the ubiquity of narratives of victimization told in the 1940s and 1950s, see Robert G. Moeller, *War Stories: The Search for a Usable Past in the Federal Republic of Germany* (Berkeley: University of California Press, 2001).

51. Institut für Zeitgeschichte, Munich, ED 106/97, undated report, "Bericht über das Judenhilfswerk des 'Bundes' Gemeinschaft für sozialistisches Leben." The report refers to discussions in the holidays that led to its writing, which might mean it was written after the summer of 1946. It was certainly already available by the time Artur wrote to Kurt Desch in

May 1947. See AAK, Weisenborn 366a, Artur Jacobs to Kurt Desch, Zinnen Verlag, May 30, 1947.

52. Institut für Zeitgeschichte, Munich, ED 106/97, undated report, "Bericht über das Judenhilfswerk des 'Bundes' Gemeinschaft für sozialistisches Leben," 6.

53. It was not all hypocrisy; for a discussion of youth in postwar society see Benjamin Möckel, *Erfahrungsbruch und Generationsbehauptung: Die "Kriegsjugend-generation" in den beiden deutschen Nachkriegsgesellschaften*, Göttinger Studien zur Generationsforschung (Göttingen: Wallstein Verlag, 2014), 163–72.

54. BAE, "Aufruf an die Jugend nach dem Zusammenbruch des Nationalsozi-alismus. Aus Artur Jacobs Nachlass" (typed manuscript, no date), 1, 3. Henceforth referred to as "Aufruf an die Jugend." The title of the manu-script suggests that it comes from Artur. But Ernst's letter to Dore in *Mit-teilungen*, June 1947, 17, "Deine Jugendschrift" makes clear it is Dore's, as does another version of the manuscript in the BAE, titled "An die Jugend."

55. BAE, "Aufruf an die Jugend," 4.

56. LAN, NW 17, 172–3, "Bericht über die Pfingstfreizeit des Bundes vom 26. Mai bis 5. Juni 1950 in Oberhundem (Sauerland)"; BAE, "Aufruf an die Jugend," 7, 10, 14–16; BAE *Mitteilungen* June 1947, Artur Jacobs, "Wohin steuern wir? Gedanken zum Beginn der VHS Arbeit," 11.

57. AB2; AAK, Nachlass Weisenborn, AJ to Kurt Desch, May 30, 1947; BAE, "Aufruf an die Jugend," 42.

58. See the discussion of the Women's International League for Peace and Freedom, BAE, folder Rundschreiben 1947–8, Doris Braune Rund-schreiben an die Gruppen, July 5, 1948. And see note 45 above.

59. Description of Bund conference, Haltern, summer 1947, on "Deutschland als Brücke zwischen Ost und West" in BAE, *Mitteilungen*, August 1947, 17. See also BAE, Karin Morgenstern to Tove and Wasja, August 28, 1947.

60. BAE, AJD May 4, 1945, and May 8, 1945. Carsten Dutt, *Die Schuldfrage: Untersuchungen zur geistigen Situation der Nachkriegszeit* (Heidelberg: Manutius Verlag, 2010), 7–16. BAE, "Aufruf an die Jugend," 1, 7; StAR, N41, 3, AJD, "Mai 45, 2. Teil"; BAE, *Mitteilungen*, 1948, Issue I, 13–14; BAE, folder "Dore Jacobs, Personalien," Doris Braune, Worte auf einer Gedächtnisfeier."

61. Hannah Arendt, "Organisierte Schuld" [1946], reprinted in *In der Gegenwart: Übungen im politischen Denken II* (Munich: Piper Verlag, 2000), 26–37.

62. BAE, AJD entry for January 6.

63. "Aus Aufzeichnungen von Artur Jacobs: 1948," reproduced in DJGU, 128.

64. AB1.

65. BAE, *Mitteilungen*, November 1947. And see Ernst Jungbluth's comments in BAE, *Mitteilungen*, 1948, issue I, 66.

66. BAE, *Mitteilungen*, 1948, issue I, 29, 66.
67. BAE, *Mitteilungen*, June, October, and November 1947; BAE, AJD, May 1948; *Mitteilungen*, issue I/1948, 36A, report on Volkshochschule Essen; LAN, NW 17, 168, Der Bund: Gemeinschaft für sozialistisches Leben, "Zur Jugendarbeit des Bundes," Essen, February 6, 1951. See also attached reports on subsequent events; and interviews with Helmut Lenders, Kurt Schmidt, and Alisa Weyl. Ellen's note to Dore in JP, folder "Fragen zur Zukunft des Bundes, Frage nach den Jungen."
68. Hoffmann, "Besiegte."
69. AB1, 7. Institut für Zeitgeschichte, ED 106/97, "Bericht über das Judenhilfswerk des 'Bundes' Gemeinschaft für sozialistisches Leben," typewritten manuscript, no date; BAE, *Mitteilungen*, 1948, I, 66; JP, undated handwritten text "Gestern stellten Inge und Helmut zum wievielten Mal mir die Frage, warum sind keine jungen Menschen im Bund" (probably 1950, in Ellen's handwriting); LAN, NW 1022 L 32201 Gisela Lenders; interviews with Helmut Lenders, Düsseldorf, June 1999; Kurt Schmidt, Wuppertal, May 1999; second interview with Ursula Jungbluth, Wuppertal, June 24, 1999; LAN NW 17, 172–73, "Bericht über die Pfingstfreizeit des Bundes vom 26. Mai bis 5. Juni 1950 in Oberhundem (Sauerland)."
70. BAE, "Aufruf an die Jugend," 36.
71. BAE, *Mitteilungen*, 1948, issue I, 66.
72. Interview with Änne Schmitz, January 1997. And see BAE transcript of Tove Gerson broadcasts on Südfunk II, Stuttgart, titled "Lebenserfahrungen" (six installments, beginning August 4, 1987).
73. Interview with Kurt Schmidt, Wuppertal, May 1999.
74. Interview with Friedl Speer, Wuppertal, April 2000.
75. BAE, EB to DJ, October 6, 1946.
76. BAE, AJD, August 15, 1948.
77. "Why is no one being sworn in to the commitment and why must we, for the sake of the mission, take the step of excluding everyone from the commitment who does not lead a committed life." BAE, "Aus der Ansprache zum Verpflichtungstage 1948," no author, no date.
78. BAE, folder Rundschreiben 1947–8, Dore to the Bundesgruppen, March 30, 1948; Ceremony admitting Friedl in AJD, August 15, 1948, and a letter from Ernst in BAE, folder "Rundschreiben 1947–8," circular to all Bundesgruppen, October 28, 1948.
79. BAE, folder "Rundschreiben 1947–8," circular to all groups, July 11, 1948, signed "Liese."
80. ASP, Karlos and Karin Morgenstern to all Bundesgenossen, May 30, 1949; Tilde Stürmer to Karin Morgenstern, June 4, 1949; JP, folder "Fragen zur Zukunft des Bundes, Frage nach den Jungen," typed page titled "Aus

einem Brief von Ellen an Karin (der aber nicht geschickt wurde, weil die anderen meinen, Ellen müsste es sagen)."

81. From an extended discussion on this in an interview with Gustav Zenker, Mülheim, February 1988 (conducted by Monika Grüter).

82. BAE, *Chronik*, October 1952, "Kleine Mitteilungen"; conversation with Huberte Arnsmann, Essen, October 2015; Mark Roseman, "Ein Mensch in Bewegung: Dore Jacobs, 1894–1978," *Essener Beiträge: Beiträge zur Geschichte von Stadt und Stift Essen* 114 (2002): 73–109. Conversations with the later school director, Karin Gerhard, Essen, May 1999 and subsequently.

83. BAE, "Verpflichtungstag 1952, Mitschrift der Ansprache"; manuscript "Verpflichtungstag 1950, Gang der Aussprache"; "Erste Gedanken zum Verpflichtungstag 1951" in Else Bramesfeld's handwriting; WE to SSch, March 14, 1952.

84. JP, undated letter from Ernst to Artur.

85. JP, EJ to AJ, February 2, 1960.

86. Interview with Tove Gerson, Essen, January 1997.

10. Beyond Recognition

1. Susanna Schrafstetter, "Von der Soforthilfe zur Wiedergutmachung: Die Umsetzung der Zonal Policy Instruction Nr 20 in der britischen Besatzungszone," in *"Arisierung" und "Wiedergutmachung" in deutschen Städten*, ed. Christiane Fritsche and Johannes Paulmann (Köln: Böhlau Verlag, 2014), 309–34, specifically 311–15. Volmer-Naumann, "'Betrifft: Wiedergutmachung': Entschädigung als Verwaltungsakt am Beispiel Nordrhein-Westfalen," in *"Arisierung" und "Wiedergutmachung" in deutschen Städten*, 335–62, specifically 338.

2. StAE, WG 158, J103 (Artur Jacobs), Fragebogen. June 6, 1946.

3. StAE, WG 158, J103, AJ to Militärregierung Fürsorgeamt für politische Opfer, July 22, 1946.

4. Ibid.

5. Ibid.

6. StAE, WG 158, J103, Beschluss des KSHA in der Sitzung vom July 30, 1946.

7. Schrafstetter, "Von der Soforthilfe zur Wiedergutmachung," 333; Kristina Meyer and Boris Spernol, "Wiedergutmachung in Düsseldorf: Eine statistische Bilanz," in *Die Praxis der Wiedergutmachung: Geschichte, Erfahrung und Wirkung in Deutschland und Israel*, ed. Norbert Frei, José Brunner, and Constantin Goschler (Göttingen: Wallstein, 2009), 690–727, specifically 709.

8. StAE, WG 158, J30, LJ, letter March 15, 1948.

9. StAE, WG 158, J103, AJ to Rat der Gemeinde, zu Hd. von Herrn Stadtinspektor Neuner, March 4, 1948.

10. StAE, WG 158, J103, AJ to WGA Essen, January 3, 1950. Meyer and Spernol, "Wiedergutmachung in Düsseldorf," 710.

11. Volmer-Naumann, "'Betrifft: Wiedergutmachung,'" 339–42.

12. LAN, BR 3000, Nr 72, Sitzung, Kammer für Haftentschädigung (KfH), May 27, 1953.

13. LAN, RW58 19223, Der Oberpräsident der Rheinprovinz, Abteilung für höheres Schulwesen, Koblenz to Police president, Essen, June 2, 1933, and subsequent correspondence and reports. LHAK, 405A—3216, AJ to Städtische Kommissar für Schulangelegenheiten Bubenzer, June 16, 1933. ASE, Bestand 45-2AS, Nachlaß Friedl Jacobs, Gottfried Jacobs to Artur, no date, but evidently July 1933.

14. StAE, WG 158, J103, Eidestattliche Erklärung, gez. Luise Speer, June 29, 1949.

15. StAE, WG 158, J103, AJ to Rat der Gemeinde, zu Hd. von Herrn Stadtinspektor Neuner, March 4, 1948.

16. StAE, WG 158, J103 Fragebogen, June 6, 1946, and AJ to Militärregierung Fürsorgeamt für politische Opfer, July 22, 1946.

17. StAW, WG, Jungbluth Ernst 115, 24, EJ to Betreuungstelle für politische Häftlinge, November 2, 1945; Fragebogen, additional sheet, dated Wuppertal, March 20, 1946; Kreissonderhilfsausschuß, Wuppertal, Entscheidung, July 2, 1949.

18. Correspondence in StAE, WG 158, J153 (Dora Jakobs [*sic*]), Dore Jacobs to Amt for Wiedergutmachung, May 9, 1949, and following.

19. StAE, Bestand 158, File J30, Elisabeth Jacob, Affidavits from Emmi Schreiber, December 15, 1949, and Medi Heilwagen, December 17, 1949.

20. StAE, WG 158, J153, Dr. Walter Hurwitz, "Ärtzliche Bescheinigung," May 10, 1949; memo, May 13, 1949; letter from DJ, May 29, 1949. Being over sixty-five, Artur did not need to demonstrate impaired working ability and in August 1951 was awarded the full pension. LAN, BR 3000, Nr 73, Zentralkartei für Wiedergutmachungsleistungen, Nr 7423.

21. StAW, WG Jungbluth Ernst 115, 24, Kreissonderhilfsausschuß, Wuppertal, Entscheidung, July 2, 1949.

22. LAN, BR 3000, Nr 74, Innenministerium NRW to EJ, April 13 1950, and EJ to Arbeitsministerium, October 6, 1950.

23. Hermann Fischer-Hübner, "Zur Geschichte der Entschädigungsmaßnahmen für Opfer nationalsozialistischen Unrechtes," in *Die Kehrseite der "Wiedergutmachung": Das Leiden von NS-Verfolgten in den Entschädigungsverfahren*, ed. Helga Fischer-Hübner and Hermann Fischer-Hübner (Gerlingen: Bleicher, 1990), 9–42, specifically 32.

24. Meyer and Spernol, "Wiedergutmachung in Düsseldorf," 721.

25. LAN, BR 3000, Nr 74, EJ to Arbeitsministerium, October 6, 1950.

26. On Artur's battles, see StAE, WG 158, J103, AJ to WGA Essen, August 18, 1949; WGA to AJ, January 16, 1950; AJ to WGA Essen, January 1950; copy, letter from Kreissonderauschuss to AJ, August 31, 1950; AJ to Stadverwaltung Essen, January 25, 1951; KfH beim Inneministerium, Düsseldorf, Beschluss, December 10, 1951; LAN, BR 3000, 73, AJ to Interior Ministry, Abteilung V.I. KfH, November 10, 1950.

27. LAN, BR 3000, 73, AJ, Antrag auf Entschädigung, July 28, 1954.

28. StAE, WG 158, J153, undated attachment "Begründung meines Antrags," carries a date stamp from the receiving authority of December 20, 1949. A later note makes clear this is an attachment to an application for compensation for loss of liberty dated December 19, 1949.

29. StAE, WG 158, J153, DJ to WGA, November 11, 1950; Ausschuss für die Entschädigung für Freiheitsentziehung, Beschluss, December 12, 1950; LAN, BR 3000, Nr 72, Anlage zum Protokoll, Sitzung KfH, December 16, 1952. The payments covered the periods September 1, 1939–May 30, 1943; June 2, 1943–September 15, 1943; and February 22, 1944–February 14, 1945.

30. LAN, BR 3000, Nr 72, Paul Grundmann to WGA Essen, October 22, 1952.

31. LAN, BR 3000, Nr 72, Anlage zum Protokoll, Sitzung KfH, December 16, 1952.

32. Ibid.

33. Ibid.

34. StAE, WG 158, J153, Vermerk, Düsseldorf, May 3, 1954.

35. LAN, BR 3000, Nr 74, EJ to KfH beim Innenministerium, November 30, 1950; Auschuß für die Entschädigung der Freiheitsentziehung Essen für den Stadtkreis Wuppertal, Beschluss, February 20, 1952.

36. LAN, BR 3000, Nr 70, Zentralkartei für Wiedergutmachungsleistungen, Nr 6588; an undated sheet labeled "Leistungen nach dem BEG" records the later payment of DM 900 in 1959.

37. By now she was Marianne Ellenbogen (ME), married and living in Liverpool, England.

38. EP, copy, ME to Carl Hermann, January 9, 1956 [*sic*; should be 1957].

39. EP, Carl Hermann to ME, June 4, 1957.

40. EP, copy, ME to Carl Hermann, June 8, 1957.

41. Volmer-Naumann, "'Betrifft: Wiedergutmachung,'" 351–56; Marlene Klatt, "Die Entschädigungspraxis im Regierungsbezirk Arnsberg und die Reaktion jüdischer Verfolgter," in *"Arisierung" und "Wiedergutmachung" in deutschen Städten*, 363–86.

42. On the striking case of Tilde Stürmer, see LAN, BR 3000, 76 (Stürmer, née Hoeger), Tilde Stürmer to Regierungspräsident, September 29, 1964; Tilde Stürmer to Regierungspräsident, August 15, 1965; court session, Krefeld, May 20, 1969, testimony from Alfred Stürmer. Conversation with Alfred Stürmer in Innsbruck, June 10, 2011.

43. Johannes Tuchel, "Vergessen, verdrängt, ignoriert: Überlegungen zur Rezeptionsgeschichte des Widerstandes gegen den Nationalsozialismus im Nachkriegsdeutschland," in *Der vergessene Widerstand: Zu Realgeschichte und Wahrnehmung des Kampfes gegen die NS-Diktatur*, ed. Johannes Tuchel (Göttingen: Wallstein, 2005), 7–38, specifically 10.

44. Ernst Jungbluth, "Unbewätigte Vergangenheit in der Praxis der Erwachsenenbildung," *Volkshochschule im Westen* 11, nos. 11–12 (1960): 346–48.

45. Tuchel, "Vergessen, verdrängt, ignoriert," 7–38, specifically 10.

46. Steinberg, *Widerstand und Verfolgung in Essen, 1933–1945*, 13; Tuchel, "Vergessen, verdrängt, ignoriert," 9; Christine Hikel, "Erinnerung als Partizipation: Inge Scholl und die 'Weisse Rose' in der Bundesrepublik," in *Lieschen Müller wird politisch: Geschlecht, Staat und Partizipation im 20. Jahrhundert*, ed. Christine Hikel, Nicole Kramer, and Elisabeth Zellmer (München: Oldenbourg, 2009), 105–14, specifically 108–9. For a quite brilliant exploration of a real case of discrimination against heroes of the left-wing resistance, though explored in fiction, see Friedrich Christian Delius, *Mein Jahr als Mörder* (Berlin: Rowohlt, 2004).

47. The Zinnen Verlag. In the end the book would be published by Rowohlt, in Hamburg.

48. "Der Bund Gemeinschaft für politisches Leben to Zinnen-Verlag," Kurt Desch, May 30, 1947, Nachlass Weisenborn, AAK, Berlin, File 366 IV. I am very grateful to Kobi Kabalek, who brought this letter to my attention, and to the AAK for providing a copy. Joachim Scholtyseck, "'Mit alten Kräften und im alten Stile'? Die Überlebenden des deutschen Widerstandes gegen Hitler und der politische Neubeginn in der Bundesrepublik," in *Die Überlebenden des deutschen Widerstandes und ihre Bedeutung für Nachkriegsdeutschland*, ed. Joachim Scholtyseck and Stephen Schröder (Münster: Lit, 2005), 11–32.

49. Steinberg, *Widerstand und Verfolgung in Essen, 1933–1945*, 13; Klotzbach, *Gegen den Nationalsozialismus*; Kuno Bludau, *Gestapo, geheim! Widerstand und Verfolgung in Duisburg, 1933–1945*, Schriftenreihe des Forschungsinstituts der Friedrich-Ebert-Stiftung (Bonn-Bad Godesberg: Verlag Neue Gesellschaft, 1973).

50. Steinberg, *Widerstand und Verfolgung in Essen, 1933–1945*, 23.

51. Oblique hints of the book's impact come, as we will see, in Dore Jacobs's manuscript on the history of the Bund, "Gelebte Utopie," written in the 1970s. See the section "A Spiritual Journey."
52. Kabalek, "The Rescue of Jews and the Memory of Nazism in Germany," 96ff. On the rewriting of Ursula Kardorff's wartime diary to accentuate help for Jews, for example, see Kabalek, 125, and Ursula von Kardorff and Peter Hartl, *Berliner Aufzeichnungen, 1942–1945* (München: C. H. Beck, 1992).
53. Ernst von Salomon, *Der Fragebogen* (Hamburg: Rowohlt, 1951), 456.
54. Kabalek, "The Rescue of Jews and the Memory of Nazism in Germany," 144.
55. Kurt Richard Grossmann, *Die unbesungenen Helden: Menschen in Deutschlands dunklen Tagen* (Berlin: Arani Verlags-GmbH, 1957), and Kabalek, "The Rescue of Jews and the Memory of Nazism in Germany," 241.
56. The following history of the recognition of the righteous draws heavily on Sarah Gensburger, "L'émergence de la catégorie de Juste parmi les nations comme paradigme mémoriel: Réflexions contemporaines sur le rôle socialement dévolu à la mémoire," in *Culture et Mémoire*, ed. Carola Hähnel-Mesnard, Marie Liénard-Yeterian, and Cristina Marinas (Paris: Éditions de l'École Polytechnique, 2008), 25–32; Sarah Gensburger, *Les Justes de France: Politiques publiques de la mémoire*, Gouvernances (Paris: Presses de Sciences Po, 2010); and Kobi Kabalek, "The Commemoration Before the Commemoration: Yad Vashem and the Righteous Among the Nations (1945–1963)," *Yad Vashem Studies* 39, no. 1 (2011): 169–211.
57. On all this, see Kabalek, "The Commemoration Before the Commemoration," 197ff.
58. Inge Deutschkron, *Ich trug den gelben Stern* (Köln: Verlag Wissenschaft und Politik, 1978).
59. On the ISK, see the references in chapter 1, note 8.
60. Letter from Heinz Putzrath to Gustav Streich, April 10, 1985. Copy in the hands of Norbert Reichling, Essen.
61. Conversation with Mordecai Paldiel, July 29, 1998.
62. Ibid.
63. Artur Jacobs, "Ansprache zur Maifaier 1945," in DJGU, 175; see also BAE, "Aus einem Brief von Dore an Wasja vom 22. Mai 1945."
64. For example, Ernst's efforts to gain the attention of the British Military Government; SLC, MC 447, Box 2-46, EJ to the military government, May 1945.
65. AAK, Berlin, Weisenborn 366a, Artur Jacobs to Kurt Desch, Zinnen Verlag, May 30, 1947.

66. Institut für Zeitgeschichte, Munich, ED 106/97, undated report (probably late 1946), "Bericht über das Judenhilfswerk des 'Bundes' Gemeinschaft für sozialistisches Leben."
67. AAK, AJ to Desch, May 30, 1947.
68. Not to be confused with the Bund's publication of the same name—see below and note 73.
69. A completion date of 1975 is given in the later published version of *Gelebte Utopie*. However, at the time, the Bund reported that the manuscript was completed only in 1977, and even then not all parts were finished. BAE, "Chronik des Bundes," 1977, 1, 25–26.
70. Artur Jacobs, *Die Zukunft des Glaubens: Die Entscheidungsfrage unserer Zeit* (Frankfurt am Main: Europäische Verlagsanstalt, 1971).
71. DJGU, 5.
72. DJGU, 232.
73. Dore Jacobs, Else Bramesfeld, et al., *Gelebte Utopie: Aus dem Leben einer Gemeinschaft* (Essen: Klartext, 1990).
74. BAE, "Mitteilungen an die Bundesfreunde, No. 9. Herbsttagung, November 9, 1988," 10.
75. Copy of a letter to Mordecai Paldiel, September 3, 2003, in the author's possession.
76. Announcement from Yad Vashem, dated April 18, 2004, sent, along with other documents, to the author.
77. Announcement, Embassy of the State of Israel, Berlin, September 2005.
78. Friedrich Ebert Stiftung, brochure, *Einladung: Gerechte unter den Völkern*, copy in the author's possession. Düsseldorfer Nachrichten, "Ehrung für eine Gerechte," January 21, 2006.
79. The narrative can be found on the Yad Vashem website at: http://db .yadvashem.org/righteous/family.html?language=en&itemId=5082687 (accessed January 27, 2019).
80. Copy of a document from the Israeli Embassy, Berlin, "Fritz and Maria Briel—Emilie Busch—Hanni Ganzer—Hedwig Gehrke—Meta Kamp-Steinmann—Karin Morgenstern—Änne Schmitz und Grete Ströter sowie Constantin Kradja," dated September 2005. Copy in the author's possession.

Conclusion: The Rescue of History

1. Schoppmann, "Rettung von Juden," 115.
2. Schrafstetter, *Flucht und Versteck*, 9–11. How small these figures were is underlined by the fact that they include those in mixed marriages who were endangered only later in the war.

3. Beate Kosmala, "Überlebensstrategien jüdischer Frauen in Berlin: Flucht vor der Deportation (1941–1943)," in *Alltag im Holocaust*, ed. Löw, Bergen, and Hájková, 29–47, specifically 46.

4. Schoppmann, "Rettung," 120–21.

5. Comment by Herr Jost in an interview with Herr Jost and Maria Briel by Jochen Bilstein, November 9, 1990.

6. AB3, 9ff. Klär, "Zwei Nelson-Bünde."

7. Christl Wickert, "Frauen zwischen Dissens und Widerstand," in *Lexikon des deutschen Widerstandes*, ed. Wolfgang Benz and Walter H. Pehle (Frankfurt am Main: S. Fischer, 1994), 141–56; Schoppmann, "Rettung," 122–23.

8. Schoppmann, "Rettung," 120–21; Rudolph, *Hilfe beim Sprung ins Nichts*.

9. Hans Rothfels, *The German Opposition to Hitler: An Assessment* (London: O. Wolff, 1961). For Rothfels's definition of resistance, see *Die Deutsche Opposition Gegen Hitler: Eine Würdigung*. Bücher des Wissens (Revised edition, Frankfurt am Main: Fischer, 1958), 10.

10. Interview with Änne Schmitz, Wuppertal, January 1997.

11. Kershaw, *The Nazi Dictatorship*, 199–200.

12. Broszat, "Resistenz und Widerstand," 697. Hartmut Mehringer, "Die Bayerische Sozialdemokratie bis zum Ende des NS-Regimes: Vorgeschichte, Verfolgung und Widerstand," in *Bayern in der NS-Zeit*, vol. 5, *Die Parteien KPD, SPD, BVP in Verfolgung und Widerstand*, ed. Hartmut Mehringer and Martin Broszat (München: Oldenbourg, 1983), 287–432, specifically 429–32.

13. Jacobs, "Ansprache zur Maifaier 1945," reprinted in in DJGU, 175; See also BAE, "Aus einem Brief von Dore an Wasja vom 22. Mai 1945."

14. Paul and Mallmann, *Milieus und Widerstand*.

15. AB3, 10.

16. AB3, 21.

17. AB3, 2.

18. AB3, 3.

19. John M. Cox, *Circles of Resistance: Jewish, Leftist, and Youth Dissidence in Nazi Germany*, Studies in Modern European History (New York: Peter Lang, 2009), 96.

20. Just how challenging it was to maintain this kind of stance emerges strongly from Janosch Steuwer, *"Ein Drittes Reich, wie ich es auffasse": Politik, Gesellschaft und privates Leben in Tagebüchern 1933–1939* (Göttingen: Wallstein Verlag, 2017).

21. Wolfgang Benz, "Solidarität mit Juden während der NS-Zeit," in Kosmala and Schoppmann, *Solidarität und Hilfe für Juden während der NS-Zeit*, vol. 5, 9–16, specifically 13; Arno Lustiger, *Rettungswiderstand: Über die Judenretter in Europa während der NS-Zeit* (Göttingen: Wallstein, 2011). For an earlier

attempt to include rescue in the resistance category, see an essay by the sociologist Manfred Wolfson: "Der Widerstand gegen Hitler: Soziologische Skizze über Retter [Rescuers] von Juden in Deutschland," *Aus Politik und Zeitgeschichte* 15 (1971): 32–39.

22. For the evolution of historiography in France, see Renée Poznanski, "Rescue of the Jews and the Resistance in France: From History to Historiography," *French Politics, Culture & Society* 30, no. 2 (2012): 8–32; and Sarah Gensburger, "From Jerusalem to Paris: The Institutionalization of the Category of 'Righteous of France,'" *French Politics, Culture & Society* 30, no. 2 (2012): 150–71. For a discussion of what is at stake in distinguishing rescue from resistance, see Saul Friedländer's comments in the foreword to Lucien Lazare, *Rescue as Resistance: How Jewish Organizations Fought the Holocaust in France* (New York: Columbia University Press, 1996), ix–x. For examples of active resistance groups also involved in rescue, see Winfried Meyer, *Unternehmen Sieben: Eine Rettungsaktion für vom Holocaust bedrohte aus dem Amt Ausland/Abwehr im Oberkommando der Wehrmacht* (Frankfurt am Main: Hain, 1993), and the discussion in Lazare, *Rescue as Resistance,* 25–28.

23. Schoppmann, "Rettung," 126.

24. Unpublished paper, Natan Sznaider, "Zwischen Liebe zur Welt und politischer Verantwortung: Das Neinsagen in der Diktatur," given at the conference "Helfer, Retter und Netzwerker des Widerstands. 3. Internationale Konferenz zur Holocaustforschung / Praxisforum: Zivilcourage lernen," held in Berlin, 2011.

25. Mordecai Paldiel, *German Rescuers of Jews* (London: Vallentine Mitchell, 2017).

26. Grabowski, *Rescue for Money: Paid Helpers in Poland, 1939–1945;* Paulsson, *Secret City;* Simon and Bell, *Underground in Berlin;* and Moore, "The Rescue of Jews from Nazi Persecution."

27. Beate Kosmala and Claudia Schoppmann, "Überleben im Untergrund: Zwischenbilanz eines Forschungsprojekts," in *Solidarität und Hilfe für Juden während der NS-Zeit,* vol. 5, ed. Beate Kosmala and Claudia Schoppmann, 17–32, specifically 22–23; Angela Borgstedt, "Hilfe für Verfolgte: Judenretter und Judenhelfer," in *Widerstand gegen die nationalsozialistische Diktatur 1933–1945,* ed. Peter Steinbach and Johannes Tuchel (Berlin: Lukas, 2004), 307–21, specifically 311; and Barbara Schieb, "Die Gemeinschaft für Frieden und Aufbau," in *Der vergessene Widerstand: Zu Realgeschichte und Wahrnehmung des Kampfes gegen die NS-Diktatur,* ed. Johannes Tuchel (Göttingen: Wallstein, 2005), 97–113.

28. These were crucial, for example, in "Aryan" Warsaw. Paulsson, *Secret City.*

29. Marten Düring, *Verdeckte soziale Netzwerke im Nationalsozialismus: Die Entstehung und Arbeitsweise von Berliner Hilfsnetzwerken für verfolgte Juden* (Berlin: De Gruyter Oldenbourg, 2015).

30. Oliner and Oliner, *The Altruistic Personality;* Monroe, *The Hand of Compassion;* Monroe, *The Heart of Altruism;* and Peter Suedfeld and Stefanie de Best, "Value Hierarchies of Holocaust Rescuers and Resistance Fighters," *Genocide Studies and Prevention* 3, no. 1 (2008): 31–42.

31. Tec, "Toward a Theory of Rescue."

32. Institut für Zeitgeschichte, Munich, ED 106/97, undated report (probably late 1946), "Bericht über das Judenhilfswerk des 'Bundes' Gemeinschaft für sozialistisches Leben," 6.

33. See Michael Gross's book on Le Chambon: *Ethics and Activism: The Theory and Practice of Political Morality* (Cambridge: Cambridge University Press, 1997).

34. As well as Gross, see also Christian Gudehus, "Helping the Persecuted: Heuristics and Perspectives (Exemplified by the Holocaust)," *Online Encyclopedia of Mass Violence* (2016).

35. Schrafstetter, *Flucht und Versteck*, 78; Schoppmann, "Rettung," 120–21; Marnix Croes, "The Holocaust in the Netherlands and the Rate of Jewish Survival," *Holocaust and Genocide Studies* 20, no. 3 (2006): 474–99, specifically 485; Richard Lutgens, "Jews in Hiding in Nazi Berlin, 1941–1945: A Demographic Survey," *Holocaust and Genocide Studies* 31, no. 2 (2017): 268–97, specifically 270–71; and Beate Meyer, "*Jüdische Mischlinge*," 25.

36. Kwiet and Eschwege, *Selbstbehauptung und Widerstand;* Moore, *Survivors: Jewish Self-Help and Rescue in Nazi-Occupied Western Europe.* AJD, January 23, 1945. Undated, unpublished bound volume dedicated to the memory of Lisa Jacob (1989).

37. Tec, *When Light Pierced the Darkness*, 204.

38. One additional reason for the contrast is that different *kinds* of records survive from different eras. During the Nazi years, the Bund could not express itself publicly. If Bund members put pen to paper, they did so in the intimate medium of letter or diary. Afterward, they must have decided that these private sources, as the only surviving testament to the Nazi era, were worthy of preservation. This also held true the first year or so after the war. From this period, too, a rich trove of letters has been preserved. Later, however, when the Bund finally had the ability to disseminate collective reports and manuscripts, many of which have been carefully preserved, its members deposited fewer personal documents in the archive.

39. BAE, AB1, 1–2; Artur Jacobs, "Ansprache zur Maifaier 1945," in DJGU, 175; and BAE, copy, DJ to WE, Meersburg, May 8, 1945.

40. As both Robert Moeller and David Crew have pointed out, war stories and Holocaust accounts were for a long time mutually exclusive. Moeller, *War Stories*; Jörg Echternkamp, "Von Opfern, Helden und Verbrechern— Anmerkungen zur Bedeutung des Zweiten Weltkrieges in den Erinnerungskulturen der Deutschen, 1945–1955," in *Kriegsende 1945 in Deutschland*, ed. Jörg Hillmann and John Zimmermann (Munich: R. Oldenbourg Verlag, 2002), 301–18; and David F. Crew, *Bodies and Ruins: Imagining the Bombing of Germany, 1945 to the Present*, Social History, Popular Culture, and Politics in Germany (Ann Arbor: University of Michigan Press, 2017). Even now, the recent expanding literature on Germans as victims in the war remains for the most part quite separate from work on the Holocaust or resistance. See also William John Niven, *Germans as Victims: Remembering the Past in Contemporary Germany* (New York: Palgrave Macmillan, 2006). Some important exceptions that have begun to interweave the two narratives include Atina Grossmann, *Jews, Germans, and Allies: Close Encounters in Occupied Germany* (Princeton: Princeton University Press, 2007), and Stargardt, *German War*.

41. Published in English as W. G. Sebald, *On the Natural History of Destruction* (New York: Random House, 2003).

42. See Crew, *Bodies and Ruins*.

43. Though the collective memory did then determine the story Bund members narrated individually.

44. On hindsight and moral judgment in the Holocaust generally, see Mariot and Zalc, "Reconstructing Trajectories of Persecution," 85–112. For German Jews, see also the introduction to Matthäus and Roseman, *Jewish Responses to Persecution*.

45. Sarah Gensburger, "La création du titre de Juste parmi les Nations," *Bulletin du Centre de recherche français à Jérusalem* 15 (2004): 15–37, and Kabalek, "The Commemoration Before the Commemoration."

46. Sznaider, "Zwischen Liebe zur Welt und politischer Verantwortung." For a few examples among very many, see Cecilie Felicia Stokholm Banke, Anders Jerichow, and Paul Larkin, *Civil Society and the Holocaust: International Perspectives on Resistance and Rescue* (New York: Humanity in Action Press, 2013); Facing History and Ourselves, "Decision Making in Times of Injustice Unit" for educators; N.C. Civic Education Consortium, "The Holocaust: Exploring Active Citizenship Through Resistors and Rescuers," viewed at https://civics.sites.unc.edu/files/2012/05/ResistorsRescuers.pdf.

47. Daniel Rothbart and Jessica Cooley, "Hutus Aiding Tutsis During the Rwandan Genocide: Motives, Meanings, and Morals," *Genocide Studies & Prevention* 10, no. 2 (2016): 76. More generally, see Gensburger, "From

Jerusalem to Paris," and Gensburger, "L'émergence de la catégorie de Juste parmi les nations comme paradigme mémoriel."

48. For example, Oliner and Oliner, *The Altruistic Personality;* Monroe, *The Hand of Compassion;* and Monroe, *The Heart of Altruism.*

49. Beer, "Aid Offered Jews in Nazi Germany." The difficulty of capturing motives in retrospect emerges also from Michael Gross's discussion of Pierre Sauvage's documentary about Le Chambon; see Gross, *Ethics and Activism,* 132.

ACKNOWLEDGMENTS

I have been thinking about the Bund on and off for twenty years. During that time, I was helped by a great many people. I can't thank them all personally here, but I am very conscious of my debt.

It is a pleasure to name the Bund members I interviewed: Fritz Briel, Tove Gerson, Ellen Jungbluth, Hermann Schmalstieg, Änne Schmitz, and Reinhold Ströter were inspiring interlocutors, and Ellen in particular was a fount of knowledge. I also interviewed those who had themselves been helped and inspired by the Bund: Marianne Ellenbogen née Strauss and Hanna Jordan. I am sad that none are alive to see the finished book. I am grateful, too, to those who talked to me about encountering the Bund after the war, including Helmut Lenders and Kurt and Jenni Schmidt, and to the children or other relatives of Bund members who had often vivid memories to share, notably Wolfgang Briel, Ursula Jungbluth, Elfriede Nenadovic, Armgard Schubert, Friedl Speer, Ernst Steinmann, and Alfred and Eberhard Stürmer. Sadly, many of this generation, too, are no longer alive. Through their involvement with the Dore Jacobs School, Huberte Arnsmann and Karin Gerhard encountered many of the Bund members in later life and gave me a great deal of interesting information. Karien Anstadt, the daughter of Milo Anstadt, and Susi Cohen shared memories and stories of Friedl Jacobs in Holland. Susi also told me about her mother's years in the Bund. François de Beaulieu gave me information about his father.

The Bund left its papers in many places. The Alte Synagoge archive in Essen contains the Jacobs family's letters and photos. My thanks to Edna Brocke, Uri Kaufmann, and Martina Strehlen for pleasant and unbureaucratic assistance in gaining access, and to Angela Genger, Judith Hess, and Monika Josten for helping me understand the collection. The official Bund depository is in the Essen City Archive, and Klaus Wisotzky made working there a pleasure. The most important official papers are in the North Rhine–Westphalian State archive in Duisburg, and over the years many different archivists have been extremely helpful. I'm grateful to the half dozen other archives that made their papers available. The biggest trove of papers was, however, not in any of these official repositories but in cupboards and boxes in the Bund's Blockhaus. My thanks to Karin Gerhard for making it easy and pleasant to work there among these remarkable documents. My interactions with her have been one of the joys of this project. I am indebted to children or grandchildren of Bund members, or of those whom they helped, for making private papers available, notably Stefan Brandt, Wolfgang Briel, Vivian Ellenbogen, Ursula Jungbluth, Florian and Annette Speer, and Alfred Stürmer.

Monica Grüter wrote an excellent MA dissertation on the Bund before I had even heard of them and spoke to people who were no longer alive by the time I came on the scene. She generously made interviews and knowledge available. Heidi Behrens-Cobet and Norbert Reichling similarly preceded me, met Bund members I could not, and have been equally generous. Of all the people named here, there is none to whom I owe a greater debt than Norbert. We have shared materials, manuscripts, ideas, and leads for almost twenty years. His commitment to public education in the form of the Humanistische Union, which he headed for many years, as well as his humanity and insight, provided an inspiring subtext as I learned about the Bund. Completing the project involved many trips to the Ruhr. My thanks to my friends Jola and Ricky Colman, Gabriele Musebrink, Alexander and Alice von Plato, and Falk Wiesemann and Martha Giannakoudi for making every visit a homecoming as well as a voyage of discovery.

Historians, archivists, and others with deep knowledge of the region's Jewish and non-Jewish history shared their wisdom, notably Angela Genger,

Dieter Nelles, Benno Reicher, Falk Wiesemann, and the late Michael Zimmermann. Many historians of rescue and resistance provided essential insights or knowledge, including Sarah Gensburger, Christian Gudehus, Kobi Kabalek, Susanna Schrafstetter, Johannes Tuchel, and Harald Welzer. For the larger German and Jewish scene during the Nazi and postwar eras, I profited particularly from conversations with Frank Bajohr, Volker Berghahn, Anna Hajkova, Stefan-Ludwig Hofmann, Jürgen Matthias, Alexander von Plato, Nick Stargardt, Falk Wiesemann, and Michael Wildt. I'm particularly indebted to Laura Hobson Faure, Stefan-Ludwig Hofmann, Joan Roseman, and Susanna Schrafstetter, who read part of the manuscript, and to Nick Stargardt, who read all of it, for their suggestions and corrections.

Many colleagues and institutions gave me the chance to present the work in progress. I'd like to particularly acknowledge the opportunity to lecture at the Hamburger Institut für Sozialforschung in 2006, and the ensuing publication in *Mittelweg*; two public lectures I gave as the 2010–2011 Ina Levine Invitational Scholar at the United States Holocaust Memorial Museum's Center for Advanced Studies; a presentation to the European History Seminar at the University of Oxford around the same time; and the special seminar on the book, then titled "Rescued Lives," for the seminar *Histoire et historiographie de la Shoah* cohosted by Centre de recherches historiques and EHESS-CNRS in 2017. Each gave the book impetus and new direction.

When I first encountered the Bund, I was at Keele University. I made my first research forays while at Southampton, and I completed the book at Indiana University Bloomington. In each institution I profited from conversations with smart and convivial colleagues and from institutions committed to support research. At IU, I have benefited enormously from the generosity of Jay and Marsha Glazer in endowing my chair, in honor of Jay's mother, and of Bob and Sandra Borns, in endowing the Borns Jewish Studies Program as a whole. Until I came to direct the program, I hadn't realized quite how much my colleagues and I are in their debt. I was also assisted by graduate assistants, notably Melissa Saferstein, who scanned all the documents, and Denisa Jashari, who read early chapters with the eye of an insightful outsider to German and Jewish history.

My ever-patient and supportive agent, Peter Robinson at Rogers,

Coleridge & White, helped me craft the case for the book and to find a home for it. I am grateful to Luciana O'Flaherty and OUP for believing in it and publishing the UK edition. Sara Bershtel and her team at my US publisher, Metropolitan Books, especially Connor Guy, were responsible for editing the English-language editions. The manuscript benefited enormously from their editing and copyediting. Thanks, too, to Hannah Campbell, Bonnie Thompson, Sarah Bowen, and Rima Weinberg for the wonderful copyediting and proofing, to Jordan Blekking for the map, and to Rebecca Carter-Chand for the index.

My life and my work are shared with Roberta Pergher. Chapters in every stage of undress landed on her desk and returned always with a new air of respectability. Her influence and insights are evident everywhere, as they are indeed everywhere in my life. I dedicate this book to her.

INDEX

ABOUT THE AUTHOR

MARK ROSEMAN is the author of *A Past in Hiding* and *The Wannsee Conference and the Final Solution*. He is the recipient of a number of prestigious prizes, including the Mark Lynton History Prize, the Fraenkel Prize in Contemporary History, and one of Germany's foremost literary prizes, the Geschwister Scholl Prize. He teaches at Indiana University, where he is a distinguished professor and director of the Borns Jewish Studies program.